THE GREAT DIONYSIAK MYTH

BY ROBERT BROWN, JUN., F.S.A.

> 'I strive and struggle to deliver right
> That music of my nature, day and night,
> With dream and thought and feeling interwound,
> And inly answering all the senses round
> With octaves of a mystic depth and height
> Which step out grandly to the infinite
> From the dark edges of the sensual ground'
>
> — ELIZABETH BARRETT BROWNING

VOL. I.

LONDON
LONGMANS, GREEN, AND CO.
1877

Kessinger Publishing's
Rare Mystical Reprints

THOUSANDS OF SCARCE BOOKS ON THESE AND OTHER SUBJECTS:

Freemasonry * Akashic * Alchemy * Alternative Health * Ancient Civilizations * Anthroposophy * Astrology * Astronomy * Aura * Bible Study * Cabalah * Cartomancy * Chakras * Clairvoyance * Comparative Religions * Divination * Druids * Eastern Thought * Egyptology * Esoterism * Essenes * Etheric * ESP * Gnosticism * Great White Brotherhood * Hermetics * Kabalah * Karma * Knights Templar * Kundalini * Magic * Meditation * Mediumship * Mesmerism * Metaphysics * Mithraism * Mystery Schools * Mysticism * Mythology * Numerology * Occultism * Palmistry * Pantheism * Parapsychology * Philosophy * Prosperity * Psychokinesis * Psychology * Pyramids * Qabalah * Reincarnation * Rosicrucian * Sacred Geometry * Secret Rituals * Secret Societies * Spiritism * Symbolism * Tarot * Telepathy * Theosophy * Transcendentalism * Upanishads * Vedanta * Wisdom * Yoga * *Plus Much More!*

DOWNLOAD A FREE CATALOG
AND
SEARCH OUR TITLES AT:

www.kessinger.net

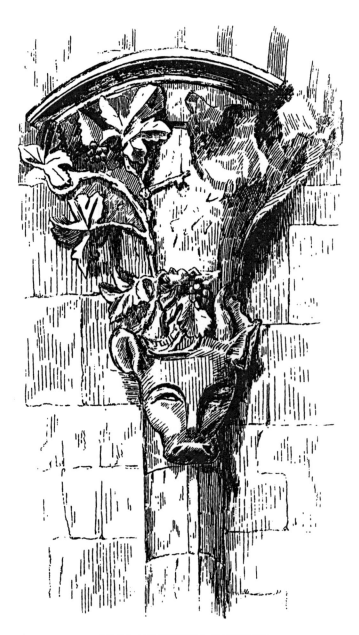

DIONYSIAK REPRESENTATION AT SOUTHWELL.

PREFACE.

In the midst of other and varied occupations I have amused some leisure hours with the consideration of the Dionysiak Myth,—a study which has at length taken a tangible form in the following pages. Whilst the outline of the subject is sufficiently familiar, its present treatment will, it is believed, be found to be novel to a great extent, and, moreover, to be in accordance with the recent and splendid discoveries whose magical force has reduced to uselessness vast quantities of earlier effort in this direction. Those who have not followed the thought and progress of the age are naturally unable to understand the present immense importance of Religious-mythology, and too generally regard it as a mass of idle, unmeaning, and often highly objectionable, fables; or, again, suppose that the subject has been exhausted by the efforts of luminaries long since extinguished. But the keener minds on all sides, whether religionists or not, are becoming fully alive to the magnitude of such enquiries in a religious point of view; and the study has, at the same time, claims no less strong upon the archaeologist, the psychologist, and the historian. One of the vastest questions which can be submitted to the mind—a question, moreover, which is rapidly coming to the front in the great debates of the age—is, Whether Religion and all that it entails sprang from man's unaided cogitations upon himself and the material world around? An answer to this momentous enquiry is supplied by the scientific consideration of the historic course of religious thought.

With respect to my chief modern authorities, and in order to satisfy the reader at the outset that the views of various important writers have not been overlooked, I have consulted the leading Assyriologists and Egyptologists of the time, such as Baron Bunsen, Sir J. G. Wilkinson, Sir H. C. Rawlinson, Canon Rawlinson, and Messieurs Birch, George Smith, Fox Talbot, Sayce, Cooper, Lepsius, Brugsch, Chabas, Lenormant, and Maspero. Acquaintance also with the admirable *Transactions of the Society of Biblical Archaeology*, and with the *Records of the Past*, must be possessed by all writers on Mythology who do not confine themselves exclusively to Aryan studies or to the beliefs of modern savages. I have also, as far as is necessary in the treatment of the subject, considered the standpoint of Payne Knight, Dulaure, and the phallic school, down to the late Dr. Inman; and the researches of D'Hancarville, Lobeck, Creuzer, Movers, Gesenius, Welcker, Rolle, Donaldson, K. O. Müller, Mure, Grote, Sir G. C. Lewis, Maury, Preller, Deutsch, Professor Ruskin, Mr. Gladstone, Dr. Schliemann, Dr. Tylor, Sir John Lubbock, Professor Max Müller, the Rev. G. W. Cox, Messieurs Herbert Spencer, C. W. King, A. S. Murray, F. A. Paley, and others.

In a subject so wide and so replete with difficulty all dogmatism, especially on minor points, is altogether out of place, yet I cannot but own my strong confidence in the correctness of the general conclusions arrived at; and I gladly take this opportunity of expressing a deep sense of thankfulness to those great minds of the past and of the present, whose previous labours have alone rendered the compilation of this work possible.

BARTON-UPON-HUMBER:
Jan. 1, 1877.

CONTENTS

OF

THE FIRST VOLUME.

CHAPTER I.

THE SUBJECT AND ITS TREATMENT.

	PAGE
Design of the Work; objections considered	1
Recent undue extension of Aryan principles	4
Unity of man and of God	5
The sources of Religious-mythology	6
Its essentially compound character	8
Treatment of the subject adopted	10
Style of nomenclature	11
Relation of the enquiry to present questions	12

CHAPTER II.

THE DIONYSOS OF THE THEOLOGERS.

SECTION I.
THE HOMERIK DIONYSOS.

Subsection I.—The Episode of Lykourgos.

Consideration of *Il.* vi. 128-41	15
Homerik consistency as shown in the conduct of Diomedes	17
Real meaning of the legend	19
Overthrow of opposers of the Dionysiak cult	21

Subsection II.—Dionysos Son of Semele.

Consideration of *Il.* xiv. 325	22
Important historic element in the legend of Kadmos	23
Dionysos as a source of joy	24

Subsection III.—*Dionysos and Naxos.*

	PAGE
Consideration of *Od.* xi. 321	24
Nysa and Dionysos	25

Subsection IV.—*Dionysos and the Tyrsenoi.*

The legend of the Homerik Hymn	26
Savage side of the cult	27

Subsection V.—*The Youth of Dionysos.*

The impersonation of joyous country life	27

Subsection VI.—*General Character of the Dionysos of the Homerik Hymns.*

Dionysos a Semitic divinity	28
His solar aspect	29
Progress of historic research	30

Subsection VII.—*Dionysos and the Kyklik Poems.*

Survival of the *Ilias* and *Odysseia*	31
Dionysos as Zagreus	31
Myth of Roio and her sisters in the *Kyprian Verses*	32
Care required in drawing explanations from names	33

Subsection VIII.—*Eikon of the Homerik Dionysos.*

The two aspects of the Earth-god	34
Dionysos not the Homerik Wine-god	35

SECTION II.
THE DIONYSOS OF HESIODOS.

Subsection I.—*Dionysos Son of Semele.*

Consideration of *Theog.* 940-2	36
Dionysos as Phanes and Phaidimos	37

Subsection II.—*Dionysos and Ariadne.*

Phoenician character of Minos	38
Pompeian fresco of Dionysos and Ariadne	39

Subsection III.—*Grapes the Gift of Dionysos.*

Double aspect of wine	40

Subsection IV.—*Eikon of the Hesiodik Dionysos.*

His foreign and kosmogonic character	40

THE FIRST VOLUME.

SECTION III.

THE ORPHIK DIONYSOS.

Subsection I.—Thrake and Orphik Mysticism.

Mythical Thrakian bards	41
Asiatic connection of Thrake	42
The Orphik ritual not derived from Kam	43
Quotation from the *Batrachoi*	44

Subsection II.—Dionysos and Apollon.

Theory of Macrobius	44
Oracle of Apollon Klarios	45
Bunsen and Bishop Browne on the Oracle	46
The Aryan and Semitic Sun-gods	47

Subsection III.—Dionysos the Demiurge.

Consideration of Orphik Fragment vii.	48
Pantheism, or God in All as opposed to All in God	50
The Demiurge reduces the Universe to order	51
And is manifested chiefly in a Solar aspect	52
Bishop Colenso on the Iao-myth	54
Iao a name of the Hebrew Yahveh	55
The circumstance no assistance to the anti-religionist	57
Iao in Gnostic art	59

Subsection IV.—Dionysos and Zeus.

The Orphik concept of Zeus	60
The kosmic Zeus-Dionysos	61

Subsection V.—The Neo-Platonik Orphik Hymns.

Dionysos son of Persephone	62
Various Dionysiak epithets	63
Seilenos	65
Adonis	66

Subsection VI.—Neo-Platonism.

Cause of its rise	67
Taylor, the last Neo-Platonist	68
Worthlessness of the system	69

Subsection VII.—Eikon of the Orphik Dionysos.

The solar Demiurge	70

CONTENTS OF

CHAPTER III.
THE LYRIC DIONYSOS.
SECTION I.
THE DIONYSOS OF PINDAROS.

Subsection I.—Dionysos Son of Semele.

	PAGE
Professor Ruskin and the Rev. G. W. Cox on Semele	72
Her kosmogonic character	74
Consideration of the myth of Zeus and Semele	75
The symbolism of flowing locks	78
The cheated Semele	79

Subsection II.—Dionysos and the Dithyramb.

Bakchik cult of the North Dorik cities of the Peloponnesos	80
The legend of Arion	80

Subsection III.—Dionysos Associate of Demeter.

Demeter and Kybele	81
Dionysos Eurychaites	84
Effect of geographical affinity	85

SECTION II.
OTHER LYRIC DIONYSIAK ALLUSIONS.

Subsection I.—Vinal Allusions.

Manifestations of the Theoinos	86

Subsection II.—Non-vinal Allusions.

Iakchos Thriambos	88
The bull-faced god	89

SECTION III.
EIKON OF THE LYRIC DIONYSOS.

His foreign character	90

CHAPTER IV.
THE DIONYSOS OF THE ATTIK TRAGEDIANS.
SECTION I.
THE DIONYSOS OF AISCHYLOS.

Subsection I.—Dionysiak Allusions in Extant Plays.

Eumenides, 24-6	91
Zagreus the Guest-receiver	92

Subsection II.—The 'Lykourgeia.'

Legend of Lykourgos 93
The Edonian cult 94

Subsection III.—Other Dionysiak Allusions in the 'Apospasmatia.'

Dionysos and the Kabeiroi 96
The *Dionysou Trophoi* 97

SECTION II.
THE DIONYSOS OF SOPHOKLES.

Subsection I.—Dionysos and Nysa.

Consideration of the *Triptolemos*, Frag. xi. 98

Subsection II.—Dionysos and Thebai.

Bakchos Chrysomitres 99
The pine-cone 100
The Invocation in the *Antigone* 101
Progress of Dionysos in the West 102

SECTION III.
THE DIONYSOS OF EURIPIDES.

Subsection I.—Dionysos and the Dance.

The joyous Bakchik dance 103
The orgiastic Bakchik dance 104
The universal mystic nature-dance 106
Cyclic phenomenal motion 108
Circular erections 110
'The impious *dinos*' 113

Subsection II.—The 'Bakchai.'

Argument of the Play 114
Eastern travels of Dionysos 116
The bull-horned god 120
Axiokersos at Elis 121
Karneios the Horned-sun 123
Dionysos serpent-crowned 125
Dionysiak adjuncts 127
The Kouretes and Korybantes 128
The Satyroi 133

CONTENTS OF

	PAGE
The Dionysiak goat	134
Dionysos Omestes and human sacrifices	135
The Aryan concept Pan	137
Kosmogonic symbolism	140
Dionysiak materialism	142
Dionysos the Prophet	144
'The Bakchik branch'	148

Subsection III.—*The Sufferings of Dionysos.*

Dionysos-Adonis	149
The Linos-Maneros dirge	151
Self-sacrificing divinities	153

Subsection IV.—*The 'Kyklops.'*

Mr. W. W. Lloyd on the Kyklopes and Aetna	154
Seilenos	155
Antagonism between Here and Dionysos	155
War with the Giants and Titanes	156
Maron	157

Subsection V.—*Dionysiak Allusions in the 'Apospasmatia.'*

Consideration of the *Kretes*, Frag. ii.	159

SECTION IV.
EIKON OF THE TRAGIC DIONYSOS.

Solar and kosmogonic character of the god	160
His foreign origin	162

CHAPTER V.
THE DIONYSOS OF HERODOTOS.

SECTION I.
DIONYSOS AND THRAKE.

Ares Bendis and Dionysos	163
Samothrake and the Pelasgoi	165
Bassareus	167

SECTION II.
DIONYSOS IN THE NORTH.

The Episode of Skylas	168
Sabazios at Olbia	170

SECTION III.

DIONYSOS IN HELLAS.

	PAGE
Bakchik portents before the battle of Salamis	172
The Bakchik cult said to be introduced by Melampous	173
Birth of gods computed from the time when they are first known	174
Melampous instructed by Kadmos	175

SECTION IV.

DIONYSOS AND NYSA.

Notices of Nysa by Herodotos 175

SECTION V.

DIONYSOS AND UASAR.

Subsection I.—Theory of Herodotos on the Historic Connection between the Divinities of Hellas and Kam.

Aryan and Semitic divinities of the Hellenik Pantheon	176
Herodotean identifications of Hellenik and Kamic divinities	178
Identity of the Dionysiak and Uasarian myths	178

Subsection II.—Dionysos considered by Herodotos as identical with Uasar, but the Dionysiak cult not supposed by him to be derived from the Uasarian.

The Bakchik cult introduced into Hellas by the mythic Kadmos . . 180

Subsection III.—Outline of the Uasarian Myth.

Its vastness and intricacy	182
Assistance afforded by the Bakchik myth	183
Basis-concept of Uasar	184

Subsection IV.—Identity of the Uasarian and Dionysiak Myths.

Consensus of ancient Authors	187
Uasar and Dionysos warriors and conquerors	190
Connected with Nysa	190
Suffering divinities	190
Of Asiatic origin	190
Many-named and manifold in nature	191
Chested	192
Connected with ivy	195
Both the youngest of the gods	196
Connected with spotted animals and garments	196

	PAGE
Vinal divinities	196
Tauric divinities	197
Solar divinities	200
Chthonian divinities	201
Grote's view respecting the introduction of Kamic religious ideas into Hellas	202
Grote on Onomakritos and the Zagrik myth	204
Rejection of the theory that the Zagrik and Dionysiak myths were borrowed from Kam	205

Subsection V.—*Basis and Starting Point of the Uasario-Dionysiak Cult.*

The religion of Kam Asiatic in origin	209
Divinities common to Kam and Aram	210
Derivation of divinities from Kaldea	214
An objection of Mr. Kenrick to the theory of a Phoenician Dionysos considered	215

SECTION VI.
DIONYSOS IN ARABIA.

Orotal and the Great Goddess Alilat	217
The Great God	220
Solar character of Dionysos-Orotal	221
Connection between Dionysos and Arabia	224

SECTION VII.
EIKON OF THE DIONYSOS OF HERODOTOS.

Wide-spread worship and compound nature of the god	224

CHAPTER VI.
THE HELLENIK CULT OF DIONYSOS.

SECTION I.
THE FESTIVALS OF DIONYSOS.

Subsection I.—*The Attik Cult.*

The Rural Dionysia	227
The phallic element in Religious-mythology	229
The Dionysia Lenaia	231
The Anthesteria	232
Signification of its symbolism	234
The Dionysian Megala	236

	PAGE
The Dionysia Brauronia	239
The Oschophoria	241

Subsection II.—The Boiotik Cult.

The Agrionia	243
Horned Kabeirik divinities	245
Legend of Athamas	246
Its underlying signification	247
Melikertes-Melqarth	251
Ino	253
Consideration of *Od.* v. 333-53	256
The Omaphagia	258
The Trieterika	259

Subsection III.—Other Festivals of the God.

The Lampteria	260
Phanes the Theban	261
The Thyia	262
The Dionysia Arkadika	262
Argolik contests between Here and Dionysos	263
The Lernaia	263
Dionysiak lakes	264
Festival of Dionysos Melanaigis	267
Contests between Perseus and Dionysos	268
Spartan Dionysiak ritual	269
Naxian Festivals of the god	270
Other Bakchik Festivals	270
Festival at Parnassos and consideration of *Od.* xi. 581	271

SECTION II.
DIONYSOS AT ELEUSIS.

Subsection I.—The Legend of the Homerik Hymn.

The rape of Persephone	273
Demeter or the Earth-mother	276
Basis-ideas of her cult	278
Persephone	278
Her companions	280
Signification of the concept of Persephone	281
Her change of character in the Under-world	282
The mystic pomegranate	284
Various statements respecting the locality of the rape	285

Subsection II.—The Union of the Cults.

Position of Dionysos at Eleusis	285
Identity of Dionysos and Iakchos	287

	PAGE
Illustrations of the connection between Dionysos and the Two Goddesses	289
Harmony of ideas in the concepts	290

Subsection III.—*The Eleusinian Ritual.*

The Lesser Mysteries	292
The Greater Mysteries	292
The Assembling	293
The March to the Sea and Sacrifices	293
The Basket-procession	294
The Torch-procession	294
The Day of Iakchos	296
Eleusinian cult at Pheneos	297
The Epopteia	299
Demeter Kidaria	301
Apparitions of the Furies	303
Their dance and canine character	305
Later Eleusinian ideas	308
Erinys and Saranyu	309
The Maniai and the Charites	311
The Fury in Art	312
Final efforts of Paganism at Eleusis	314
Later manifestations of the gods	316
Sol Inferus and his golden boat-cup	317
Appearance of Uasar-Adon	318
The Return and Day of the Epidaurians	319
The Day of Earthern Vessels	319
Principal personages at Eleusis	320

SECTION III.
DIONYSOS AND THE DRAMA.

Reason of our interest in the Drama	320
Its necessary connection with Dionysos	321
Tragedy, what	323
Comedy, what	324
The Dionysos of Comedy	325
Double aspect of the Drama and of Dionysos	326

CHAPTER VII.
DIONYSOS IN ART.
SECTION I.
VASES OF THE DIONYSIAK CYCLE.

Paucity of historic Vase-scenes	328
Vast number of Dionysiak Vases	329

	PAGE
The Dionysos of the Vases	330
With Ariadne	332
Dionysos Pelekys	332
The Gryphon-myth	334
The ass Eraton	337
Other Vase-scenes	338
The Iÿnx-myth	339
Dionysos in galley-shaped car	342
Other Vase-scenes	343
The flying Eros	344
The Bakchik Thiasos	345
Its kosmic grouping	347
Members of the Dionysiak Train	348
Instances of the grotesque	349

SECTION II.

DIONYSIAK STATUARY.

Early instances of pillar-cult	350
Unanthropomorphic statues	352
Ideas connected with the pillar-stone	353
The statuary's art Semitic—Daidalos	355
Archaic statues of Dionysos	357
Dionysos Agyios	358
Hellenik divinities always anthropomorphic	359
The four-armed Kouridios	360
The four-headed Dionysos of the Kerameikos	362
The horned Sun	363
Evolution of the human form in statuary	364
Instances of Dionysos Stylos	365
Dionysos Katapogon	366
Dionysos Ephebos	367
Statues of the god noticed by Pausanias	369
Statues of the Dionysiak Train	370
The Arkadian Pan	371

SECTION III.

DIONYSIAK COINS.

The archaic obol	374
Pecunia and *kesitah*	376
Coins bearing the head or figure of Dionysos	378
Interest of numismatic study—importance of the reason of facts	380
Concept of Dionysos as deduced from the Coins	381
Semitic and Aryan Sun-gods—coins of Rhodos	383
Coins of Thasos	385
The bovine coin-type—the river Acheloös	387

	PAGE
Euboik coins	389
The Gelan demi-bull or sun in the Under-world	390
Other bovine coin-types	394
Other Dionysiak coins	398
The andro-sphinx of Chios	400
The bee of Ephesos	401
Jewish and Numidian coins	404
Kilikian coins	404
Other Dionysiak coins	405
The Gryphon of Teos	409
Etrusco-Roman coins	411

SECTION IV.

DIONYSIAK GEMS.

Various Bakchik gems	413
The Gnostic Abraxas	416
Symbolic figures	418
Legend of the Phigaleian Demeter	419
Contests between Aryan and Semitic divinities	424
Oscilla	426

LIST OF ILLUSTRATIONS.

PLATE

I. Dionysiak Representation at Southwell	*Frontispiece*
II. Helios Karneios	*to face* 123
III. The Gryphon in Burmah	„ 336

THE GREAT DIONYSIAK MYTH.

CHAPTER I.

THE SUBJECT AND ITS TREATMENT.

To trace to its original source, and, in so doing, to explain and illustrate the underlying meaning and significance of that vast and varied mythologico-religious concept the Great Dionysiak Myth, is the object of the present work. The Hellenik Dionysos, with his endless train of Seilenoi, Satyrs, Nymphs, Fauns, and Bakchanals, is familiar to every student of antiquity; and a superficial acquaintance with the subject has reduced 'the worship of Bacchus' in popular idea to the use of wine, and that chiefly in excess. Facts and beliefs are, however, frequently well known, while at the same time their causes are very obscure; and though it is undoubtedly necessary to know that a thing Is, before we can consider, Why it is, or, Why it is as it is, yet an examination of the reason of actualities is the chief difference between the intellectual and the animal life. Finding, then, the concept of Dionysos, we are next impelled to ask why it exists, and in this particular form. To the enquiry it may be objected *in limine* that the subject is (1) unimportant, or (2) already sufficiently investigated.

To the first objection, I reply that the belief of great numbers of mankind during many centuries, and the reasons for such belief are always, as is now more generally recognised than formerly, well worthy of the attention of the philosopher, since inasmuch as the mind of man is practically a unity,[1] we are but studying ourselves in the persons of distant ages. We thus also notice what root ideas or principles are common to all minds in all times, and so if any reliance can be placed upon consciousness and its attendant phenomena (and if not, the less said or done the better) we are enabled to obtain a more correct approximation to truth.[2] The subject, moreover, possesses a special literary and historical interest of its own, and that of a high order. There are numerous other considerations illustrative of the genuine importance of such an enquiry, and deducible from the foregoing; but he who loves the study of religious-mythology and archaic idea, either considered separately or in connection with all religious ideas, will require but slight excuse to justify his investigations. To the second possible objection—that this particular subject has already been exhaustively treated—it is enough to reply that whilst the vast amount of scholarly labour bestowed since the era of the Reformation on Hellas and Rome, their history, literature, manners, arts, and arms, considered as isolated and all-important nationalities, leaves comparatively little to be accomplished in this particular direction; yet that modern historical research has deposed the lofty pair from their lonely mediaeval position as the beginning and end of the studies of antiquity. The historic telescope is almost daily revealing to us more and more of the distant empires of the Euphrates and the Nile, stars vast, brilliant, and remote, embedded in time as Sirius or Aldebaran in space. The whole mighty family of the Aryan

---

[1] 'There is one mind common to all individual men.' Emerson, *Essay on History*. Complete works, i. 1.

[2] Vide the general argument on this point in Mr. Herbert Spencer's *First Principles*, part i. chap. i.

Nations, with Hellas and Rome as but two younger sisters of the house, now demand the attention of the student of the Past. The dim figures of Arabia, Syria, and Phoenicia, are gradually becoming plainer through the scattering mists of ages; and, in a word, we have no longer only to compare Hellas with Rome, or Rome with Hellas, but must consider in connection the history and mutual relations of many empires and nationalities—Kaldea,[1] Assyria, Syria, Phoenicia, Arabia, Egypt, Persia, India, Hellas, Italy. Something, but how little, has long been known of Kaldea, Assyria, and Egypt; we have had the fragmentary notices of the Old Testament, the hearsay histories of Herodotos and Diodoros, and the traditional accounts of later writers such as Justinus. But the combined information of all Hellenik and Latin authorities, even were it reliable in every particular, which is far indeed from being the case, would be chiefly remarkable as illustrating the scantiness of our knowledge of the subject. Modern energy and talent, however, have revolutionised the position; the Sphinx has broken her majestic silence, and hieroglyph and cuneiform reveal their long-hidden secrets. These considerations might readily be greatly amplified, but the reader can easily follow out for himself the conclusions to which they point; sufficient to remark here, that time has recently brought to light a great quantity of fresh and most important material, which not only requires treatment, but also may modify or otherwise alter our views respecting that which we already possess. It is obvious that the force of these considerations is not restricted to the Dionysiak Myth, or to any other particular study; in each case a greater acquaintance with the sources of knowledge warrants, or rather demands, a

---

[1] 'Dans les documents cunéiformes, Kaldi est une tribu de la grande nation d'Accad.' (Lenormant, *La Magie*, 270.)

fresh adjustment of facts, and probably a consequent alteration of opinion.

But it may perhaps be hastily asked: What has the Hellenik Dionysos to do with hieroglyph or cuneiform, with Egypt or Kaldea? The present work must be an answer to the question; and I urge the reader to weigh the evidence carefully, and not to conclude at the outset that any particular theory which he may chance to hold is necessarily correct or exhaustive. Time was when men believed that the sun moved round the earth, and that all languages were derived from the Hebrew; and it is quite possible that many opinions which now pass unchallenged, and as a matter of course, may ultimately be found to be as wanting in truth as numbers of admitted errors long since consigned to the limbo of the past. When the great discoveries of Professor Max Müller and his fellow-labourers in the field of Aryan comparative philology and mythology had demonstrated the family connection between the divinities of the Vedas and of Olympos, the fresh truth was, in accordance with the tendency of the human mind, pushed beyond its proper limits. It became an axiom that an Aryan nation must have Aryan divinities and *none others*, in disregard of the obvious and undeniable fact that commerce, conquest, colonisation, and local proximity, as well as original unity of nationality, all necessarily exercise a vast influence on communities. Nations in history are not observed to change their gods by formally discarding the old, but they constantly add strange divinities to their elastic Pantheons. I am, however, quite willing to admit that, in the abstract, the probability is that any divinity of an Aryan nation is Aryan in origin; any divinity of a Semitic nation, Semitic; and that consequently the *onus probandi*, which I willingly accept, is on any one who asserts the contrary. A few years ago when the above-mentioned views respecting Aryan divinities were even more pronounced than at present, I endeavoured to test the general correctness of the theory by its application to a particular Hellenik god, Poseidon.[1] Whatever the shortcomings of this little monograph may have been, and it undoubtedly took the side of the question then unpopular, I am pleased to find that the leading principles which it advocated are not likely to be impeached by subsequent investigation, and that a juster view on this important question has recently gained ground.

The unity and uniformity of man, both in his physical and in his mental aspect,[2] and of the world in which he is placed, suggests, and even necessitates, an intrinsic unity of his ideas; a circumstance which emboldens us to enquire into the belief of far-off ages with a good hope of being able to unfold and to understand it. The principle of comparison, so ably and successfully applied in modern times, reveals endless similarity and resemblance, a family likeness and a consequent common parentage, of all mythologico-religious conceptions. Man in all ages, possessing a consciousness and sensations equivalent to our own, has been surrounded by the same external phenomena. It is a great achievement to have discovered the intrinsic unity of the religious ideas of the Aryan race, or of any other particular family of mankind; but it will be a still greater accomplishment to reveal and to demonstrate the grand unity into which the religious ideas of all nations and tribes are necessarily resolvable. From the unity of man and of the Kosmos, as well as otherwise, thinkers of all creeds and in all ages have accepted the idea of the unity of the Supreme Being, deducing, as S. Athanasios expresses it, 'the unity of the workman from the unity of the work.' Atheism doubtless exists, and has

---

[1] *Poseidon.* By the writer. London: Longmans & Co. 1872.

[2] 'A double-faced unity.' Bain, *Mind and Body*, 109.

existed, although its genuine disciples are few indeed; but its chief dogma will not bear any philosophical test, for if it be an unwarrantable assumption to affirm that God is, it is still more so to declare that He is not. The unity of God, by whatever name He may have been known, or however regarded, shines through the most complicated religious systems, whether archaic or comparatively recent. Much has been written about Semitic Monotheism, but Aryan Monotheism is a fact equally obvious. Ilu, Il, El, Allah, Amen, Yahveh, Iao, Dyaus, Deus, Theus, Zeus, 'Jehovah, Jove, or Lord,' are all in reality identical, and names for the Monad and First Cause. This doctrine is the central point and principal feature in the *Timaios*, ' the greatest effort of the human mind to conceive the world as a whole, which the genius of antiquity has bequeathed to us,'[1] and in which, ideas Platonik and Pythagorean meet not inharmoniously. The idea of a First Cause, it is also to be noted, is an hypothesis necessarily consequent upon the act of thinking.[2]

No religious-mythology, therefore, is utterly erroneous; and, again, there is in reality but one religion, however at different times and in various places obscured or debased. Worship, or the expression of the reverent respect paid by the human mind to a potency admittedly superior and intelligent, is necessarily either of the invisible, or of the visible, or of both; and the less the former is reverenced, the more the latter will be. The Supreme is hidden from the votary by the infinity of His being and the intervention of His other creations; secondary causes obscure the primal, which remains shadowy and indefinable because definition, having nothing tangible to grasp, subsides into rhetorical expression, and idea is paralysed beneath illimitable capacities and apparent contradictions. The Visible,

---

[1] Jowett, *The Dialogues of Plato*, iii. 598.
[2] Vide Herbert Spencer, *First Principles*, part i. chap. ii. 12.

then, considered Platonikally as a living animal containing living animals, comes with overwhelming prominence before the mind of the worshipper; and naturally divides itself into (1) the external world and its phenomena, or Nature; (2) the mental capabilities of man as viewed in their products, or Art; and (3) the principle of renewal and reproduction, or Phallicism. The cult of these, or any of them, is idolatry, or the worship of the Visible, which is thus (1) nature-worship; (2) man-worship, or primitive Euemerism; and (3) anthropo-nature-worship. Nature-worship is (1) celestial, or the cult of the heavenly bodies, and of the air[1] and aether; and (2) telluric, or the worship of the earth and the things connected with it; which are (*a*) terrestrial, or upon the earth, and (*b*) chthonian, or under the earth. Man-worship is (1) that of the individual or Euemerism proper, and (2) that of his productions, either mental or physical, as distinct from himself, which latter branch includes image-worship. Anthropo-nature-worship is divided into (1) the cult of the male principle, and (2) the cult of the female principle.[2] Any branch of the worship of the Visible may be, and indeed is, connected to a certain extent with the worship of the Invisible; and the cults of the various branches are generally unantagonistic as between themselves. Celestial worship, again, is solar, lunar, planetary, astral, zodiacal, and astrological, or combinations of these. The sun, as the most remarkable of natural phenomena, is the pro-

[1] 'Neanthes of Cyzicum writes that the Macedonian priests invoke Bedu, which they interpret to mean the air, to be propitious to them and to their children.' (Clem. Alex. *Strom.* v. 8.)

[2] In the present work addressed to general readers, the Phallic element, though sufficiently indicated, will be very lightly touched upon. It is undoubtedly an important feature in ancient religious idea, although its *rôle* is much exaggerated. It has been illustrated by the writings of R. P. Knight and his recent Editor. Inman, Davenport, Westropp, Wake, Rolle (*Recherches sur le Culte de Bacchus*); Lajard (*Recherches sur le Culte de Vénus*); Dulaure (*Histoire Abrégée des Différens Cultes*); and others. Vide also Rev. G. W. Cox, *Mythol. of the Aryan Nations*, ii. 107, 130.

tagonist of religious-mythology, and appears in three principal connections as (1) light, (2) fire, and (3) the generator or life-quickener of the face of the world. The sunlight has two principal and closely connected aspects, light (1) physical and (2) mental. Fire has also two principal aspects, the flame (1) grateful and (2) terrible. These materials, to which must be added the amount of abstract truth possessed at any time by man, and his deviations from it, compose the sources whence all religious-mythology is derived. Whilst, on the one hand, a similar mind, an originally common stock of ideas, and the same surrounding universe, necessitate the pristine unity of, and produce the resemblances and parallels between, the various branches of religious-mythology; on the other, variety of disposition, different degrees of knowledge and intelligence, and dissimilar habitations and fortunes have occasioned their varieties and contrasts.

The elements, which thus, in proportions varying in different localities, unite to compose religious-mythology being so numerous and diverse, the nature of their production cannot but be correspondingly compound and intricate. For this simple reason, systems which purport to supply a key to all mythologies by the aid of a single secondary principle, whether that happen to be the cult of light and darkness, or of storm and wind, the worship of ancestors or of animals, the cult of the dead and deified great or Euemerism, phallicism, astrolatry, the zodiacal cult, or any other, are necessarily essentially incorrect in principle and correspondingly erroneous in general theory of interpretation. That which is a perfect explanation of one fact becomes idle when applied to another. Thus the mode of treatment here pursued is not based upon the exclusive application of any particular method of mythological investigation, nor again, has any school been wholly rejected, as being altogether beside the mark. As great writers have constantly given the world much that was unworthy of them, so very inferior scribes have occasionally left us things truly valuable.

To descend from general principles to the particular subject, it is to be observed that in studying a single important divinity or mythic cycle we are, to a considerable extent, studying Mythology as a whole. As the greater includes the less, so the more complicated mythic legend or idea when understood renders the simpler almost immediately transparent. The real history and nature of the mysterious Dionysos have perplexed many investigators in different ages. Thus Diodoros Sikelos expended great erudition upon the subject only to arrive at no conclusion; while Nonnos, who seems to have devoted the chief part of his life to the study and harmonisation of Dionysiak traditions almost innumerable, may well have doubted whether he really understood anything of the true meaning of the myth which he has succeeded in compressing into an amorphous unity. Theories of language utterly incorrect, a crude Euemerism, a wholesale and unreflecting acceptance of the statements of ancient authors without reference to their probable means of knowledge or trustworthiness, and a desire to support various preconceived opinions, chiefly religious, are rocks upon which many adventurers in these waters in modern times have been fatally shipwrecked. But if the failures of others in any department of knowledge were to be accepted as conclusive reasons for making no efforts ourselves, progress would cease to be a reality. Nothing is really useless, and we may learn much from previous errors. I do not intend to write a mythic life of Dionysos after the fashion of Nonnos, or as may be found shorn of poetical form and adjuncts in a Classical Dictionary: because a large amount of such detail would be of comparatively late date and unimportant character, and would in no way assist in enabling us to obtain a true concept of the god and a knowledge of his more archaic history. The treatment of the subject here adopted is as follows:—

I. The statements of early Hellenik writers from Homeros to Herodotos concerning Dionysos are examined and analysed in four chapters, respectively devoted to

1. The Dionysos of the Theologers, a title bestowed on Homeros, Hesiodos, and the imaginary Orpheus.[1]

2. The Lyric Dionysos, in which the representations of the god by Solon, Alkaios, Theognis, Anakreon, Simonides of Keos, Pratinas, Ion, Pindaros, and others, are considered.

3. Dionysos as he appears in the

> Tragic triad of immortal fames,
> Aischulos, Sophokles, Euripides.

4. Dionysos as he appears in the great work of Herodotos. It is unnecessary to extend the analysis after B.C. 400; the archaic idea of the god is, by that time, fixed and determined, and Herodotos himself is mainly valuable in this connection on account of his travels in the Outer-world. The Dionysiak allusions of later writers down to Nonnos, A.D. 550, will be noticed from time to time throughout the enquiry as may be requisite. At the conclusion of each chapter the Eikon, or personified idea of the god, to be found in the particular author or authors, will be given.

---

[1] Cf. Professor Max Müller, *Chips from a German Workshop*, ii. 127; Rev. G. W. Cox, *Mythol. of the Aryan Nations*, ii. 239 *et seq.* Aristoteles in a lost work declared that 'there never was such a person as Orpheus the poet.' Cic. *De Nat. Deor.* i. 38; vide also K. O. Müller, *Introduction to a Scientific System of Mythology. The Orphica*, 310 *et seq.* Some writers strangely continue to speak of Orpheus as a veritable Hellenik sage, who travelled in Egypt, India, &c. Platon calls him and Mousaios, Children of the Moon and the Muses. (*Rep.* ii.)

II. Turning from individual authorities to the course of daily Hellenik life, I shall next consider the god as he appears in the general Dionysiak cult of Hellas, at the festivals in connection with the divinities of Eleusis, and lastly in connection with the Drama.

III. Dionysos will next be noticed with reference to Art, as he appears in statuary, and on vase, coin, and gem.

IV. His principal epithets, about 150 in number, and the chief accompaniments of his cult, Bakchic words and things, will then be given alphabetically; and lastly, his seven protagonistic phases will be examined. At this point in the investigation, we shall be able to determine the Eikon of the Hellenik Dionysos, considered as an entirety.

V. Regarding the god as a divinity non-Hellenik in origin, I shall subsequently discuss the obscure question of the introduction of his cult into Hellas; shall notice his position in the Phoenician Outer-world; and finally, trace his worship to its origin in the earliest home of civilisation and religious-mythology. In an undertaking of such difficulty and intricacy, some minor matters may escape the most searching attention, but the plan of enquiry proposed probably omits no point of much importance.

As regards names, following the example of authorities of the greatest weight, I adopt forms approaching as nearly as possible to those originally employed. Thus, as the Hellenes did not call themselves Greeks, I have not so styled them.[1] The baneful practice of bestowing on Hellenik divinities the names of Latin divinities, which latter generally do not even represent the same personages under other appellations, is fortunately

---

[1] 'The name of Greeks is too firmly established to be changed [?]; but it is not a correct name.' (Glads. *Juv. Mun.* 31.)

rapidly becoming obsolete. But, as it is generally admitted that to call Athênê Minerva, is erroneous; so, similarly, it must be conceded that the divinities of Kaldea, Phoenicia, or Egypt, should not. be obscured under the names of Hellenik gods supposed to be their equivalents; or even under Hellenik forms of their own original appellations. Osiris and Isis are household words in mythology, but they must be made to give way to the more correct forms Uasar and Uasi. The same rule is applied to other names, and as these, when Hellenik are now generally and properly written in an Hellenik, instead of in a Latin form, so, in turn, Xerxes must yield to its original Khshayarsha, and Nebuchadnezzar reappear as Nabu-kudur-uzur. This, at first, may seem somewhat strange alike to ear and eye, but time will soon familiarise us with the change, which, being correct in principle, will gradually prevail. Its early supporters must expect to have the groundless charge of pedantry and affectation brought against them—a hardship which, however, they will probably be able to endure.

In the present age, so distinguished for mental activity in connection with religion, the importance of early religious-mythology and archaic belief is being rapidly recognised. Works long and learned have recently appeared, in which attempts have been made to resolve all religious systems into phallicism, ancestor-worship, or sun-worship in connection with the signs of the zodiac. These are dreams, as baseless as the long-exploded efforts of those investigators who regarded all mythology as merely an echo of the Noachian deluge. But both those who accept any particular creed, and those who do not, may alike find ample food for reflection in studying the human mind in past ages. The enquiry may be found to give some assistance on the important discussions respecting the foundations of belief, basis of a creed, supernatural religion, government of the world, and the like, which are at present so widely agitated amongst the thoughtful. There are certain questions of primary importance which will constantly recur throughout all time, although various ages impress their special characteristics upon particular aspects of them; such are enquiries respecting the nature of God and the world, time and space, good and evil, the relations between God and man, and the destiny of the latter. At present, the champions of orthodoxy and the contrary (I use these terms as best fitted to express my meaning, although in themselves far from unobjectionable), confront each other like Hector and Aias fairly matched, and it is impossible for an unenlightened spectator to decide which will ultimately prevail. There is, however, widely prevalent, a sort of spurious unorthodoxy which thinks it fashionable to profess to be a thinker, as the term is; to doubt this and deny that, and yet which at the end is sure to be found voting tamely with the orthodox majority, simply because they at present compose the larger crowd; a state of mind which dreads above all things expulsion from the social synagogue. Whilst every sympathy should be extended to honest doubt or disbelief, and its fearless expression in becoming language merits respectful attention, all earnest advocates of either side should unite in exposing the hypocritical religionist and the hypocritical unbeliever. Again, a narrow-minded and ignorant orthodoxy clinging to erroneous and obsolete interpretation and untrustworthy tradition, constantly makes itself ridiculous by crying out when in no way really injured. All truth, religious and scientific, must be harmonious; no truly honest mind will shrink from any amount of test or investigation being applied to its beliefs. An age or an individual may have a faulty concept of astronomy or of Christianity, yet these may in reality be perfect, for man's errors affect himself, not the truth at which he aims. A calm investigation of facts is almost always distasteful to an ardent partisan, but will commend itself to the judgment of that large moderate majority whose consistently steady action preserves the balance of things.

15

CHAPTER II.

THE DIONYSOS OF THE THEOLOGERS.

SECTION I.

THE HOMERIK DIONYSOS.

Subsection I.—The Episode of Lykourgos.

The first direct, and indeed the most important, notice of Dionysos in the Homerik Poems[1] occurs in the speech of Diomedes to Glaukos.[2] 'Who art thou?' enquires the former, and continues:—

> But if really one of the Immortals thou hast come from heaven
> I would not fight with the heavenly gods.
> For neither did even the son of Dryas, strong Lykourgos
> Live long, who truly strove with the heavenly gods,
> He who once the attendants of Raving Dionysos
> Pursued down the most-holy Nyseïan [Mount]. But they together all
> Their sacred-implements cast on the ground, by man-slaying Lykourgos
> Smitten with an ox-goad. But Dionysos being-terrified
> Sunk under the wave of the sea, and Thetis received him to her bosom
> Frightened; for strong trembling seized him at-the-angry-tone of the man.

---

[1] The belief that an actual historic individual, Homeros, composed the two great epic poems which have come down to us, is now again decidedly gaining ground. In this view, after considering the arguments of Wolf and his followers, and of Thirlwall, Grote, Mure, Gladstone, F. A. Paley, Cox, Köchly, and others, I respectfully concur. The question, however, does not directly concern the present enquiry.
[2] Il. vi. 123 et seq.

With him [Lykourgos] the gods who live in ease were afterwards enraged,
And the Son of Kronos made him blind : nor truly much longer
Did he live, since he was hated by all the immortal gods.
Neither should I wish to fight with the blessed gods.

Chapman translates :—

If heav'n be thy divine abode,
And thou a Deity thus inform'd, no more with any God
Will I change lances. The strong son of Dryus did not live
Long after such a conflict dar'd, who godlessly did drive
Nysaeus' nurses through the hill made sacred to his name,
And called Nysseius; with a goad he punch'd each furious dame,
And made them ev'ry one cast down their green and leavy spears.
This th' homicide Lycurgus did; and those ungodly fears,
He put the froes in, seiz'd their God. Ev'n Bacchus he did drive
From his Nysseius; who was fain, with huge exclaims, to dive
Into the ocean. Thetis there in her bright bosom took
The flying Deity; who so fear'd Lycurgus' threats, he shook.
For which the freely-living Gods so highly were incens'd,
That Saturn's great Son strook him blind, and with his life dispens'd
But small time after; all because th' Immortals lov'd him not,
Nor lov'd him since he striv'd with them; and his end hath begot
Fear in my pow'rs to fight with heav'n.

The first question which arises on this very remarkable legend is, Whether it should be treated as an addition to the original poem, an interpolation of a much later date? There appears to be nothing special in the phraseology to point to such a conclusion, nor have these lines generally been included amongst the more doubtful passages of the *Ilias*. But to the view of their genuineness, it has been objected that the whole speech and its sentiments are glaringly opposed to the character and conduct of Diomedes, who had shortly before contended triumphantly against two of the immortals, Aphrodite and Ares, and had even rushed undauntedly upon Aineas when under the immediate and visible protection of Apollon himself. The careful reader of the Homerik Poems will, however, be struck by the perfect harmony of the whole representation and the wonderful consistency of the author.[1] Diomedes pursues Kypris because Athene has ordered him to do so,[2] and because he knows her to be a strengthless divinity.[3] Encouraged by this success, he is emboldened to oppose Apollon, but receives a terrible check, and is reminded of the dissimilarity of the races of men and of gods.[4] He retires appalled, and Athene, afterwards finding him at some distance from the fight, chides him as being inferior to Tydeus, his sire, and urges him to attack Ares with her immediate personal assistance, by means of which he escapes death, and wounds the god.[5] The powers of Diomedes has been much overvalued alike by the timid Helenos,[6] who was suitably promoted in mediaeval times as Bishop of Troy, and by many moderns. Throughout the whole episode the Argeian warrior is merely the instrument of Athene, his father's patroness;[7] and she, having returned to the abode of Zeus,[8] the son of Tydeus, is naturally very undesirous to fight with the gallant Glaukos until assured that the latter is a mortal like himself. Apollon's warning is yet ringing in his ears, and he bethinks him of the fate of Lykourgos. It would have been a strange artistic blunder had the poet really per-

---

[1] According to some writers, if the Poems exhibit any inconsistency, the circumstance is proof positive of diversity of authorship; but if they are consistent, then the circumstance shows that they have been artificially harmonised. Thus there is no escape. 'Here Papists swing, there Protestants are burnt.'
[2] Il. v. 132.
[3] Il. v. 330.
[4] Il. v. 441.
[5] Cf. Ruskin, *Queen of the Air*, i. 36.
[6] Il. vi. 90.
[7] Il. iv. 390.
[8] Il. v. 907.

mitted any Hellenik hero seriously to vie with his protagonist Achilleus, 'much the best of the Achaioi;' and in the hour of their deepest distress the son of Peleus scornfully observes that Diomedes, by some erroneously supposed to be his rival in warlike prowess, cannot save them.[1] These considerations, which in the main did not escape the ancient commentators, illustrate the perfect propriety of the introduction of the Episode of Lykourgos by Diomedes at the particular place and time in which it appears, and thus being satisfied that the passage is of equal authority and antiquity with its immediate surroundings, we may next proceed to consider its statements.

And first, it is no Ogygian legend of remote antiquity which is referred to by the king of Argos. Nestor, in his youth, had personally known Dryas, the father of Lykourgos, and classes him among that band of heroes, Peirithoös, Kaineus, Exadios, and Polyphemos, king of the Lapithai, whom the old man declares were superior to all men whom he had seen or was likely to see.[2] Hence the incident is represented as having taken place in times then comparatively recent. We next notice the extraordinary delineation of the god, the reality of whose divinity is at the same time most fully acknowledged; he is represented as a terrified child, or even infant, and yet as having allies or protectors so powerful that the opposition of Lykourgos is hopeless, and his temporary success only the more delusive. Zeus, god amongst gods, acknowledges the raving stranger as his son,[3] and personally avenges him with the full assent of the other divinities; and the strong son of the mighty Dryas, and his fellow-sufferer, Pentheus, remain for ages as monuments of the wrath and power of Dionysos.[4] Dionysos flies to Thetis, 'the recon-

---

[1] *Il.* xvi. 74.
[2] *Il.* i. 263.
[3] *Il.* xiv. 325.

[4] Cf. Ais. *Lykourgeia*; Soph. *Antig.* 955; Eur. *Rhesos.* 972.

ciler between the conflicting creeds,'[1] who, in like manner, 'received to her bosom'[2] another Oriental divinity, Hephaistos, when, like Dionysos, a temporary outcast from Aryan regions.[3] The son of Semele requites the kindness of Thetis by the gift of the golden urn in which the bones of Achilleus were placed, and which was made by his brother Semite Hephaistos.[4] It will be observed that Dionysos is not expressly stated to be, but is represented as if he were, a child or infant. Here are two distinct ideas (1) that of the god as youthful, in consequence of his cult being yet of recent introduction; and (2) that of the god as ever fresh and young as connected with all green and growing things,[5] as representative of the powers of reproduction and resurrection, as Orthagoras[6] and Erikapeios, in a word, as the 'puer aeternus,'[7] or Ever-Youth. The Thrakian Edonoi, over whom Lykourgos is said to have ruled, were celebrated for their devotion to the Dionysiak cult,[8] and, as Niebuhr notes, 'the southern coast of Thrace is one of the countries in which the nobler kinds of wine were produced at a very early period.'[9] As to the most holy mount of Nysa, we shall find that wherever the Bakchik cult prevailed, whether in Thrake, Boiotia, Euboia, Naxos, or elsewhere, this name is found,[10] and that, therefore, it is not originally connected with any particular Hellenik locality.[11] Such being the principal incidents of this remarkable myth, how is it to be understood? It may be boldly affirmed that the legend is inexplicable unless received historically, *i.e.*, that it more or less truthfully commemorates certain actual historical facts; which are (1) the foreign, *i.e.*,

---

[1] Glads. *Juv. Mun.* 338.
[2] *Il.* vi. 136; xviii. 398.
[3] Cf. *Il.* xviii. 393 *et seq.*; *Poseidon*, xiv.
[4] *Od.* xxiv. 74.
[5] Vide *inf.* VIII. i.; *Dendrites, Karpios, Kissous*, &c.
[6] Aristoph. *Ek.* 916.
[7] Ovid. *Metam.* iv. 17.
[8] Cf. Hor. *Car.* ii. 7.
[9] *Lectures upon Ancient Ethnography*, i. 233.
[10] Vide *inf.* VIII. i. *Nysios.*
[11] Ibid. IX. viii.

non-Hellenik, origin of Dionysos; (2) the introduction of his cult into the West; and (3) the violent but unsuccessful opposition which it excited. Whether Lykourgos was a real or an imaginary king of the Edonoi, or of any other kindred or neighbouring tribe, or whether, as has been conjectured, the name is that of a rival native deity 'worshipped perhaps with phallic rites like the Roman Luperci,'[1] is quite immaterial; the purport and general bearing of the legend cannot be mistaken. I am not aware that anyone has attempted to explain it by the aid of the Natural Phenomena Theory, but any such attempt, if made would be about as rational as the assertion that the campaigns of Kudurlagamer[2] represent astronomical allegories. Colonel Mure, who somewhat arbitrarily transfers the scene of the tale to Boiotia, very properly regards Lykourgos as 'a type of the resistance offered to the spread of those extravagant (Bakchik) orgies.'[3] Mr. Gladstone remarks, 'What is most clear about Dionusos in Homer is, first, that his worship was extremely recent; secondly, that it made its appearance in Thrace; thirdly, that it was violently opposed on its introduction, a fact of which we have other records, as, for example, in the *Bakchae* of Euripides;'[4] and even Mr. Cox admits that 'the opposition of the Thrakian Lykourgos and the Theban Pentheus to the cultus of Dionysos is among the few indications of historical facts exhibited in Hellenik mythology.'[5] In this brief Homerik sketch the god appears, somewhat as we are accustomed to see him in the Attik dramatists, as Bakcheios the Exciter-to-phrensy, accompanied by his attendant Bakchai (not the Nymphs his nurses), with their Thysthla or sacred implements, not merely the Thyrsoi. The circumstance, however, affords no proof of the

---

[1] Mr. F. A. Paley, *in loc.*
[2] *Gen.* xiv.
[3] *Crit. Hist.* i. 151.
[4] *Juv. Mun.* 319.
[5] *Mythol. of the Aryan Nations*, ii. 294.

spurious character and comparatively late date of the passage; but, on the contrary, illustrates at once the antiquity of Bakchik worship, and the fidelity with which earlier traditions were preserved to later ages. Nor, again, can it be said, that the pristine cult of the god was merely that of Dionysos Theoinos, giver of wine and lord of the vine, and that on this primitive Aryan idea the Semitic orgies of the East were grafted. Homeros is quite innocent of any such notion. It is not to an Aryan Dionysos metamorphosed into a Semitic Sabazios that the ruler of the Edonoi objects, but to Dionysos altogether, in origin and in growth. Again, the Dionysos of the *Ilias* in no way differs from the Dionysos of the *Homerik Hymns*. The god of each is the son of a Kadmeian, *i.e.*, Oriental, not of a Boiotik, mother; is connected with the mysterious Nysa; is supposed to be weak, but in reality is most potent; is opposed and insulted, and terribly avenged. In each case his would-be oppressors are smitten with blindness; not the mystic blindness of the great poets and prophets, Teiresias, Thamyris, and others, but the blindness of Pentheus, which is unable to foresee the coming vengeance of the god, that heaven-sent mania under the impulses of which the guilty wretch fulfils his doom, according to the familiar saying, 'Quem vult perdere Deus prius dementat.' And so, we do not find Lykourgos represented in other legends as having been physically blinded, but merely has having been smitten with Bakchik madness, in which state he kills his son Dryas, supposing that he was pruning vines.[1] Such, then, are the principal features in the Episode of Lykourgos; other points, more or less connected with it, I shall have occasion to notice again in the course of the enquiry; but let the reader always bear in mind the important fact which will receive

[1] Apollod. iii. 5.

ample confirmation as we proceed, and which is set forth with unanswerable force by this the earliest of Helleniko-Dionysiak legends, altered and trimmed as it may have been from time to time by rhapsodist or grammarian, that *Dionysos in origin is a non-Hellenik divinity, whose whole cult breathes of that Semitic East where first it originated.*

Subsection II.—*Dionysos, son of Semele.*

In *Ilias*, xiv. 317–27, a passage which, although probably of genuine antiquity, is yet not quite beyond the reach of suspicion, having been doubted, amongst others, by some of the Alexandrine critics; Zeus gives a list of some of his most illustrious children and their mothers. Amongst these occur, side by side, the two Theban divinities Herakles and Dionysos, the former son of Alkmene, the latter of Semele. Both gods are stated to have been born in Thebai, and Semele is mentioned in a Homerik Hymn[1] as one of the family of Kadmos, who himself is only directly alluded to in the Poems on the occasion where Odysseus is assisted by his daughter, the once mortal but afterwards deified Ino Leukotheë,[2] The inhabitants of the Thebais, however, are called Kadmeioi and Kadmeiones,[3] after Kadmos, their reputed ancestor. 'I loved Semele in Thebai,' says Zeus, 'and she bore Dionysos, a-source-of-joy to mortals.' The Episode of Lykourgos had left us in ignorance of the race of Dionysos, but this important passage links him with the house of the Phoenician Kadmos, and the mystic City of the Seven Gates; in other words, with the Semitic East. As to the legend of Kadmos, which Bunsen truly calls 'a wonderful myth,' suffice it to say here that the unanimous

---

[1] *Eis Dionyson*, v. 57. *inf.* VI. i. 2.
[2] *Od.* v. 333. As to Ino, vide [3] *Il.* iv. 385 *et seq.*; v. 804 *et seq.*

voice of antiquity describes him as an Oriental stranger, Phoenician or Egyptian, the founder of the legendary Thebai; nor does the Homerik version differ from others, for Zethos and Amphion founded the Lower City, Hypothebai,[1] described as Eurychoros, Spacious,[2] like Sparte; while Kadmos founded the Upper City, or comparatively small Kadmeia. Homeros distinguishes, as Pausanias observes,[3] between the Lower City and the Kadmeia.[4] That this tradition contains very important historic truth, sound modern opinion, in harmony with the universal belief of antiquity, admits.[5] Dionysos, therefore, in Homerik mythic genealogy, is a Phoenician by the mother's side, and adopted by the Aryan Zeus, into whose realm he has penetrated. But he is also said to be 'a-source-of-joy to mortals,' and the wonderful propriety of this description will only become apparent when we fully realise his various phases. Once for all, let me caution the reader against simply regarding Dionysos as Theoinos the Wine-god, and supposing that he is merely a source of joy as making glad the heart of man with the juice of the grape. This would, indeed, be a sadly incomplete concept of the son of Semele. As well might we suppose that Zeus was naught but Ombrios, the Rain-god, or Poseidon only Kyanochaites, the Lord-of-the-dark-blue-sea. Moreover, all the aspects of Dionysos Theoinos are by no means joyful, since wine has a double influence, producing, on the one hand, happiness and exhilaration, and, on the other, misery and madness. The Wine-god might thus have been properly represented as

---

[1] *Il.* ii. 505.
[2] *Od.* xi. 263.
[3] Paus. ii. 6.
[4] Vide *inf.* X. ii.
[5] Cf. Niebuhr, *Ancient Ethnography*, i. 114; Kenrick, *Phoenicia*, 97 *et seq.*; Donaldson, *Theatre of the Greeks*, 14 *et seq.*; Thirlwall, *Hist. Greece*, i. 58, 60; Bähr in *Herod.* v. 57; Creuzer, *Symbolik*, iv. 236; Mure, *Crit. Hist.* iii. 490; Rawlinson, *Herod.* ii. 78; Lenormant, *La légende de Cadmus*, and *Ancient Hist. of the East*, ii. 160, 204; Gladstone, *Juv. Mun.* 122; Grote, *Hist. Greece*, ii. 357; and Rev. G. W. Cox, *Mythology of the Aryan Nations*, ii. 86.

Janus-faced, and so at times we see him as Psychodaiktes, the Destroyer-of-the-soul,[1] or Hypnophobes, the Terrifier-during-sleep, *i.e.* by sending dreadful dreams. Thus Dionysos as Theoinos would be by no means a source of unmixed joy to mortals.[2] But Homeros calls him *Charma*, a mystic charm, soothing as the Nepenthe of Polydamna;[3] (1) as aye fresh and young, the Ever-Youth, a new-fledged Eros in perennial vigour; (2) as Hymeneïos, god of marriage and rejoicing; (3) as Karpios and kindred epithets, which connect him with the beautiful green earth in its might of strength and growth; (4) as Melpomenos, the Singer and leader of the cheerful song-and-dance; (5) as Hygiates, the Healer, and restorer to sound health and vigour; and (6) as Theoinos, the Exhilirater-by-wine. Let the reader consider the combined force of epithets such as these, and he will see how truly Dionysos was regarded as a source of joy, and how rightly Hesiodos calls him Polygethes the Much-cheering, and Ploutarchos, Charidotes the Joy-giver.

Subsection III.—*Dionysos and Naxos.*

Odysseus, when recounting his adventures in the Under-world, states that he saw 'beautiful Ariadne, daughter of Minos, whom once Theseus was conducting to the cultivated soil of sacred Athenai; but Artemis slew her in sea-girt Dia, through the testimony of Dionysos.'[4] The common tradition about Ariadne, daughter of the Phoenician Minos,[5] represents her as having been abandoned by Theseus in Naxos, and found there by Dionysos, who makes her his wife. But in this Homerik legend the chaste Artemis avenges the profanation of a sanctuary by the flying lovers, as Kybele had done in the

---

[1] Cf. Hos. iv. 11.
[2] Cf. Hesiod. *Aspis Herak*, 400.
[3] *Od.* iv. 220
[4] *Od.* xi. 321.
[5] Cf. *Il.* xiv. 321; *Juv. Mun.* chap. v.

THE DIONYSOS OF THE THEOLOGERS.

case of Hippomenes and the Boiotik Atalante; and she does so on behalf and at the instigation of Dionysos, who was, therefore, the god of the place. The sea-girt Dia, otherwise called Dionysias, or the Isle-of-the-Zeus-of-Nysa, is Naxos, also known as Strongyle the Circular,[1] and noted for its devotion to the cult of the god, whose sacred Kanthar, or two-handled Drinking-Cup,[2] appears on its coins; and which, like all Bakchik localities in Hellas, contained a Nysa.[3] Thus the Theban Chorus[4] allude to the Naxian maids :—

> Who all night long with phrensied spirit sing
> And dance in honour of their Bakchik King.

As the cult of the Semitic Kypris slips along from isle to isle of the Aigaion, until, as Aphrodite Anadyomene or Rising-from-the-sea, she passes over from Kythera to Lakonike on the mainland, where the hardy Spartans, while receiving her, put her in chains;[5] so the Semitic Dionysos advances by degrees, subduing Ikaros,[6] Naxos, Thasos,[7] and Euboia, where was also a Nysa,[8] and landing at length on the shores of Thrake and Boiotia.[9] 'Planxerunt te Nysa ferax Theseaque Naxos.'[10] As the poet suggests no direct connection between Dionysos and Ariadne, it is unnecessary for me here to notice the position of the latter in the Natural Phenomena Theory as the deserted bride of the solar hero Theseus; but it may be observed that if Ariadne, the Very-holy-one,[11] was represented as deserted in Naxos, and as being subsequently found there by Dionysos,[12] there must have been some special connection between the god and the island.[13]

---

[1] Cf. Diod. Sik. v. 50, 51; *Poseidon*, x.
[2] Vide *inf.* VIII. ii. *Cup*.
[3] Cf. Hesychios *in voc. Nysa*.
[4] Soph. *Antig.* 1150.
[5] Cf. K. O. Müller, *Doric Race*, i. 420.
[6] Cf. Hom. Hym. apud Diod. Sik. iii. 66.
[7] Herod. vi. 47.
[8] Soph. *Antig.* 1150; Schol. Apollon. Rhod. iv. 540.
[9] Cf. Eur. *Bak.* 20.
[10] Statius, *Thebais*, vii. 685.
[11] Cf. Bunsen, *Egypt's Place*, iv. 246.
[12] Cf. Pherekydes, *Frag.* cvi.
[13] Cf. Diod. Sik. iv. 61, v. 52.

Subsection IV.—*Dionysos and the Tyrsenoi.*

In the first of the Homerik Hymns [1] to Dionysos, we read how the god appeared as a youth on the sea-shore, and was seized by Tyrsenian pirates, who in vain attempt to bind him. The fetters fall from his hands and feet [2] 'and he continued sitting smiling with dark blue eyes.' The wise pilot, Medeides, warns the infatuated crew that the beautiful stranger must be a god, Zeus, Apollon, or Poseidon; but they, like Lykourgos and other contemnors of Dionysos, are stricken with blindness, and bring him on board their ship. Then wonders appear. Wine trickles down the deck, ivy twines round mast and oars, and the vine covers the sails. The god changing into a lion,[3] and further alarming the pirates by the apparition of a phantom bear, seizes on the captain while the terrified crew leap overboard and are changed into dolphins;[4] and the wise pilot is crowned with good fortune and encouraged by the god who reveals himself as 'Dionysos Eribromos, the Loud-shouting,[5] whom a Kadmeian mother Semele bore, being embraced by Zeus.'

> And thus, all excellence of grace to thee,
> Son of sweet-count'nance-carrying Semele.
> *Chapman.*

This story is exactly parallel to that of Lykourgos, and occurs somewhat later in the history of Dionysos, who no longer appears as a child taking refuge with the friendly Thetis, but as a youth confident in his own power to resist and avenge. As usual, however, he seems to be weak, and is insulted accordingly; but this time by strangers of the West, wandering Tyrsenoi or Etruscans, who live far

---

[1] These compositions may contain some few passages later than B.C. 600.
[2] Cf. Eur. *Bak.* 445.
[3] Vide *inf.* VIII. ii. *Lion.*
[4] Vide VIII. ii. *Dolphin.*
[5] Vide *inf.* VIII. i. *Bromios.*

THE DIONYSOS OF THE THEOLOGERS.

away in lands near the setting sun, where the Dionysiak cult has not yet penetrated. But the time has gone by when father Zeus had to avenge his adopted son, and all the savage Semitic element in the god's composition rushes to the front. The beautiful youth disappears, and Dionysos Agrionios, or the Savage,[1] stands before us in wild-beast fury, as his ancient Boiotik worshippers saw him in his festival at Orchomenos.[2] No longer Antheus the Blooming youth, he becomes Omestes the Raw-flesh-eating, and death and horror seize the ill-fated despisers, for in the words of Euripides, he is 'to men both most terrible and most mild.'[3] This is no myth of the power of wine on man. Neither the god or his enemies are represented as being in any way influenced by the grape. The tale has the same moral as the legends of Lykourgos, Pentheus, Damaskos,[4] and others,—death and ruin to the despisers and opponents of the new god, the son of Semele.

Subsection V.—The Youth of Dionysos.

In *Homerik Hymn*, xxiv., the poet sings how Dionysos Kissokomes, the Ivy-Chapleted, was nurtured by the Nymphs[5] in a cave[6] in the dells of the mysterious Nysa, which only appears to vanish, like the oriental gardens of Irem; a myth connected with the tale of the Bakchik city of Libye which no one could find twice,[7] and with inaccessible paradises and shadowy isles of delight in East and West.[8] Ivy 'never-sere' is a fitting ornament for the

---

[1] Vide *inf.* VIII. i. *Agrionios*.
[2] Vide *inf.* VI. i. 2.
[3] *Bak.* 861.
[4] An imaginary personage very unnecessarily excogitated as the founder of the ancient city of Damesek. He was said to have resisted the introduction of the vine, and to have been flayed alive by the god. The legend is a copy of others, late, and unimportant.
[5] Cf. Ais *Dionysou Trophoi*, Diod. Sik. v. 52.
[6] As to the Mithraik cave and its solar connection, vide *inf.* XII. i. 4.
[7] Strabo, vii. 3.
[8] Vide Rev. S. B. Gould, *Curious Myths of the Middle Ages*, The Fortunate Isles; Southey, *Thalaba the Destroyer*, book i.; Washington Irving, *Life of Columbus*, Appendix.

28 THE GREAT DIONYSIAK MYTH.

Ever-Youth, who 'is numbered with the immortals,' as the after-chosen Matthias was among the Apostles. The wood resounds with the wild mirth of the growing deity Dionysos Dasyllios the Dweller-in-the-thickets, and the poet concludes with a prayer to him, as Polystaphylos the Rich-in-grape-clusters, that, as a source of joy, he would grant long and happy life to his votaries. Here the god is represented as having received immortality, and in his character of Kissokomes, his locks bound with the deathless ivy, as being himself a giver of life to his faithful worshippers.

Subsection VI.—General character of the Dionysos of the Homerik Hymns.

As Aristoteles is the philosopher of the ancients, and Strabo the geographer, so is Homeros the poet, and to the poet is erroneously ascribed the composition of a vast number of ancient verses and hymns, the scattered productions of various rhapsodists and Orphiks, dating from the later heroic epoch down to the times of Kleisthenes. One fragment of a Hymn to Dionysos [1] celebrates him as Eiraphiotes the Thigh-sewn,[2] and another as Gynaimanes the Erotic, 'the son of Semele, whom men call Thyone,' the Inspired. Nysa, or Nyse, his birthplace, is a lofty wood-crowned mountain, 'far from Phoinike, near the flowings of Aigyptos,' i.e. Neilos.[3] 'Others,' says the Hymn-writer, 'falsely say that he was born in Thebai.' This testimony is true, and all these traditions point unanimously to some portion of the Semitic East as the real birthplace of the god, who lives in his cult far and wide over the Hellenik world. To ascertain the exact age of this or that particular myth is a difficulty frequently

[1] Apud Diod. Sik. iii. 66.
[2] Vide VIII. i. Eiraphiotes.
[3] Cf. Od. xiv. 25; vide inf. VIII. i. Nysios.

amounting to impossibility, but be it remembered that the most familiar version of a legend, Homerik or otherwise, is not necessarily the oldest; and that legends *do not originate at that point in history when we first meet with them*, but have almost invariably been in existence previously, possibly for centuries. Tales have often been classed amongst late inventions or introductions, as being supposed to be contrary to the spirit or knowledge of more primitive ages, when in reality our acquaintance with such earlier times is probably insufficient to enable us to judge whether this or that particular assumption or idea is in harmony with them or not. Thus without being dogmatic about dates, like the writers who once informed us that Troia was taken June 22, B.C. 1184, we may safely consider some of these Homerik Fragments as of very high antiquity, and as embodying conceptions necessarily older than themselves; for the real poet, whether a writer of hymns or drinking-songs, never arbitrarily invents, but takes some portion of existing truth or fact, and moulds it into a new and distinct shape of beauty or power. Thus when we find Diodoros alluding to the Bakchik Hymns of Eumolpos the Thrakian, a contemporary in mythic history with Erektheus of Athenai, also said to have been the founder of the Eleusinian Mysteries, and priest of Demeter and Dionysos, and quoting the line, 'Dionysos, with face of flame, glitters like a star with his rays,' although we are not in the least bound to recognize the existence of a particular Eumolpos, yet that there was an ancient *Good-singer* we need not doubt; nor does it necessitate any violent effort of imagination to believe that some few fragments of his muse may have been preserved to us. Dionysos Pyropos, or the Fiery-eyed, who
                    Flings
From each plumed arc, pale glitterings
And fiery flakes,

widely differs from an Hellenik concept, as will probably be acknowledged; but this fact by no means necessarily implies the late date of the idea, as belonging to the time when Hellas was invaded by a vast wave of Oriental cults, that passing over it broke upon Imperial Rome beyond. The early, not to say the prehistoric, connection between East and West is becoming ever more apparent, as patient research slowly unveils the buried annals of Kam,[1] and Phoenicia, of Assur and Bab-ilu;[2] and, as it were, unearths from the recesses of immemorial tombs ever-burning lamps whose rays, like those from Dionysos Pyropos, cast new light and meaning on the course of Hellenik history. Let the Agnostics, for whom ante-Olympiak time in Hellas is but a blank and void, Tohu-and-Bohu, be content to accept the curtain as the picture, and to pass by miracle at a bound from legend to history in the wonderful year B.C. 776.[3] But let not their want of faith on the one hand, or the vast credulity of former enquirers on the other, deter the student of the Earlier Time from the quiet pursuit of his researches; it being his duty, as Bunsen well says, ' to throw out piquets into the empire of history which is to be conquered, as far as his means will permit.' It is unnecessary to allude further to the ancient Hymn Fragments; they all tell us, either directly or by implication, that Dionysos was not *originally* born in the Boiotian

---

[1] Egypt. 'Called in the hieroglyphics Kam, or the Black, from the colour of the alluvial mud of the Nile. To the Hebrews it was known as Mitsraim, or the Two Mitsrs, an appellation found also in the Assyrian as Musr, and the Persian as Mudraya; but the Greeks called it Aiguptos, a word of uncertain derivation retained at the present day as Egypt.' (Birch, *Egypt from the Earliest Times*, Introduction, i.)

[2] Babylon, *i.e.* Gate of God.

[3] Even this magical date is somewhat doubtful. Vide *The Olympiads in connection with the Golden Age of Greece*; W. R. A. Boyle, in the *Transactions of the Society of Biblical Archaeology*, ii. 289–300. Well, says Mr. H. Spencer, 'The assumption that any decided division can be made between legend and history is untenable. To suppose that at a certain stage we pass suddenly from the mythical to the historical, is absurd' (*The Principles of Sociology*, No. 40, Appendix).

Thebai, though the city of Kadmos, was his Hellenik birthplace; or, in other words, that his cult reached it from the Outer-world. The god is thus, in another sense, Dimetor, Bimater, Son-of-two-mothers.

Subsection VII.—Dionysos and the Kyklik Poems.

The *Ilias* and the *Odysseia* are the sole standing columns of the great temple of the Epik Cycle, and around their bases lie a few fragments of their once companions, deemed by some to have been of almost as fine a workmanship as the two survivors, though I doubt not but that these were 'the two middle pillars upon which the house stood,' and that their preservation is an instance of the 'survival of the fittest.' This great Cycle contained a history of the world from the marriage of Heaven and Earth down to the death of Odysseus by the unwitting hand of his son Telegonos, and treated at length of the Wars of the Titanes, of Thebai, and of Troia. Three at least of the Epik poems, the *Oidipodeia*, the *Thebais*, and the *Epigonoi*, were devoted to the history of the Kadmeis, and one of the very few surviving lines of the later work speaks of

Venerable Earth, and "Zagreus" highest of all gods.

A glimpse such as this enables us to imagine to some extent what has been lost, and how much easier it would have been to trace the progress of an obscure and shadowy divinity like Dionysos, did we possess the complete works of the Epik poets, of Pindaros, Anakreon, Aischylos, Sophokles, Euripides, Aristophanes, and others, instead of only a comparatively small portion of them, not to mention numbers of interesting, perhaps admirable, writers whose every line has perished. Mr. Grote, when speaking of the writings of the Ancient World, truly says,

'We possess only what has drifted ashore from the wreck of a stranded vessel.' That Semitic influence, still very perceptible in Hellenik history, although so coldly admitted by some, and so boldly denied by others, would, had we the materials of antiquity, have been far more apparent; but fortunately sufficient traces of it remain to enable us to construct, to a considerable extent, an account of its early progress, as the fragments of colouring found in ancient churches recall to the skilled restorer the period when the shades of the walls corresponded with the hues of the windows. That Zagreus is a phase of the mystic Dionysos, is sufficiently well known,[1] and his intimate connection with the venerable Earth-mother, De-meter, will become more apparent when we consider the combined cult of Demeter and Iakchos in the historical Eleusinian Mysteries.[2] But it will be observed that Zagreus is represented as a Zeus Hypsistos, Jupiter the Highest, god of gods; and so, Dionysos, although in Aryan regions, son of the Aryan Zeus, whom he was unable to dethrone, is himself a Zeus, but in Hellas only the Zeus of Nysa.[3] His place in the Aryan pantheon, into which he was admitted as a stranger divinity, was much lower than the one occupied by him in the land where his cult first originated, and hence, he might easily be regarded esoterically by his worshippers as being far greater than he appeared by comparison with other deities of the earlier Aryan religion,[4] and so, in the *Bakchai* the barbarian Chorus declare that he 'is inferior to none of the gods.'[4] Only one other allusion to him is preserved amongst the few surviving fragments of the Kyklics. Isaac Tzetzes, cir. A.D. 1150, author of the Commentary on the *Kassandra* of Lykophron, mentions that the writer of the Epik poem called the *Kyprian*

---

[1] *Inf.* IX. vi. *Zagreus.*
[2] Ibid. VI. ii.
[3] Cf. Diod. Sik. iii. 64.
[4] V. 777.

THE DIONYSOS OF THE THEOLOGERS. 33

Verses, who may have been Stasinos of Kypros, related the story of Roio, the beloved of Apollon and the daughter of Staphylos the Argonaut, son of Dionysos and Ariadne. Roio was shut up in a chest by her father, and thrown into the sea, a repetition of the legend which related that Semele had been so treated by Kadmos on his discovery of her intrigue with Zeus. The chest was cast up on the shore of Euboia, and broken by the waves; and Roio, saved from the sea, called her newborn son Anios, the Ben-oni or Son of Sorrow. Anios became the father of three daughters, Oino, Spermo, and Elais, to whom Dionysos gave the magic power of producing any quantity of wine, corn, and oil, with which they supplied the Achaioi during the first nine years of the Troian War. The general purport of the myth is sufficiently evident. Staphylos or Bunch-of-grapes, is the father of Roio, the Flowing-wine, beloved by Apollon, whose genial rays ripen the fruit. Then follows the familiar idea of the outraged and revengeful sire who, like Kadmos or Akrisios, shuts the frail fair one in a chest and casts her into the sea. The child is naturally Anios, the Son of Sorrow, but he is the great grandson of Dionysos, and, his mother's troubles being over, the genial element re-appears in the story, and his daughters, Oino, wine, Spermo, seed, and Elais, oil, support the Achaian host before Troia. Dionysos, it will be observed, is not merely the father of Wine alone. Seed and Oil are equally his daughters, for he is the lord of the producing vitality of the venerable Earth-mother. The principle of explaining legends from the signification of the names of personages mentioned in them is frequently both sound and serviceable, but may easily be overstrained. Thus Eumolpos may, in the abstract, be merely a general term for a Poet or Good-singer, and Homeros for a Stitcher-together of lays and ballads; but

Argos is not necessarily the Land of Whiteness, nor Lykia that of Light, in any aërial or heavenly sense.[1]

Subsection VIII.—Eikon of the Homerik Dionysos.

The Homerik Dionysos appears as the son of Zeus, and Semele daughter of Kadmos; as a stranger opposed and injured on his first entry into the regions of the West; as enrolled among the cycle of Aryan and Hellenik divinities, to which he did not originally belong;[2] as a god apparently feeble, yet potent to revenge himself; and as locally connected with Naxos, Thrake, and the Boiotik Thebai. He is a charm or soothing joy to mortals, and crowned with the deathless ivy can grant life to his votaries, himself the dark-eyed, smiling, blooming, and eternal youth. Women minister in his orgies, and the wine is consecrated in his worship. The green earth-mantle is his robe of freshness and beauty, adorned with the embroidery of flowers which chaplet the brows of Dionysos Antheus, and he breathes of sunny skies, pure air, ever-verdant meadows, and flowing streams. Father is he of grape-clusters, of corn, and wine, and oil, and of the fatness of the earth beneath. But, like Janus, he has another face. The dark and smiling eyes can deepen and intensify till they burn and scorch with the fierce rays of Dionysos Pyropos. The perfect vigour of the beautiful youth can develope into the fierce bound of the savage beast of prey, Dionysos Omestes, the Raw-flesh-eating;[3] Dasyllios, the apparently innocent rustic deity, can also appear as Agrionios, the ruthless and savage. This curious two-fold character, this face at

---

[1] Cf. De Quincy on the conclusions to be drawn from the meanings of Hellenik names. *Works*, v. 316 *et seq.*

[2] Cf. Clem. Alex. *Strom.* i. 21. 'Dionysos was deified in the thirty-second year of the reign of Perseus, as Apollodorus says, in his [truly valuable] *Chronology*.'

[3] Vide *inf.* IV. iii. 2; VIII. i. *Omestes.*

once grim and smiling, 'Dionysos, son of Zeus, a god at once most terrible and most gentle to mortals,'[1] we shall see developed throughout his career; its closer consideration belongs to another stage of the enquiry. With reference to the introduction of the Dionysiak cult into Hellas, Mr. Gladstone well remarks: 'We cannot, perhaps, treat the Dionusos of Homer as the discoverer of wine, and father of its use, in Greece; for it is universal and familiar, while he appears to be but local and as yet strange. The novel feature, which connects itself with his name, seems to be the use of wine by women; and the effect produced, in an extraordinary and furious excitement, which might well justify not only jealousy, but even forcible resistance to demoralising orgies. It seems, then, as if this usage was introduced by immigrants of a race comparatively wealthy and luxurious, and was resisted by, or on behalf of, the older and simpler population.'[2] Professor Mayor, commenting on *Od.* ix. 197, where allusion is made to the skin of excellent wine given to Odysseus by Maron, priest of Apollon, remarks: 'Neither here, nor in the vineyard of Alkinoös, nor in the vintage scene on the Shield of Achilleus, do we find Dionysos; *hence he cannot have been the god of wine to Homer.*'[3] I think it will clearly appear that this inference is amply justified. There is one more incident in the description of the Homerik Dionysos which is not without a special significance. The poet never admits him to that wide heaven, the peculiar home and abode of Zeus Hypsistos,[4]

---

[1] Eur. *Bak.* 860.
[2] *Juv. Mun.* 319.
[3] *The Narrative of Odysseus,* i. 108.
[4] I have endeavoured to show (*Poseidon,* xxix.) that the customary Homerik formula for the Aryan divinities is 'the gods who possess the wide heaven.' Mr. Gladstone (*Juv. Mun.* 318) quotes Nagelsbach to the effect that Homeros places neither Dionysos or Demeter in Olympos by any distinct declaration. As Demeter is unquestionably an Aryan divinity, this must seem an exception to the principle above suggested. Even if it be an exception, the reason of it is not far to seek, as it would seem to us to be a strange clashing of ideas to place Earth in

that clear blue aether which is far removed from the career and independent of the sway, alike of the terrestrial Dionysos and of the chthonian Zagreus, whose lurid torches, though for a time they may obscure, can never vie with, the pure beauty of its incorruptible stars.[1]

SECTION II.

THE DIONYSOS OF HESIODOS.

Subsection I.—Dionysos, son of Semele.

'To Zeus,' says the poet of Askra,[2] 'Semele, daughter of Kadmos, bore a famous son Dionysos, the Much-cheering,[3] an immortal though she was mortal. But now both are deities.' The Hesiodik account is thus in perfect accord with the Homerik; Dionysos is a Kadmeion, *i.e.* a Son of the East. The primary meaning of the word *phaidmos*, 'famous,' is that which is brought to light or made to appear, and hence that which strikes the eye remarkably. Some of its fellow words are *phaino*, 'to bring to light;' *phane*, 'a torch,' *i.e.* that-which-brings-things-to-light; and Phanes, the Apparent-one, the Orphik Demiurge, who has made, and in making has brought to light, all created things which form his 'living

Heaven; but Demeter in Homerik idea probably had too much anthropic personality to make the concept incongruous, and as all the gods are said to possess Olympos (*Il.* i. 606), it is likely that he regarded both Dionysos and Demeter as at times present there. The distinction is between the two formulas—'the gods who possess Olympos,' or the entire Pantheon; and 'the gods who possess the wide heaven,' or the Aryan members of it only.

[1] The originally protagonistic solar phase of the god (*Inf.* sec. iii. 2, XII. i.) does not appear directly in Homeros, though clearly developed in the Hymns. In Phoenicia and Egypt the kosmogonic element became very pronounced, and consequently, to some extent, interfered with the former.
[2] *Theog.* 940-2.
[3] Polygethes (cf. Pind. *Frag.* cxxx.

THE DIONYSOS OF THE THEOLOGERS.

visible garment.'[1] Whether Hesiodos uses *phaidimos*, one of his epithets for Dionysos, in this primary sense, or merely in the secondary sense of 'famous,' is of course doubtful; but it should be remembered that Phanes in the Orphik Theogony[2] is identified with Dionysos, and this circumstance illustrates the exceedingly important kosmogonic aspect of the Dionysiak Myth.[3] Phaidimos occurs in Homeros[4] as the name of the king of the Sidonians, who gave Menelaos the splendid bowl wrought by the Phoenician Hephaistos, and presented by the king of Sparte to Telemachos. Some subtle links of connection between East and West may be traced in these circumstances. That remarkable Thrakian symbolic religious mysticism subsequently known as Orphik, and afterwards overshadowed by the parasitic growth of Neo-Platonism, appears to have coalesced, perhaps in Kabirik Lemnos, past which the head and harp of Orpheus were carried in tradition to Lesbos[5] early home of the lyric muse—with the Semitic religious element, chiefly represented by the world-colonising Phoenician. The Orphik Demiurge and the kosmogonic Phoenician divinity, known in Hellas as Dionysos, are one and the same. One is Phanes, the Spirit-of-the-Apparent the other is Phaidimos the Illustrious-apparent, a Sidonian or Phoenician hero. These Aryan names are really the same, as is the Semitic concept which they embody, namely, that of the Creator becoming apparent pantheistically in his works. Hence Dionysos is Phaidimos more truly than perhaps ever entered into the mind of the author of the Hesiodik Theogony who, nevertheless, had a wonderful, although shadowy apprehension of certain great root-truths, which

---

[1] Vide *inf.* VIII. i. *Phanes.*
[2] *Frag.* viii.
[3] Vide *inf.* sec. iii. 3.
[4] *Od.* iv. 617, xv. 117.
[5] 'His gory visage down the stream
　　was sent,
Down the swift Hebrus to the
　　Lesbian shore.'
　　　　Milton, *Lycidas.*

gleam and pierce through all their cumbrous trappings and disguises.[1]

Subsection II.—Dionysos and Ariadne.

'Dionysos Chrysokomes [the Golden-haired] made the blonde-haired Ariadne, daughter of Minos, his blooming spouse, and for him Kronion [Zeus] made her immortal and ever-young.'[2] Dionysos here appears in one of his solar aspects, Chrysokomes, the Golden-haired Sun, as the rival divinity the Aryan Apollon is Akersekomes, the Unshorn, undeprived of his far-reaching beams. Minos, the mighty king of Krete, whose 'name is *man*, the measurer or thinker, the Indian Manu,'[3] and whom Homeros speaks of as 'possessed of awful wisdom,'[4] is the son of Zeus and Europe the daughter, either of Phoinix son of the Phoenician king Agenor, or of Agenor himself. He is thus of direct Phoenician descent, and his daughter Ariadne, whose name is perhaps Phoenician,[5] forms by relationship a suitable bride for her Phoenician cousin Dionysos. His rival is the Aryan Theseus,[6] who is defeated in the competition, and Dionysos confers immortality on his consort as on his mother.[7] The root of the story is probably some contest or connection between the Phoenician powers of Krete and Naxos, and the Hellenik Attike. Pausanias speaks of Dionysos as having had a much superior force,[8] and, so far as the god represents in the legend the Phoenician Navy, this was doubtless correct. Minos has been regarded as a solar hero

---

[1] As to the connection between Hesiodos and Phoenician Kosmogonies, vide Bunsen, *Egypt's Place*, iv. 245 *et seq.*
[2] *Theog.* 947.
[3] *Mythol. of the Aryan Nations*, ii. 87.
[4] *Od.* xi. 322.

[5] Cf. Bunsen, *Egypt's Place*, iv. 246. Bunsen remarks, 'The strictly Greek derivation, however, Ariadne, equivalent to Ariagne, the Very Holy, is palpable.'
[6] Vide *inf.* X. iv.
[7] Cf. Pherekydes, *Frag.* cvi.
[8] Paus. x. 29.

because there is a tradition that he was slain in the West by a king of Sikelia. If all solar heroes, like their prototype, closed their careers in the West, their histories would present a gratifying consistency; but since heroes who travel from West to East, such as Achilleus, and die in Oriental regions, are equally supposed to be solar, it is evident that, let them die where they may, they cannot escape a solar character.[1] The Episode of Dionysos and Ariadne formed one of the favourite subjects of ancient art, and is thus treated on a fresco discovered at Pompeii: 'Bacchus, after his arrival at Naxos, finds Ariadne sunk in a profound slumber. Her face is hid in the pillows; over her head stands Sleep, with outspread wings, and bearing in his left hand a torch reversed, a symbol common to him with his brother Death. A young faun lifts the sheet, or veil, in which Ariadne is enveloped, in an attitude expressive of surprise at her beauty, and looks earnestly at the god, as if to discover what impression it makes upon him. Bacchus, crowned with ivy and berries, clothed in a short tunic and flowing pallium, having on his legs rich buskins, and holding in his right hand the thyrsus bound with a fillet, appears to be approaching slowly, and cautiously, for fear he should awake the nymph.[2] Seilenos and the Bakchik train follow. Mr. King, after having illustrated the custom of honouring a deceased friend ' by sculpturing his portrait in the character of a Bacchus,' remarks, 'from all this it is allowable to conjecture that the heads of Bacchus and Ariadne, in which the Roman glyptic art so conspicuously displayed itself, may not in every instance be ideal, but may often perpetuate the features of deceased friends.'[3]

---

[1] For illustrations of the Phoenician character of Minos, vide *Juv. Mun.* 110 *et seq.*, and for the early history and non-Aryan character of Krete, vide *Poseidon*, secs. xxx.-xxxiv.

[2] Dyer, *Ruins of Pompeii*, 80–1; Adams, *Buried Cities of Campania*, 211–2.

[3] *Antique Gems*, i. 218, 265.

Subsection III.—Grapes, the gift of Dionysos.

The remaining allusion to Dionysos in the Hesiodik Poems states that 'he gave grapes to men, a source of joy and grief.'[1] This passage excellently illustrates the two-faced character of Dionysos Theoinos, the Wine-god.[2] In one aspect he is Luaios, the Deliverer-from-care; in the other he is Psychodaiktes, Destroyer-of-the-soul, frantic, and raging. The rustic author of the Shield of Herakles gives quite an Aryan aspect of the god, just as an Attik husbandman of the age of Perikles might have done, accustomed to connect him only with the rural Dionysia and the sports of the Askoliasmos or Leaping-on-the-wine-skin; and had we nothing more about the god than such a passage as this, we should unhesitatingly ascribe to him an Aryan origin. But even the Hesiodik allusions to Dionysos, brief as they are, would fully warrant us in regarding him as a foreign importation. In the time of Hesiodos the contests with Lykourgos and Pentheus were things of the past, and the son of Semele was universally acknowledged as a member of the Aryan Pantheon.

Subsection IV.—Eikon of the Hesiodik Dionysos.

The Hesiodik Dionysos appears as the son of Zeus, and Semele daughter of Kadmos the Oriental, and as the husband of Ariadne, daughter of the Phoenician Minos. His wife and mother are both deified, or received into the Aryan Pantheon, through his agency; and he is the giver of the grape to mortals, inasmuch as he is Chrysokomes, the Golden-haired Sun, whose beams cause the earth to yield her increase. He is thus foreign in connection and kosmogonico-solar in character.

---

[1] *Aspis Herak.* 400.   [2] Cf. *sup.* sec. i. 2.

SECTION III.

THE ORPHIK DIONYSOS.

Subsection I.—Thrake and Orphik Mysticism.

Down to the time of the Peloponnesian War Thrake extended on the eastern side of the Bosphoros, as far as Herakleia, on the coast of the Euxine, and this country, at once European and Asiatic, appears in legendary history as the home of a peculiar school of mythical poetry and religious symbolism. Orpheus, one of the three Theologers or Writers on the Nature of Divinity (Homeros and Hesiodos being the other two), Mousaios the Muse personified in the poet, said to be a son of Orpheus or of Eumolpos, and reputed author of various poems connected with the cult of the Eleusinian Demeter; Eumolpos, the Good-singer, founder of the Eleusinian Mysteries and first high priest of Demeter and Dionysos ; Linos, or Song personified, either plaintive as the Dirge, or lively, all these, and many other similar personages, appear in tradition as either actually Thrakian, or else in some way linked with Thrake. The Asiatic connection of Thrake is illustrated in the Homerik Poems where the Eastern Thrakians appear in the Catalogue among the Troian allies ;[1] and the Western Thrakians, who subsequently arrive with Rhesos, their king, in like manner join the Troian array.[2] The antagonism between the Thrakian and the Ionik schools of poetry is seen in the allusion to the fate of the Thrakian bard Thamyris, who, with the arrogance of Marsyas and Linos, both of whom challenged Apollon to musical contests, boasted that he could conquer even the Muses in song, on which they struck him with blindness,

---

[1] *Il.* ii. 844.   [2] *Il.* x. 434 ; Eur. *Rhesos.*

and deprived him of his skill.[1] In sculpture he was represented holding a broken lyre. The singular compound Thrakian character and phase of thought is produced by and resolvable into a blending of the Aryan and Turanian elements, combined with a Semitic tinge, imported by the adventurous Phoenician colonists. Orpheus himself is identified by Professor Max Müller[2] with the Sanskrit Ribhu, used in the *Veda* as an epithet of Indra and name for the sun,[3] and in this case he is of Aryan origin. Eumolpos is Aryan in name; but his name, like that of Mousaios, who is sometimes spoken of as his son, or like that of the earliest Hellenik lyric poet who is called Olen, or Flute-player, is merely a descriptive epithet; while his being represented as a son of Poseidon points to a Semetic connection. Linos, or the Genius of Song, is also represented as a grandson of Poseidon,[4] and not unnaturally his cult obtained especially in the form of very similar Dirges, alike in Egypt, Phoenicia, Hellas, and 'other places;'[5] a circumstance which, although so surprising to the worthy Herodotos, is not in itself mysterious when the underlying links between those countries are brought to light. Another incident connecting the Thrakian poets with the Semitic East is their intimate relation to Dionysos. Thus Orpheus is torn to pieces by the Thrakian Bakchanals, not like Pentheus, as a despiser of the god, but as being indifferent to the attractions of his worshippers, and his death is avenged by Diónysos, who transforms the infuriate matrons into trees.[6] Again, all four poets, Orpheus, Mousaios, Eumolpos, and Linos, are credited with having written poems relating the exploits, or otherwise connected with the rites and in

---

[1] *Il.* ii. 595.
[2] *Chips*, ii. 127.
[3] Cf. Bunsen, *Egypt's Place*, iv. 452.
[4] Paus. ix. 29; vide *Poseidon*, xxvii, xxviii. The Children of Poseidon.
[5] Cf. Herod. ii. 79.
[6] Ovid, *Metam.* xi.

honour of Dionysos. So we find Diodoros quoting certain Bakchik Hymns attributed to Eumolpos,[1] and which, be it observed, appear to have represented the god in a decidedly Oriental phase. Herodotos declares that 'the rites called Orphic and Bakchic are in reality Egyptian and Pythagorean,'[2] and Diodoros represents Orpheus as introducing the greatest part of his mystical ceremonies and orgies from Egypt.[3] It is thus to be observed that the early Orphik and Bakchik rites were practically identical; 'Orphean and Bacchian orgies expressed quite the same thing... The worship of Bacchus formed the central point of this religious brotherhood.'[4] But the theory which derives Orphik mysteries direct from Egypt may be unhesitatingly rejected. Herodotos himself declares that the knowledge of Bakchik rites came through Kadmos the Tyrian, *i.e.* through a Phoenician medium. The undescriminating acceptance of the statements of Herodotos respecting the influence of Egypt on Hellas has been productive of many misconceptions and much confusion. Almost all early Hellenik travellers in Egypt accepted with perfect good faith and childish credulity any sayings and opinions of the priests, and we may quite believe that Solon received with all respect the celebrated legend about the Island of Atlantis, the great deluge, the wars which were stated to have occurred 9,000 years ere his time, and other equally authentic traditions.[5] When speaking of Dionysos, as he appears in Herodotos,[6] I shall have occasion to consider to what extent and with what modifications the Egyptian theories of the great historian have been confirmed, and are to be received. Any strictures of this kind on Herodotos apply still more strongly to Diodoros. The historical connection between the

[1] *Sup.* sec. i. 6.
[2] Herod. ii. 81.
[3] Diod. i. 96.
[4] K. O. Müller, *Scientific Mythol.* 317.
[5] Platon, *Timaios.*
[6] *Inf.* V.

44 THE GREAT DIONYSIAK MYTH.

various elements of the Thrakian phase of thought is a subject highly interesting but exceedingly obscure, and it is unnecessary to notice it further at present, merely premising that the extant Fragments of the Orphik Theogony, whether remodelled or even in part composed by Onomakritos the Athenian in the time of Hipparchos,[1] or of prior date,[2] appear to have preserved an earlier, and, at the same time, in some respects, a far more correct, view of the concept of Dionysos than is to be found in the general aspect of the god as he appears in the popular religion of historic Hellas. The high position in Hellenik opinion of the three Theologers and the personified poet, Mousaios, is well illustrated by a passage in the *Batrachoi*[3] of Aristophanes:—

> Orpheus instructed mankind in religion,
> Reclaimed them from bloodshed and barbarous rites;
> Musaeus delivered the doctrine of medicine,
> And warnings prophetic for ages to come;
> Next came old Hesiod teaching us husbandry,
> Ploughing and sowing, and rural affairs,
> Rural economy, rural astronomy,
> Homely morality, labour and thrift.
> Homer himself, our adorable Homer,
> What was his title to praise and renown?
> What but the worth of the lesson he taught us,
> Discipline, arms, and equipment of war.—*Frere*.

Subsection II.—Dionysos and Apollon.

The first phase of the Orphik Dionysos which requires special notice is his connection with the Sun-god, and hence with the Dorik Apollon. Thus Macrobius[4] quotes Aristoteles, Euripides, Aischylos, and others, as showing by many arguments that 'Apollo and Liber were one and

---

[1] Vide *inf.* IX. vi.
[2] Cf. Grote, *Hist. of Greece*, i. 21.
[3] V. 1032 *et seq.*
[4] *Saturnalia*, i. 18.

THE DIONYSOS OF THE THEOLOGERS.   45

the same god;' and alludes to the use of ivy by the Lakedaimonioi at the sacreds of Apollon in Bakchik manner, and to the joint worship of Apollon and Dionysos by the Boiotoi at Parnassos. He then says, 'That the Sun was Liber, Orpheus plainly lays down in this verse:'

The Sun whom men call Dionysos as a surname.

And again,—

One Zeus, one Aïdes, one Helios, one Dionysos,[1]

'the authority of which verse is founded on the oracle of Apollo Clarius [or of Klaros, a small town on the Ionik coast near Kolophon, where was a renowned temple and oracle of the god,] in which another name also is applied to the Sun, who in the same sacred verses amongst other names is called Iao. For Apollo Clarius, being asked which of the gods should he who is called Iao be considered to be, replied thus:

Much it behoves that the wise should conceal the unsearchable orgies:
But if thy judgement is weak, and thy knowledge is quickly exhausted,
Know that of gods who exist the highest of all is Iao.
He is Aïdes in winter, and Zeus at the coming of spring time,
Helios in summer heat, and in Autumn graceful Iao.

The force of which oracle and the signification of the deity and of the name by which Liber [Dionysos] is plainly meant, while the Sun is intended by Iao, Cornelius Labes has explained in his work " Concerning the Oracle of Apollo Clarius."' In the Orphik verse the four varient phases of the one great divinity are Zeus, Aïdes, Helios, and Dionysos, and in the oracle of Apollon Klarios, Zeus, Aïdes, Helios, and Iao, who is thus represented as the equivalent of Dionysos. In further proof of the real

[1] *Frag. iv.*

unity of Apollon and Dionysos, Macrobius proceeds to quote the celebrated Orphik Fragment which describes the sacred dress of the initiated,[1] but which, in reality, far from supporting the theory of a purely solar Dionysos, wonderfully illustrates the kosmogonic character of the god. Of course, the whole idea of the absolute unity of the two divinities is as inadmissible as the next step in the theory of Macrobius, by which Father Liber and Mars are identified; but he is practically right in so far as Apollon and Dionysos are both solar divinities, although the one is a Semitic, and the other an Aryan, study of the Sun; and his knowledge of the subject is greatly superior to the ordinary conception of Dionysos as simply Theoinos, the Wine-god. The root of the Dionysiak Myth, is, however, in Phoenicia and Egypt not merely solar, but also kosmogonic;[2] and rightly does Mr. Cox include the god among the earth-deities.[3] As regards the oracle of Apollon Klarios, and the mystic name Iao, Bunsen observes, 'Lobeck admits the antiquity of the celebrated answer of the oracle of Apollo Clarius, which Jablonsky doubted without any foundation.[4] Iao is there said to be the general name of the Sun-god, "the highest of all gods;"' Hades, of the Winter sun; Zeus, of the Vernal sun; Helios, of the Summer sun; Adonis

---

[1] Vide subsec. iii.
[2] Ibid.
[3] *Mythol. of Aryan Nations*, ii. 293.
[4] Bishop Browne, speaking of the appellation Yahveh (Jehovah), remarks, 'Some of the German writers have tried to trace the name to an attempt at expressing in Hebrew letters the name of the Phoenician god *Iao*,' and says that the chief support of the theory is this 'response of the Clarian Apollo, which has been clearly proved by Jablonsky to have originated in a Judaising Gnostic' (*Speaker's Commentary*, i. 26). There is, however, no reason to doubt the antiquity of this oracular response; but the circumstance is not in itself any proof that the name Yahveh is derived from Iao, which later title is nevertheless undoubtedly of extreme antiquity (vide subsec. iii.). The mistake of Jablonsky is shown, amongst others, by Movers (*Phönizier*, i. 539). Mr. King well observes, 'The titles *Iao* and *Abraxas*, instead of being recent Gnostic figments were indeed holy names, borrowed from the most ancient formulae of the East' (*The Gnostics*, 79). Mansel (*The Gnostic Heresies*), somewhat singularly, does not mention Iao.

(Dionysos), of the Autumn sun.[1] Iao is, of course, a Semitic name, and a strong Semitic tinge must have overspread the oracle of the Klarian god, if, indeed, he were identical with the Dorik Apollon, before such a response could have been possible. But how was it, then, that men called the Sun Dionysos as a surname? Apollon, as we know, is a purely Aryan and Ouranik divinity, distinct and separate from the Semitic and chthonian Dionysos. There could be no real, but only apparent, affinity between such opposite concepts. But Dionysos, as we have already seen, has undoubtedly a most important solar phase and aspect, and so Donaldson rightly asserts that he 'first appeared to the Greeks as a tauriform sun-god;'[2] as in the Eumolpik verses we read 'Dionysos, with face of flame, glitters like a star with his rays.'[3] And this solar phase and character of Dionysos at once explain how ancient philosophical investigators, ignorant of those laws of linguistic affinity which it is the triumph of modern research to have developed, and of the gaps which separate the concepts of Aryan and Semite, not unnaturally confounded divinities essentially distinct. To the ordinary philosopher, the creed of the multitude generally appeared gross and absurd. He regarded the gods as either the arbitrary creations of man's fancy, or as expressions denoting the forces of nature; or again, as the attributes of a great and unknown divinity. To believe in Apollon and Dionysos as distinct divine beings, would appear childish to a philosophical pagan, or perhaps to any pagan, of the age of Macrobius, A.D. 390. He would regard the two divinities as in reality merely two solar impersonations, and therefore as identical. But this view is historically considered incorrect, since (1) Pyropos, the Fiery-eyed, is not the entire Dionysos, but one only of his many phases;

---

[1] *Egypt's Place*, iv. 193, *note*.
[2] *Theatre of the Greeks*, 17.
[3] Subsec. i. 6.

and (2) Apollon is an Aryan, Dionysos Pyropos a Semitic, study of the sun; they are distinct alike in origin and in line of thought.[1]

Subsection III.—*Dionysos the Demiurge.*

A very prominent feature of the Orphik Dionysos is that of the Demiourgos, or Maker-of-the-world, in fact, of the entire Kosmos. Thus the Orphik poet, speaking of the sacred dress to be worn in the Bakchik Mysteries, says:

To accomplish all these things, clad in a sacred dress
The body of God, a representation of the bright-rayed Helios,
Let the worshipper first throw around him a crimson robe
Like flowing rays resembling fire.
Moreover from above the broad all-variegated skin of a wild
    fawn
Thickly-spotted should hang down from the right shoulder,
A representation of the wondrously-wrought stars and of the
    vault of heaven.
And then over the fawn-skin a golden belt should be thrown,
All-gleaming, to wear around the breast, a mighty sign
That immediately from the end of the earth the Beaming-one
    springing up
Darts his golden rays on the flowing of ocean,
The splendour is unspeakable, and mixed with the water
Revolving it sparkles with whirling motion circularly
Before God, and then the girdle under the unmeasured breast
Appears as a circle of ocean, a mighty wonder to behold.[2]

Here we have a full-length portrait of the kosmogonic Dionysos. The sacred rites are proceeding; the principal worshipper, who in the symbolism represents the god himself, is in the Thronismos or State-of-enthronement, clad in the mystic dress, and surrounded by the chorus of votaries dancing in a ring. His crimson robe and *peplos*, with its flaming rays, symbolise the heat and

[1] Vide *inf.* subsec. iii.
[2] *Frag.* vii.

THE DIONYSOS OF THE THEOLOGERS.

fierce beams of the sun, Dionysos Pyropos; and, had the mystic dress consisted of the peplos only, there might have been some foundation for the theory of the absolute unity of Helios and Dionysos. But this is merely the first article of the attire. Next, the all-variegated,[1] much spotted, faun-skin, typifying the starry vault of heaven, is to hang down from the shoulder.[2] Over the faun-skin is thrown a golden belt, typifying the Homerik ocean-circle, when gleaming with splendour beneath the rays of Phaëthon, the Beaming-sun, who corresponds with Dionysos Antauges, the Sparkler.[3] The ocean-girdle, it will be observed, is placed in the symbolism without the stars, because they in Hellenik idea sink into it; and Okeanos is, like Poseidon Gaieochos, the Earth-encircler, and holds the Kosmos in his all-surrounding arms. Thus, the sacred dress typified sun, starry vault, and ocean, all indeed of matter that exists, except the earth; but this latter is not omitted from the mystery-play, for the worshipper himself is at once the earth and Dionysos, or the kosmogonic spirit of the world; sexless, or of both sexes, for the result is the same, clad in the woman's robe, *peplos*, and the man's belt, *zoster*. Hence the close affinity and the connected historic worship of Dionysos and Demeter, the Aryan Earth-mother, anthropomorphic, emerging into human form from the huge and shadowy Gaia. This Orphik Dionysos is truly a colossal concept, and let those who are inclined to condemn the study of Mythology as frivolous and unimportant endeavour to estimate the value and interest of the light which it throws alike upon the mind of man and the general history of the world. The great subject of Pantheism—the higher and the lower: its truth and error, truth—that all things are in God; error—that God is in all things, as if Deity were

---

[1] Vide *inf.* VIII. i. *Aiolomorphos*.
[2] Cf. Diod. i. 11.
[3] *Frag.* vii.

nought but animated and eternal matter, is and ever must be of the highest importance, especially in these days when Agnosticism exults in its ignorance, and a deepening Materialism finds constantly increasing favour with numerous sages. How apparently delicate are many of its distinctions, yet how important their differences! Thus with equal truth and beauty may the Deity, especially when considered anthropomorphically and in His more active operations, be figuratively represented as clad with the immediately surrounding visibility, not with the entire Kosmos, 'as with a garment,' from which, nevertheless, He must ever be kept distinct and separate in idea. He animates the All, not as soul does body from within, but, being essentially external and distinct in His infinity, He looks upon the whole world, not as His tabernacle, but 'as a very little thing.'[1] It is not true, as the friend and pupil of Bolingbroke has asserted, that

> All are but parts of one stupendous whole,
> Whose body nature is, and God the soul;
> That changed thro' all, and yet in all the same,
> Great in the earth as in the etherial frame;
> Warms in the sun, refreshes in the breeze,
> Glows in the stars, and blossoms in the trees;

that the Creator is but the animated creation, no more than the Platonik 'Soul of the World,' the Neo-Platonik Hippa. This is not God, but Dionysos. But,

> The sun, the moon, the stars, the seas, the hills and the plains—
> Are not these, O Soul, *the Vision* of Him who reigns?

that is,

> In contemplation of created things
> By steps we may ascend to God,—

not find God indwelling in them.

[1] 'God could have made other worlds.' S. Athanasios.

THE DIONYSOS OF THE THEOLOGERS. 51

Earth, these solid stars, this weight of body and limb,
Are they not sign and symbol of thy division from Him?

Not of forming 'parts of one stupendous whole.'

Speak to Him thou, for He hears, and spirit with Spirit can meet— .
Closer is He than breathing, and nearer than hands and feet.

For 'in Him we live, and move, and have our being;' we in Him the Creator, not He in us His creatures.

Worlds without number
Lie in His bosom like children.

He lies not concealed in them, as a principle of inherent vitality.

'This Being governs all things, not as the soul of the world, but as Lord over all.' (Newton). And this is not Dionysos, but God. Such then is the root-idea of the Kosmogonic Dionysos.

But the Orphik poet, while thus pantheistically clothing Dionysos with the visible universe, is no mere crude materialist. He fully admits Mr. Martineau's canon, that 'mind is first and rules for ever,' and so, in another Fragment, he tells how the Demiurge, whom 'men call both Phanes, and Dionysos, and King Eubouleus the Wise-counselling, and the widely-known Antauges the Sparkler,' and whom 'others of the men who dwell on the earth call by other names, first came to light;' and how this mysterious power 'melted down,' *i.e.* resolved into form and shape, 'the divine ether that before was motionless, and lit it up for the gods to see, most beautiful to behold;'[1] or, in other words, established order out of a pre-existing chaos. This demiurgic force is not external to the matter in and through which it works, and through which it becomes known as Phanes the Apparent,[2] identi-

[1] *Orphik. Frag.* vii. [2] Cf. *sup.* sec. ii.

fied with Dionysos, and representing the visible creation in its vitality. As the sun is the eye of the universe, the most prominent and remarkable object of the Visible, and as the mind looks out through the human eye, so the demiurgic Dionysos looks down through the great solar eye upon his worshippers and the world; and thus, being peculiarly associated with the sun, naturally appears as Pyropos the Fiery-faced, and Antauges the Sparkler. That all nations, and especially the children of the glowing East, should have solar gods and solar myths is natural and even necessary; but, at the same time, the kosmogonic aspect of the Uasar-Dionysos Myth is even vaster here than the solar, while the relations between Dionysos and Helios are fully explicable by the protagonistic position of the latter in the material universe, and the kosmic concept of the former as its animating essence, and all-pervading daemon. Hence the poet, while saying that men call the Sun Dionysos, does not thereby absolutely identify the two; and he clearly distinguishes between them in his account of the enthroned worshipper and his dress.

But, as may be readily conceived, the idea of a solar, being simpler than that of a kosmogonic, deity, when Dionysos had become thus connected with the Sun, the light of the solar phase threw the broader conception somewhat into the shade. Dionysos the Demiurge was lost sight of, but his character is so far impressed upon Dionysos Pyropos, that the latter chiefly appears, not in an astral or purely solar phase, as being distinct and distant from the earth, but, as the lord of the changing seasons, whose power affects and alters the visible world on which he looks down. And so the poet tells us:

> He has surnames for each of his changes,
> Manifold as the year rolls, and they suit with the change of the seasons.

THE DIONYSOS OF THE THEOLOGERS.

These names, as we have seen,[1] are Zeus, Aïdes, Helios, and Dionysos, and all of them are said to belong to Iao, who, like Zagreus,[2] is 'the highest of all gods.' But the Semitic Iao, of whom, according to the Klarian oracle, Zeus and the three other deities are but annual phases, is not merely a solar divinity, but the life-heat power of nature as imparted through the solar orb.[3] The very fact that he is the 'highest of all gods' shows this, for neither in Kaldea, Assur, Phoenicia, or Egypt, or in Aryan Hellas or India, does the Sun-god, merely as such, head the list of divinities. Joannes Laurentius, who from having been born in Lydia is commonly called Lydus, and who lived A.D. 490–560, in his work 'Peri Menôn' (De Mensibus), states that 'the Chaldaeans call God Iao,' and the name itself in the form Iau, occurs in the cuneiform inscriptions.[4] Iao, in fact, somewhat corresponds in place and position with the Aryan Zeus, from whom he is, of course, utterly and absolutely distinct. And thus, as was noticed,[5] all investigations into the nature and history of Dionysos tend to show how lofty is the place among divinities which he occupied in the Outer-world. No longer, as in the Homerik Olympos, an inferior personage, he is in Phoenicia Iao, and Zagreus 'highest of all gods;' and as the solar concept, as distinguished from the kosmogonic, becomes still stronger in the mind, the poet invokes him in the words: O brilliant Zeus; O Dionysos, sire of sea, sire of earth; O Helios, sire of all.' Phanes, the pervading demiurge, has here become centred in the most remarkable piece of visibility, 'that nebulous star we call the sun.' But all this is

---

[1] Subsec. ii.
[2] Vide sec. i. 7.
[3] Cf. Movers, *Phön.* i. 550.
[4] *Trans. Soc. Bib. Archaeol.* iii. 505. Cf. Bunsen's remark, 'Rawlinson thinks he has found the Fire-God, Iah or Iao in the arrow-headed inscriptions.

'There are, moreover, many traces of an old name of God, Iau, which Greek form leads to Iahu, *i.e.* Iah with the archaic nominal ending U' (*Egypt's Place*, iv. 194).
[5] Sec. i. 7.

essentially Semitic in thought and feeling; no purely Aryan bard could for an instant have confounded Zeus the All-father,

> The constant heaven with its deep blue eyes,

with solar divinities. But the poet has come to regard the Sun as being the first and highest of gods, or rather perhaps, Semitically, as containing the spirit and intelligence of the first of divinities;[1] and hence he applies to the Sun whatever names were given to the Supreme, Zeus, Iao, All-father, &c. And so, incidentally, we see that Dionysos ranks with these, and is second to none. In another passage he describes the god as keeping the visible world together, *i.e.*, 'upholding all things by his power;' and in consequence, being called Phanes, the Spirit-of-the-Apparent, who gives surrounding matter, form, and shape, and Erikapaios, an epithet, apparently meaning Spring-time-garden-growth, or the vital force of life-heat of the vast visible world. It may possibly, however, be equivalent to Protogenes, Primeval, the one who 'first came to light.' Such is Dionysos, the Orphik Demiurge, the spirit of material visibility, a Kyklops giant of the universe with one bright solar eye.

As the mysterious Iao is a very important phase of Dionysos, and has of late been employed in the attempted injury of the ordinary belief in Yahveh, some further observations on his occult concept are here added. I have already noticed [2] that a groundless alarm arose in some orthodox quarters at certain supposed serious consequences which would arise from accepting the view of the genuine antiquity of the answer of the oracle of Apollon Klarios. Bishop Colenso thus comments on the view of Bishop Browne, 'Land [3] maintains the genuineness of

---

[1] Vide *inf.* XII. i.
[2] *Sup.* subsec. ii. *note.*
[3] *Theol. Tijdschr.* March, 1868.

this oracle, since after the closest examination there appears not a trace in it of later Greek or of defective versification, of anything whereby the fictitious oracles of a later age always betray themselves.' Dr. Colenso then quotes Movers in support of the genuineness of the oracle, and gives Land's explanation of it as follows : ' Iao is the highest of all the gods, because he gives life to all, and his dwelling is in heaven which spreads over all. Yet in heaven he reveals himself specially by the Sun. In winter, when the nights are longest, the god prefers to dwell in the Under-world as Zeus Chthonios, and rules over the shades in Hades. In the spring-time, when the grain harvest is at hand, all depends upon the weather, upon sufficient rain and sunshine; and the god is addressed as Zeus, as especially the god of heaven and of the weather. In the summer, he is the scorching Helios, which burns up everything, and is tempered by no cloud. Lastly, in the autumn, comes the ripeness of the fig, pomegranate, and above all of the grape, with its mysterious life-awaking juice; and now is the god known as the tender Iao, the spring of all beauty, love, and life.' This is a truly admirable interpretation of the oracle, and Dr. Colenso adds: ' It is obvious how closely this corresponds to the worship of Dionysos.'[1] The genuine antiquity of the oracle being thus established beyond all reasonable doubts, do any evil consequences follow to ordinary belief? Certainly not. Yahveh or Jahve may have been, and indeed undoubtedly was, as the Bishop suggests, ' a very ancient name in the land of Canaan.' Il or El is a very ancient name of God in all the countries adjacent, and of course, long anterior to the time of Moses; but this circumstance is in no way prejudicial to religion. The identity of Yahveh and Iao, moreover, cannot be denied; and Diodoros states that, amongst the Jews, Moses called God

[1] *The New Bible Commentary critically examined*, i. 656.

Iao.[1] We have the express testimony of Eusebios [2] that the Phoenicians called Yahveh Ieuo,[3] and the identification of the two is frequently made in ancient writers.[4] Fürst is probably often a very doubtful authority,[5] but his observations on this question are well worthy of note. He says, ' the very ancient name of God, Yaho, in Hellenik Iao, appears to have been an old mystic name of the supreme god of the Semites. In the ancient religion of the Chaldaeans, whose remains are to be found amongst the Neo-Platonists,[6] the highest divinity enthroned above the seven heavens, representing the spiritual-light principle, and also regarded as the Demiurge, was called Iao,[7] who was like the Hebrew Yaho [*i.e.* Yahveh] mysterious, and unmentionable,[8] and whose name was communicated only to the initiated. The Phoenicians had a supreme god, whose name was triliteral and secret.[9] He was Iao.[10] This Phoenician Yaho, a knowledge of whom spread farther, represented the Sun-god in a four-fold variety, according to the oracle of Apollon Klarios, *i.e.* he represented [the four-faced] Baal (according to an account in Eustathios), whose image was set up in the temple by Manasseh.'[11] The Chaldaeans, according to Cedrenus, adored the physical and intellectual light. The diffusion of this throughout the region of the seven planets was represented by the letters I A Ω, the first of which represented

---

[1] Diod. i. 94.
[2] *Euan, Apod.* i. 6.
[3] Cf. Gesen. *Script. Ling. Phoe.* 408; vide also the Phoenician myth of the sacrifice of the only son Ieoud; Cory, *Anct. Fragments*, 17; Bunsen, *Egypt's Place*, iv. 280 *et seq.*
[4] Tacitus, *Hist.* v. 5, Plout. *Symp.* i. 4; Julianus (the Apostate), *Orat. in Matrem Deorum*, and his Christian opponents.
[5] Vide *Trans. Soc. Bib. Archaeol.* iii. 105, *note.*
[6] In illustration of this, vide *inf.* XI. iii.

[7] Lydus, *ut ante*; Cedrenus, *ut inf.*
[8] Proklos. *In Tim.* ii.
[9] Sanchou. i. 8.
[10] ' Cui litera trina
    Confirmet sacrum nomen, cognomen et omen.'
Martianus Capella, *Hymn to the Sun.*
[11] *Inf.* VII. ii. Fürst, *Lexicon*: ' Jehovah.' A Gnostic gem given by Montfaucon, tome ii. part ii. pl. clix. fig. 2, represents a Janus-headed figure, and is inscribed I A W on the reverse.

THE DIONYSOS OF THE THEOLOGERS. 57

the Sun, and the second and third, the Moon and Saturn, the two extremes of the planetary system.[1] This is the Panaugeia or Universal Light of Philon, whose theories so greatly assisted Neo-Platonism. 'There is no doubt,' observes Movers, 'that Iao is Adonis,'[2] and Adonis, again, is the Semitic and Mosaic Adonai, the Lord. Here, too, we find another of the names of the Supreme God of the Hebrews applied to a Phoenician divinity. But what, in the abstract, more probable 'since the Phoenician language was almost identical with the Hebrew'? It has been asserted that the Hebrews borrowed their divinity Yahveh from Phoenicia, but this neither has been, nor will be, proved; and, apart from any religious conclusions, it would be quite as sensible to assert that the Latins borrowed their Jupiter from the Hellenik Zeus, since the two names are really identical, and belong in fact to but one divinity. But this is absurd; there is no borrowing in the matter; the forms spring up together and independently. Again, it is said: 'Jehovah is the Sun, for if he is identical with Iao, and Iao is the Sun, Jehovah must be the Sun,' and so nearly all the religion of the Old Testament would thus fade away into a mere solar cult of a physical Sun of righteousness Was it this idea which alarmed the opponents of the genuineness of the oracle of the Klarian god? Let us, however, test the remarkable, and to some apparently conclusive, argument: *Yahveh is Iao, the Sun is Iao*, argal, *Yahveh is the Sun;* or again, *water is a liquid, wine is a liquid*, argal, *water is wine*. To leave this argument and proceed: Iao, as we have noticed, is far more than the sun, and I shall be quite willing to agree that Yahveh is the Supreme God, Iao is the Supreme God, argal Iao is Yahveh. Neither name is derived from the other; they are simply varient forms of the same identical appellation. Next, as to the

[1] Cedrenus, i. 296.   [2] *Phön.* 542.

meaning of the name; Clemens Alexandrinus says, 'the mystic name of four letters,' the sacred Tetragrammaton YaHVeH, 'which was affixed to those alone to whom the adytum was accessible, is called Iaou, which is interpreted, "Who is and shall be."'[1] Mr. King observes, 'Theodoret states that the four letters of the Holy Name were pronounced by the Samaritans I A B E; by the Jews, I A Ω. Jerome (Ps. viii.), "The name of the Lord amongst the Hebrews is of four letters, Jod, He, Vau, He; which is properly the name of God, and may be read as I A H O, and is held by the Jews for ineffable."'[2] Bunsen, very reasonably, considers it questionable whether the real etymology of the word is Hebrew, but remarks, 'The sublime idea, "I am that I am," *i.e.* the Eternal, is certainly the right one in a Hebrew point of view.'[3] As Iau appears in the cuneiform, it has very probably a further meaning. The Rev. J. M. Rodwell[4] translates 'exalter of Yav,' 'by the help of Assur and Yav the great gods &c.,' and observes, 'The god Yav may be the *Yaveh* of the Moabite stone.' But this reading is exceedingly doubtful. Professor Oppert prefers Bin; the Rev. A. H. Sayce, Rimmon; and Mr. George Smith 'has given Daddi, Teiseba, and Vul as the Syrian, Armenian, and Assyrian values.' Movers connects Iao (pronounced with an aspirate) with IAkchOs, with the Bakchik cry 'Eua,' with Hyes, the name of Dionysos connected with fertilising moisture, and with the Phrygian cry 'Hyes Attes,' or 'Atys lives,' which belonged to the rites of

---

[1] *Strom.* v. 6.
[2] *The Gnostics*, 84, note 1.
[3] *Egypt's Place*, iv. 193, note. 'The existent,' Bishop Browne, *Speaker's Commentary*, i. 26. 'He is, or He makes to be,' Bishop Colenso, *New Bible Commentary critically examined*, i. 66. 'In the scrolls entombed with the [Egyptian] dead in those days [*i.e.* the time of Moses] the name of God is never mentioned save in the guise of the phrase Nukpu-nuk, which means *I am that I am*,' *Literary Remains of Emmanuel Deutsch*, 166.
[4] *Records of the Past*, iii. 37 *et seq.* Annals of Assur-nazir-pal [Sardanapalos].

THE DIONYSOS OF THE THEOLOGERS. 59

Sabazios and the great Mother.[1] This view possesses a very high amount of probability; Iao is more especially the autumn-sun-power 'with its mysterious life-awaking juice.' Iao, again, is identical with Sabazios,[2] or the more especial Thrakian and Phrygian varient of Dionysos; and 'that Adonis was known also by the name Iao cannot be doubted.'[3] Iao in Gnostic Art, which is mainly interesting as illustrative of more archaic ideas, frequently appears as identified with Abraxas.[4] The name I A W, when it appears on gems surrounded with the time-serpent tail in mouth, typifies the endless course of the supreme solar power through the ever-revolving year.[5] Another gem[6] is explained by Mr. King as 'the Gnostic Pleroma, or combination of all the Aeons; expressed by the outline of a man holding a scroll, or perhaps serpent, and filled in with innumerable letters, in which the name only of Iao may be recognised.' Mr. James Fowler elegantly illustrates the application by mediaeval Christendom of some of the earlier thoughts respecting Time and his Master. After noticing various mediaeval Zodiacal representations, and emblems of the months, he observes, 'The course of the sun through the Zodiac . . . represented the course of the Sun of Righteousness through the festivals of the Church, which marked the divisions of the ecclesiastical year as the signs of the Zodiac did the divisions of the natural. . . . As the natural sun is replaced in these examples by the Sun of Righteousness, so are the signs of the Zodiac by the Apostles, the first to reflect the light from Our

---

[1] Vide *inf.* VIII. i. *Hyes, Iakchos*. ii. *Eua*. As to Atys, vide *inf.* IX. vi.

[2] *Inf.* V. ii. VIII. ii. *Sabazios*.

[3] *Mythol. of the Aryan Nations*, ii. 113. As to Adon-Tammuz, vide *inf.* subsec. v., XI. ii. XII. i. 1.

[4] Vide King, *The Gnostics*. Plate opposite title-page, fig. 4; plate opposite page 36, fig. 7; *inf.* VII. iv. No. 37. Vide also the numerous Iao-Abraxas gems in Montfaucon, tome ii. part i. pl. cxlv. *et seq.*

[5] Vide *inf.* VIII. ii. *Serpent*.

[6] *The Gnostics*, pl. iii. fig. 11.

Lord; and as the stars of the Zodiac possessed an interest to the ancient astronomer which no other stars possessed, so the Apostles here shine forth as a kind of synecdoche of that greater company of Saints which are as the stars in multitude.'[1]

Subsection IV.—*Dionysos and Zeus.*

The connection in the Orphik Theogony between Dionysos and Zeus is naturally exceedingly close, for all things in God or Zeus, and God in all things or Dionysos, though so widely different in meaning and effect, may seem to many almost interchangeable phases and phrases. We have seen Dionysos represented as the Spirit of the Kosmogony, which, as our great Pantheistic poet tells us, appears in sun and star, in wind and tree.

How, then, does the poet describe Zeus? Zeus is ' the first and the last '—the Alpha and Omega. 'He is head and middle, the origin of earth and of starry heaven, the breath of winds, the fury of the tireless flame, the root of sea, sun, and moon, First Cause of all things, oneness of force, unity of divinity, mighty ruler of all, one kingly frame from whom all things have sprung, fire and water, earth, air, night and day. He is Mind, and Love delighting in its works.' How is he these? and, if he be these, is he not the equivalent of the kosmic Dionysos? No; for the poet connects him with the manifestations of visibility because he is their maker. They breathe and whisper to the wise of a divine origin, declare his glory and show his handiwork, so that in the beautiful words of Mr. Martineau, 'We must look upon the sublime face of the Book of Nature as the living appeal of thought to thought.' Zeus is not their inherent and indwelling

---

[1] *Archaeologia,* xliv. 1; *Mediaeval Representations of the Months and Seasons,* 184-5.

THE DIONYSOS OF THE THEOLOGERS. 61

divinity; on the contrary, they have sprung from him, and he is their origin, not their vital force. He is not merely the working demiurge who brings order out of chaos and sustains the course of nature; he is the great First Cause of all things, a oneness of force, and a unity of divinity. 'All these things' are not Him, but 'are encircled in Him, for *all things lie in the mighty frame of Zeus.*'[1] This is a grand old creed,[2] a noble declaration of faith, a belief in the one God and Father of whom are all things, whose luminous and ever-present divinity encircles His great store of starry worlds, which 'lie in His bosom like children,' and whose vastly delighting love eternally rejoices in His works, and sees with divine satisfaction

> In gradual growth His full-leaved will
> Expand from world to world.[3]

Pindaros truly tells us that 'Zeus obtained something more than what the gods possessed.' But, although the nature of Zeus is here nobly described, and clearly distinguished from that of Dionysos, yet the two concepts, at once so similar and dissimilar, soon necessarily clash in the mind of the poet and become intermixed and confounded. Zeus assumes a kosmogonic phase, and Dionysos becomes a kind of Zeus. In the line

> So father Zeus governs all things, and Bakchos, he governs also,

the poet labours hard to give both divinities a kind of equal sway. And, again, when the solar concept pre-

---

[1] *Orphik Frag.* vi.
[2] Platon alludes to the passage as 'an archaic statement' (*Laws,* iv.).
[3] The *Voluntas Dei* may be thought by some but a poor reason for the constitution and course of the universe, but no other can be suggested; for the view of Spinoza 'that God is the Universe, producing a series of necessary movements or acts, in consequence of intrinsic energy' (Draper, *Conflict between Religion and Science,* 179), is merely a re-statement of things as they are, or, at most, an imaginary reason drawn only from nescience.

dominates, both Zeus and Dionysos fade away into Helios, who becomes 'Zeus Dionysos, sire of sea, of earth, of all things.' The poet thus concludes his description of the kosmic Zeus-Dionysos:—

> Would you behold his head and his fair face,
> It is the resplendent heaven, round which his golden locks
> Of glittering stars are beautifully exalted in the air.
> On each side are the two golden taurine horns,
> The risings and settings, the tracks of the celestial gods;
> His eyes the sun and the opposing moon;
> His infallacious mind the royal incorruptible ether.[1]

The golden horns or track of the solar photosphere belong to Dionysos as Chrysokeros.[2]

Subsection V.—The Neo-Platonik Orphik Hymns.

The eighty-eight so-called Orphik Hymns which have come down to us are evidently the work of Neo-Platonists, though, perhaps, some fragments of them may be of earlier date; but they are, nevertheless, interesting in many respects as presenting to a considerable extent 'a faithful reflection of ancient ideas.'[3] Many points relating to Dionysos which occur in them I notice elsewhere. Hymn xxix. describes him as the son of Persephone, and Hymn xliv. as the son of Semele. This, however, is not contradictory, even supposing that Persephone and Semele are two distinct personages; for the god is also said to be Dimetor, Bimatris, Son-of-two-mothers.[4] He is the son of Semele from his connection with the Phoenician house of Kadmos, and he is the son of Persephone, daughter (Kore) of earth (Demeter), in consequence of his kosmogonic affinities. The Awful Damsel 'represents what we might really expect from

---

[1] Cory, *Ancient Fragments*, 290.
[2] Vide *inf.* IV. iii. 2, VIII. i. IX. iii. iv.
[3] Cf. *Poseidon*, xl.
[4] Hymn l. 1, lii. 9.

THE DIONYSOS OF THE THEOLOGERS. 63

her position as Queen of the Under-world: a mixture of Pelasgic and Eastern traditions.'[1] But the concept of Dionysos as son of Persephone, though not contradictory, is necessarily posterior to that of Dionysos as son of the daughter of Kadmos. The foreign god, as such, is the son of a Phoenician mother; and afterwards, when his nature is found to be kosmogonic, he becomes with equal propriety the son of a mysterious kosmogonic and chthonian goddess. In Hymn xxiv. 10, the poet, addressing the Nereïdes, says:—

> You at first disclosed the rites divine
> Of holy Bacchus and of Proserpine.—*Taylor.*

What possible connection there can be between the innocent sea-nymphs, daughters of Nereus, the true Aryan sea-god and rival of the Semitic Poseidon,[2] and the Phoenician Dionysos, and Persephone the 'majestic' and 'terrible,' it is difficult to say, unless, indeed, the statement is the poetic expression of the fact that the cult of the two mysterious divinities came *by sea* into Hellas. Many of the lines of the Hymns consist of strings of adjectival epithets illustrating the almost numberless phases of the god, some very ancient, some comparatively modern. All the more important of these will be separately noticed under the head of Dionysiak Nomenclature.[3] Hymn xxxi. connects the Kouretes, legendary inhabitants of Akarnania, Kyretis (Aitolia), and Krete, with Dionysos and Persephone. The connection is not Hellenik, and points towards Phoenicia, and Asia Minor, the home of 'mingled people,' Semitic, Aryan, and Turanic.[4] Hymn xlii. invokes Dionysos under the name of Mise, as the sexless spirit of kosmic life, who, like Zeus Kerastes, is 'the mixer of all things.' The Law-giver[5] I

---

[1] Cf. Gladstone, *Juv. Mun.* 300 *et seq.*
[2] Cf. *Poseidon,* vi.
[3] Vide *inf.* VIII. i.
[4] Cf. IV. iii. 2.
[5] Vide *inf.* VIII. i. *Thesmophoros.*

64   THE GREAT DIONYSIAK MYTH.

invoke, narthexbearing [1] Dionysos, many-named Eubouleus,[2] and holy Mise,[3] mysterious queen, male and female, two-natured Iakchos.'[4] And the poet proceeds to connect this strange being particularly with Phrygia, Kypros, and Egypt. Hymn xlv. is inscribed to Dionysos Bassareus[5] Trieterikos, in whose honour a *trieteris*, or triennial festival, was held. The epithet also applies to several other deities, especially Poseidon. Various epithets, also, connected with the Bull[6] are ascribed to Dionysos in the Hymns; this connection, again, is entirely Semitic, and will be fully noticed and illustrated subsequently.[7] Hymn xlvi. is addressed to Dionysos as Liknites, *i.e.* bearing the *liknon*,[8] or fan-shaped basket, which, filled with fruit and offerings, was carried in the Bakchik festivals.[9] Hymn xlvii. is addressed to Dionysos as Perikionios, or the Twiner-round-the-pillars,[10] because, when he shook the Theban land,[11] he preserved the house of Kadmos. Hymn xlviii. is addressed to Sabazios, the Phrygian phase of Dionysos,[12] who is here described as having, like Zeus, inserted the infant Dionysos in his thigh. Thus, at a comparatively late date, varient forms of the same divinity came to be regarded as distinct beings. Hymn l. is addressed to Dionysos as Lysios,[13] Lenaios,[14] the god of the wine-press, who frees men from care. In Hymn li. 3, the Nymphs are called the Nurses of Bakchos.[15] This connection is older than the Homerik Poems.[16] Hymn lii. addressed to Dionysos as Trieterikos,[17] is almost one continued string of epithets, including Bakcheus, Taurokeros,

---

[1] Vide *inf.* VIII. i. *Narthekophoros*.
[2] Vide ibid. *Eubouleus*.
[3] Vide ibid. *Mise*.
[4] Vide ibid. *Iakchos*.
[5] Vide *inf.* V. i. VIII. i. *Bassareus*.
[6] Vide *inf.* VIII. ii. *Bull*.
[7] *Inf.* IV. iii. 2, IX. iii. *Taurokeros*.
[8] Vide *inf.* VIII. i. *Liknites*.
[9] *Inf.* VI. i.
[10] Vide *inf.* VIII. i. *Perikionios*.
[11] Vide ibid. *Elelichthon*.
[12] *Inf.* V. ii. VIII. i. *Sabazios*.
[13] Vide *inf.* VIII. i. *Lysios*.
[14] The Festival of the Lenaia is noticed, *inf.* VI. i.
[15] Vide *inf.* IV. i. 3.
[16] Cf. Hom. Hymn, xxiv. *Sup.* sec. i. 5.
[17] Vide *sup.*

THE DIONYSOS OF THE THEOLOGERS.

Nysios, Eubouleus, Liknites, Protogonos, Erikepaios, Omadios, Keros, Dimetor, Bassareus, Nebridostolos, Polyparthenos, many of which have already been more or less illustrated, and all of which will be again referred to.[1] Hymn liii. is addressed to Dionysos as Amphietes, or Having-a-yearly-festival, an epithet to which the god was well entitled.[2] This is Dionysos Chthonios,[3] a divinity of the Under-world, who, for a season, 'sleeps in the sacred abode of Persephone.' Hymn liv. is addressed to the Satyr Seilenos, the nurturer or foster-father of Dionysos. The Satyroi and Seilenoi appear to be conceptions more Aryan than Semitic, and their connection with Dionysos is not one of the earliest features in his history. Mr. Cox, however, with considerable probability, regards the ass of Seilenos as a link between him and the East, and observes, 'The grotesque form which Seilenos is made to assume may be an exaggeration of the western Greeks, who saw in the ass which bore him a mere sign of his folly and absurdity, while it points rather to the high value set on the ass by Eastern nations. It was, in fact, the symbol of his wisdom and his prophetical powers, and not the mere beast of burden which, in Western myths, staggered along under the weight of an unwieldly drunkard.'[4] Hymn lv. addressed to the Semitic Aphrodite, Kyprogenes,[5] or Kypros-born, describes her as 'the associate of Bakchos.' Both divinities are alluded to as personages, and not as mere representatives of Love and Wine, and the connection is altogether Semitic and Phoenician.[6] Hymn lvi. is addressed to Adonis, the well-known Phoenician god Adon, the Hebrew Adonai or Lord. Adonis, be it observed, is with the Hymn-writer only another name for Dionysos, and so he is Polyonymos,

---

[1] Vide *inf.* VIII. i.
[2] Vide *inf.* VI. i.
[3] V. i.
[4] *Mythol. of the Aryan Nations,*
ii. 316.
[5] V. xv.
[6] Vide *Juv. Mun.* viii. 14, *Aphrodite.*

the many-named, 'the best of heavenly beings,' as Zagreus and Iao are 'the highest of gods.' So Adonis is Eubouleus, the Wise-counselling, and Dikeros, the Two-horned, 'nourisher of all,' *i.e.* vital power of the world, 'male and female;' or, as Shelley says, 'a sexless thing it seemed,' in fact the 'two-natured Iakchos.' Ever fresh and vigorous, he is, like Dionysos, both solar and kosmogonic.

> Adonis, ever flourishing and bright;
> At stated periods doom'd to set and rise
> With splendid lamp, the glory of the skies.
> 'Tis thine to sink in Tartarus profound,
> And shine again thro' heaven's illustrious round.
> *Taylor.*

Dionysos, Adonis, Iao, 'these three agree in one.' Hymn lxxiv. is addressed to Leukotheë, daughter of Kadmos, 'a nurturer of Dionysos,' and also called Ino; and Hymn lxxv. to her son Paleimon, 'nurtured with Dionysos,' and also called Melikertes.[1] It is unnecessary to enter more fully into the varied detail of these Hymns. Many points connected with them will be noticed and illustrated in different parts of the Work; and they are here referred to, not as being themselves of high antiquity, but as having preserved to a considerable extent the aroma of an archaic period, although mingled with, and often almost overpowered by, the stupifying incense of a comparatively modern mysticism.[2]

Subsection VI.—*Neo-Platonism.*

The learned reader will observe that I have carefully avoided and shall not, except in this subsection, allude to the arbitrary mysticism rightly styled Neo-Platonism, that

---

[1] As to Ino and Melikertes, vide *inf.* VI. i. 2.
[2] Vide subsec. vi.

is, something entirely different from the philosophical ideas of Platon and the Hellenes of the great ages. The diffusion of the divine truths and doctrines of Christianity throughout the ancient world naturally stimulated the learned who remained constant to heathenism to attempt to discover a corresponding grandeur, and sublimity, and depth of mystery, in the writings, traditions, and practices of their own religion. Before the Christian era the speculations and belief of the wiser heathen, in their feeling after God and divine realities, are sufficiently intelligible, and their discoveries and errors can alike be understood and appreciated. But the vain endeavour to bring to light, from the confused mass of heathen belief, knowledge, and tradition, a depth of splendour and of truth corresponding to the revelation of the Deity and his principles in the sacred books of the Hebrew and the Christian, only produced a system of the most uncertain belief and midnight obscurity, mainly founded on unsupported fancy and arbitrary assertion. The chiefs of the Neo-Platonists were Ammonios, the founder of the School, who died A.D. 243, and who was the son of Christian parents; Longinos, the friend of Zenobia, put to death by Aurelian; Plotinos, often considered as the originator of the system; Porphyrios, the great anti-Christian controversialist; the Emperor Julianus; Saloustios, his friend, author of an occult treatise *About the Gods and the Kosmos*; Proklos, the chief luminary of the School, surnamed Diadochos, the Successor, as being the true representative of Platon; Marinos, his pupil, and who wrote his life; Olympiodoros the elder; and Olympiodoros the younger, a contemporary of the Emperor Justinianus; and Simplikios, who, persecuted by the Christians, took refuge with six other philosophers at the Court of Kosru of Persia, and through his assistance obtained from the Christian Emperor license for the fugitives to return and practise their religion undisturbed. The last, and possibly not the least of the School, was the late Thomas Taylor, translator and commentator on the Orphik Hymns, Platon, Iamblichos, Pausanias, Plotinos, Proklos, Julianus, and others, and Author of a *Dissertation on the Eleusinian and Bacchic Mysteries*.[1] He speaks of Proklos as being 'incomparable,' which he probably was, and as 'the man that unfolded the theology and philosophy of the Greeks in the most consummate perfection.' The 'ancient fables,' he tells us, 'are replete with the most philosophical and mystic information,' and at once 'scientific and sublime;' and that, thanks to Proklos and the younger Olympiodoros, we can have them explained at our pleasure. He then proceeds to pass a severe censure on Euemerism, and praises the Baconian method of dealing with the myths,[2] remarking that Bacon 'has done all in attempting to unfold them that great genius without the assistance of *genuine philosophy* is able to effect.' The anxious enquirer may now perhaps congratulate himself on having met with a sage who, apparently, has thoroughly fathomed the whole subject, and sounded all its depths and shoals. A few illustrations of what Neo-Platonism can bring up *de profundis* will suffice. Bakchos is, that is, represents, 'the mundane intellect.' What is that?—and why does he represent it?—may perhaps be asked. The first question I am altogether unable to answer, but the reply to the second is, Because Proklos says so. Similarly the talons of the Sphinx, according to Lord Bacon, represent 'the axioms and arguments of science.' This, again, is of course quite arbitrary and unphilosophical, although perhaps more intelligible; and, as Dr. Tylor well observes, 'any of us may practise this simple art, each according to his own fancy. If, for

---

[1] Recently edited by Dr. Wilder. New York Bouton. 1875.
[2] Cf. *Mythol. of the Aryan Nations*, 28.

instance, political economy happens for the moment to lie uppermost in our mind, we may with due gravity expound the story of Perseus as an allegory of trade: Perseus himself is Labour, and he finds Andromeda, who is Profit, chained and ready to be devoured by the monster Capital. But when it comes to sober investigation of the processes of mythology, the attempt to penetrate to the foundation of an old fancy will scarcely be helped by burying it yet deeper underneath the new one.'[1] For further information about Neo-Platonism I would respectfully refer enquirers to the great originals, and conclude this notice with the wise remark of a living sage: 'Simple and credulous persons are, perhaps fortunately, more common than philosophers; and it is of the highest importance that you should take innocent testimony as it was meant, and not efface, under the graceful explanation which your cultivated ingenuity may suggest, the evidence their story may contain of an event having really taken place.'[2]

Subsection VII.—Eikon of the Orphik Dionysos.

The Homerik portrait of Dionysos chiefly consists of detail, the Orphik of general features, amongst which the primary and leading characteristic is a kosmogonico-solar phase. Dionysos the Demiurge fills and sustains the universe of matter; he is Phanes the Apparent, and Erikepaios [3] the Growth-Power of the world, not yet

---

[1] *Primitive Culture*, i. 251.
[2] Ruskin, *Queen of the Air*, i. 3. The third period of Hellenik Philosophy, comprising the (1) Hebreo-Alexandrian, (2) Neo-Pythagorean, and (3) Neo-Platonik, is ably summarised by Ueberweg, *History of Philosophy*, i. 222-59.
[3] 'I take
That popular name of time to shadow forth
The all-generating powers and genial heat
Of Nature, when she strikes thro' the thick blood
Of cattle, and light is large, and lambs are glad,
Nosing the mother's udder, and the bird
Makes his heart voice amid the blaze of flowers.'
Tennyson, *Lucretius*.

degraded into a Priapos, he is also a solar divinity, Pyropos the Fiery-eyed, and Antauges the Sparkler; and so becomes, on the one hand, naturally but erroneously connected with Aryan sun-gods, and, on the other, is properly linked with such Semitic personages as Sabazios, Iao, and Adon. So, again, he is Eubouleous the Wise-counselling, like Helios who 'sees and hears all things,' and thus becomes the possessor of mystic wisdom. Again, he is a chthonian divinity, or connected with the Under-world, in his kosmogonic phase, as being the concealed earth-power; and in his solar, as sinking at close of day into the chambers of Persephone,[1] from which he rises as her son in renewed splendour. Unanthropomorphic in shape, horned and bovine, and nursed by the Ocean Nymphs, he is the tauriform god from the lands of the morning. Like the great earth-goddess Demeter, he is Thesmophoros, the Law-giver, who regulates religious ritual, civil relationship, and the general order of things. He is connected locally with Krete, Kypros, Phrygia, Syria, and the Semitic East generally, and with the Kypros-born Aphrodite. He is a Kadmeion, and son of Semele. His vast and vaguely defined power and sway place him almost, if not quite, on a level with the highest of gods. By the side of Zeus and Iao he stands as a brother deity, 'every inch a king.' His stern and savage aspect is not prominent here, as in the case of the Homerik Dionysos, for the Poems are the productions of his humble worshippers, to whom he is ever graceful and kindly, written in his honour, and not to record his early struggles in Aryan regions. Lord of the vine is he, but this phase is not a very prominent one. All these concepts and connections of the god are separate and distinct from the Neo-Platonik mysticism which has twined itself around them, and are also in perfect harmony with the

---

[1] Cf. *Od.* x, 509 with Hymn liii.

THE DIONYSOS OF THE THEOLOGERS.

Dionysos of Homeros and of Hesiodos. Each new detail adds a fresh touch to the portrait, and, while explaining or expanding, is in uniformity with previous outlines, and assists us in obtaining a juster concept of this gigantic and mysterious divinity. The choric voices of the three Theologers, in different tones, raise a harmonious song in honour of the Zeus of Nysa. Homeros shows him as in youth, at once strong and weak, he leaped Protesilaos-like upon the hostile shore. Hesiodos, while preserving the traditions of his birth, shows him as he became when established on the banks of the Asopos and Ilisos; the Orphik Poet reveals his solar and kosmogonic character, which previously had been but indirectly apparent, and displays the towering stature to which he attained in an earlier home.

CHAPTER III.

THE LYRIC DIONYSOS.

SECTION I.

THE DIONYSOS OF PINDAROS.

Subsection I.—Dionysos, son of Semele.

THE writings of the prince of Hellenik lyric poets have been hardly dealt with by Time; we know them but in fragments, for the *Epinikia* or *Triumphal Odes*, although complete in themselves, form but a detached group in the original starry cluster of the Muse of Pindaros. The *Hymns*, the *Choric Songs*, the *Dithyrambs*, the *Processional Odes*, the *Lays of the Virgins*, the *Hyporchemes* or *Pantomimic Dancing Ditties*, the *Banquet Melodies*, the *Panegyrics*, the *Dirges*; combining in the whole a perfect cycle of lyrics, domestic, festive, religious, survive only in unconnected fragments; and since we can but deal with existing material, it is as impossible to fully realise the complete Pindarik concept of Dionysos as it is to thoroughly estimate the genius of the Theban bard himself.

There are only three direct allusions to Dionysos in the *Epinikia*. In the second Olympik Ode the Poet shows how the woes of the daughters of Kadmos redounded to their advantage; how—for Pindaros constantly uses language and lines of thought of striking similarity with those of our own Sacred Books—they were made perfect

THE LYRIC DIONYSOS.

through suffering. 'There lives amongst the Olympians, Semele with-the-flowing-locks, who died in the roar of the thunder.[1] But Pallas loves her ever and Father Zeus much, and her child Kissophoros [the ivy-bearer][2] loves her.' Here we have the Phoenician parentage of Dionysos as in the Theologers, with a notice of the death and deification of Semele, who finally appears as the Pambasileia or Universal Queen.[3] Semele, according to Professor Ruskin, ' is the cloud with the strength of the vine in its bosom, consumed by the light which matures the fruit; the melting away of the cloud into the clear air at the fringe of its edges being exquisitely rendered by Pindar's epithet for her, " Semele with-the-stretched-out-hair." '[4] This is elegantly imaginative, and may be accepted as being true as far as it goes; but it is only a mikrokosmic view of the subject. According to a somewhat wider concept, we find that 'the myth of Koronis precisely corresponds with the legend of Semele. Like Dionysos, Asklepios is born amongst and rescued from the flames; in other words, the light and heat of the sun which ripen the fruits of the earth, scorch and consume the clouds and the dew, or banish away the lively tints of early morning.'[5] Semele here becomes a kind of impersonation of the more delicate phenomena of morning, dawnlight, clouds, and dew, and generally of the frail yet material supports of the infant earth-vigour of her son. But our concept of the daughter of Kadmos, the Man-of-the-East, the Ogygian, or Man-of-Ancient-Times, and of Harmonia, who appears in the myth 'dressed in a robe studded with stars and wearing a necklace representing the universe,'[6] our idea of the mother of the mighty Dionysos must be far wider even

---

[1] Cf. Soph. *Antig.* 1139; Eur. *Hippol.* 558; *Bak.* 3.
[2] Vide *inf.* VIII. ii. *Ivy.*
[3] *Orphik Hymn,* xliv. 1.
[4] *Queen of the Air,* i. 30.
[5] *Mythol. of the Aryan Nations,* ii. 34.
[6] Bunsen, *Egypt's Place,* iv. 231.

than this. It will include these, as the greater does the less, but they are in themselves quite inexhaustive of the meaning of the ancient legend. The cycle of Dionysiak myths, as noticed,[1] appears to have had a peculiar fascination for Diodoros, who made great but futile efforts to unravel them. After having rightly explained that Demeter was usually used by the ancient poets and mythologists as a name for Mother-Earth, and having alluded to the sacred rites, 'which it is not lawful for any ordinary person to treat of,' he continues, 'And likewise they refer the birth of Dionysos from Semele *to the beginnings of nature*, having shown that the earth was named Thyone by the ancients; and the reason of the nomenclature, Semele from being splendidly worshipped (semnê), and Thyone from the sacrifices (thyomenôn) and offerings made to her.'[2] Declining these etymologies, but accepting the view of the ancients on the matter, we find that the concept of Semele has greatly enlarged. She is not now merely the more delicate phenomena and accompaniments of morning that assist in expanding the strength of the grape-god; but the earth itself, and as such is an equivalent of Demeter. We have no difficulty, therefore, in understanding how Demeter herself appears in some legends as the mother of Dionysos. But we have even yet hardly reached the root idea of Semele, for Demeter, again, is a derivative concept, representing the earth in a state of order and civilisation, and as such she is Thesmophoros, the Law-giver, the establisher of agriculture, marriage, and the arts of life. But over her is flung the vast shadow of the huge and unanthropomorphic Gaia, the Earth without form and void, colossal and chaotic, as it seemed to the Hebrew prophet when he exclaimed, 'I went down to the bottoms of the mountains; the earth with her bars was about me.' At the

---

[1] *Sup.* I.   [2] Diodoros, iii. 62.

bottoms of the mountains, at the very basis and root of material phenomena, in 'the beginnings of nature,' to use the expression of Diodoros, and in the very place where we should expect to find the mother of the kosmogonic Dionysos and daughter of the universe Harmonia, clad in her starry robe,[1] we discover Semele or Themele, *themethlon*, that which is first laid or placed, the foundation,[2] *i.e.* the foundation of materiality; the expanding might of which, as it

> Warms in the sun, refreshes in the breeze,
> Glows in the stars, and blossoms in the trees,

bounds in the dance, boils in the blood, flows in the song, echoes in the shout, is her son Dionysos, the kosmic spirit of the world.[3] She is the vital centre of that growth-power of which her son Dionysos, Karpios or Erikepaios, is the personified incarnation; and so when Zagreus, mystic son of Zeus and Persephone, Queen of the Under-world, another phase of Semele the Foundation-of-things, is at the instigation of the jealous Here slain by the Titanes, his heart is given to Semele; that is, the Earth receives from Zeus the principle of vitality, the seeds of being, and Zagreus who was dead becomes alive again in the person of Dionysos.[4] That Pindaros really entertained this view of the kosmic nature of Dionysos is made absolutely certain by a very valuable passage in Ploutarchos, who wrote with the Theban Bard's Works before him. He observes, 'That the Hellenes consider Dionysos as the lord and first cause not only of wine but

---

[1] *Inf.* X. ii.
[2] 'There is also a legend which says that Dionysos was born of Zeus and Gê (Earth); from Earth called Themele, because all things are so to speak placed in it as a *foundation*, which by the change of one letter, the S, the poets call Semele.' (Apollod. *Frag.* xxix. apud Ioan. Lyd. Cf. Hesychios *in voc. Semele.* Vide also remarks on the Hebrew *Semel, inf.* VII. ii.)
[3] Cf. Welcker, *Götterlehre*, i. 536; Donaldson, *Theatre of the Greeks*, 20.
[4] Cf. Grote, *History of Greece*, i. 19; *Mythology of the Aryan Nations*, ii. 294; *inf.* IX. vi. *Zagreus.*

of the whole humid nature,[1] Pindaros is an excellent witness when he says, "Dionysos, the much-cheering,[2] increases the nourishment of trees,[3] the holy splendour of the later summer."[4] It is unknown from what Work of the Poet the quotation is taken,[5] but the whole passage is peculiarly valuable as showing the general view of the earlier writers on the subject; and, in so doing, as absolutely disproving the theory which regards Dionysos as a simple wine-god. Ploutarchos speaks of the fact as well known, and could evidently with equal facility have quoted a dozen passages to illustrate it. Truly, says D'Hancarville, that amongst the Hellenes Dionysos was quite as much 'god of water' as 'god of wine.'[6] But how and why does Semele, the foundation of materiality, 'die in the thunder's roar?' Is her fate merely the scorching of clouds and dew by the rays of the morning sun? This view, although perhaps true in itself, yet seems quite inadequate as a full explanation of the myth. Zeus, the Most High, draws near to Semele the Foundation-of-things; and amid thunders and convulsions is born Dionysos, the Spirit-of-the-material-world. This is the gist of the myth; the jealousy of Here, and the stratagem by which she procures her rival's death,[7] are mere afterthoughts springing from the introduction of the Semeleian myth in anthropic form into Aryan regions. There appears to be an occult reference in the legend to a state of pristine chaos from which was produced the form, beauty, and order of the material world, itself a combination of Semele and Dionysos, for the injury to Semele is merely temporary. She becomes immortal, and as Thyone the Inspired, mother of Dionysos Thyoneus, is conducted by her son to heaven.[8] The following

---

[1] Vide *inf*. VIII. i. *Phlias*.
[2] Polygathes, *sup*. II. ii. 1.
[3] Vide *inf*. VIII. i. *Dendrites*.
[4] *Peri Is.* xxxv.
[5] Bergk. *Poet. Ly. Grae.* i. 340.
[6] *Arts de la Grèce*, i. 223.
[7] Ovid. *Metam*. iii. Fab. 4, 5.
[8] Apollod. iii. 4, 5.

extract from the Phoenician Kosmogony of Sanchouniathon, may perhaps to some extent illustrate this very obscure myth [1]:—

'When the air began to send forth rays of splendour, through the fiery influence both on sea and land, there were winds and clouds and mighty flowings and torrents of heavenly waters. And when they were separated and carried out of their proper place by the fiery influence of the sun and all met again in the air and were dashed together, thunders and lightnings ensued.'[2]

The sound arouses certain mysterious intelligent existencies named Zophasemim or 'the sentinels of heaven,' 'as the great constellations or Decans of the Chaldees were called,'[3] and the orderly procession of material phenomena commences. The external creative force (Zeus) shoots fiery splendour on sea and land, themselves emerging into form from the pristine Mot, Mokh, or Mud, the foundation of things (Semele), which has been personified as a Phoenician sage Mochos.[4] Strange chaotic convulsions follow, and amidst the roar of their thunder and the lightning flashes of the enkindling power the earth, temporarily eclipsed in a transition period of Tohu-and-Bohu, passes through it into a state of augmented splendour, a resurrection vitality also typified by the changes of the seasons; and Semele in restored beauty stands forth, the All-mother, the All-queen, combination of Demeter and Persephone, Thyone the Inspired;[5] breathing of the Invisible God, and an early impersonation and concept of that Kingdom-of-the-Heavens spoken of by Apostles and Evangelists, and which appeared to the Seer of Patmos in its developed splendour as 'a woman clothed with the sun, and the moon under her feet,' the

---

[1] As to the authenticity of Philon, cf. Bunsen, *Egypt's Place*, iv. 162 et seq.
[2] Sanchou. i. 2.
[3] Bunsen, *Egypt's Place*, iv. 182.
[4] Cf. ibid. 176.
[5] *Hom. Hymn*, xxvi. 21; Pind. *Pyth.* iii. 176.

time of night, darkness, chaos, and confusion passed, and on her head a starry crown; a feature which leads to the mention of another Pindarik epithet of Semele, namely, Helikampyx,[1] Curling-hair-circlet-girt. Both this name and Tanuetheira have special reference to her flowing locks. And why? Because the hair, the glory of the woman-earth, is, like the Samsonian locks, the sign and symbol of the force and vigour of vitality; and as such is dedicated to the River-gods as representatives 'of the strength and daily flow of human life,'[2] and Semele is thus fitly the mother of Dionysos Eurychaites,[3] the Flowing-tressed; not the unshorn tresses of Apollon Akersekomes, but the earth-vigour of the telluric spirit of the world Kallietheiros,[4] Adorned-with-lovely-locks. Such appears to be the root idea of the myth of Semele, but since Hesiodos and Pindaros pictured her as a mortal maiden, daughter of the Phoenician Kadmos, it may easily be perceived how the elements of the myth came to appear in their present form. Zeus has already an Aryan consort, Here, who naturally resents his preference for another and plots her destruction. The kosmical chaos becomes in the anthropomorphic concept the death of Semele, its restoration to order and ever-renewing beauty her resurrection and investiture with immortal life; and, being immortal, she naturally joins her fellow-deities in the etherial abodes of Olympos through the instrumentality of her son, the favourite of Zeus and youthful member of the Aryan Pantheon. These circumstances are easily embellished by the arbitrary and meaningless imaginations of later writers; Ovidius can give us a detailed history of the intrigue, while Nonnos records how the deified Thyone sits at the same heavenly

---

[1] Dithyrambs, *Frag.* iii.
[2] *Queen of the Air*, i. 12; cf. *Il.* xxiii. 142; Hes. *Theog.* 347; Ais. *Choe.* 6.
[3] Pind. *Isth.* vi. 4.
[4] *Orphik Hymn*, i. 7.

table with Zeus and Hermes, Ares and Aphrodite.[1] But while we cast aside the comparatively modern and worthless fiction which entwines itself round the original idea, we may well admire the fullness of meaning of these strange stories of the Earlier Time, which seem as deathless as the truths they represent. Nor are we bound to see in them only the thoughts and ideas which they may have reflected upon the gifted minds of antiquity. But in the story of Semele we may find an adumbration of the truth that the creature cannot bear to behold the unveiled glories of the Creator; that if He look upon the earth it trembles, if He touch the hills they smoke; that we must be covered with the hand and set in the cleft of the rock while the brightness of the Infinite passes by; and, lastly, that all changes in created things shall ever be from the lower to the higher, from glory to glory, until at length in place of Semele, the present mortal and melancholy earth that shall wax old as a garment, will arise the deathless splendour of a happier creation, Thyone, inspired to show forth the glory of the true Zeus Hypsistos, when He shall make all things new. As regards the historical cult of Semele, Hesychios[2] mentions a festival in her honour, which is apparently identical with the Herois, a singular celebration performed by the Delphians once in nine years, and in which, according to Ploutarchos, 'was a representation of something like Semele's resurrection,' with many mysterious rites illustrating the restoration to life of a great heroine who was doubtless a personification of the Earth-mother. The inhabitants of Brasiai on the Argolik Gulf had a local tradition that Kadmos enclosed Semele and her infant in a chest, which was cast into the sea, and at length thrown up on that coast; from which circumstance the place was said to have received its more modern name, *i.e.* from

[1] *Dionys.* viii. 418.   [2] *In voc. Heroai.*

brasso, to thrown up. Semele, they reported, died and was splendidly buried upon the sea shore, and the youthful Dionysos was nurtured by his aunt Ino, who had opportunely arrived there in the course of her wanderings.[1] The legend is a link between Dionysos and the Semitic Adonis, who 'was placed in a chest and put into the hands of Persephone,'[2] herself another phase of Semele. This mystic chest is a kind of ark or kosmic egg, from which the powers of growth, heat, and life-beauty come forth in the procession of existence.[3]

Subsection II.—Dionysos and the Dithyramb.

In *Olymp.* xiii. 22, the Poet, recounting the glories of Korinthos, exclaims, 'Where else appeared the delights of Dionysos and the ox-capturing Dithyramb?' The North Dorik cities of the Peloponnesos, Korinthos and Sikyon, were more addicted to the Bakchik ritual than Argos and Sparta. The Sikyonians worshipped the god with many peculiar ceremonies as Bakcheios, the Exciter-to-phrensy; his cult having been originally introduced from Thebai about the time of the Dorik invasion.[4] The Dithyramb, or ancient Bakchik choral hymn, is said by the almost unanimous voice of antiquity to have been invented, or rather remodelled and greatly improved, by the lyric poet Arion of Lesbos, who passed the greater part of his life at the court of Periandros, despot of Korinthos, who ruled B.C. 625-585.[5] This circumstance explains the allusion of Pindaros, and, as the Scholiast informs us, a bull was the prize and sacrifice at the Bakchik festival. The fact is interesting as an early instance of the cult of Dionysos Taurokeros.[6] According

---

[1] Paus. iii. 24.
[2] *Mythology of the Aryan Nations*, ii. 7.
[3] Vide *inf.* V. v. 4.
[4] Müller, *Doric Race*, i. 419; *inf.* VI. i. 3.
[5] Cf. Herod. i. 23.
[6] *Inf.* IX. iii., VIII. ii. *Dithyramb*

to the natural Phenomena Theory Arion is an unhistoric personage, whose harp represents the wind.[1] This view, like that of the Eumeristik interpreters of his history,[2] is much more easily advanced than satisfactorily supported; nor is it indeed at all material to the present enquiry, the important fact remaining undoubted that a Bakchik cult was introduced at Korinthos from Thebai, and was subsequently enlarged and improved by strangers from the neighbourhood of the eastern shores of the Aigaion. The circumstance mentioned by Mr. Cox that Arion 'is represented as a son of Poseidon,' is in perfect accordance with the Semitic character of the worship and the foreign nature of the god. Pausanias, alluding to the account in Herodotos of Arion and his dolphin, states that he knew a dolphin which would carry a certain boy who had cured it of a hurt wherever he liked.[3]

Subsection III.—Dionysos Associate of Demeter.

The sixth Isthmian Ode opens, 'With which of the former glories of thy country, O fortunate Thebai, does thy mind chiefly delight itself? Was it when thou broughtest forth to light the associate of bronze-rattling Dameter, Dionysos Eurychaites?' From this important passage we learn (1) that Dionysos was born in Thebai,[4] that is, that his cult was introduced there from the Outerworld; Thebai, as above noticed,[5] was one of the chief centres from which it spread through continental Hellas; (2) that Dionysos became the associate of Demeter; (3) in his character of Eurychaites, Lord-of-the-flowing-tresses. The first point is already familiar in the enquiry,[6] and, as regards the second, the connection between Diony-

---

[1] Cf. *Mythology of the Aryan Nations*, ii. 26, 245.
[2] Vide Rawlinson, *Herod.* i. 136.
[3] Paus. iii. 25.
[4] Cf. *Hymns, Frag.* i.
[5] Subsec. i.
[6] *Sup.* II. i. 2.

sos and Demeter has already been partially illustrated.[1] We have seen how Semele in her phase as the earth is necessarily an interchangeable concept with Demeter the Earth-mother, the earth in a state of order and civilisation; and how therefore, in this point of view, Dionysos becomes the son of the latter. But he is not originally her son, and it is only when the recognition of his character gives a suitability to the idea that he thus becomes connected with her and the assistant at her Mysteries. There is a singular appropriateness in the epithet by which Pindaros describes the union between them. He calls Dionysos the Paredros or Associate of Demeter, literally one who sits with or by the side of another to assist, not the original authority; and thus, for example, the term is applied to the inferior Archons at Athenai, where each of the three premier Archons had two assistants or associates. Here the original authority is the Aryan Demeter and the associate, also 'of the commission,' is the Semitic Dionysos. And it will further be noticed that even the undoubtedly Aryan divinity Demeter has, in this passage, an Oriental aspect, arising from her similarity of position to that of certain other Earth-mothers and Great Mothers; for the epithet Chalkokrotos, Bronze-rattling, connects her cult with that of the Phrygian Kybele, the goddess of furious and orgiastic ritual, whose service was constantly accompanied with the beating of drums, playing on the loud sounding cymbals,[2] blowing of horns, and clashing of armour, and whose worship was fully established at Thebai in the time of Pindaros,[3] and also with that of Dionysos as the noisy god, Bakchos, Bromios, and Mainomenos.[4] The ancient earth-goddess Rhea, daughter of Ouranos and Gaia, and in mythologic pedigree the mother of Zeus and others of

---

[1] *Sup.* subsec. i.
[2] Cf. Eur. *Hel.* 1308.
[3] Cf. *Pyth.* iii. 78.
[4] Cf. Dithyrambs, *Frag.* v.

the chief divinities of Olympos, is another important concept in this group of telluric personages, of whom Dionysos is the Associate. She appears Aryan in origin, and her name seems to be merely another form of Gê, Gaia, or of Era, Terra, the Earth. This, however, is not beyond doubt, for Canon Rawlinson is of opinion that she may be identical with the Kaldean Bilta (Beltis), 'the Great Goddess,' whose numerical symbol was fifteen, pronounced Ri.[1] The point, however, is not one of immediate importance; but we notice that being all earth goddesses, Semele, Demeter, and Rhea, are in phase at least identical, the Earth, 'whose names are many but her form the same;'[2] and Rhea, whether originally Aryan or not, was early identified by the Asiatic Hellenes with Kybele, an undoubted phase of the Great Goddess of the East. Perhaps, however, we must only understand from this identification that Rhea and Kybele were corresponding divinities in their respective Pantheons, for the general Hellenik fashion of indiscriminately identifying the gods of different nations and races is to be carefully avoided.[3] But although the two figures may be distinct, yet the connection between them both in idea and historically is very close. Rhea 'worshipped as the great reproductive force of the world, as producing life through death,'[4] identified with and an Aryan copy of Kybele the 'mother of the gods,' the great goddess of the Eastern world, whose innumerous phases reach back to the most remote antiquity; Semele, the Foundation-of-things; and Demeter, Mother-earth, are appropriately connected with Dionysos the great earth-spirit whose almost countless epithets answer harmoniously to the characteristics and properties of his mythologic mother. And this leads to

[1] *Ancient Monarchies,* i. 120, *note.*
[2] Ais. *Prom. Des.* 210.
[3] Cf. *Poseidon,* v.
[4] *Mythology of the Aryan Nations,* ii. 312.

the third point in the passage, namely, that it is in his character of Eurychaites, the Flowing-tressed, that Dionysos is connected with Demeter. We noticed[1] how the descriptive epithets of Semele referred to her long locks as symbolising the strength and flow of life, the vital earth vigour; and how appropriately her son, the lord of vitality and reproduction, is described as Eurychaites.[2] This is the phase of Dionysos as Phleon or Phloios, the fullness or overflowing of the life-force of nature; the hair, a symbol of which, is dedicated to the divinities of the everflowing streams. And Rhea herself, whose historic cult is so closely connected with that of Dionysos, may be the Flowing-one, the earth goddess as the representative of the constant course and fullness of life; and, if so, Dionysos Phleon will in reality be identical with her, the pair forming two distinct concepts, male and female of the same root idea. It might be urged that if Dionysos were the Associate of the Aryan Demeter, then he must in all probability be himself of Aryan origin. But the analysis of their histories prevents such a conclusion, and the different divinities group themselves in orderly fashion in their respective Pantheons. On the Aryan side we find Gaia, Rhea, Demeter, representatives of the Earth, mother of all; on the Semitic side we have Kybele and Semele,[3] representatives of the Earth-mother; and Dionysos, when known as the child of the Semitic Earth, naturally and necessarily becomes the Associate of the Aryan Earth. I have classed Kybele among Semitic divinities, for even if it be admitted that the Lydians and Phrygians were members of the Indo-European Family of nations, yet the concept of the Great Goddess is undoubtedly Semitic. The scientific labours

---

[1] *Sup.* subsec. i.
[2] Cf. Eur. *Bak.* 493-4.
[3] The *name* Semele is Hellenik. It may, however, be identical with the Hebrew *semel* and Assyrian *simallu* (vide *inf.* VII. ii.).

of Comparative Mythologists will ever be of the highest value; but they are at times apt to forget, in the ardour of discovery, and in their zeal for philological and ethnic affinities, that there are also geographical and commercial affinities which to some extent run counter to the former, and in their operation at times produce apparent breaches in scientific laws of language and classes of religious ideas. Semitic influence in Hellas is a remarkable instance of this fact, and thus it appears that some Hellenik names and words being, like some English words, adopted from foreign sources, do not belong to the Aryan family of languages; and therefore the idea that all Hellenik words are necessarily Aryan, and so cannot have a Semitic derivation, is simply based on a misapprehension of the facts. Thus, if there be a single Hellenik name, Melikertes for instance, which is admittedly Semitic in derivation, there are, apart from any investigation, in all probability a considerable number of kindred terms.[1] 'We do not,' said an opponent of the notion of a Phoenician colony at Thebai, 'meet with the slightest trace of Phoenician influence in the language of Boeotia.'[2] A bold and unsupported assertion of this kind forms an admirable groundwork for a theory. Assuming the point in discussion, we may argue: The Phoenicians left no traces in Thebai; but had they ever been there they would have left traces; therefore, they were never there. Keightley appears either to consider that 'the letters Cadmus gave' were thoroughly Aryan, or else that a nation may adopt the alphabet of another and yet show us no trace of the influence of the latter in its language. Either opinion is as reasonable as the other, and possibly ultimate anti-Semitic investigation

---

[1] For a list of such words, being chiefly names of various productions of the East, musical instruments, weights, and measures, vide Lenormant, *Les Premières Civilisations*, ii. 425-6.

[2] Keightley, *Mythology*, i. 327.

may result in the discovery that the Phoenicians obtained their letters from the Hellenes, not the Hellenes from the Phoenicians. In the meantime, however, we must be content to take things as we find them; and meeting assertion by assertion, it will be sufficient to reply that the Phoenicians left traces in Thebai; but had they never been there, they would have left no traces; therefore, they were once there. And that these are no mere idle assertions the patient investigator will discover.

SECTION II.

OTHER LYRIC DIONYSIAK ALLUSIONS.

Subsection I.—Vinal Allusions.

As the Hellenik Lyric Poets, like most of their fellow bards in all ages, appear to have fully appreciated the good things of the present material life, gifts, which may be briefly expressed by the triad Demeter, Aphrodite, and Dionysos; it is not surprising that the latter divinity generally appears in their works as Theoinos the Wine-god. It is far from my intention to ignore this important though strictly subordinate part of his character, in which he is seen as Botryokosmos the Grape-decked, Lenaios the Lord-of-the-wine-press, Polystaphylos the Rich-in-grape-clusters, Protygaios or Protryges the Presider-over-the-vintage, Lyaios or Lysios the Deliverer-from-care, Choöpotes the Gallon-drinker, Oinops the Wine-faced, and in other similar phases.[1] Such is his constant aspect in the Odes so long ascribed to Anakreon, and well translated by Moore otherwise 'Little, young Catullus of his day,' in which the height of happiness is placed in a

[1] Vide *inf.* VIII. i.

kind of modern music-hall enjoyment, the quaffing of wine forming the most important feature. To notice such passages in detail is unnecessary, but I may refer to several which somewhat illustrate the general character of the god. Solon links Dionysos with the Kypros-born Aphrodite and the Muses, as being cheering deities,[1] and Theognis, cir. B.C. 544, alludes to wine as the gift of the former divinity;[2] Alkaios, too, cir. B.C. 608, declares that 'care-banishing wine the son of Zeus and Semele gave to men;'[3] and thus all the earlier writers agree in connecting the god with Kadmos and Thebai. Archilochos, cir. B.C. 700, in a passage noticed subsequently,[4] exclaims, 'I know how to lead off the dithyramb, the beautiful strain of King Dionysos, when my mind is struck with wine as with a thunderbolt;' and Ion, the friend of Aischylos, and also a tragic poet, addresses the god as 'father Dionysos,' which recalls the 'Liber Pater' of the Latin writers, and connects him with wine-banquets and thyrsos-bearers.[5] Simonides[6] 'describes the dithyramb as sung by noisy Bacchanalians, crowned with fillets and chaplets of roses and bearing the ivy-wreathed thyrsos.'[7] There are many similar passages scattered throughout the fragments of Lyric Poets;[8] but should the reader feel inclined to give undue prominence to Dionysos Theoinos, and to imagine that the tauric, solar, and kosmogonic character of the god is entirely a later and non-original phase, he will probably be convinced on pursuing the enquiry that the Dionysos of the Lyric Poets, like the Dionysos of the Theologers and the Tragics, is no mere wine-god, but, as we shall see him throughout the course of the investiga-

---

[1] *Frag.* xxvi.; cf. *Il.* xiv. 325; Anakreon, *Frag.* ii.
[2] Theog. 076.
[3] *Frag.* xli.
[4] *Inf.* IV. iii. 1.
[5] *Frag.* i.
[6] *Frag.* cxlviii.
[7] *Theatre of the Greeks*, 38.
[8] Cf. Dionysios Chalkous, *Frag.* v.; Bakchylides, *Frag.* xxviii.; Philoxenos, *Frag.* iv.; Telestes, *Frag.* i.; Simonides, *Frag.* lxxxviii.; Anakreon, *Frags.* lv. ciii. &c.

tion, one of the vastest and most wonderful concepts that ever entered the imagination of a thinker or received the homage of a devotee.

Subsection II.—*Non-Vinal Allusions.*

Pratinas, cir. B.C. 500, alluding to the god as Bromios the Noisy, a common epithet with the Lyric Poets, connects him with clamour and choric dances, and calls him by the sounding epithet of Thriambodithyrambos, the Trumpher-in-the-dithyramb;[1] and, similarly, Anakreon speaks of him as 'the loud-shouting Deunysos,'[2] and in an Anonymous Fragment[3] he is addressed 'O Iakchos Thriambos the chorus-leader.'[4] It may be objected that the noisy phase of the god is connected with wine; but this is only partially the case, for noise is linked with song and dance; and these, especially the latter, have other aspects and significations than mere vinal hilarity.[5] Moreover, the cult of many Oriental divinities, *e.g.* the Great Mother, is distinguished by noise which has no connection with the excitement produced by wine. Anakreon[6] connects the Bassarides[7] with Dionysos, and calls the god Aithiopais,[8] Child-of-the-sun-burnt-land, *i.e.* the East; while Hipponax, cir. B.C. 530, associates the Bakchanals with Kithairon.[9] Another Anonymous Fragment[10] apparently identifies or closely links the god with Ares. 'O Bromios spear-bearing Enyalios [the Warlike], father Ares rousing-the-din-of-war,' but the full meaning of the passage is probably uncertain. Euripides says similarly that Dionysos 'has something of Ares in him.'[11] His

---

[1] Pratin. *Frag.* i.
[2] *Frag.* xi.
[3] No. cix. Bergk.
[4] Cf. Soph. *Antig.* 1147; Eur. *Bak.* 141.
[5] Vide *inf.* IV. iii. 1.
[6] *Frag.* lvi.
[7] Vide *inf.* IV. i. 2.
[8] Vide VIII. i. *Aithiopais.*
[9] *Frag.* xci.; cf. Eur. *Bak.* 751; Aristoph. *Thes.* 996.
[10] No. cviii. Bergk.
[11] *Bak.* 302.

savage and warlike phase frequently appears.[1] An obscure passage from Kastorio[2] addressed to the god, apparently exhibits him in a solar connection. We next come to a cluster of Fragments which show Dionysos in his tauric aspect. Thus Simonides[3] alludes to 'the ox-slaying priest of King Dionysos;' and Ion, in his Dithyrambs,[4] addresses him as 'Inexorable youth, bull-faced, young not young, sweetest assistant of tempestuous loves, cheering wine, lord of men.' This passage exhibits, perhaps, the most perfect instance of the almost absolute blending of the Oriental aspects of Dionysos Tauropos with his familiar phase as the Wine-god. The divinity is actually treated as the very personification of wine, and yet is also styled inexorable, bull-faced, young and not young. This latter point in the description is of doubtful meaning, but it may well signify that the establishment of his cult in Hellas was comparatively recent, while at the same time its origin was lost in antiquity; that, in fact, he was much younger in Hellas than in the Outer-world. The epithet 'inexorable' is fully explained when we realise the Phoenician sternness and ferocity of his cult; and with respect to the remaining feature in the description, perhaps the adherents of the extreme vinous theory can explain why wine personified is called bull-faced. Failing to supply any satisfactory reason for the use of this very singular epithet, they must needs abandon their theory. Those who accept the true origin and character of Dionysos Taurokerôs can easily comprehend the poet, follow the obscure course of the historic phases of the god, and understand the invocation of the women of Elis, which describes him as the 'Worthy Bull.'[5]

---

[1] Vide *inf.* IV. iii. 2.
[2] *Frag.* i.
[3] *Frag.* clxxii.
[4] *Frag.* ix.
[5] Vide *inf.* IV. ii. 1, iii. 2, VI. i. IX. iii.

SECTION III.

EIKÔN OF THE LYRIC DIONYSOS.

The Lyric Dionysos appears as born in Thebai, and as the son of Zeus and Semele, the daughter of Kadmos; and his mother, beloved by her son, is at length exalted to an equality with the elder Aryan divinities of the country. As the lord of ever-renewing life and vitality he is Kissophoros the Ivy-bearer, Kissodotas the Ivy-crowned, and Eukissos the Ivy-girt. As a kosmogonic divinity he is the Assistant of Demeter, the great Earth-mother; and appears as Eurychaites the Flowing-tressed, son of Semele the foundation of material existence, who is addressed as Tanuetheira the Long-haired, and Helikampyx Curling-hair-circlet-girt, these flowing locks of mother and son typifying the flow and force of the life-vigour of the world. As an Oriental divinity he is connected with the bull the prize of the successful dithyramb in which he triumphs, is styled 'bull-faced,' and hymned as the 'Worthy Bull;' and thus appears as Taurokerôs the Bull-horned, and the Ox-horned Iakchos of the Mysteries. As fits a divinity of eastern votaries he is the choir-leader of the heated dance wild and orgiastic, and as such is Bromios the Noisy, and Eriboas the Loud-shouting, the fit Associate of the Great Goddess, who is herself Chalkokrotos the Bronze-rattling. He is also the Wine-god, and has something of the War-god in him, an aspect occasionally stern and savage. These notices, comparatively few as they are, sufficiently embrace the salient points of the character of the god, a stranger of Oriental associations and Phoenician introduction, a solar, igneous, kosmogonic earth-power, yet making his way into the Aryan Olympos, the lord of vitality and the son of Zeus.

CHAPTER IV.

THE DIONYSOS OF THE ATTIK TRAGEDIANS.

SECTION I.

THE DIONYSOS OF AISCHYLOS.

Subsection I.—Dionysiak Allusions in Extant Plays.

But a tithe of the works of the son of Euphorion have descended to us, and the seven extant Plays contain only three direct Dionysiak allusions. In the opening speech of the *Eumenides*, the scene of which is at Delphoi, the Pythia or Priestess of Apollon recounting the divinities of the country, says, 'And Bromios possesses the land *from the time when* the god marshalled the Bakchai, having contrived death for Pentheus like a hare.'[1] Lykourgos,[2] and Pentheus the grandson of Kadmos and King of Thebai, afford the two most remarkable instances of hopeless opposition to the introduction of the Bakchik cult. The episode of the latter will be considered when examining the *Bakchai* of Euripides,[3] but the present allusion is important as showing that the worship of Dionysos Bromios, the noisy and orgiastic god, was not indigenous, but was introduced into the Kadmeis at an early but still sufficiently known period, and that on its introduction it was unsuccessfully opposed.

In their opening speech in the *Iketides*, the Chorus,

---

[1] *Eumen.* 24–6.
[2] *Sup.* II. i. 1.
[3] *Inf.* sec. iii. 2.

consisting of the daughters of Danaos the Egyptian, exclaim, 'But if not [*i.e.* if they did not escape from their persecutors], a blackened sunburnt race[1] to Zagreus[2] the many-guest-receiving Zeus of the dead we will go.'[3] The epithet Zagreus has been interpreted 'Mighty Hunter,' as if from *za*, intensive, and *agreus* the hunter, an epithet of Apollon, Pan, and several other divinities; but from the context the poet seems to have understood it as derived from *zogreo*, to take alive, He-that-makes-numerous-captives, *i.e.* the Dead, called euphemistically the Majority.[4] We have already, in a surviving line of the *Epigonoi*,[5] caught a glimpse of 'Zagreus highest of all gods,' the chthonian Dionysos, and shall have occasion again to refer to him when speaking of some special phases of the god.[6]

In the *Hepta epi Thêbas* the messenger tells Eteokles that Hippomedon 'raves (βακχᾷ) for fight like a Thyiad,'[7] *i.e.* a Rager, a term technically applied to a Bakchante.[8] Such are the slight Dionysiak allusions in the extant Plays of Aischylos; and if we knew nothing further about his writings, and placed confidence in that broken reed the 'argument from silence,' we should undoubtedly conclude that Dionysos was a divinity about whose legendary history Aischylos was either comparatively ignorant or indifferent.

Subsection II.—*The Lykourgeia.*

But it would have been strange if the citizen of Eleusis, whose father, moreover, was personally connected with the cult of Demeter, the great goddess and associate

---

[1] Vide *inf.* VIII. i. *Aithiopais.*
[2] This reading has been truly called 'a splendid emendation.'
[3] *Iket.* 144 *et seq.*; cf. *Frag.* ccxlii. noticed *inf.* subsec. 3.
[4] Cf. *Dan.* xii. 2; vide *inf.* VIII. i. *Zagreus.*
[5] *Sup.* II. i. 7.
[6] *Inf.* IX. vi.
[7] V. 493; cf. Eur. *Troi.* 500.
[8] Cf. Vir. *Aen.* iv. 302.

THE DIONYSOS OF THE ATTIK TRAGEDIANS. 93

of Dionysos, and who himself also is said to have been initiated into the mysteries of the goddess which he was accused of having divulged,[1] had not treated the Dionysiak Cycle more copiously than appears from his surviving Plays; and accordingly we find that the history of Dionysos was one of his favourite themes. For, not to take into account the numerous Dionysiak allusions which many of the lost Plays must have doubtless contained, both the great opponents of the god, Lykourgos and Pentheus, were honoured by the Poet with trilogies. The trilogy forming the *Lykourgeia* consisted of the *Edonoi*, the *Bassarides*, and the *Neaniskoi*, with the *Lykourgos* as a satyric afterpiece, the whole forming a tetralogy. The *Edonoi* appears to have contained an account of the arrival of Dionysos in Thrake, the victory of Lykourgos over his train, and the captivity of the god. Strabo, in his remarks on the Kouretes,[2] has preserved three Fragments of the Play. The first alludes to 'the revered Kotys, who dwells among the Edonoi.' The Thrakian Kotys, 'dark-veil'd Cotytto, to whom the secret flame of midnight torches burns,'[3] and whose worship was introduced at Athenai and Korinthos in comparatively late times, like the Attik Konisalos,[4] and similar concepts, represents the life-vigour of Dionysos Dendrites, Karpios, or Phleon, running wild in the form of personal licentiousness, a still further development of the coarse idea of Priapos.[5] The second Fragment introduces the Bakchai with their *bombykes* or booming flutes, and hollow bronze-bound kettledrums, fit instruments for the cult of Dionysos Bromios; and the third graphically describes their effect:—'The burst of music is poured forth,[6] terror-striking sounds

---

[1] Cf. Aristoph. *Bat.* 886; Aristot. *Eth.* iii.
[2] Strabo, x. 3.
[3] Vide *inf.* VIII. i. *Lampter. Nyktelios.*
[4] Cf. Aristoph. *Lysist.* 982.
[5] Cf. *Mythol. of the Aryan Nations*, ii. 318.
[6] Ἀλαλάζει. Cf. VIII. i. *Eleleus. Nyktelios.*

imitating the bellowing of bulls blare in concert from unseen recesses, and the echo of the drum is borne along like terrific subterranean thunder.' In this very Aischylian passage the Chorus are represented as mimicking the bellowing of bulls, and it would seem that at times the Bakchik votaries imitated bulls in their attire also,[1] like the Bullards or Bull-baiters of modern times.[2] The cult of Dionysos Taurokerôs appears persistently throughout the investigation.

Another Fragment alludes to the 'Edonian faun-skins,' the peculiar garb of the Bakchai. It will be remembered that an important part of the mystic Orphik dress of the votary of the kosmogonic Dionysos was 'the all-variegated skin of a wild faun much spotted, a representation of the wondrously-wrought stars and of the vault of heaven.'[3] With this agrees the statement of Diodoros that Dionysos is represented as clothed in a faun-skin on account of the stars.[4] Strabo observes that the Orphik ceremonies had their origin among the Thrakians, and, on the strength of their resemblance to the Phrygian ritual, conjectures that the Phrygians were a Thrakian colony, and adds, ' From the song, the rhythm, and the instruments, all Thrakian music is supposed to be Asiatic.'[5] The Edonian worship, says Niebuhr, 'is in a certain sense Thrakian, especially in regard to women, and existed by the side of the Phrygian.'[6] This common character necessitates a common origin. Phrygians and Thrakians alike belonged to the Aryan family of nations; but their cult is by no means purely Aryan, each of them having been brought into contact with both the Turanian and Semitic elements. Nor can the conjecture of Strabo that the settlement of

---

[1] Cf. Eur. *Bak.* 922.
[2] Vide an interesting account of the Bullards of Stamford with their 'uncouth and antic dresses' in Timbs' *Abbeys, Castles, and Ancient Halls of England and Wales*, i. 380 et seq.
[3] *Sup.* II. iii. 3.
[4] Diod. i. 11.
[5] Cf. Eur. *Bak.* 1168, 'O Asiatic Bakchai.'
[6] *Lectures on Ethnography*, i. 288.

the Phrygians was the result of an emigration from West to East be allowed; but, on the contrary, the Bryges or Phryges who inhabited Thrake and bordered on Makedonia, 'must be regarded as colonists of the Phrygians, the stream of Indo-European colonisation having set westward from Armenia into Phrygia, and from Phrygia across the straits into Europe.'[1]

The *Bassarides* appears to have contained an account of the escape of Dionysos and his companions from their bonds, the madness of Lykourgos, and his slaughter of his son Dryas. The Bassarides themselves are the Chorus of Bakchai, dressed in fox-skin tunics. *Bassara*, a Thrakian word, but Semitic in origin, is equivalent to the Hellenik *alopex*, fox. The Play also perhaps contained the punishment of Lykourgos. According to Homeros, the gods took away his life;[2] according to Sophokles, he was imprisoned alive in the rocks, where 'the dreadful strength of madness is ever ebbing away.' He discovered that 'in his madness he had touched a god with jeering words, for he would have put a stop to the inspired women and the flame of Euios, and he angered the lay-living Muses.'[3] The *Neaniskoi* or Youths, forms the third Play of the trilogy, and seems to have recounted the founding of the cult of Lykourgos in connection with that of Dionysos,[4] and perhaps the fate of the former. The Neaniskoi or Chorus of Youths probably represented the Mystics, or those initiated in the rites of the god,[5] a cyclic Dionysiak Chorus such as in early historic times danced around the altar of Zeus to the sound of Phrygian flutes and orgiastic music.[6] Ploutarchos has preserved a Fragment apparently chanted by the Chorus in celebration of the joint rites of Dionysos and Lykourgos, 'It is fitting

---

[1] Rawlinson, *Herodotus*, iv. 57, note.
[2] *Sup.* II. i. 1.
[3] *Antig.* 950 et seq.
[4] Cf. Eur. *Rhesos*, 972; Strabo, x. 3.
[5] Cf. Aristoph. *Bat.* 318 et seq.
[6] Cf. *Theatre of the Greeks*, 35.

that the mixt-sounding dithyramb familiar to Dionysos should accompany.'[1]

Subsection III.—Other Dionysiak Allusions in the Apospasmatia.

In the *Kabeiroi*, almost every line of which is lost, and which formed one in the trilogy of the *Iasoneia*, the poet appears, from a passage in Athenaios, to have recounted the revelry of the Argonautai in Lemnos,[2] where, according to the myth, they arrived on their outward voyage shortly after the Lemnian women had murdered the males on the island.[3] Orgies seem to have been described as having been performed in honour of Dionysos and the Kabeiroi. The same episode was treated in the *Lemniai* of Sophokles, and the loss of both Plays is much to be regretted, as they would certainly have afforded important illustration of the Semitic character of Dionysos the associate of the Kabeiroi, most mysterious personages of undoubted Semitic extraction,[4] and appropriately found as the presiding daemons of Lemnos, an isle sacred to the Semitic Hephaistos,[5] and a Phoenician colony.

The story of Pentheus was treated by the Poet in a trilogy, consisting of the *Semele*, *Pentheus*, and *Xantriai* or 'wool-carders.'[6] Of these Plays almost every line has perished, but in the latter[7] 'the goddess Lussa was introduced stimulating the Bacchae, and creating in them spasmodic excitement from head to foot.'[8] Lussa, Attik Lutta, is a personification of phrensy.[9] Another Play, *Dionysou Trophoi*, 'the nurses of Dionysos,' of which

---

[1] Ahrens, *Aischylos, Frag.* xxiii.
[2] Athen. x. 7.
[3] Cf. Herod. iv. 145.
[4] *Inf.* X. i.
[5] Cf. *Poseidon*, xiv.
[6] Cf. Ovid, *Metam.* iv. 34.
[7] *Frag.* i.
[8] Grote, *Hist. of Greece*, i. 35, note.
[9] Cf. Eur. *Herak. Mai.* 823.

some ten words have been preserved, recounted the youth and early nurturing of the god.[1] The nymphs of Dodona, to whom he was entrusted by Zeus, were seven in number, Ambrosia, Koronis, Eudora, Dione, Aisyle, Polyxo, and Phyto.[2] They were persecuted by Here and the impious Lykourgos, and were placed by Zeus among the stars, where they appear as the Hyades, or Rainy-ones,[3] the seven stars in the horns of Taurus.

> Ora micant Tauri septem radiantia flammis,
>   Navita quas Hyadas Graius ab imbre vocat,
>   Pars Bacchum nutrisse putat.[4]

This incidental circumstance curiously illustrates the intimate connection between that animal and Dionysos, who is himself called Hyes, and his mother Semele Hye, in their phase of the Earth-life, as connected with fertilising moisture.[5] (Tzetzes, in his Commentary on Lykophron,[6] quotes the line, 'Father Theoinos, yoker of the Mainades,' from some unknown play of the poet.) Another passage,[7] refers to him as 'Bakcheios the prophet,' and another from the *Sisyphos Drapetes*, the Fugitive, speaks of 'Zagreus who receives many guests;'[8] and the foregoing comprise all the surviving allusions of Aischylos to the god and his cult. This is a slight residuum, but still we may truly say, 'Egregie Aeschylus Bacchi laudem declaravit,' since no less than eight or nine of his Plays were devoted to Dionysiak subjects. As the three great Attik Tragedians give a most harmonious and closely connected account of the god, I shall notice the combined Eikon which they present, after having referred to the Dionysiak allusions of Sophokles and Euripides.

---

[1] Cf. Eur. *Kyk.* 4; *sup.* II. i.
[2] Pherekydes, *Frags.* xlvi. lxxiv.; Schol. in Hom. *Il.* xviii. 486; Apollod. III. iv. 3; Hygin. *Poet. Astron.* ii. 21.
[3] Cf. Hor. *Car.* I. iii. 14, 'Tristes Hyadas;' Vir. *Aen.* i. 744, iii. 516, 'Pluvias Hyades.' They were much observed by 'ancient mariners.' Cf. Eur. *Ion*, 1156.
[4] Ovid, *Fast.* v. 165-7.
[5] Vide *inf.* VIII. i. *Hyes. Phlias.*
[6] V. 1247.
[7] Apud Macrob. *Sat.* i. 18.
[8] *Frag.* ccxlii. edit. Ahrens.

SECTION II.

THE DIONYSOS OF SOPHOKLES.

Subsection I.—Dionysos and Nysa.

In a fragment of the *Triptolemos* quoted by Strabo, we read—'I beheld the famed Nysa, the abode of Bakchik fury, which the ox-horned Iakchos inhabits as his best beloved retreat; where no bird screams.'[1] The speaker in this passage is probably Triptolemos himself, who, according to the myth, was carried over the earth in a winged chariot, the gift of his patroness Demeter, and from which he distributed seeds of wheat to mankind.[2] From this it is probable that the Nysa referred to in the passage was not one of the places of that name within Hellenik or neighbouring regions,[3] as the Euboian Nysa alluded to in the invocation to the god in the *Antigone*,[4] or the Thrakian Nysa of Lykourgos.[5] Later writers, such as Diodoros, give full accounts of Nysas in India, Arabia, and elsewhere; but this passage is peculiarly important as showing that Dionysos Boukerôs, the Ox-horned Iakchos, had in early tradition a distant and favourite abode, the renowned Nysa, evidently his original home and the true starting-point of his cult, deep in the Outer-world and as un-Hellenik as the ox-horned god himself.

Among the numerous writers who treated of Dionysos and the legendary history of Thebai, was the celebrated Antimachos, an epic and elegiac poet of Klaros,[6] a place already noticed as possessing a celebrated temple and oracle of Apollon.[7] Antimachos, who lived at the time of the Peloponnesian war, was the author of the *Thebais*,

---

[1] Strabo, XIV. i. 7.
[2] Cf. ib. I. ii. 20.
[3] Cf. Eur. *Bak.* 556.
[4] Vide subsec. ii.
[5] *Il.* vi. 133.
[6] Cf. Ovid, *Trist.* I. vi. 1.
[7] *Sup.* II. iii. 2.

a great epic poem which we may presume was of high merit, as the Alexandrian grammarians assigned to him the second place among epic writers. He, together with some other of the poets, held that Lykourgos was not king of any part of Thrake, but of Arabia, and that Nysa accordingly was in Arabia.[1] His opinion about Lycourgos is untenable, but as regards Nysa he is in perfect agreement with Sophokles. Where Dionysos is there is always a Nysa,[2] and hence, if he came into Hellas from the Outer-world, the original Nysa was there also.[3]

Subsection II.—Dionysos and Thebai.

In the *Oidipous Tyrannos* the Chorus invoke the god as follows :—' Chrysomitres [the Golden-mitred], too, I call, surnamed of this our land, the wine-faced Bakchos Euios, companion of the Mainades,[4] flaming with beaming fir-torch.'[5] There is a double Oriental reference in the epithet Chrysomitres: (1), an allusion to the Eastern head-dress, the turban;[6] and (2), as being a solar epithet, like Chrysokomes,[7] and Chrysopes,[8] and referring to the golden- haired, faced, or crowned Sun or Mithra.[9] It will next be observed that the poet represents the Theban Chorus, supposed to be speaking in the time of Oidipous, that is, in the fourth generation from Kadmos, as asserting that the god had already received the name of Bakchos Euios at Thebai. It has been said that the epithet Bakchos ' does not occur till *after* the time of Herodotos,' whose death has been placed as late as about B.C. 407. It appears, however, more probable that the historian died about B.C. 423,[10] and he himself, as well as Aischylos,[11]

---

[1] Cf. Diod. Sik. iii. 65.
[2] Cf. *Sup.* II. i. 1, 5.
[3] Vide *inf.* VIII. i. *Nysios.*
[4] Cf. *Sup.* sec. i. 3, ' Yoker-of-the-Mainades.'
[5] *Oid. Tyr.* 209-14.
[6] Cf. Herod. i. 195.
[7] Hesiod, *Theog.* 947.
[8] Eur. *Bak.* 553.
[9] *Inf.* XII. iv.
[10] Cf. Rawlinson, *Herodotus*, i. 26.
[11] *Frag.* cccxi.

speaks of Dionysos as Bakcheios,[1] the Exciter-to-phrensv,[2] while the name Baccheus occurs in the *Antigone*,[3] which was brought out at least as early as B.C. 440, and Bakchos in the passage before us. The obvious inference is that this whole class of epithets originated at a much earlier date.[4] The god is further addressed as 'flaming with beaming fir-torch.'[5] Here we have an igneous cult, which also includes the solar and astral phases. The kosmogonic, igneous divinity is lord equally of day and night, at once Pyropos the Fiery-faced, and Chrysokomes the Golden-tressed, Lampter the Torch-bearer, and Nyktelios the Nightly-one. The flaming resinous fir-torches, moreover, symbolise the bright lights of heaven, and so in the *Antigone* the god is addressed by a double reference, as 'chorus-leader of the fire-breathing stars.'[6] The torch-bearing, faun-skin-girt worshipper thus represented the starry vault by a two-fold symbolism, and Dionysos becomes a fit companion for Kotytto.

Connected with the fir- or pine-torch of Dionysos is the mystic pine-cone which, according to a passage in the Orphik Poems,[7] was among the symbols used in the Bakchik mysteries. It was also carried at the end of the Thyrsos or budding-rod,[8] itself the emblem of vitality, as a symbol of fruitfulness and productive power;[10] and, according to Porphyrios,[11] was an emblem of the Sun, 'the great vivifying and procreative power in nature;'[12] and thus is most appropriately connected with Dionysos in his phase as Dendrites and Karpios, and also in his solar aspects, as it is with the cone-shaped, sacred stones of

---

[1] Herod. iv. 79.
[2] Cf. ib. 108.
[3] V. 1122.
[4] Vide *inf.* IX. i.
[5] Cf. Eur. *Archelaös, Frag.* iii.; Aristoph. *Bat.* 340 *et seq.*
[6] *Antig.* 1146.
[7] *Frag.* xvii.; apud Clem. Alex. *Protrept.* ii.
[8] Cf. Eur. *Bak.* 145.
[9] Vide *inf.* VIII. ii. *Wand.*
[10] Cf. Bunsen, *Egypt's Place*, iv. 233.
[11] Euseb. *Euan. Apod.* iii. 7.
[12] *Poseidon*, xxxvi.

THE DIONYSOS OF THE ATTIK TRAGEDIANS. 101

Phoenicia, and the cone in the hand of the hierakephalic Assyrian Genius and other figures at Nimrûd and Khorsabad.¹ There is also a connection between the fir-cone and Dionysos Theoinos, as the turpentine yielded by the fir was one of the seasonings mixed by the ancients with wine, a practice which still prevails in the interior of Hellas. In the *Trachiniai* we meet with the expression, 'Bakchik Thebai.'² The 'Bakchik vine' is also alluded to,³ and the exciting ivy, which 'hurries one along like a Bakchik contest.'⁴ Again, in the *Oidipous Tyrannos* reference is made to the 'Bakcheian god dwelling on the mountain heights,' and to 'the Helikonian nymphs with whom he chiefly sports,'⁵ in his phase as Dionysos Polyparthenos,⁶ a passage which connects one of his favourite abodes with the vicinity of Thebai. But the most remarkable Dionysiak allusion in Sophokles is the beautiful invocation of the Chorus in the *Antigone*,⁷ which I venture to translate:—

> O Thou of many-a-name, who aye hast been
> The glory of the fair Kadmeian Queen,
>   Son of loud-thundering Zeus, whose sway
>   Renowned Italia⁸
> And Eleusinian vales Demeter's shrine obey!
> O Bakcheus, who at Thebes dost dwell,
> Thebes, mother-city of each Bakchanal:
> Where the Ismenos flows with gentle tone,
> Where once the savage dragon's teeth were sown .
>   Above the double-crested mount⁹
> The smoke and flame beheld thee as they rose,¹⁰
>   Where the Korykian Nymphs at the Kastalian fount
>   Thy votaries repose.

---

¹ Cf. Rawlinson, *Ancient Mons.* ii. 0, 29; Lenormant, *Ancient Hist. of the East*, ii. 229 et seq.
² V. 510.
³ V. 706.
⁴ V. 218.
⁵ *Oid. Tyr.* 1105 et seq.
⁶ Vide *inf.* VIII. i. *Gunaimanes*.
⁷ Vs. 1115–54.
⁸ Cf. *Hom. Hymn, Eis Dionuson.*
⁹ Cf. 'The two-topt mount divine,' Milton. From *An Epitaph*, an unpublished poem discovered by Professor Morley.
¹⁰ Cf. Eur. *Ion*, 1125.

The Nysian hills,[1] with ivy covered o'er,
The many-clustering vines on the green shore,
Behold thy progress to thy Theban shrine,
Amid immortal words of Evoe divine!
    For Thebes thou honourest
    Of cities most and best,
With thy mother who, mid lightning and mid thunders
    passed to rest.[2]
And now, since 'neath the plague thy seat
Is perishing, with healing feet
    Swift to our succour flee,[3]
From the Parnassan slopes[4] or o'er the sounding sea.[5]
O leader of the stars that breathe and burn,[6]
Lord of the voices of the night,[7] return;
    Offspring of Zeus! reveal again
    Thy glory with thy Naxian train,[8]
Who all night long with phrensied spirit sing
And dance in honour of their Bakchik king.[9]

This passage contains in itself almost all the principal features in the character of the god. His cult has long been established in the isles of the Aigaion; and speeding westward like the beacon-light that revealed the fall of Troia to the watchman at Mykenai, it has leaped the narrow straight of the Euripos, and fixed its seat at

---

[1] Nysa in Euboia; cf. *Thy en Sik. Frag.* vii.

[2] Cf. Pindar, *Olymp.* ii. 38; Eur. *Hippol.* 558.

[3] As Hygiates the Healer, and Soter the Saviour.

[4] Cf. Eur. *Iph. in Tau.* 1243; *Ion,* 716; Aristoph. *Neph.* 603.

[5] 'The wild Euripus;' cf. Ais. *Ag.* 283.

[6] The fiery kosmogonic Dionysos by day gleaming from the solar eye as Pyropos or Chrysopes, by night becomes the Choragos of the 'starry quire,' mystically symbolised by the torches, though these had also other significations. This astral cult breathes the true spirit of the Semitic East, and finds a remarkable Western echo in the celebrated Seven Gates of Thebai, each dedicated to a planet. Cf. Nonnos, v. 69 *et seq.*; Bunsen, *Egypt's Place,* iv. 252; Gladstone, *Juv. Mun.* 123, 315.

[7] As Nyktelios the Nightly-one, and Nyktipolos the Night-wandering; cf. Eur. *Ion,* 718, 1049; *Kretes, Frag.* ii.

[8] Cf. *sup.* II. i. 3. The neighbouring islands of Keos, Seriphos, Oliaros, Thera, Anaphe, and Amorgos, were all known Phoenician colonies. Vide Dr. W. Smith's *Ancient Atlas,* map ix.

[9] Lit.—'their lord Iakchos.' The cult of the tauriform Dionysos or 'Ox-horned Iakchos' (*sup.* subsec. i.), is thus positively connected with Naxos.

Thebai, his best beloved abode, the 'metropolis' of the Bakchai. But it has also made wide progress thence in other parts of continental Hellas. He sports with the Nymphs of Helikon and Kastalia, rules at Delphoi enthroned by the side of Apollon, and, passing southward, surmounts the rugged range of Kithairon, and descends into the Thriasian plain to become the associate of Demeter in the vale of Eleusis; thence eastward into Attika, and westward to Korinthos and Sikyon, and so to the regions of Magna Graecia beyond.

> The jolly god in triumph comes,
> Sound the trumpets, beat the drums.

In the *Antigone*, the Chorus propose to approach the temples of the gods with dances that shall last all night long, and exclaim, 'Let Bakcheios, shaker of Thebai, lead off'[1] the dance. These are the nightly Naxian dances; and I shall next refer to the connection between Dionysos and motion.[2]

SECTION III.

THE DIONYSOS OF EURIPIDES.

Subsection 1.—Dionysos and the Dance.

In speaking of Dionysos and the Dance, I shall notice (1) the dance of Bakchik votaries, either simply joyous, or furious and orgiastic; and (2) the universal mystic nature-dance, as connected with the kosmogonic divinity. The dance of the Eumenides is spoken of as being 'joyless,'[3] literally without-Bakchik-fire;[4] but the dances of Dionysos are either joyous, such as that in which the

---

[1] V. 153.
[2] *Inf.* sec. iii. 1.
[3] *Orest.* 319.
[4] Cf. *Herak. Mai*, 891.

Theban maidens are represented as celebrating the birth of the god,[1] or furiously orgiastic, as those of the Mainades or Ravers.[2] Speaking merely of the joyous dance, the poet says :—'His mother wedded to Zeus bore Bromios, whom the twisted ivy instantly twining round whilst yet an infant, blessed and covered with verdant shading branches, a subject of Bakchik choral dance for Theban virgins and inspired women.'[3] And, again, 'Why, O Arês, art thou hostile to the festivals of Bromios? Thou dost not in the beautiful circling dance of youthful maids, with flowing locks, on the breath of the flute, sing the song in which are dance-stimulating delights.'[4] But mere mirth easily becomes fast and furious, and then the joyous dance deepens into the orgiastic or raving dance, such as is constantly referred to in the *Bakchai*, the wild, circular whirling of the thyrsos-maddened and faun-skin-clad votary,[5] the phrensied Naxian cult, in which the god is the 'leader of the revel.'[6] Dionysos, like Poseidon Ennosigaios, is Elelichthôn, the Earth-shaker,[7] and the epithet appears to include among its meanings the idea of the ground being shaken by, or moving in concert with, the orgiastic dancers.[8] And the further this dancing cult is traced into the Semitic East, the wilder and more furious does it become, until passing through the Korybantic and Kourêtik phases of Asia Minor and Krêtê, it culminates in Phoenician regions in the form of Baalic leapings on the very altar itself, accompanied with self-wounding and mutilation,[9] the grim worship of those who—

> With cymbal's ring
> Call the grisly King,
> In dismal dance about the furnace blue.

[1] *Phoinis*, 655.
[2] *Bak.* 1060.
[3] *Phoinis*, 649 *et seq.*
[4] Ibid. 784 *et seq.*; cf. *Kyklops*, 63.
[5] Cf. *Phoinis*, 792.
[6] *Orphik Hymn*, lii. 7.
[7] Cf. *Bak.* 587 *et seq.*; Soph. *Antig.* 153; *Orphik Hymn*, xlvii.
[8] Cf. *Bak.* 727.
[9] Cf. 1 *Kings*, xviii. 26.

THE DIONYSOS OF THE ATTIK TRAGEDIANS. 105

In early Hellenik history, too, the furious and orgiastic character of the Bakchik dance is well sustained. Thus Archilochos, cir. B.C. 700, exclaims—'I know how to lead off the dithyramb, the beautiful strain of king Dionysos, when my mind is struck with wine as with a thunderbolt,'[1] a singular expression, appearing to refer to the mystic birth of the god, and to imply that as he sprang to light amidst the thunder and lightning of Zeus, so his cult is best sustained by the corresponding mental fury and confusion produced in the heated votary by wine. Similarly speaks Epicharmos, B.C. 500, in a Fragment preserved in Athenaios—'There is not a dithyramb if you drink water.'[2] 'The dithyramb,' says Donaldson, 'originally was nothing more than a Comus, and one, too, of the wildest and most Corybantic character. A crowd of worshippers, under the influence of wine, danced up to and around the blazing altar of Jupiter.'[3] Singing as they danced the birth, the adventures, the sufferings, and the glories of Dionysos, they typified the grand kosmic circular dance-movement of material phenomena, which is headed by their king as 'the choir-leader of the fire-breathing stars.' Far different from these wild Dionysiak revelries are the sterner and purer Dorik dances, the cult of the worshippers of the Aryan Sun-god, the far-darting king Apollôn, who himself leads the stately choir, not with maddened foot, but with noble and lofty steps,[4] the 'sort of dancing' which 'aims at preserving dignity and freedom,'[5] and thus

> Triumphs in victorious dance
> O'er sensual folly and intemperance.

Next, as to the universal mystic nature-dance in con-

---

[1] *Frag.* lxxvii.; *sup.* III. i. 1.
[2] Athen, xiv. 6; cf. Simonides, *Frag.* cxlviii.
[3] *Theatre of the Greeks*, 35.
[4] Cf. *Hom. Hymn, Eis Apoll.* 514 *et seq.*
[5] 'Emmeleiai,' or dances of order. Plat. *Laws*, vii.

nection with the kosmogonic Dionysos, Spirit-of-the-Apparent. The first passage from our philosophical poet relating to this somewhat occult subject, is as follows:—
'I am ashamed of the god honoured-by-many-hymns, if around the Kastalian founts[1] he by night, lying sleepless, shall behold the torch, a spectator of the Eikads when the starry-faced ether of Zeus is wont to begin the choric dance. And the Moon dances and the fifty daughters of Nêreus who are in the sea and in the eddies of the ever-flowing rivers, celebrate in choric dance the golden-crowned Damsel and her awful Mother.'[2] The meaning of the passage is, that the Chorus would be ashamed of Dionysos if he did not duly hasten from his favourite abode to take part in the Eleusinian Mysteries, when all nature combined to honour Demeter the Earth-mother, and her daughter Persephonê the Damsel. The Eikads are the Twenties, for the sixth day of the Eleusinian Mysteries, which was dedicated to Iakchos, fell on the twentieth day of the Attik month Boedromiôn, September-October, in which the Mysteries were celebrated. Dionysos, therefore, is supposed to be under an obligation to attend at Eleusis on the Eikas, or twentieth day of the month. On this sixth day of the Mysteries, which was the most solemn of all, when at Athenai, in historic times, the image of Iakchos, torch in hand and crowned with myrtle, was carried along the sacred road of the Kerameikos, or Potters' Quarter, to Eleusis, moon, stars, seas, and streams are said to dance in honour of the Earth-mother and her Child; and, therefore, also in honour of their associate Dionysos, for he also is the son of Dêmêter, of Persephonê, or of both.[3] The 'etherial dances of the stars Pleiads and Hyads'[4] are represented as adorning the shield of Achilleus;[5] and in another passage the poet

[1] Cf. Soph. *Antig.* 1130.
[2] *Ion*, 1074 *et seq.*
[3] *Sup.* II. iii. 5, III. i. 3.
[4] *Elektra*, 467.
[5] Cf. *Il.* xviii. 486 *et seq.*

speaks of 'the eddyings of the stars.'[1] A doubtful chorus in the *Helenê*,[2] in which Dêmêter and Kybele are incorrectly identified, treats of the search of the former for her lost daughter Persephonê, and concludes—'Of much power [*i.e.*, of mighty occult influence] are the all-variegated garments of faun-skin, and the green ivy wound on the sacred wands, and the circular shaking of the magic wheels in the whirling ether. And the hair flowing like a Bakche, for Bromios, and the nightly vigils of the goddess.' Here we have a terrestrial representation of the etherial starry dance; everything turns, revolves, circles, and eddies; while the spotted dress and tresses flowing in honour of Dionysos Eurychaites, with their mystic meanings, are familiar incidents. The sacred wands are the stalks of the Narthex, or Fennel-giant, in a hollow stem of which Prometheus was said to have conveyed the spark of heavenly fire to earth, and which was carried at the Bakchik festivals.[3] The Rhomboi, or magic Wheels, literally anything that has a spinning or circular motion, are like the cone[4] among 'the symbols of the Dionysiak Mysteries.'[5] Other writers, such as Maximus Tyrius, speak of the 'chorus of stars;'[6] and the Pleiads, according to Hyginus, were 'thought to lead the starry chorus.'[7] We have then, in passages such as these, the idea of a circular kosmic nature-dance, arising from a perception more or less real of cyclic movement in surrounding phenomena. Thus as regards the sun, moon, and stars, themselves, all circular in form, they pass across the semi-circle of the sky, apparently moving circularly round the earth; and so Professor Ruskin observes, that one of the meanings of the Dolphin in Hellenik symbolism is 'the ascending

---

[1] *Hellene*, 1408.
[2] Vs. 1301-68.
[3] Cf. *Bak.* 147; vide *inf.* VIII. 2, *Wand*.
[4] *Sup.* sec. ii. 2.
[5] Cf. *Orphik Hymn, Frag.* xvii.; vide *inf.* VIII. ii. *Wheel.*
[6] Cf. Ais. *Ag.* 4.
[7] *Poet. Astron.* ii. 21.

and descending course of any of the heavenly bodies from one sea-horizon to another—the dolphin's arching rise and replunge (in a summer evening, out of calm sea, their black backs *roll round with exactly the slow motion of a waterwheel*),' the mystic Rhombos,' being taken as a type of the emergence of the sun or stars from the sea in the east, and plunging beneath in the west.'[1] Again, as regards the seas and rivers, the Homerik ocean-stream into which all the rivers run, surrounds the earth as it did the shield of Achilleus,[2] which displayed a pictorial representation of the Kosmogony. Okeanos is thus the vast 'circle of the earth,' the belt of the kosmogonic Dionysos, without the stars even, inasmuch as they sink into it, and when the Beaming Sun, Phaethôn, darts

     Golden rays on the flowings of Ocean,
Wondrous the splendour appears on the surface and mixed with
 water,
Whirling around and around, in circles revolving it sparkles,
Full in the presence of God: while, beneath the breast boundless, the girdle
Shows as a circle of Ocean, an infinite wonder to look at.

And, again, this cyclic phenomenal movement is clearly connected with the circularity in the flight of time and the recurrence of the seasons, 'seed-time and harvest, cold and heat, summer and winter, day and night;' and it was this cyclic recurrence alike of seasons and phenomena which 'certain philosophers' of the present day are fond of dignifying under the name of 'Laws of Nature,' which smote with such weariness upon the heart of the aged Solomon, and made him exclaim, 'the sun ariseth, and the sun goeth down, and hasteth to his place whence he arose.'—(First Circle.) 'The wind goeth toward the south, and turneth about unto the north; it

---

[1] *Queen of the Air*, i. 39.   [2] *Il.* xviii. 605.   [3] *Sup.* II. iii.

whirleth about continually, and the wind returneth again, according to his circuits.'—(Second Circle.) 'All the rivers run into the sea, yet the sea is not full; unto the place whence the rivers come, thither they return again.' —(Third Circle.) 'The thing that hath been, it is that which shall be; and that which is done is that which shall be done.'—(Fourth Circle.) But this Solomonian feeling of weariness is alike far removed from the immortal chorus of stars singing together, and from the Dionysiak freshness of the earth, which, in comparison with her children, abideth ever. The stars in their courses are tireless; and on earth the Bakchik votary, representative of the unflagging earth-life, can dance and sing the live-long night in honour of his divinity. How exquisitely Milton, in that wonderful poem named after the impersonation of the band of Bakchik revellers, describes this universal kosmic dance:—

>We that are of purer fire,
>Imitate the starry quire,
>Who in their nightly watchful spheres,
>Lead *in swift round* the months and years.

Observe the close connection between the natural phenomena, circles, and the time or season-circles, and how all nature joins the mystic ritual:—

>The sounds and seas, with all their finny drove,
>Now to the moon in wavering morrice move;
>And, on the tawny sands and shelves,
>Trip the pert fairies and the dapper elves.

The Bakchic votary must in his cult symbolise this nature-dance, so

>Come, knit hands, and beat the ground,
>In a light, fantastic round.

Again, to quote from modern poetry in illustration of 'the stars' concentric rings,' 'Thou,' says the Morning

Star to Lucifer, in the words of the greatest of English poetesses:—

> Did'st sting my *wheel of glory* [*Rhombos*]
> Along the God-light by a quickening touch!
> *Around, around the firmamental ocean*
> *I swam,* expanding with delirious fire!
> Around, around, around, in blind desire
> To be drawn upwards to the Infinite—
> Until, the motion flinging out the motion
> To a *keen whirl* of passion and avidity,
> To a *dim whirl* of languor and delight,
> *I wound in girant orbits* smooth and white
> With that intense rapidity.
> *Around, around,*
> *I wound and interwound,*
> *While all the cyclic heavens about me spun.*
> Stars, planets, suns, and moons dilated broad,
> Then flashed together in a single sun,
> And wound, and wound in one,
> And as they wound I wound, around, around,
> In a great fire I almost took for God.'

'Nature,' says Emerson, 'centres into balls. The eye is the first circle; the horizon which it forms is the second; and throughout nature this primary figure is repeated without end. It is the highest emblem in the cipher of the world. St. Augustin [following earlier sages] described the nature of God as a circle whose centre was everywhere and its circumference nowhere. We are all our lifetime reading *the copious sense of this first of forms.*'[1] Elsewhere, when alluding to Phoenician architecture, and especially to their circular tower-pillars and to the circular form in which even cities, such as Hagmatana,[2] or the Phoenician settlement at Caere in Italia, called Argylla, the Round Town, were sometimes

---

[1] *Works,* i. 125. For illustration of this passage, vide *inf.* VIII. ii. *Circle.*

[2] Agbatana, Herod. i. 98. Ekbatana is the general Hellenik form.

constructed, I ventured to suggest that the mysterious Kyklôpes, in illustration of whose single eye so many ingenious theories have been offered, were, as the name may fairly be interpreted, Circle-builders. And as the cyclic nature of things appears equally in human thought and action, according to the common saying, 'history repeats itself,' and in the material phenomena around, so it was most natural that man, whose inventions are never entirely original, but always more or less imitations of, or adaptations from, something beyond him, should in his works strive to copy and perpetuate this 'first of forms,' and hence, probably, circular cities and temples, and stone circles, not peculiar to one race or country, but widely scattered through the world.[1] It matters comparatively little who built them, and how, if we know why they were built and what they symbolise. The Phoenicians were famous in the art of circle-building; but it would be most erroneous to suppose that all circular erections are Phoenician, for some are found in regions where probably the Phoenician never penetrated, and it is idle to imagine that proficiency in an art implies its monopoly. Yet at the same time, when we find such erections, or their connected symbolism, in regions within the limits of Phoenician enterprise, we have strong *primâ facie* evidence to connect the world-colonising nation with the work. Thus, one of the ancient names of the Dionysiak isle of Naxos was Strongylê the Circular, or Kyklôpian.[2] The word implies that which is tightly pressed together, so that the angles are rounded off, and it becomes ball-shaped like 'the round world.' Of course, the natural shape of the island suggested the name, but

---

[1] It is somewhat singular that, considering the attention which is now bestowed on 'rude stone monuments,' the circular character of many of them should not be more noticed in connection with its accompanying symbolism. It is no sufficient explanation of a stone-circle that it was used as a burying-place. Why should the dead be buried *in a circle?*

[2] *Sup.* II. i. 3.

it may fairly be asked, Was it not this circular shape which induced the Semitic colonists to appropriate it to the special worship of the kosmogonic divinity, the representative of the cyclic heavens, and of the round world? For, be it remembered, the Hellenes of the great ages, like ourselves, considered the world to be round, but as being a flat plain, ocean-circled. So we find Dikaiarchos, writing, cir. B.C. 310, a few years after the restoration of the walls of Thebai on the old site by Kassandros; describes the city as 'circular (strongylê) in form';[1] a most interesting illustration of what was doubtless the original shape of the city of the Phoenician Kadmos,[2] which with its seven gates and their planetary symbolism was an architectural representation of the Kosmogony, and as such was the suitable abode of the kosmic Dionysos.[3]

But these are merely particular instances of a principle which is that Circle-building generally was originally an imitation of the natural circularities of the universe, and that, therefore, the root-idea of the cult attached to such erections is not simply solar or igneous, though these are doubtless often included in it, but is more or less kosmogonic.[4] Circularity being thus, so to speak, an attribute of nature, and motion being one of the principal characteristics of surrounding materiality, we thus obtain the idea of circular motion, which, when phenomena are personified, and we speak anthropically, becomes Dance, which has been defined as 'the poetry of motion.' Hence the kosmic dance of suns and seasons, stars and streams, the dance which, as the poet says, 'the whole earth joins,'[5] the 'dancers of the heavens,' 'starry nymphs that dance around the pole,' and the symbolic cyclic chorus dancing

---

[1] *Peri tôn en Helladi Poleôn*, xii.
[2] Cf. Eur. *Bak.* 653.
[3] *Inf.* X. ii.
[4] It is, of course, not denied that other and special causes may have occasioned the erection of some circular edifices. The plan of the ruins of Mugheir (Rawlinson, *Ancient Mons.* i. 17) is an instance of a circular burying-place.
[5] Eur. *Bak.* 113.

wildly around the altar where burns the life-heat and divine fire of the world, or wandering wine-flushed over hill and vale, hymning the praises of the spirit of material existence. And this Dionysiak Chorus, like the daughters of Nereus who dance in the sea, generally consisted of fifty members. The kosmik dance is an illustration of what is termed in modern philosophic language 'the rhythm of motion,'[1] and in its mental phase it becomes 'the impious "*dinos*," [circular dance, hence dizziness, vertigo] and tumult in men's thoughts, which,' according to Professor Ruskin, 'have followed on their avarice in the present day, making them alike forsake the laws of their ancient gods, and misapprehend or reject the true words of their existing teachers.'[2] The furious dance is well described in the *Bakchai*, where the very mountain, the wild beasts, and all nature are said to join in it.[3] The allusions in the Comedies of Aristophanes to the Bakchik dance are numerous, and its circular character is frequently noticed. Thus the Chorus of Mystics in the *Batrachoi* exclaim, 'the knee of the old men moves swiftly,'[4] which is exactly illustrated in the case of Kadmos and Teiresias,[5] and the dance itself is called 'the sacred circle of the goddess,'[6] *i.e.*, Demeter. Again, we read in reference to the Bakchik dance, 'But come, dance with head and foot like a deer, and at the same time make a noise chorus-cheering.'[7] Here the allusion is to the Bakchik devotee as clad in the mystic faun-skin *nebris*.[8] So *nebrizo* signifies (1) to wear a faun-skin, and (2) to dance at the Dionysiak Festivals. In the *Thesmophoriazousai* we naturally find various notices of the Demetrian and Dionysiak dance. 'Rise, come on lightly with your feet

---

[1] Cf. Herbert Spencer, *First Principles*, part ii. cap. 10.
[2] *Queen of the Air*, i. 20.
[3] *Bak.* 726.
[4] *Bat.* 345.
[5] *Bak.* 181 *et seq.*
[6] *Bat.* 441.
[7] *Lysist.* 1316-7.
[8] Vide *inf.* VIII. i. *Nebridopeplos.*

in a circle, join hand-in-hand, move to the rhythm of the dance, go with swift feet. It is right that the choral order should look about, rolling the eye in every direction,'[1] *i.e.*, lest there be a hidden Pentheus.[2] Again, the poet alludes to 'the graceful step of the well-circled [*i.e.*, elegant] dance;'[3] and the Chorus exclaim, 'Sing aloud the whole ode, and do thou thyself lead, ivy-bearing Bakchos, our lord, Bromios, child of Semele, delighting in dances. And about thee resounds the clamour of Kithairon and the mountains dark-with-leaves, thick-shaded, and the rocky dells re-echo. And in a circle about thee, the ivy, beautifully-leaved, flourishes in its curl.'[4] Allusion is also made to a peculiar movement called the Diple, 'the grace of the dance;'[5] the term conveys the idea of doubling, and the dancers perhaps formed two combined circles like the figure 8. Hesychios somewhat obscurely defines it as 'the figure of a dance, or of beating time.'[6] Aristophanes, 'the constant servant of Dionysos,'[7] might have been Pindaros, had he not been Aristophanes.

Subsection II.—*The Bakchai.*

The *Bakchai* of Euripides possesses a peculiar interest and importance as being the only Dionysiak Play which has come down to us entire, and I shall, therefore, enter into a somewhat detailed examination of the more remarkable passages in it. The argument is as follows:—Dionysos, with his train of Asiatic Bakchants, arrives at Thebai, where Pentheus, the grandson of Kadmos, rules. The aged Kadmos and the seer Teiresias determine to honour the new divinity, but the infatuated Pentheus, despite their warnings, resolves to put a stop to the

---

[1] *Thes.* 953 *et seq.*
[2] Cf. Paus. ii. 2.
[3] *Thes.* 968.
[4] Ibid. 986 *et seq.*
[5] Ibid. 982.
[6] Hesych. in voc. *Diple*; cf. Ioul. Pol. iv. 105.
[7] Platon, *Sympos.*

THE DIONYSOS OF THE ATTIK TRAGEDIANS. 115

Bakchik cult, and to slay the ringleader. Dionysos, in mortal form, is brought before Pentheus, who in vain attempts to imprison him, and like the deluded Aias,[1] fastens up a bull instead. In the meantime, Dionysos shakes the earth around, and a messenger freshly arrived from Kithairon recounts the wondrous doings of the Bakchai, the leaders of whom are the three surviving daughters of Kadmos, Autonoe, Agaue, and Ino. Dionysos now persuades Pentheus to dress like a woman, and promises to conduct him to the haunts of the Mainades. They depart, and a messenger arrives and recounts to the Chorus the fate of Pentheus, who is torn in pieces by the Bakchai.[2] Agaue then joyfully enters, supposing in her madness that her son, whom she had slain, was a young lion, and afterwards Kadmos comes on the stage with the remains of the body of Pentheus. Agaue's reason returns, and Kadmos explains to her the vengeance of Dionysos, who, appearing, reveals the destiny of Kadmos, and asserts his own divinity. The Play, which is pronounced by some critics to be the poet's masterpiece, was finished a few months before his death in B.C. 406, and afterwards brought out by his son, the younger Euripides.

Verses 1–63, Introductory Prologue, spoken by Dionysos: the arrangement of the piece is somewhat awkward, as is customary in the Plays of Euripedes. 'I, Dionysos, son of Zeus, whom Semele, the daughter of Kadmos, bore, delivered by the lightning-bearing fire, am come to this land of the Thebans. And I see the monument of my thunderbolt-stricken mother, here near the dwellings, and the fallen ruins of the house smoking, and the still living flame of the fire of Zeus, the deathless insult of Here[3] against my mother.'[4] He praises the piety of

---
[1] Cf. Soph. *Aias*, 51 et seq.
[2] Cf. Paus. ii. 2.
[3] Cf. subsec. iv.
[4] Cf. Vs. 244, 577; *Hippol.* 558; sup. III. i. 1.

Kadmos, who has covered his daughter's shrine with vine-leaves, and continues in what Strabo calls 'a boasting speech,'[1] 'having left the wealthy lands of Lydians and Phrygians, and having come o'er the sun-stricken plains of the Persians, and the Baktrian walls, and the dangerous country of the Medes, and Arabia the happy, and all Asia which lies by the salt sea, having fair-towered cities filled with Hellenes and Barbarians mingled together, and there having danced,[2] and established my Mystic Rites in order that I might be an evident divinity among mortals, I have arrived at this city first of Hellenik cities.' Euripides, at times, somewhat arbitrarily alters the mythic legends, but he does not seem to have taken many such liberties with the history of Dionysos, who here appears in his accustomed character as the Wanderer. Why is he said to wander? Mr. Cox remarks on this phase of the god, 'In the Homeric Hymn the Tyrrhenian mariners avow their intention of taking Dionysos to Egypt, or Ethiopia, or the Hyperborean land; and this idea of change of abode becomes the prominent feature in the later developments of the wandering wine-god. When the notion was once suggested, every country, and even every town, would naturally frame its own story of the wonderful things done by Dionysos as he abode in each.'[3] But what parallel is there in the case? In the Homerik Hymn strangers meet with the god in Hellenik regions, attempt to carry him into the Outer-world, and fail. Here, having wandered at will *first* over the Outer-world, he at length arrives at Hellas. Even supposing that the Hymn attained an almost universal popularity, why, because it depicted a vain attempt to withdraw him from Hellas, should he therefore be supposed to have become the exact opposite, an actual, voluntary wanderer? And,

[1] Strabo, xv. 1.
[2] Cf. subsec. i.
[3] *Mythol. of the Aryan Nations,* ii. 294.

further, what is the meaning of the Hymn itself? and why should men be represented as being desirous to carry him away to distant lands? How simple is the answer to such questions from the historical point of view. We need not suppose, contrary to possibility and apart from evidence, that on account of the legend of the ancient Hymn, every town invented tales about the god's travels; but just as the territorial contests of Poseidon, otherwise inexplicable, illustrate the introduction of his cult into fresh regions and the opposition which it encountered there,[1] so the travels of Dionysos symbolised the progress of his worship throughout the world, until at length he arrives in Thebai, the first of Hellenik cities of the continent reached by him; and there finds himself unhonoured and his cult violently opposed. Even Mr. Cox himself admits, as we have seen,[2] that 'the opposition of the Theban Pentheus to the cultus of Dionysos is among the few indications of historical facts exhibited in Hellenic mythology.' But while thus interpreting Euripides in an historic sense, we are not bound to accept in all its details his historical account of the Dionysiak cult; to suppose, for instance, that it was originally identical with the worship of the Phrygian Kybele, or that Lydia was the point from whence it passed over into Hellas. So, again, when he speaks of the cities of maritime Asia as inhabited by a mingled population of Hellenes and Barbarians, he is evidently thinking more of his own times than of the mythical era of Pentheus, as the earliest Hellenik colonies in Asia Minor were according to tradition, founded subsequently to the Dorik conquest of the Peloponnesos.[3] Seven eastern regions are mentioned by the god as having been visited by him, Lydia, Phrygia, Persia, Media, Baktria, Arabia, and maritime Asia, and the names are not

[1] Vide *Poseidon*, xxi.
[2] *Sup.* II. i. 1.
[3] Cf. Tyrrell, *The Bacchúe of Euripides*, Introduction, xxxiii. *note* 2.

uninteresting, as they appear to contain the Euripidean theory of the localities in which the Dionysiak cult obtained. He refers its origin, as Bunsen observes, 'to the fanatical physiolatries of Asia Minor,'[1] and consequently Lydia, Phrygia, and Asia, are three of the places visited by Dionysos; and the poet apparently mentions Persia, Media, and Baktria, the first of which was the dominant Oriental power, chiefly to show that the worship of the god had penetrated deep into the regions of the extreme East. Euripides can scarcely have possessed any definite knowledge, even traditional, of any Dionysiak ritual in immediate connection with either of the three last-mentioned countries. The mention of Baktria is somewhat singular, but there seem to have been various early Hellenik traditions of the ancient greatness of that kingdom;[2] and the Baktrians, who were noted for their valour, had come in contact with the Hellenes in consequence of the invasion of Khshayarsha (Xerxes).[3] But the poet's list is more remarkable for its omissions than for what it contains. As the Baktrians are mentioned, we should naturally have expected that the Indians, most distant of men, and who fought by their side at Plateia, would have been also included, more especially since one of the most famous epithets of Dionysos is Indoletes, the Indian-slayer, while his renowned campaign against the Indians has been celebrated by numerous writers from the age of Euripides to that of Rabelais.[4] Thus Antimachos, whose *Thebais* I have already referred to,[5] writing a few years earlier, related how Dionysos, after three years' absence in India, entered Thebai in triumph on an elephant, and from that circumstance instituted the Trieteris, or Triennial Festival, performed in his honour,[6]

---

[1] *God in Hist.* ii. 235.
[2] Cf. Rawlinson, *Herodotus*, iv. 166.
[3] Cf. *Herod*. vii. 64, ix. 31.
[4] Vide *inf.* IX. vii. *Indoletes.*
[5] *Sup.* sec. ii. 1.
[6] Antimachos, apud Diod. Sik. iii. 65.

and from which he is called Trieterikos.¹ The mention of Arabia is interesting, and he subsequently alludes to Nysa,² which, as he does not connect it with any particular locality, he may, like Antimachos, have supposed to be in Arabia.³ But the other Semitic countries, Kaldea, Assur, Aram, and Phoenicia, are unmentioned in consequence of his theory of a Dionysos Phrygian in origin. He also appears to have deliberately rejected the Kamic theory of Herodotos,⁴ with which he must have been familiar. It is amusing to notice the scepticism with which writers such as Strabo, who consider Dionysos to have been an individual man, naturally regard his traditional travels and exploits.⁵ The Mystic Rites, Teletai, connect the Dionysiak cult with that of the Eleusinian Demeter.⁶

Verses 64–177, Introductory Speech by the Chorus of Barbarian Bakchanals. 'Who is beneath the roof? Let him be out of the way ("Procul, O procul este profani") and let everyone use well-omened words, for I will ever hymn Dionysos according to custom. O blessed one! whosoever being fortunate, knowing the mystic rites of the gods, lives piously, and has his soul imbued with Bakchik revelry, raving among the mountains with holy purifications; and observing the orgies of the Mighty Mother Kybele, and shaking the thyrsos crowned with ivy, serves Dionysos.'⁷ The natural connection between Dionysos and the Earth-mothers, Demeter, Rhea, and

---

¹ *Orphik Hymn*, xlv.
² V. 556.
³ *Sup.* sec. ii. 1.
⁴ *Inf.* V. v.
⁵ I regret that Mr. Tyrrell in his excellent edition of the Play (Longmans, 1871) has not devoted more attention to this passage. He contents himself with the observation: 'Bacchus, Musgrave well remarks, was reared in Lydia and Phrygia, and when he reached man's estate, invaded Persia,' &c. (*note* in v. 14, p. 2). So far as legend goes the youth of Dionysos is not principally connected with either Lydia or Phrygia; but if it is meant to assert that his cult originated there, evidence should be offered on the point.
⁶ Cf. Herod. ii. 171.
⁷ Vs. 60–82; cf. *Hom. Hy. Eis Dem.* 485 *et seq.*; Aristoph. *Bat.* 356 *et seq.*

Kybele, has already been partially noticed,[1] how the Demeter and Rhea of the West corresponded to, but were not originally identical with, the Kybele or Great Goddess-Mother of the East; and how Dionysos, as Associate of the Aryan goddess-mother, naturally becomes the Associate of the Semitic goddess-mother, a circumstance which, combined with the foreign nature of his worship, caused Euripides to incorrectly impute a Phrygian origin to the Dionysiak cult. Having related the death of Semele, and how Zeus enclosed the infant Dionysos in his thigh, the Chorus continue, 'And he brought him forth when the Fates had perfected the Bull-horned [Taurokeros] god, and crowned him with crowns of serpents, whence the thyrsos-bearing Mainades twine their hair around their prey.'[2] We are here introduced to Dionysos as the horned, bovine god, whose dithyramb chanting votaries receive a bull as a prize,[3] and who is identical with Zagreus Eukeraos,[4] the Beautifully-horned. Thus Pentheus says to Dionysos, 'You seem like a bull, and horns seem to grow on your head. But were you ever a wild beast? for you look like a bull. *Di.* The god accompanies us; and now you see what you should see.'[5] In the stable Pentheus fastens up a bull, supposing he is binding Dionysos,[6] and the Chorus call upon the latter to 'appear as a bull, or as a many-headed dragon,[7] or a

---

[1] *Sup.* III. i. 3.
[2] Vs. 100–4.
[3] *Sup.* III. i. 2.
[4] Nonnos, vi. 209.
[5] Vs. 920–4.
[6] V. 618.
[7] This is a non-Aryan characteristic, and reminds us of the non-Aryan Indian votaries of the Naga or sacred five- or seven-headed hooded snake, sculptured at Sanchi and Amravati (vide Fergusson, *Tree and Serpent Worship*). The mystic Kamic snake, 'Ruhak the great charmer,' is also sometimes represented as trikephalic. But Akkad is the original home of the Many-headed-serpent myth, and so we read in a very ancient Akkadian Hymn, 'The *thunderbolt* of seven heads, like the huge serpent of seven heads (I bear); like the serpent that beats the sea (which attacks), the foe in the face' (*Records of the Past*, iii. 128). M. Lenormant well compares the Akkadian serpent with the seven-headed Indian serpent Vasonki, which was doubtless derived from it (*Les Prem. Civilisations*, ii. 137; vide also his remarks in *La Magie*, 207). The 'Lernaeus turbâ

flaming lion.'[1] Oppianos the Syrian, cir. A.D. 210, in his *Kynêgetika*, or Poem-on-hunting, says that Pentheus himself was transformed into a bull, and the Bakchai into panthers, who tore him to pieces. The Eleian women at the festival of Dionysos used to chant a Hymn to the god, which ran, 'O Dionysos! come as a sea hero to the holy shrine, with the Graces, rushing to the shrine with bovine foot;' ' and then,' says Ploutarchos,[2] 'they twice sing " Worthy Bull."'[3] And he asks whether they do it because the god is addressed both as ox-sprung and as a bull, for Dionysos, as he elsewhere tells us,[4] was known among the Argeioi as Bougenes the Ox-sprung. So Clemens Alexandrinus, in his exposition of the Mysteries, says, 'Pherephatta (Persephone) has a child, in the form of a bull, as an idolatrous poet says, "The bull the dragon's father, and the father of the bull the dragon, on a hill the herdsman's hidden ox-goad," alluding, as I believe, under the name of the herdsman's ox-goad, to the reed wielded by the Bakchanals.'[5] Now we learn from the Scholiast on the *Argonautika* of Apollonios of Rhodos, that Mnaseas the Grammarian of Alexandria, a disciple of Eratosthenes, in his work on the Delphik Oracles, called two of the mystic Kabeiroi of Samothrake Axiokerse and Axiokersos, evidently male and female divinities, whose names signify Worthy Horned Goddess and Worthy Horned God.[6] Here, then, we have a short and simple proof of the Semitic origin of Dionysos. The 'worthy-horned god' of the Phoenician colony of Samothrake is identical with the '*worthy* bull' of Elis and the

---

capitum anguis' which, according to the Natural Phenomena Theory, represents the many-headed changing storm-clouds (*Mythol. of the Aryan Nations*, ii. 48), and which appears as merely a monster and unconnected with divinity, may very probably be a purely Aryan concept.

[1.] V. 1017; cf. v. 1159; *Hom. Hy. Eis Dionuson*, 44.
[2] *Qu. Gr.* xxxvi.
[3] Cf. Bergk. *Poet. Ly. Gr.* iii.1200.
[4] *Peri Is.* xxxv.
[5] *Protrept.* ii. 16.
[6] Cf. Lobeck, *Aglaoph*. III. v.; Bunsen, *Egypt's Place*, iv. 440.

ox-sprung divinity of Argos, the hero not indigenous but from the sea, *i.e.* from beyond it. But the bull of Elis and Argos is Dionysos, who is therefore the Horned-god from beyond the sea;[1] the ox-horned Iakchos of Sophokles whose home is the mysterious Nysa, deep in the Outer-world. But as we have also seen, this Horned Stranger is in one of his phases a solar divinity,[2] and as such is Antauges the Sparkler, Chrysomitres the Golden-turbaned, Chrysokomes the Golden-haired, Chrysopes the Golden-faced, Pyriphenges the Fire-blazing, Pyrisperos the Fire-sowing, Pyropes the Flame-faced. The god is beginning to appear before us as a fiery, tauriform being,[3] representing a solar, astral, igneous, phallic, and kosmogonic cult, eddying, flickering, vibrating, burning; and Euripides, however much he may at times have wandered from old traditions, yet caught more than a glimpse of his hero when he wrote:—

Semi-Chor.—Iô, Iô, O master, master, come now to our band. O Bromios, Bromios! Shake the ground holy earth. Quickly will the roofs of Pentheus be shaken in ruins!

Semi-Chor.—Dionysos is beneath the roofs: worship him.

Semi-Chor.—We worship him. See those stone architraves reeling around with the pillars! Bromios will shout aloud in the chambers.

Di.—Kindle the thunderbolt like a fiery torch! Burn, burn together the dwellings of Pentheus.[4]

The least investigation into the phase of Dionysos as Taurokeros shows at once its Semitic origin.[5] His fellow divinity Poseidon, another non-Aryan member of the Hellenik Pantheon, appears similarly as peculiarly con-

---

[1] Cf. Creuzer, *Symbolik*, part i. iii. 153.

[2] *Sup.* II. i. 6, ii. 2, 3, IV. ii. 2.

[3] Cf. Macrob. *Sat.* i. 21. 'Taurum vero ad solem referri multiplici, ratione Aegyptius cultus ostendit.' He then mentions various instances of Kamic solar-bull worship.

[4] Vs. 582-95.

[5] For its more detailed examination, vide *inf.* IX. iii. Mr. Tyrrell apparently does not think the matter worthy of even a passing allusion.

HELIOS KARNEIOS.

nected with the bull.¹ And so, again, even the great Dorik and Aryan divinity Apollon becomes not unnaturally somewhat connected with Semitic solar beings, and consequently appears in several Semitic phases, one of the principal of which is Karneios, the Horned-Sun. Thus Kallimachos, after noticing that Apollon had numerous names, calls him Karneios, and states that at his festival in Libye many bulls were sacrificed to him by the Hellenik colonists,² thus illustrating the continued connection between the sun and the bull.³ He also tells how Apollon constructed an altar with goats' horns; 'with horns he laid the foundations, he built the altar from horns, and horns as walls he placed under it around.'⁴ No sailor, he says,⁵ ever passed the sacred isle of Asterie,⁶ afterwards called Ortygia, and finally Delos, without stopping to be beaten before the altar of Apollon, a penance at once recalling Oriental modes of invoking and propitiating stern and ruthless deities;⁷ and which, while exactly corresponding with the Diamastigesis or severe scourging inflicted before the altar of his sister goddess Artemis Orthia, herself another instance of a Semitic phase having been fastened upon an Aryan divinity,⁸ is peculiarly opposed to the innocent cult of the bright Aryan sun-god. And how came this phase of Karneios, the Horned-sun, among the Dorians of the Peloponnesos? Observe the answer. 'We have as yet,' says K. O. Müller in his great work, 'omitted the mention of two national festivals celebrated at Amyclae by the Spartans in honour of the chief deity of this race, viz., the *Hyacinthia* and the *Carnea*, from a belief that

---

[1] Cf. *Poseidon*, xxiv.
[2] *Hymn, Eis Apol.* 70.
[3] Cf. Virg. *Aen.* iii. 119.
[4] *Hymn, Eis Apol.* 62.
[5] *Hymn, Eis Del.* 310.
[6] The name contains a remarkable Phoenician connection. Thus the bovine Minotauros was called Asterios, the Starry, for the explanation of which occult epithet, vide *inf.* IX. iii. *Taurokeros*.
[7] Cf. Herod. ii. 61.
[8] Cf. *Mythol. of the Aryan Nations*, ii. 144; vide *inf.* VI. i. 1.

they *do not properly belong to Apollo,*' that is, that they are Semitic grafts upon an Aryan stock. 'The worship of the Carnean Apollo in which both were included, *was derived from Thebes,*'[1] that is, the Horned Sun-god came, as we should have anticipated, from the place which, as our poet tells us, first among Hellenik cities received the cult of Dionysos Taurokeros. Thus Apollon is called Dikeros, the Two-horned;[2] and Karneios is a male sungod Ashtar Karnaim,[3] corresponding to the ancient Syrian lunar goddess Ashtareth Karnaim,[4] Astarte the Twohorned. Speaking of the ruins of Kenath in Argob,[5] the Rev. J. L. Porter says, 'A colossal head of Ashtaroth, sadly broken, lies before a little temple, of which probably it was once the chief idol. The crescent moon which gave the goddess the name Carnaim is on her brow.'[6] Again, the unanthropomorphic character of a horned god is a circumstance in itself almost negativing an Hellenik origin,[7] for, as I have remarked elsewhere, "Greek art and Greek mythology are *essentially anthropomorphic with respect to their divinities.*" The Greek mind accepts the idea of monsters, numerous and horrible, but never forgets that they are monsters; to the Hamitic mind monsters are often gods.'[8] The instance of the crescent moon, however, a phenomenon necessarily familiar alike to Semite and Aryan, might possibly have caused an exception to this rule, and therefore the cow-horned Io, whose story, moreover, is illustrated with peculiar felicity by the Natural Phenomena Theory, and who, it should be remembered, is not a divinity, is, in the abstract, not necessarily related to Uasi or Ashtareth. But this excep-

[1] *Doric Race*, i. 373.
[2] *Orphik Hymn*, xxxiv. 25.
[3] Cf. Moabite Stone, 17.
[4] Cf. *Gen.* xiv. 5.
[5] Cf. 1 *Kings*, iv. 13.
[6] *Giant Cities of Bashan*, 12, 43.
[7] The instance of Pan is considered below, and also *inf.* VII. ii. His earliest representations were probably entirely anthropomorphic.
[8] *Poseidon*, xxxiv.; vide *inf.* VII. ii. I know of no real exception to this principle.

tion, even admitting it to be one, only applies to a particular lunar myth ;[1] male horned solar gods are certainly unknown to Hellenik Aryan mythology.

The Bull-horned god, when brought forth, is 'crowned with crowns of serpents,' which also often appear on Vases and elsewhere in the snakebound locks of the Bakchai.[2] The wide field of Ophiolatry, or the 'worship of serpents devoid of wisdom,[3] will be subsequently noticed ;[4] suffice it to observe here that two of the principal aspects of the Serpent in religious-mythology are (1) a deadly venomous beast, a creature hateful and hostile to man and to good divinities, such as the Vedic Ahi, the choking-snake; the Azidahâka, or biting snake of the Persians; and the Giant Apap, or great serpent of Egypt; and (2) a creature

---

[1] As to Iô, whose story is of high antiquity since Homeros constantly calls Hermes Argeiphontes, it is to be observed that she was connected with the Outer-world generally, and with Kam in particular at a very early period. Her son Epaphos (cf. the Phoenician Pappa, Paphos, and the Egyptian Apepi or Apap, the Great Serpent. The Bull-horned god is serpent-crowned, Eur. *Bak.* 100) in mythic history is discovered by Io in Syria, becomes king of Egypt, and marries Memphis, daughter of Neilos (cf. Ais. *Prom. Des.*). It has been doubted whether Io and Dionysos appeared on the Hellenik stage as horned, or whether they were merely supposed to be so, but on the whole I think that horns were actually represented (vide Elmsley in *Bakchai*, v. 920. Speaking of the stage Dionysos he remarks, 'Oui similem Ioni tribuerat Aeschylus in Prometheo.' Io says, 'Forthwith my form and senses were distorted, and I became horned as ye see,' *Prom. Des.* 691-1), as on the Vases (British Museum, Nos. 580, a. 1423). It is generally said that the connection between Io and Kam 'seems to be an invention of later times,' but there is no proof of this; and, on the other hand, an early historic intercourse between Kam and Hellenik regions is being revealed by modern investigation (vide as an instance 'the brilliant red terra-cotta hippopotamus found at a depth of 23 feet' by Dr. Schliemann at Hissarlik, *Troy and its Remains*, 228). It is also to be observed that in Kam we meet with a divinity 'Ioh, or Pioh, the god of the moon, figured with a crescent on his head' (Murray, *Manual of Mythology*, 342). Bunsen similarly mentions 'a deity called after the moon, Aah, Copt. Ooh, Ioh' (*Egypt's Place*, i. 407). The Kamic, Phrygian, and Kaldean moon-divinities were male, but the two former were also androgynous. Sex, therefore, presents little difficulty in identification. Sir Gardner Wilkinson remarks that the name Io 'is evidently connected with *Ehe*, the "Cow" of the Egyptians' (Rawlinson, *Herodotus*, ii. 62). Apparent exceptions to the anthropomorphic canon respecting Hellenik religious-mythology will, on examination, only tend to illustrate and confirm it.

[2] Cf. V. 698.

[3] *Wis.* xi. 15.

[4] *Inf.* VIII. ii. *Serpent.*

friendly to man, connected with life, love and heat, such as the Egyptian serpent of good, the divine serpent of Phoenicia, the healing serpent of Moses, symbol of the All-healer, the serpent of the Hellenik goddess Hygieia, the personification of health, the twining serpents of the kerukeion (caduceus) of Hermes, and the harmless denizens of the Epidaurian temple of Asklepios, 'the blameless physician,' and son of Apollon, whose staff is serpent-twined, as are those of the Boiotik Trophonios and Herkyna.[1] 'The sun-god, as the giver of life, was represented under the type of a serpent,'[2] and serpents were prominent features in the Dionysiak processions,[3] and in the cult of the horned Sabazios, the Phrygian phase of Dionysos. 'Tree and serpent worship,' again, so widely spread, and so much discussed, is undoubtedly, to a great extent, phallic in nature.[4] The sun, the bull, and the serpent in his friendly aspect, are all vivifying and life-producing, and therefore the serpent of life is fitly twined around the horns of the tauriform sun-god, whose very solar phase even is but an expression of his deeper and wider life-power and vital heat, as the spirit of the breathing and animated universe. 'It is not, perhaps, altogether clear,' remarks Canon Rawlinson, '*why* the serpent has been so frequently regarded as an emblem of life. Some say, because serpents are long-lived; others, because the animal readily forms a circle, and a circle was the emblem of eternity. But, whatever the reason, the fact cannot be doubted.'[5] 'The Zulus,' says Dr. Tylor, 'work out in the fullest way the idea of the dead becoming snakes, a creature whose change of skin has so often been associated with the thought of resurrection and immortality.'[6] And similarly, we read in a curious passage

---

[1] Paus. x. 39.
[2] *Theatre of the Greeks*, 18.
[3] *Inf.* VI. i. 1.
[4] *Inf.* VIII. ii. Serpent.
[5] *Ancient Mons.* i. 122, note.
[6] *Primitive Culture*, ii. 7.

of Sanchouniathon, 'Taautos, and in common with him the Phoenicians and Egyptians, attributed divinity to the nature of the dragon and of snakes; for he esteemed the animal the most spiritual of all living things, and of a fiery nature, because it shows an unsurpassed quickness of motion through its spirit, without feet and hands, or any other external members, by means of which other living things effect their movements. And it is also exceedingly long-lived, and not only retains its youth by putting off old age, but also it is wont to receive a great increase of strength, and when it has fulfilled its apportioned span of life it is dissolved into itself, as in the sacred books likewise Taautos himself has recorded.'[1] 'And be ye crowned, as ye rave with wreaths of oak or pine, and adorn your garments of spotted faun-skins with fleeces of white-haired curls [or 'sheep,' according to another reading], and purify yourselves with the insulting wands; immediately the whole earth will join the choric dance.'[2] As the infant Dionysos was snake-crowned, so the Bakchai are to be wreath-crowned. Dionysos is said to have invented buying and selling, the diadem or royal crown, and the triumph.[3] All three inventions point to the East; buying and selling reminds us of the commercial Phoenicians; while the diadem and the triumph speak of the ancient monarchies of the Nile and Euphrates, and of those oriental nations who 'put beautiful crowns upon their heads.'[4] There must have been some reason why Dionysos was traditionally credited with such inventions, and if, as the combined force of the evidence shows was the case, his cult was imported from localities where they were in use, the solution is at once obtained. The connection between the pine and Dionysos

[1] Sanch. ii. 12; vide *inf.* VIII. ii. *Dragon, Serpent.*
[2] Vs. 100-14.
[3] Plinius, vii. 57.
[4] *Ezek.* xxiii. 42.

has been already noticed.¹ The spotted faun-skins are to be still further variegated by being ornamented with little tufts of wool, a favourite style of adornment among the ancients, and which has been well compared with the spots of ermine now similarly used.² The fleece of wool, *pokos*, according to Clemens Alexandrinus, was one of the symbols in the Dionysiak Mysteries.³ The 'insulting wands' are the narthex stalks,⁴ and the purification which they afford is one apparently connected with fire, since, as before noticed, Prometheus was said to have stolen the sacred fire from heaven in a narthex stem; they are styled insulting probably with a double reference (1) to the conduct of Prometheus as regards Zeus, and (2) to the use made of them by the Bakchai against their opponents.⁵ The choric earth-dance has been noticed.

The Chorus, identifying the cult of Dionysos, Rhea and Kybele, proceed to connect it with the Island of Krete,⁶ which presented an extraordinary mixture of races and consequently of religions.⁷ The mysterious Kouretes and Korybantes are represented as the ministers of this joint ritual, and it is therefore necessary to refer to some extent to their origin. I may first remark that the Kabeiroi, Kouretes, Korybantes, Daktyloi, Idaioi and Telchines are, according to the Natural Phenomena Theory, simply—clouds; and those who desire to see the reasonings which lead to this misty conclusion should refer to the Rev. G. W. Cox's important work, the *Mythology of the Aryan Nations*. I have thought it unnecessary to allude to his views on this

---

¹ *Sup.* sec. ii. 2; vide *inf.* VIII. ii. *Cone.*
² Vide VIII. ii. *Spots.*
³ *Protrept.* ii. 18.
⁴ Cf. *Hel.* 1361; vide *inf.* VIII. ii. *Fennel-giant.*
⁵ Cf. v. 147 with v. 702; vide Loukianos, *The Dionysiak Discourse.*
⁶ V. 121.
⁷ Cf. *Poseidon*, xxx. xxxi. My conclusions were, 'that the Mizraimic Kaphtoureem first colonised the island at a remote period; that the Kydones, a Japhetic tribe, subsequently established themselves in the north-western portion of it; that these two races were both found there by the Phoenician colonists; and that, lastly, other Hellenik tribes settled in the country.'

point in detail, inasmuch as the arguments in favour of the Semitic connection of these personages and of Dionysos, when viewed in their totality, present the same kind of evidence which is available in support of the right way of putting together a child's dissected map ; we feel convinced that it is correctly done by a double proof, namely, (1) every piece fits exactly in its place, and (2) will not fit elsewhere. I trust that the reader, while duly observing detail, will also as he proceeds weigh the *combined* force of the connected evidence. To return to the Kouretes and Korybantes. The family pedigree of the latter is as follows. From Zeus, the broad, bright heaven, and the nymph Elektra, a feminine personification of Eliktor the Beaming-Sun, also called Phaethon, and corresponding with Dionysos Antauges the Sparkler, proceed three children, Dardanos, Iasion, and Harmonia.[1] Dardanos sailed to Samothrake, the special home of Semitic Mysteries, and, crossing thence to the Troad, received a grant of land from Teukros, son of the river Skamandros and the nymph Idaia, and first king of Troia. He thus became the ancestor of the Troians, and was an associate of Kybele and initiated in her Mysteries. Iasion is represented as the beloved of Demeter and of Kybele, a circumstance shewing the early identification of the two: the myth is of great antiquity, for the passion of Demeter for him is alluded to by Homeros[2] as a familiar instance of the danger of association between mortals and immortals. To Iasion Zeus discovers the celebrated Samothrakian Mysteries, and his son is Korybas, the child of Kybele and ancestor of the Korybantes, who crosses with his mother into Asia and introduces her worship there, a circumstance illustrative of the fact that the cult of the Mother of the Gods was not Phrygian in origin. Harmonia, the sister of Dardanos and Iasion,

[1] Cf. *Schol.* Apoll. Rhod. i. 916.   [2] *Od.* v. 125.

receives from Athene the celebrated necklace and *peplos*, 'the star-bespangled robe,' so famous in the mythic history of Thebai, and is married to Kadmos, the Man-of-the-East, its founder and the son of the Phoenician king.[1] It is not difficult to estimate the true value of Hellenik mythic genealogies;[2] they have evidently some meaning, and are founded on certain facts. But this signification is to some extent esoteric. Thus the pedigree in question illustrates (1) the natural connection between the two earth-goddesses, Demeter and Kybele, which has been already noticed, (2) that the mystic Korybas is born in the home of non-Hellenik mystery, and that many of his connections are Phoenician; (3) that the whole family are descended from the beaming sun of Eastern climes, Dionysos Pyropos, the Fiery-faced, are in fact the children of a flame-cult. But in order that the pedigree may be correct in form, the Sun is changed into a female, the bright-beaming nymph Elektra, and as such, is duly wedded to Zeus, the Aryan All-father. Thus the Elektran, the fourth of the Seven Gates of Thebai, was dedicated to the Sun.[3] Strabo gives an interesting dissertation on the Kouretes and Korybantes, in which he notices that Pindaros[4] and Euripides identify the Bakchik and Phrygian rites. He states that the names Kabeiroi and Korybantes were invented to designate the ministers, dancers, and servants employed about the sacred rites, that these beings were not only ministers of the gods, but were themselves also called gods.[5] Quoting many authorities, he says that there were nine Telchines in Rhodos, who accompanied Rhea to Krete; that Korybas was one of them, and that certain Rhodians held that the Korybantes were daemons,

---

[1] Cf. Ephoros, Frag. xii.; Diod. v. 48–9.
[2] Cf. *Poseidon*, xxvii.
[3] Cf. Ais. *Hept. epi The.* 418;
[4] Eur. *Phoi.* 1129; Nonnos, v. 76.
[5] *Dithyrambs.* Frag. ix.
[5] Cf. *Hippol.* 143.

children of Athene and the Sun; that they were the same as the Kabeiroi and that they went to Samothrake. He further states that the Kouretes were Kretans, that in the Kretan history they are called the nurses and guardians of Zeus, and that Demetrios of Skepsis, cir. B.C. 160, who wrote a very learned work entitled *Troikos Diakosmos*, 'The Troian Array,' held that the Kouretes and Korybantes were identical. Quoting Pherekydes the celebrated logographer, cir. B.C. 470, he says that there were nine Korybantes who lived in Samothrake, and three Kabeiroi, children of Hephaistos and the nymph Kabeira, who were especially worshipped at Lemnos, Imbros, and in the Troad. He adds that Rhodos was anciently called Telchinis, from the Telchines, who according to many writers, excelled in the mechanical arts, and were found also in Krete and Kypros.[1] Pausanias gives the names of the Kouretes, one of whom is Iasios, and states that they came from Mount Ida in Krete.[2] Thirlwall is of opinion that the Telchines were Phoenicians, and that the legends respecting them 'embody recollections of arts introduced or refined by foreigners who attracted the admiration of the rude tribes whom they visited.'[3] That their connection is Phoenician is highly probable, although not matter of absolute history. The Bishop's views have been objected to as unsupported by evidence, but there is still less evidence that the Telchines were clouds. The Emperor Julianus states that Korybas is, *i.e.* represents, the Sun.[4] The Pseudo-Orphik Hymns, xxxi. and xxxviii. are addressed to the Kouretes, and Hymn xxxix to Korybas, who is called one of the Kouretes, who are themselves identified with the Korybantes. They are said to dwell 'in the sacred region

---

[1] Strabo, x. 3, xiv. 2.
[2] Paus. v. 7.
[3] *Hist of Greece*, pt. I. iii.
[4] *Orat. in Mat. Deorum.*

of Samothrake.' Taylor's translation is not without merit:—

> Deathless Curetes, by your pow'r alone,
> *The greatest mystic rites to men at first were shown,*
> Who shake old Ocean thund'ring to the sky,
> And stubborn oaks with branches waving high.
> 'Tis yours in glittering arms the earth to beat
> With lightly leaping, rapid, sounding feet;
> Then every beast the noise terrific flies,
> And the loud tumult wanders through the skies.
> The dust your feet excites, with matchless force
> Flies to the clouds amidst their whirling course;
> And every flower of variegated hue
> Grows in the dancing motion formed by you.
> Immortal daemons, to your pow'rs consign'd
> The task to nourish and destroy mankind—
> Curetes, Corybantes, ruling kings,
> Whose praise the land of Samothracia sings.

This curious passage clearly indicates their close affinity with Dionysos, as assistants in the vast kosmic dance,[1] and at once the nurturers and destroyers of mankind, as he is to men at the same time the mildest and most terrible of divinities. It is unnecessary to analyse these legends and myths in detail; they are all evidently harmonious, and teach the non-Hellenik character of the Kouretes and Korybantes, thus connected by Euripides with the Dionysiak ritual. Among other points, may be noticed, (1) Their solar connection as the children or associates of Helios, not as the Clouds against whom he wages war, and the implication of this connection as pointing to a foreign cult; (2) Their connection with Phoenician personages such as Kadmos, Hephaistos and the Kabeiroi, Phoenician arts such as metallurgy, and Phoenician localities such as Kypros, Rhodos, Krete,

[1] Cf. *Kretes*, Frag. ii.; *Sup.* subsec i.

THE DIONYSOS OF THE ATTIK TRAGEDIANS. 133

Lemnos, Imbros and Samothrake; (3) Their mutual close and intimate affinity, though not absolute identity, as perhaps being different phases of the same personages, and (4) Their connection with the kosmogonic Dionysos, both as ministers of death and life, and as choir-leaders in the universal nature-dance or rhythm of motion.[1] Strabo sagely concludes his Kouretik dissertation with the remark, 'all discussion respecting the gods requires an examination of ancient opinions, and of fables, since the ancients *expressed enigmatically their physical notions concerning the nature of things*, and always intermixed fables with their discoveries. It is not easy, therefore, to solve these enigmas exactly; but if we lay before the reader a multitude of fabulous tales, some consistent with each other, others which are contradictory, we may thus with less difficulty form conjectures about the truth.'[2]

'And hard by the raving Satyroi performed the rites of mother Rhea, and they added the dances of the triennial festivals in[3] which Dionysos rejoices, glad on the mountains when from the running bands of revellers he falls on the plain, having a sacred garment of faun-skin, hunting for the blood of goat-slaughter, a raw-eaten delight.'[4] The Satyroi, according to the Natural Phenomena Theory, are 'the phenomena of the life which seems to animate the woods as the branches of the trees move in wild dances with the clouds which course through the air above, or assume forms strange or grotesque or fearful, in the deep nooks and glens or in the dim and dusky tints of the gloaming.'[5] The objection to this view, which applies rather to Pan and the Panises,

---

[1] Souidas (in voc. Kouretes and *Koureton stoma*) calls them a nation, and says prophetic power was ascribed to them. Dionysos also is a Prophet (*Bak.* 298). Souidas (in voc. *Korubantes*) calls both Kouretes and Korybantes children of Rhea. Hesychios similarly (in voc. *Korubas*), calls Korubas a 'priest of Rhea.'

[2] Falconer's Translation, ii. 101-2.

[3] Cf. *Orphik Hymns*, xlv. lii.

[4] Vs. 130-9.

[5] *Mythol. of the Aryan Nations*, ii. 15.

is twofold; (1) it is unsupported by evidence, and (2) it does not account for the particular form under which the Satyroi are represented, *i.e.* with pointed ears, two small horns and goats' tails, or by later writers with larger horns, and goats' feet and legs. According to Donaldson, 'the Satyrs were only the deified representatives of the original worshippers, who probably assumed as portions of their droll costume the skin of the goat, which they had sacrificed as a welcome offering to their wine-god.'[1] The first point for consideration is, What is the connection between Dionysos and the Goat? Virgil says that the goat is sacrificed as a vine-injuring animal,[2] and the constellation *Aix*, the Goat, was similarly supposed to affect vines injuriously at its rising.[3] This may be one link in the case, but there are others also, for as Virgil himself notices, various animals injure the vine, and Satyroi might, if this point comprised all the affinity between the god and the goat, have been represented with bulls' or rams' tails. The Bakchik cry 'Eua' has been said to be an imitation of the goat's bleat, and the goat as horned has, like the ram and bull, a certain connection with the god. But the chief link between the Satyroi, the goat and Dionysos is the erotic character of the animal,[4] corresponding to that phase of the god when the general vigour of the earth-life, Dionysos Karpios or Erikepeios, passes into personal amorousness as Ephaptor or Polyparthenos. The Satyroi 'represent the luxuriant vital powers of nature,'[5] and hence their connection with the kosmogonic god. This does not exclude Donaldson's idea, which is probably correct in itself, but manifestly too slender a

---

[1] *Theatre of the Greeks*, 25; cf. Strabo, x. 3. Vide *inf*. VII. ii., Remarks on Pan and Heabani.

[2] *Georg*. ii. 372-83; cf. Ovid, *Metam*. xv. 114.

[3] Paus. ii. 13.

[4] Cf. Diod. i. 88; *King Lear*, i. 2, 'his goatish disposition.' Goats' flesh was sometimes eaten as a satyrion (Athen. ix. 15). Vide Payne Knight on the Goat in Art.

[5] Smith, *Class. Dict. Satyri*.

foundation to be an exhaustive explanation of the facts. Each Satyros is thus another and a lower personification of the sensuous divinity, the goat becomes a fitting sacrifice, and the god is known as Aigobolos, the Goat-smiter.[1] But Dionysos the Exarchos, or Choir-leader[2] of the revelling bands, is described as bounding down the mountain sides to the plain, clad in the sacred faun-skin[3] 'hunting for the blood of slaughtered he-goats, a raw-eaten delight.' Here we meet the god again in his ferocious aspect as appeased by blood, as Omophagos, Omestes, and Omadios,[4] the Raw-flesh-eating. Thus, in a Fragment of the *Kretes* of Euripides, quoted by Porphyrios,[5] the Mystic devoted to Zagreus, speaks of having 'completed the carnivorous feasts,' and the same writer informs us that human sacrifices were offered to Dionysos Omadios in Chios and Tenedos, when a man was torn in pieces.[6] But a more innocent cult is natural in Hellenik regions; and ultimately, when the savage Semitic element is overpowered, animals, especially the goat, take the place of human victims. Thus at Potniai, a place a little south of Thebai, the inhabitants to atone for their impiety were commanded to sacrifice to Dionysos a boy in the flower of his youth, but not many years afterwards 'they say that the god [or in reality a less noxious cult] changed the sacrifice of a boy for that of a goat.'[7] This is similar to the case of Iphigeneia, who is preserved when about to be sacrificed and a stag substituted for her,[8] and to that of

---

[1] Vide *inf.* VIII. i. *Aigobolos*. A singular instance of the direct connection between the animal and the solar divinity occurs in the case of the inhabitants of Kleonai in Argolis, who, when smitten by pestilence, under the direction of the Delphik Oracle, sacrificed a goat to the rising sun. (Paus. x. 11.)
[2] V. 141.
[3] Cf. Vs. 24, 111. 606.
[4] *Orphik Hymns*, xxx. 5, lii. 7. Vide *inf.* VIII. i. *Omestes*.
[5] *Peri Apoches Empsychon.* iv. 19.
[6] *Ibid.* ii. 55; cf. *Ion.* 1125, 'Xouthos went to the place where the Bakchik fire of god leaps forth, that he might wet the double rocks [*i.e.* "the two-topt mount divine"] of Dionysos with the blood of victims.'
[7] Paus. ix. 8.
[8] Cf. *Iph. en Aul.* 1561 *et seq.*

Isaac, all these being instances of disapprobation of the bloody cult peculiar to Kanaanite, Phoenician, and Karthaginian. At Tenedos the legend ran that the Aeolians sacrificed to Dionysos Melikertes a new-born calf instead of a new-born child, ' shoeing it with buskins and tending the mother-cow as if a human mother.'[1] So similarly the Phoenician Poseidon was appeased by human sacrifices,[2] and his children the Kyklopes are represented as cannibals.[3] Human sacrifices prevailed to a considerable extent in early Hellas, but probably only, or chiefly, in connection with the non-Aryan divinities.[4] The raw-flesh-eating god, when unable to glut himself with human victims, bounds like a were-wolf upon the he-goat, *tragos*, which, ' was another name for Saturos the goat-eared attendant of Bacchus,'[5] who ' was called by the name of the animal he resembled in character'; and ' Tragodia is not the song of a goat, but a song accompanied by a dance performed by persons in the guise of Satyrs.'[6] There may also be a further and astronomical connection between Dionysos and the goat, as Aigokoros or Capricornus the Goat-horned, one of the Kakopoioi Asteres or Stars-of-evil-influence, a sign which appears on a Babylonian Zodiac of the date of B.C. 1200.[7] Both Dionysos and Aigokoros were said to have greatly distinguished themselves in the War between the Gods and the Giants.[8] Tityrus,[9] according to Servius, signified ' aries major,' the leading ram of the flock,[10] ' lingua Laconia;' but according to others[11] a goat. ' Tituros is the Doric form of Sisuros, which also

---

[1] Tylor, *Prim. Cult.* ii. 367.
[2] *Poseidon*, xv.
[3] *Od.* ix.; Ovid. *Metam.* xv. 93.
[4] Cf. Herod. vii. 197; Plout. *Symp.* viii.; Paus. vii. 19, 21. Vide *inf.* XI. ii. Cult of Melqarth-Molekh.
[5] *Theatre of the Greeks*, 40, and authorities cited.
[6] *Ibid.* 68. Vide the various meanings of *tragos* as connected with life-vigour.
[7] Rawlinson, *Ancient Mons.* ii. 574. As to the ancient Zodiac, vide *inf.* XII. i. 2.
[8] Cf. *Ion*, 215; Diod. iii. 73, iv. 15; Hor. *Car.* i. 12, ii. 19.
[9] Vir. *Ec.* i.
[10] Cf. *Od.* ix. 431 *et seq.*
[11] Cf. *Schol. in Theok.* iii. 2.

originally meant a goat,' and by some was perhaps wrongly connected with Saturos.[1] Such are the principal points of connection between the horned, phallic, vine-destroying goat, and Dionysos with his voluptuous phase of nature and sensuous worshippers. A goat-thighed image was mutilated in the secret exhibitions at Eleusis,[2] in which the cult of Demeter and Dionysos was combined, a rite based on the same reason as the practice of the Phrygian priests of Kybele, who honoured 'the great reproductive force of the world by the sacrifice of the reproductive power in her ministers.'[3] The goat-footed, two-horned Pan, though apparently belonging to the group of Dionysos and the Satyroi, and called by Frere, 'the first Avater of the worship of Bacchus,' is in origin quite unconnected with them. The pastoral god of Arkadia is an Aryan divinity, 'the purifying breeze, the Sanskrit *pavana*,[4] a name which reappears in the Latin Favonius,'[5] and his form merely typifies his affinity with flocks and herds. This apparent connection between Pan and Dionysos is noticed in the Homerik Hymn to the former, almost every line of which illustrates his character as the gentle wind, by the statement that 'all the immortals were delighted with him, but especially Dionysos,'[6] evidently because the newly-introduced divinity so much resembled himself. But Pan being a satyr in form naturally suffers from the circumstance, and so in works of art is represented as coarse and sensuous, although there is nothing in his mythic history, in his love of Pitys the Pine-tree, or Syrinx the Reed-pipe, or Echo, 'sweetest nymph,' which justifies such a theory of his

---

[1] Cf. Müller, *Doric Race*, ii. 358, and authorities cited.
[2] Cf. Clemens Alex. apud Euseb. *Euan Proparas*, ii. 3; *Protrep.* ii. 15; Taylor, *Dissertation on the Eleusinian Mysteries*, ii.
[3] *Mythol. of the Aryan Nations*, ii. 312.
[4] Cf. Max Müller, *Chips*, ii. 159.
[5] *Mythol of Aryan Nations*, ii. 248.
[6] V. 46.

character. He is a rough, rude, jovial, rustic daemon, full of life and vigour, such as a pure Hellenik Dionysos might have been, without a trace of anything grim, sombre, savage, phallic, or occult in his character; an innocent Aryan concept, originally of the gentler winds and their doings, and subsequently of the free, merry life of the country. Our Laureate, with his usual exquisite classic taste, speaks of—

> Lands where not a leaf was dumb;
> But all the lavish hills would hum
> The murmur of a happy Pan:
> And many an old philosophy
> On Argive heights divinely sang,
> And round us all the thicket rang
> To many a flute of Arcady.[1]

This general rejoicing of rustic existence, combined with an interpretation of the god's name as signifying 'All,' which is at least as early as the Homerik Hymn, naturally produced the derivative concept of Pan as 'universal nature,' a kosmogonic spirit, and so Milton styles Christ 'the mighty Pan,'[2] *i.e.*, the true life and supporter of the world,[3] and here again is a source of confusion between Pan and Dionysos. But these two divinities are distinct in origin, in phase of thought, and in locality. When geographically contiguous they naturally become associated through an apparent close resemblance, but analysis reveals the error, and in a word, Pan is an Aryan Dionysos, Dionysos a Semitic Pan. There is hardly anything in which the Hellenes, and after them the Romans, evinced less critical acumen than in their researches into the religious cults of foreign nations. They appear to have considered that almost all the world

---

[1] *In Memoriam*, xxiii.
[2] *Hymn on the Morning of Christ's Nativity*, 8.
[3] Cf. Mrs. Browning, *The Dead Pan*.

reverenced some at least of their chief divinities. Thus Caesar tells us that the Druids worshipped Mercury, Apollo, and Minerva.[1] Herodotos, however, has probably occasioned more confusion on this account than any other writer, for, firmly impressed with the belief instilled into him by Kamic priests, that Kam had supplied Hellas with nearly all the Hellenik Pantheon,[2] he speaks of Zeus, Artemis, Ares, and other Aryan divinities as being Kamic in origin. It is not therefore surprising to find that he met with Pan in Aigyptos,[3] in the Mendesian Nome or Canton in the Delta, where he describes the god as pourtrayed 'with the face of a goat and the legs of a he-goat,' but this seems to be a double error of the historian, for 'no Egyptian god is really represented in this way.'[4] The god in question is Khem, and similarly the city Chemmo, in Upper Aigyptos, was called by the Hellenes Panopolis. Khem, 'the generative principle, and universal nature, was represented as a phallic figure. Of him is said in the hieroglyphic legend, "Thy title is father of thine own father."'[5] The Egyptians, says Herodotos, do not believe the god to be goat-shaped, or 'in any respect unlike the other gods;[6] but they represent him thus for a reason which I prefer not to relate.' His modesty is to be commended, and illustrates the connection between the Goat and Dionysos. 'The goat was the living, deified, animal-symbol of the god,'[7] and for exactly the same reason that it was connected with the Dionysiak cult. The reader will note the resemblance between Khem, the supposed Pan of Herodotos, and

---

[1] *Bell. Gal.* vi. 17.
[2] Cf. Herod. ii. 50.
[3] *Ibid.* ii. 46. 'Aiguptos renders Aquipto, the mid-point of earth, a title found in one of the Inscriptions.' (Gladstone, *Homeric Synchronism*, 270.) Thus Jerusalem, Delphoi, etc. were equally supposed to be centres of the earth.
[4] Rawlinson, *Herodotus*, ii. 72, note 4.
[5] Sir G. Wilkinson in Rawlinson's *Herodotus*, ii. 243.
[6] An interesting illustration of the purely symbolical character of unanthropomorphic divinities in Kam, Assur, and Kaldea.
[7] Bunsen, *Egypt's Place*, i. 385.

Dionysos.[1] Numberless writers have followed the Father of History in his derivation of almost the whole of the Hellenik divinities from Kamic originals; and the old belief that the gods of Hellas were all Semitic is not unnaturally followed by an undue Aryan reaction, Truth remaining at her favourite stand-point in the centre.[2]

'Bakcheus, having a flaming torch of pine on his thyrsos, rushes about at speed, arousing the wandering chorus-bands, putting them in motion with cries of Iakchos.'[3] The extraordinary Bakchik cult at once strikes the philosophic enquirer (who wishes not so much to know what is, as why it is) as being based on a mystical and symbolic view of certain great realities. Here, again, we have the kosmic symbolism imitated, probably unconsciously by the vast majority of the Dionysiak worshippers of Hellas, who deemed that their dances and ritual were at most but representations of the acts of some pre-historic hero of the Earlier Time. It is Dionysos as 'the choir-leader of the fire-breathing stars,' the spirit of the universe, who, with wild shouts and streaming locks, heads and agitates the cyclic starry groups in their aërial dance around the mighty altar of the world.[4] The chorus-leader puts his band in motion, but how does Dionysos agitate the stars? The word used, *anapallôn*, reminds us of the Queen of the Air, whose 'name, Pallas, possibly refers to the quivering or vibration of the air; and to its power, whether as vital force, or communicated wave, over every kind of matter, in giving it vibratory movement.'[5] What causes the twinkling or 'eddying of the stars?'[6] The waves of light;

---

[1] Vide note by Dr. Birch in Bunsen's *Egypt's Place*, i. 386, showing the identity of Khem with 'the Harnekht or powerful Horus,' son of Uasar.

[2] As to Pan, vide *inf.* VII. ii.

[3] Vs. 145-0. As to the cry 'Iakchos,' Vide *inf.* VIII. ii. *Iakchos*, IX. i.

[4] *Sup.* II. iii. 3; IV. ii. 2, iii. 1.

[5] *Queen of the Air*, i. 43. Others, somewhat singularly, connect the name of the stainless virgin with phallos.

[6] *Hellene*, 1408.

Dionysos, as he bounds along, comet-like, with flaming torch, a circling sun, Antauges the Sparkler. It is difficult to follow the subtle phases of this vast and wonderful divinity. His solar connection with its astronomic and igneous aspect has been noticed in part, but as he is heat, so, naturally, is he light as connected with materiality. In fact, go back to first principles, and there from the root of existence we shall exhume the mystic Demiurge, and find the basis of things personified in him: Light, Dionysos the Solar; Heat, Dionysos the Fiery; Force, Dionysos the Vigorous; Sound, Dionysos the Shouter; Motion, Dionysos the Dancer; Change, Dionysos the Many-phased; Life, Dionysos the Blooming; and Death, Dionysos the Grimly, the 'many-guest-receiving Zeus of the dead.' Well does Professor Ruskin speak of 'an instinctive truth in ancient symbolism,' and of 'mythic expressions of natural phenomena which it is an uttermost triumph of recent science to have revealed.'

The Chorus having concluded, the scene which follows, absurd enough in itself, is yet interesting in a Dionysiak connection. Kadmos and Teiresias, both very old men, come on the stage, and piously resolve to dance till they drop in honour of the new god, showing what an essential feature of his cult was the rhythm or poetry of motion, the imitation of the vibratory or eddying nature of things. A passage in the *Batrachoi* of Aristophanes, describing the mystic Bakchik dances of Eleusis, is in remarkable harmony with this description, and perhaps ridicules it, 'the knee of the old men moves swiftly; and they shake off griefs and lengthy periods of ancient years at the sacred worship.'[1]

Pentheus having, not unnaturally, expostulated with his grandfather and Tieresias on their apparent folly, the

---

[1] *Batr.* 345-8. Probably the *Bakchai* and the *Batrachoi* were both brought out in the same year, B.C. 405. The expression 'foot of time' (*Bak.* 876) is ridiculed in the latter play (*Batr.* 100).

latter is made to reply in a strain of the grossest materialism, showing that he was a worthy disciple of the sensuous god : 'Two things, O youth, are of most importance among men, the goddess Demeter, who is the Earth; by whatever name you wish to call her.[1] She with dry food nourishes mortals; but the offspring of Semele, who has come as her rival, has discovered the liquid stream of the grape, and has introduced it among the subjects of death, which frees the wretched race of man from grief, when they are filled with the flowing of the vine, and sleep an oblivion of daily evils it gives, nor is there any other remedy for woes.'[2] I am compelled to notice this unworthy passage, lest it should be said that I omit extracts which show that Dionysos was merely Theoinos, the Wine-god. It is difficult to say whether it is most wanting in truth or in nobility of feeling, why the poet introduced it, and why he fastened it upon the unfortunate soothsayer.[3] Those who remember the solemn majesty of 'King Teiresias,' in the weird scenery of the Homerik Nekyomanteia, will appreciate this gross profanation of the character of the mighty seer of Thebai. Is then the Byronic sentiment, that 'man being reasonable must get drunk,' commendable, and is there no other refuge for the ills of life than the stupefaction and heavy sleep, evil-dream-haunted, produced by excess of wine? These are the bread-and-cheese views of the mythic Sardanapalos, whose tomb was said to have borne an inscription which in Latin verse ran :—

> Haec habeo quae edi, quaeque exaturata libido
> Hausit: at illa jacent multa et praeclara relicta.

[1] Cf. Ais. *Prom. Des.* 210.
[2] Vs. 274-83.
[3] Mr. Tyrrell remarks that 'the character of Teiresias, when divested of its spurious rationalism [*i.e.* as shown in Vs. 286-305, a passage rejected by some critics as "smacking rather of Proclus than of Euripides"] is very well carried out.'(*The Bacchae*, Introd. xxxiii). I should say there is still more need to divest it of its spurious materialism. Cf. the Teiresias of the *Oid. Tyr.*

'Quid aliud,' inquit Aristoteles, 'in bovis, non in regis sepulchro, inscriberes?'

But to leave the moral, or rather immoral, sentiments of the passage, and to turn to the idea of the divinities which it contains, the sentiments apparently not merely of Teiresias, but also of Euripides himself, a philosophical freethinker and materialist. 'When we call corn Ceres, and wine Bacchus,' says Cicero, 'we make use of the common manner of speaking;[1] but do you think anyone so mad as to believe that his food is a deity?'[2] Dionysos then, is not merely Wine personified, for if so, then Demeter is merely Bread; but Demeter is the Earth: then, the Earth is merely Bread; which is absurd. But he is here said to be the discoverer and introducer of wine, and of this, as we have seen, there is not a trace in his Homerik or other early history.[3] If merely the Wine-god, why is he solar, horned, and kosmogonic? Every step of the enquiry proves the vinous theory to be utterly untenable; we might as well say that Aphrodite was only a designation of love, and not a vast and widespread concept whose name might derivatively be appropriately so used. But, in truth, it is unnecessary to slay the slain: Euripides, it would almost seem in wanton mischief, (he may possibly have been laughing at Archelaos, or perhaps such sentiments were in vogue at the Makedonian Court),[4] here holds up eating and drinking, especially the latter, as the height of happiness, and this view of Dionysos but ill fits with the rest of the Play, for if the *Bakchai* were the only Dionysiak specimen of ancient literature which we possessed, we should unhesi-

---

[1] *E.g.* the proverb 'Sine Cerere et Libero frigit Venus.'

[2] *De Nat. Deor.* iii. 16. Transubstantiation would have surprised him.

[3] Vide *sup.* II. i. 8, Mr. Gladstone on the Dionysiak use of wine by women.

[4] Where the Play would seem to have been very popular. At a subsequent period Olympias, the mother of Alexandros the Great, acted Agaue. (Plout. *Alex.* ii.) Another Agaue in later times actually brought in the head of Crassus. (Vide Mommsen, *Hist. of Rome*, iv. 337.)

tatingly assert that the Tippler was but one, and that not one of the most important of the phases of the god. It is necessary to insist strongly on this point, since it is so customary to connect the Bakchik cult with wine only.[1] Bunsen, commenting on the Hellenik Mysteries, remarks, 'More especially Orphic, again is the spiritual significance of Dionysos, who elsewhere is represented rather *as a Demiurge*, and *in later ages* again under a sensual aspect as the god of wine.'[2] But this passage of the *Bakchai* contains an important fact illustrative of the connected worship of Demeter and Dionysos. The two divinities being distinct in character and origin, and yet remarkably similar in many respects, especially in the kosmogonic phase, might with equal propriety be represented either as Associates according to Pindaros, or as Rivals according to Euripides. Rivals at first, they afterwards agreed to harmonise and buried all differences in the joint cult of Eleusis, in which Demeter as the elder, and goddess of the place, has pre-eminence and priority, while Dionysos is enthroned as her associate and assistant.

'And this divinity is a Prophet, for Bakchik phrensy and madness have much of the prophetical spirit; for when the god enters strongly into the body he causes the phrensied to declare the future.'[3] 'As the god of wine,' remarks the writer of the article *Dionysus* in Dr. Smith's Classical Dictionary, 'Dionysus is also both an inspired and an inspiring god, that is, a god who has the power of revealing the future of man by oracles.' The principle here seems to be 'wine in, wit out.' But what instance is there of any divinity or individual being inspired by wine to declare future events? Is the Delphik Apollon a wine-god, and was the ecstasy of his priestess mere drunken raving? Jolly livers, from Archilochos to

---

[1] Vide the observation of Prof. Mayor, *sup.* II. i. 8.
[2] *God in Hist.* ii. 80.
[3] Vs. 298–301; cf. *Hek.* 1267; Herod. vii. 111; Ais. *Frag.* ccccxi. 'Bakcheios the Prophet.'

Theodore Hook may have felt most inclined to sing and dance when somewhat 'dizzy with the thunder of wine,' but to suppose that the secrets of futurity lie at the bottom of the talboy is to adapt a thoroughly Rabelaisian creed; and, so believing, we may sing, with Panurge:—

> Bottle! whose mysterious deep
> Does ten thousand secrets keep,
> With attentive ear I wait,
> Ease my mind and speak my fate.
> Soul of joy! like Bacchus, we
> More than India gain by thee;
> Truths unborn thy juice reveals,
> Which futurity conceals.

Of course those who regard Dionysos as simply a wine-god are of necessity driven to explain all his phases by the aid of wine alone. The first link between Apollon and Dionysos is their solar connection, which has been already noticed;[1] and we now come to the second, the possession of prophetic power. It is therefore natural, when considering why Dionysos is credited with the possession of such power, to ask why this is an attribute of Apollon? And the answer is very simple. The wisdom of Apollon is merely that of Helios the Sun, who sees and knows all things.[2] 'He is emphatically the wise and the deep- or far-seeing god,'[3] who shares in the secret counsels of Zeus.[4] This Aryan idea is perfectly simple and innocent, and unconnected with any violent emotion: Apollon does not rave or rage. Dionysos, as we have seen, has a solar phase; but his prophetic powers are not connected with it, for the Semitic mind does not regard the Sun in so simple an aspect as that of a mere observer of what is done in the world. We therefore notice that

---

[1] *Sup.* II. iii. 2.
[2] Cf. *Il.* iii. 277; *Od.* viii. 302.
[3] *Mythol. of the Aryan Nations*, ii. 25 *et seq.*
[4] Cf. *Hom. Hymn, Eis Her.* 535.

although, in the case of the two divinities, the result is the same, namely, both are regarded as being prophetic, yet that this result is arrived at by different lines of thought; a circumstance not unnatural, since one god is Aryan and the other Semitic. When speaking of the connection between the Phoenician Poseidon and the Latin god Consus,[1] I remarked, that 'the attribute of mysterious wisdom which characterises Consus distinguishes Poseidon in a similar manner,' and that the wisdom of Zeus, Apollon, and Helios 'only represents the knowledge derived from ocular observation.' In a remarkable passage in the *Ilias*,[2] Poseidon claims to be wiser than Apollon, who does not deny the assertion, and in every way confesses his inferiority; while the subordinate of Poseidon, Proteus the Aigyptian,[3] is possessed of unerring knowledge and prophetic powers. We may fairly assume that the master was as wise as the servant; indeed, he is expressly represented as 'gifted with prophetic powers.'[4] Poseidon, Proteus,[5] Dionysos, all Oriental personages, are thus all alike possessed of mysterious wisdom and prophetic power; which, as we have seen, is distinct from the simple Aryan idea of ocular solar knowledge. We

---

[1] One of my critics supposes that I meant to derive Consus from the Kamic Khons, a piece of etymology of which I am quite innocent.
[2] *Il*. xxi. 440.
[3] *Od*. iv. 386.
[4] *Poseidon*, xxiii.; cf. *Il*. xx. 203.
[5] Proteus, the wise and prophetic Old Man of the Sea, who could change into marine reptilian forms (*Od*. iv. 418), is identical with the mythic Kamic monarch of Herodotos, 'a man of Memphis,' and, as shown by the passage, of Phoenician associations, 'whose name, in the language of the Greeks, was Proteus' (Herod. ii. 112), who was also called Ketes (Diod. i. 62), *i.e.* Great Fish, and who was said to have reigned at the time of the Troian War. This great, wise, prophetic Fish, who lived near a place called 'The Camp of the Tyrians,' and also near the temple of 'Venus the Stranger,' *i.e.* Astarte, is the Phoenician and Philistine Dagon. (Vide Sir G. Wilkinson in Rawlinson's *Herodotus*, ii. 157; *Poseidon*, xxxiv. xxxv.) Thus Mr. Cox remarks, 'This Proteus is the fish-god of Ninevites and Philistines' (*Mythol. of the Aryan Nations*, i. 183. *Note*), and that the qualities of Proteus 'are shared by the fish-god, Dagon or Onnes, of Syria' (*Ib*. ii. 26), who, again, is Kaldean in origin (*Poseidon*, xxxvii–xxxix.).

are thus of necessity driven to the conclusion, that they brought their prophetic powers with them from their earlier homes; and so we shall find on the other side the sea in that wonderful group of lands from Kam to Haiasdan,[1] seers, soothsayers, augurs, diviners, enchanters, astrologers, magicians, and schools of prophets, all in full activity. It is unnecessary here to enter into detail about them, the raving votaries of Baal, the mystic trance-excitement of Balaam, the wise men of Babylon, the myriad pseudo-seers of Israel; the thousand expedients, astronomical, astrological, and otherwise, for revealing the secrets of the shrouded Future.[2] Suffice it for the present to observe whence the Semitic Dionysos obtains his prophetic power, wherein it differs from that of his Aryan brother, Apollon; how, as he is at once the associate and rival of Demeter, he is also the associate and rival of Phoibos; and, lastly, how, when their feuds are over, the joint ritual of Delphoi, where Dionysos has 'as great a share in the Delphic oracle as Apollo,' corresponds with the joint ritual of Eleusis.

'He has also something of Ares in him.'[3] So the Orphik Hymn writer calls him 'Ares-like.'[4] Ares 'is in point of strength, divine; in point of mind and heart, simply animal. He is a compound of deity and brute.'[5] This savage wild-beast phase of Dionysos has already been referred to.[6] It is closely connected, but not absolutely identical, with the darker aspect of his Semitic cult. Thus regarded, he is Dasyllios the Shaggy and Agrionios the Savage. His partially warlike character is shown in the legends of his prowess in the fight between the Giants

---

[1] 'The primitive name of ancient Armenia.' (Cooper, *Archaic Dictionary*, 207).
[2] Cf. the Babylonian 'Tables of Omens.' (*Records of the Past*, v. 167 et seq.)
[3] V. 302.
[4] *Ophik Hymn*, xxx. 4.
[5] *Juv. Mun.* 294.
[6] Cf. V. 1017-9. Vide sup. II. i. 4.

and the Gods,[1] alluded to when speaking of his possible connection with Aigokeros, and of his conquests over the Indians,[2] and other hostile nations and individual opponents. So far as we have gone hitherto, this feature resolves itself into the violent introduction of his cult into fresh localities.

'You shall see him also on the Delphik rocks, bounding, with torches, upon the double-peaked hill-top, brandishing and shaking the Bakchik branch, and mighty in Hellas.'[3] Unless this is meant as a prophecy, which it does not seem to be, but as a relation of alleged facts, the poet, thinking more of the belief of his own day than of that of the mythic age of Pentheus, contradicts himself; for, at the outset, Dionysos is represented as saying that Thebai was the first Hellenik locality at which he had arrived, and therefore Delphoi would not then be one of his haunts. His connection with the Delphik god has just been noticed.[4] The branch which he shakes is the *thyrsos*, wreathed with deathless ivy;[5] and, according to Hesychios, Dionysos was known in the Mysteries under the name of the Branch,[6] a most appropriate symbol of the earth-life or Dionysos, Dendrites Of-the-tree, and Karpios the Growth-producing. The Assyrian sculptures have made us familiar with the Bakchik branch in earlier symbolism.[7] A fuller meaning attached to the idea is illustrated by many passages in the Old Testament.[8] The branch is also a phallic tree of life.[9]

'Come Golden-faced-one,[10] brandishing your thyrsos

---

[1] Cf. *Kyk.* 5-8; *inf.* sec. iv.
[2] *Inf.* IX. vii. *Indoletes.*
[3] Vs. 306-0.
[4] Cf. V. 550; *Phoinis*, 228; *Iph. in Tau.* 1243; *Ion.* 716, 1125; Soph. *Oid. Tyr.* 1105; *Antig.* 1120; Aristoph. *Neph.* 603; *sup.* IV. i. 2.
[5] Vide *inf.* VIII. ii. *Wand.*
[6] Hesych. in voc. *Bakchos.*
[7] Vide *inf.* VIII. ii. *Spots.*
[8] Cf. *Job*, xiv. 7, xviii. 16; *Prov.* xi. 28; *Is.* xi. 1, xiv. 19, xxv. 5; *Jer.* xxiii. 5; *Zech.* iii. 8, vi. 12.
[9] Cf. *Mythol. of the Aryan Nations*, ii. 114.
[10] *Chrysopes*, V. 553. Vide *inf.* IX. iv.

along Olympos.' ' The vivifying sun.'[1] When the Bakchai strike the earth with the thyrsos water springs up and honey drops from the ivy-wreathed wands,[2] illustrative of the power which controls ' the fatness of the earth beneath.'

' Dionysos is inferior to none of the gods.'[3] An apparently absurd assertion as applied to Dionysos in connection with the Hellenik Pantheon, but by no means unintelligible when his earlier history is considered, in tracing which we find him identified with Iao the Supreme and Zagreus ' highest of all gods.'

' Dionysos, a god to men both most terrible and most mild.'[4] Terrible to his enemies or the rejectors of his cult, and in his sterner aspects; mild, as a source of joy, to his friends and worshippers. This two-faced aspect has already been noticed.[5]

' The secret dances of the god.'[6] Pentheus having seen the Bakchai performing these, is to be slain, lest he should reveal them. They formed an important part of the mystic ritual as noticed.[7]

Subsection III.—The Sufferings of Dionysos.

' Aiai, I begin the Bakchik strain,'[8] exclaimed the widowed queen of Troia, on seeing the dead body of her son Polydoros. Although Bakchik song was usually joyous and lively, yet it had also a sad and melancholy

---

[1] Cf. *Mythol. of the Aryan Nations,* ii. 102 *et seq.*
[2] V. 704 *et seq.*
[3] V. 777.
[4] V. 861.
[5] *Sup.* II. i. 4, 8; cf. Plout. *Anton.* ' When Antony entered Ephesus, the women, in the dress of Bacchanals, and men and boys habited like Pan and the Satyrs, marched before him. Nothing was to be seen through the whole city but ivy crowns, and spears wreathed with ivy, harps, flutes, and pipes, while Antony was hailed by the name of Bacchus:

'Bacchus! ever kind and free!'
And such, indeed, he was to some; but to others he was savage and severe. Asia in some measure resembled the city mentioned by Sophocles, that was at once filled with the perfumes of sacrifices, songs, and groans.'
[6] V. 1100.
[7] *Sup.* subsec. i.
[8] *Hek.* 684.

phase, which could never have been the case if Dionysos had been merely a rustic god of vineyard merriment. Thus we find that Kleisthenes despot of Sikyon, for political purposes, put an end to the tragic choruses with which the Argeian hero Adrastos had been honoured on account of his calamities, and transferred them to Dionysos,[1] whose mythic history must therefore have contained accounts of suffering and woe.

The identity of Dionysos in his solar phase with Adonis has already been noticed,[2] and at this same city of Sikyon the poetess Praxilla (cir. B.C. 452), called one of the nine lyric Muses, sang of the joys and sorrows of the beautiful Syrian youth.[3] 'The leaders of the wild irregular Comus, which danced the Dithyramb, bewailed the sorrows of Bacchus, or commemorated his wonderful birth,'[4] for 'the worship of Dionysus partook of the same variations as that of the sun-god; and, on the one hand, his sufferings and mischances were bewailed.'[5] Adonis, the heat and vigour of the summer sun and the fruitfulness of the earth produced by the warm beams, is doomed to die nightly, and more particularly to perish by the wound inflicted by the stern wintry powers;[6] and so the story of death and resurrection is mirrored on the face of nature, and myths relating to these changes arise spontaneously in the mind from contemplation of the external. The fate of Dionysos Zagreus torn in pieces by the Titanes,[7] admits of a similar explanation. 'This slaughter and cutting up of Zagreus is the stripping off of leaves and fruits in the gloomy autumn, which leaves only the heart or trunk of the tree to give birth to the foliage

---

[1] Herod. v. 67.
[2] *Sup.* II. iii. 5.
[3] Cf. Prax. *Frag.* ii.; Zenob. *Paroi.* iv. 21; Müller, *Doric Race*, i. 420.
[4] *Theatre of the Greeks*, 39.
[5] *Ibid.* 23.
[6] Cf. *Mythol. of the Aryan Nations*, ii. 7, 113.
[7] Paus. viii. 37; Nonnos, vi. 165 *et seq.*

of the coming year.'[1] These changes in natural phenomena afford the first ground-work for the sufferings of Dionysos and the laments of Adonis,[2] and sufficiently, but probably not exhaustively, explain the myth. Connected with this mournful Bakchik strain is the song called 'the Linus, which is sung under various names, not only in Egypt, but in Phoenicia, in Cyprus, and in other places; and which seems to be exactly the same as that in use among the Greeks, and by them called Linus. It appears to have been sung from the very earliest times. The Linus in Egypt is called Maneros;'[3] and the mythic Maneros was said to have been the only son of the first Kamic king, and to have died in early youth, these 'dirge-like strains' being lamentations for his untimely death. But the Linos-song, like the Bakchik strains generally, was both lively and mournful; and so in the former phase was suitable to banquets.[4] The song of Maneros was sung by Kamic peasants, and Maneros was also said to have been the inventor of husbandry;[5] a circumstance which links him with Uasar, 'whose sufferings and death were the great mystery of the Egyptian religion;'[6] and, like those of Dionysos, Adonis and Zagreus, had a kosmogonical aspect or basis.[7] According to Pausanias, Uasi bewails Uasar at the season when the Nile begins to rise, and the peasants used to say that the tears of the goddess caused the increase of the river.[8] 'The death of Osiris was piously lamented by Isis and her sister Nephthys; and once a year the Egyptians joined their priests in a melancholy procession through the streets, singing a doleful

---

[1] *Mythol. of the Aryan Nations*, ii. 204. The Zagreus myth is noticed at length *inf.* IX. vi.
[2] Of. *Ezek.* viii. 14; Aristoph.*Lysist.* 380; Sappho, *Frags.* lxii. lxiii. cviii.
[3] Herod. ii. 70.
[4] Plout. *Peri Is.* xvii.
[5] Ioul Polydeuk. iv. 7.
[6] Sir G. Wilkinson in Rawlinson's *Herodotus*, ii. 220.
[7] Of. Bunsen, *Egypt's Place*, i. 451.
[8] Paus. x. 32.

ditty called the Maneros or *Song of Love*, which was to console the goddess for the death of her husband.'[1] Pausanias also gives an account of Linos,[2] whose foreign origin appears in (1) his connection with Thrake; (2) his being called a son of Poseidon; and (3) his unsuccessful contest with Apollon, a divinity who shrank from entering the lists with his sire.[3] 'When Linos was dead, mourning for him prevailed in every barbarous nation, so that even among the Egyptians there is a song *Linos*; and the Egyptians call the song in their own language *Maneros*.[4] But the Hellenes, and Homeros, who was acquainted with the sufferings of Linos, make the song Hellenik.' He then applies *Il*. xviii. 570 to Linos,[5] and continues, 'Pamphos, who composed the most ancient hymns for the Athenians, on account of the excessive grief for Linos, called him Oitolinos, Ill-fated Linos. And afterwards the Lesbian Sappho, having learnt the name Oitolinos from the verses of Pamphos, sings of Adonis together with Oitolinos.'[6] We have here a number of lamented personages—Dionysos, Zagreus, Linos, Maneros, Uasar, Adonis, Tammuz, and a common dirge-like Song prevailing alike in all the countries where they were supposed to have lived and where their cult obtained. We have also a kosmogonical basis for the idea, supplied by the changes of the seasons and the ever-varying phenomena of the world, the myth at one time appearing more in a solar, and at another more in a chthonian aspect. Being torn or cut to pieces is a fate commonly ascribed to Dionysos and the personages con-

---

[1] Sharpe, *Egyptian Mythol.* 10; cf. Bunsen, *Egypt's Place*, ii. 65.
[2] Cf. *sup.* II. iii. 1.
[3] *Il.* xxi. 462 *et seq.*
[4] 'In Egypt they have a tradition that their ancient chants are the composition of the goddess Isis.' (Platon, *Laws*, ii.)
[5] *Linon*, however, is generally supposed to mean the flaxen lyre-chord.
[6] Paus. ix. 29; cf. Sappho, *Frag.* cviii.; Ais. *Ag.* 121, 139; Soph. *Aias.* 638; Eur. *Herak. Mainom.* 348; *Orest.* 1395, where *Ailinon* is said to be a Barbarian word.

nected with him, such as Zagreus, Pentheus, Orpheus,[1] Uasar,[2] and others.

Demosthenes is quoted as saying that the 'spotted fawns were torn in pieces for a certain mystic reason,' which we are informed ' was in imitation of the sufferings of Dionysos,'[3] and I have noticed [4] the statement of Porphyrios that men were torn in pieces in honour of the god in Chios and Tenedos.[5] Taking the whole facts of the case into consideration, it may be fairly concluded that, in addition to the kosmogonico-solar basis of the myth, there were circumstances connected with the savage nature of the cult of the god, and with the opposition which it may at different times and in various countries have encountered, which formed a secondary or additional basis for the traditions of the sufferings of its personified head. The very old notion of martyr and self-sacrificing divinities, which we find in the writings of Berosos, Sanchouniathon, and other ancient Kosmogonists,[6] is doubtless also another aspect of the same general idea.

Subsection IV.—The Kyklops.

In the *Kyklops* of Euripides we have a solitary surviving specimen of Hellenik satyrical drama; the story is taken from the Homerik *Kyklopeia*,[7] with the introduction of Seilenos and a chorus of Satyrs who have been made captives by Polyphemos, and who, after his eye has been put out, escape with Odysseus. In a former work [8] I endeavoured to illustrate in some degree the

---

[1] Cf. Apollod. i. 3; Ovid, *Metam.* xi. 1.
[2] Diod. i. 21, 22; Plout. *Peri Is.* xlii.
[3] Souidas and Photios, in voc. *Nebridzon.*
[4] *Sup.* subsect ii.
[5] Cf. Vase No. 788 a, *Brit. Mus.*

Catal. where Dionysos is represented as holding in his hands the two halves of a fawn which he has just torn asunder. Cf. Eur. *Bak.* 734 et seq.
[6] Cf. Bunsen, *Egypt's Place,* iv.284 et seq.
[7] *Od.* ix.
[8] *Posidon,* viii.-xiv.

history of the obscure family of the Kyklopes, to explain the name, and to shew the real connection between the three great branches of the Family—the Builders, the Pastors, and the Metallurgists. I am glad to observe that Mr. W. W. Lloyd confirms my view that Homeros places the Kyklopes on the Libyan coast,[1] and not in Sikelia, though as he truly observes, 'later traditions agreed very unanimously that the Cyclops dwelt about Aetna.'[2] Mr. Lloyd offers another explanation of the story, *i.e.*, 'that this tribe of Cyclopes, each with a single eye, dwelling in hollow caves on mountain summits round about Polyphemus himself, were originally personifications of the clustered cones and craters that surround and make up Mount Aetna.'[3] 'The burnt-out eye of Polyphemus' is 'the suggestion of the crater of the bellowing mountain in violent eruption amidst blazing forests;' and the rocks cast at Odysseus are 'masses ejected by the volcano.' But if the Kyklops lived on the Libyan coast, what is the connection between him and Aetna? 'The Cyclops of Homer,' remarks Mr. Lloyd, 'it need scarcely be mentioned, knows nothing of the thunder-forging function assigned in other mythology-palpable expression of the electric phenomena of a volcanic outburst.' Then, of course, the 'Cyclops of Homer' was not a personification of Mount Aetna, and his story is independent of any explanation based on the local geography of Sikelia.

The play commences with the customary Euripidean Prologue, which is spoken by the captive Seilenos. The following extracts will illustrate the connection between him and Dionysos. 'The heavenly powers become gods

---

[1] Mr. Gladstone, after alluding to his previous opinion that the Kyklopes 'inhabited the south-eastern coast of Italy,' observes, 'But Mr. Brown, soon after, established to my satisfaction the *habitat* of the Kyklopes on the coast of Africa.'(*Homeric Synchronism*, 242–3.)
[2] *Hist. of Sicily*, 15.
[3] *Ibid.* 16.

of the earth, and it was reasonable that the co-ordinate natural causes of productiveness should also have their representatives, who would form the attendants of the personified primal causes of the same effects. The Sun-god therefore, when he roamed the earth, was properly attended by the Sileni, the deities presiding over running streams.'[1] 'The name of Seilenos as a water sprite suggests to Preller its affinity with the Italian Silanus, a word for gushing or bubbling water. As the dweller in the fertilising streams, he can bestow draughts of wonderful sweetness; and the wine which his son Evanthes gives to Odysseus is pronounced by Polyphemos to be more delicious than honey. As such, also, he is the guardian and teacher of Dionysos, for from the life-giving streams alone can the grape acquire its sweetness and its power.'[2]

'O Bromios, on thy account I have ten thousand labours, both now and when in youth my frame was strong. First, when maddened by Here you departed from your nurturers the mountain nymphs.'[3] The Aryan goddess Here, wife of Zeus, is naturally hostile to the Semitic Dionysos his illegitimate offspring,[4] whom she afflicted with madness,[5] and whose mother Semele had perished by her artifice.[6] Mythic hatred between divinities is generally illustrative of early opposition between the supporters of rival rituals, and, as Here is an undoubtedly Hellenik personage the circumstance, like a thousand others, illustrates incidentally the non-Hellenik origin of the worship of Dionysos. Thus, Grote notes from Ploutarchos that 'there was a standing antipathy between the priestesses and the religious establishments of Here and Dionysos;'[7] and similarly Argos, the

[1] *Theatre of the Greeks*, 26.
[2] *Mythology of the Aryan Nations*, ii. 318; cf. *sup.* II. iii. 5, IV. iii. 2.
[3] Vs. 1–4; cf. *sup.* II. i. 5, IV. i. 3.
[4] Cf. *Bak.* 286.
[5] Apollod. iii. 5.
[6] Cf. *Bak.* 9; Ovid, *Metam.* iii. 253 *et seq.*
[7] *Hist. of Greece*, i. 34.

favourite abode of the goddess,[1] who is represented as being 'a deity of all others the most exclusively and intensely national,'[2] 'for a long time wholly abstained from the worship of Bacchus.'[3] Euripides represents the Tyrsenik pirates[4] as having attacked Dionysos at the instigation of Here.[5]

'And afterwards being thy companion in arms on thy right hand in the battle of the spear against the earth-born race, having struck Enkelados on the midst of his target, I slew him with the spear.'[6] The prowess of Dionysos in the Gigantomachia, or Battle-with-the-Giants, has already been alluded to.[7] Vase No. 788, *Brit. Mus. Catalogue* represents Dionysos, spear-armed, with the kanthar, ivy-branch, and panther's skin, attacking the giants Eurytos and Rhoitos. The story of the Giants seems to have been confused with that of the Titanes. 'Tatans,' or 'Tutuns,' according to Bunsen, 'is the Egyptian designation for every kind of Demiurge or creative divinity.'[8] Homeros and Hesiodos are both quite ignorant of any contest between the Giants and the Gods;[9] and the Giants of the former are described as savage, godless tribes living in the Outer-world.[10] It would be somewhat beyond the present subject to speak of the Titanes, and therefore observing that the Gigantomachia is a comparatively late myth, and a mere repetition of the War between Zeus and Titanik powers, we may conclude, with Professor Ruskin, that the Giants, whether the legends relating to them have a further meaning and foundation or not, represent 'the troublous powers of the earth,'[11] volcanic or otherwise. But the true early Hellenik portrait of the god is not Dionysos

---

[1] Cf. *Il.* iv. 8, 52; Paus. ii. 22.
[2] *Juv. Mundi*, 234.
[3] Müller, *Doric Race*, i. 418.
[4] *Sup.* II. i. 4.
[5] V. 11.
[6] Vs. 5–8.
[7] *Sup.* subsec. ii.
[8] *God in Hist.* ii. 36.
[9] Cf. *Theog.* 185.
[10] Cf. *Od.* vii. 59, 206.
[11] *Queen of the Air*, i. 15.

fighting successfully on the side of Aryan divinities against opposing Giants, but the timid Being, nymph-nurtured, flying from the infuriate Lykourgos. When, however, his cult becomes established, and he himself is received into the anthropomorphic family of Zeus, and when the fierce phases of the Dionysiak concept are understood and appreciated, he can be enrolled not unfitly in the army of the Olympik King, from whom his prowess in the fight is said to have drawn the exclamation, 'Well done, son!' Seilenos, the faithful attendant of Dionysos, is naturally his assistant in the struggle, but considered in his degraded form as a drunken old satyr, his tale would necessarily appear to be a mere idle boast, and is here ridiculed as such, in the same way that Dionysos in his effeminate and voluptuous character appears to be eminently unwarlike, and by the Comic Poets is held up to derision for his cowardice.[1]

Chorus of Satyrs. 'These things [*i.e.*, Kyklopean servitude and its adjuncts] are not Bromios, these things are not choric-dances and thyrsos-bearing Bakchants, not the clang [2] of tambourines . . . not Nysa [3] with a Nymph. Iakchos, Iakchos,[4] I sing a lay to Aphrodite.' [5] *Alalagmos* is derived from *Alale*, a loud cry or shout, usually the shout of battle, a word seemingly akin to numerous familiar terms.[6]

Od. Not gold, but the drink of Dionysos I bear.
And in truth Maron gave the drink to me; son of the god.

[1] Cf. Aristoph. *Bat.* 283 *et seq.*
[2] *Alalagmos.*
[3] Cf. sec. ii. 1.
[4] Cf. the invocation of the Chorus of the Initiated in the *Batrachoi.* 'Iakchos, O Iakchos! Raise the flaming torches shaking them in your hands, Iakchos, O Iakchos! of nightly mystic rites, light-bringing star.' (*Bat.* 339-41.) An allusion, amongst other things, to Dionysos as the Sun of the Under-world. The Dionysos of Aristophanes, when the latter is serious, exactly corresponds with the god as he appears in the Tragics.
[5] Vs. 63-70.
[6] Cf. Eleleu, Ais. *Prom. Des.* 896. Dionysos Eleleus the Shouter; Hallili, the hunting shout; Hallelu-jah.

Sei. He whom once I nursed in these enfolding arms.
Od. The son of Bakchios.[1]

'I had a goat's skin of dark wine,' says Odysseus, 'which Maron, son of Euanthes, gave me, priest of Apollo, who presided over Ismaros.'[2] Ismaros is a town on the southern coast of Thrake close to Maroneia, in the region inhabited by the Homerik Kikones, and renowned from the most ancient times for its wine-producing character.[3] Maron is probably a personification of the place, like Boiotos and Tirynthos, and becomes a son or descendant of Dionysos from his connection with wine. Professor Mayor in his note on *Od.* ix. 197, has collected various references to him,[4] and he is represented by Diodoros as being a companion of Uasar.'[5] 'Many centuries after he used to appear to the Thrakian vinedressers, young and delicate, redolent of wine, tending their vines.'[6]

Subsection V.—Dionysiak Allusions in the Apospasmatia.

There are several Dionysiak allusions in the *Apospasmatia*, or Fragments of Euripides, which may be briefly noticed. In the *Antigone*,[7] we read, 'O Dionysos, in no wise endured by mortals.' This may have formed part of some protest against the cult of the god, but the sense of the passage is doubtful. In the *Archelaos*,[8] the god is invoked as 'Kisseus, King of the fruitful land,' *i.e.*, Boiotia, always proverbial for fertility; 'the champaign gleams with fire.' The latter line is illustrated and explained by Aristophanes, who writes, similarly, 'the meadow shines with flame,'[9] when describing the torch-dance of the Initiated in the sacred field. In the

---

[1] Vs. 130-43.
[2] *Od.* ix. 196-8.
[3] Cf. Niebuhr, *Ancient Ethnog.* i. 233; sup. II. i. 1.
[4] Cf. *Narrative of Odysseus*, i. 108.
[5] Diod. i. 18.
[6] Cf. Philostratos, *Heroika*, iii. 16. Nonnos, ix. 121.
[7] *Frag.* xviii.
[8] *Frag.* iii.
[9] *Bat.* 344.

Likymnios,[1] the god is addressed as 'O laurel-loving King Bakchos, Paian Apollon, skilled-lyre-player,' which is quoted by Macrobius[2] to illustrate his theory of the identity of the two divinities,[3] which, however, it by no means necessarily implies, and which the context would probably have rebutted. The connection of Dionysos with Apollon and Delphoi has already been noticed. Porphyrios[4] has preserved a curious passage from the *Kretes*,[5] addressed by the Chorus to Minos:—

'Son of Phoinikian-sprung Tyre, child of Europe and of the great Zeus, King of hundred-citied Krete[6] ... we strive after a holy life from the time when we have become a mystic of the Idaian Zeus, and having fulfilled the life of the night-wandering Zagreus, and the raw-flesh-eating feasts, and holding up torches to the mountain mother [Kybele], and having been purified, Bakchos of the Kouretes I invoked. And clad in white, I fly the race of mortals and a tomb not approaching them, and I have been guarded against the eating of living food.'

Here again, as before, we note the joint ritual of Kybele, Dionysos, and the Kouretes;[7] and Zagreus and Bakchos, nocturnal divinities, appearing together like a double star. There is also a clear intimation that the Mystics enacted the legendary history of the Rape of Persephone, according to which Iakchos assisted Demeter in her search for her daughter, and lighted her way with a torch kindled at Mount Aetna. Demeter having, as was noticed, become identified with Kybele, the Mystics who personate Iakchos and his companions,[8] are described as holding up their torches to the latter, while they appear also to have imitated Dionysos in his raw-

---

[1] *Frag*. iv.
[2] *Sat*. i. 18.
[3] *Sup*. II. iii. 2.
[4] *Peri Apoch*. iv. 19.
[5] *Frag*. ii.
[6] Cf. *Il*. ii. 649.
[7] *Sup*. subsec. ii.
[8] Cf. Aristoph. *Bat*. 340 et seq.

flesh-eating propensities.[1] Graves are avoided, because death causes a temporary, or at least an apparent, extinguishment of the flaming torch of life, a fragment of natural symbolism which has continued even to our own times, as shewn by the reversed torches sculptured on modern tombs. One of the first questions asked the candidates for initiation in the Mysteries was whether they had fasted, the state of abstinence being considered most suitable for the reception or supposed reception of supernatural communications.[2]

SECTION IV.

EIKON OF THE TRAGIK DIONYSOS.

The Dionysos of the Tragics is a horned stranger, whose original home is the mysterious Nysa, deep in the Outer-world. He is a solar divinity, Chrysomitres the Golden-crowned and Chrysopes the Golden-faced, the vivifying sun whose warm beams cause the earth to bring forth life and loveliness. He is a phallic, thyrsos-bearing, and serpent-crowned god, connected with the goat and the bull, the latter an especial emblem of vigour and productiveness. He is fierce and savage in origin, and to opponents has something of Ares in him, and appears as Omestes the Raw-flesh-eating and ferocious. He is master of prophetic power, of furious inspiration, and of that phrensied mind which can pierce the secrets of futurity. And, above all, he is the kosmogonic Demiurge, leader of the aërial chorus of the starry hosts, lord of the earth-life and reproductive power of nature; who,

---

[1] Vide *sup.* subsec. ii.
[2] Cf. *Acts.* x. 10; Porphyrios, *Peri Apoches.*

although he may die and be torn to pieces, yet, as Kisseus the Ivied, arises sun-like to immortal life, and reappears as the face of nature reclad in the green mantle of spring. He has arrived in Hellas as a stranger from the regions beyond, and first of Hellenik cities comes to Thebai, the metropolis of Bakchanals; and is made king of the fruitful Boiotia, where his cult is established in the mythic era of Pentheus. As many of his phases correspond with those of the two great Aryan divinities, Apollon and Demeter, he is by turns their rival and associate; and, at length, when firmly established in his new home, is enthroned with them in the joint rituals of Delphoi and Eleusis, in the latter of which he appears as Iakchos the Torchbearer. So closely are Semitic and Aryan mythologies intermixed, that while Apollon assumes a Semitic phase as Karneios the Horned Sun, Demeter becomes identified with Kybele the Great Goddess of the East. As the god of the wandering Phoenicians, the Axiokersos or Worthy-horned-god of the mystic Samothrakian ritual, the sacred Bull of Elis, Dionysos is himself a wanderer; the associate of such Oriental beings as the Kabeiroi, Kouretes and Korybantes, connected with the fatness of the earth beneath, with Seilenos and the Satyroi. As he suffers, so is he lamented in the Linos-Maneros dirge throughout all the countries adjoining the Eastern Mediterranean. The faun-skin, the thyrsos, the pine-cone, the wheel, the flowing locks with their mystic symbolism, are portions of his cult and illustrate his nature; in which the first principles, attributes, and adjuncts of materiality, light, heat, sound, motion, change, vigour, decay, and renewal are signified and displayed. Savage and sensuous, his human sacrifices, repugnant to Aryan instincts, are by degrees abolished in Hellenik regions; and his orgiastic revelry, gross and boisterous though it may be, yet never reaches in his new home the monstrous excesses of his Phoenician devotees.

Identical with the grim and shadowy night-wandering and chthonian Zagreus, highest of divinities, he is inferior to none of the gods; and is to mortals at once most terrible and most mild. Lastly, and perhaps least, as the lord of material enjoyment, he is a nymph-chaser and patron of the vineyard. Such, in brief, is the Dionysos of the Tragiks; and the attempt to dwarf him down into a mere wine-god becomes, under the analysis, a hopeless impossibility. How exactly this portraiture agrees with that given by the Theologers and the Lyric Poets may be easily perceived. Hellenik genius and imagination undoubtedly added vastly to the Dionysiak concept, which would never in Semitic regions alone have grown into such elaborate variegations, and assumed such phases of delicate beauty; but the original idea and root of the matter came, as we shall see still more plainly in the sequel, across the empire of Poseidon and from the birthplace of the Sun-god: and he who is wearied with the familiar aroma of the Aryan field of research may stimulate and refresh his jaded senses with new perfumes wafted from the shores of the Euphrates and the Nile.

CHAPTER V.

THE DIONYSOS OF HERODOTOS.

SECTION I.

DIONYSOS AND THRAKE.

THE connection between Dionysos and Thrake has already been partially noticed,[1] as illustrated in the episode of Lykourgos, in the vine-growing character of the country, and in the links between Orpheus, Mousaios, Eumolpos, Linos, and other similar personages of Thrakian origin or associations and the Dionysiak myth. It is not, therefore, surprising to find this connection illustrated by the writings of the earliest of Hellenik historians who, when describing the manners and customs of the Thrakians, 'the most powerful people in the world, except, of course, the Indians,'[2] states that they worship three gods 'Ares, Dionysos, and Artemis.'[3] The first point for consideration is, How is the statement to be understood, and what divinities are represented by these Hellenik names? The Thrakians mainly, or perhaps entirely, belonged to the Indo-European family of nations, and were a kind of coarse copy of the Hellenes. It is therefore extremely probable that their Ares was identical with the Hellenik divinity of that name, who from the earliest times is

[1] *Sup.* II. i. iii.   [2] Herod. v. 3.   [3] Ibid. v. 7.

represented as connected with Thrake.¹ 'In Thrace clearly was his home. Thrace appears to have been known by the name of Aria. Berkel connects the two names together.'² But if the rude savage Ares, the 'Crusher,'³ is a suitable divinity for the warlike and barbarous Thrakians, it will not be supposed that such a delicate and peculiar concept as the Hellenik Artemis would obtain amongst them;- and accordingly we find that the real name of their so-called Artemis was Bendis,⁴ apparently a darker featured and more savage counterpart of the chaste huntress-queen, but yet probably a divinity of Aryan origin. Besides these two Aryo-Thrakian personages, we find a third, called by Herodotos Dionysos. Are we to understand by this appellation some divinity of the Thrakian Pantheon who was supposed to correspond with the Hellenik Dionysos, or the god himself? We may in this case, I think, consider that Herodotos was undoubtedly correct in his identification, and for the following reasons: (1) The Thrakian Ares seems to have been identical with the Hellenik god of that name, and Bendis is practically a coarser Artemis; the probability, therefore, is that the Thrakian Dionysos was identical with the Hellenik. (2) As Homeros expressly notices the introduction of the Dionysiak cult on the northern shores of the Aigaion, we are not surprised to find it there in the time of Herodotos. (3) The important non-Aryan element in

---

¹ Cf. *Od.* viii. 301. Thus Gray, with his usual classic propriety—
'On Thracia's hills the Lord of War
Has curbed the fury of his car.'

² *Juv. Mun.* 297. Canon Rawlinson seems somewhat inclined to connect the name Ares with Aria, a Semitic title of Nergal, the Kaldean Mars (*Anct. Mons.* i. 138); but, on the whole, the weight of evidence is most decidedly in favour of the Aryan origin of Ares and his name.

³ Cf. *Mythol. of the Aryan Nations*, i. 32.

⁴ Hesych. in voc. *Bendis.* So Strabo speaks of the Thrakian rites called Bendideia (Strabo, x. 3). Her cult was introduced at Athenai towards the close of the Peloponnesian War. 'I wanted to see in what manner they would celebrate the festival of Bendis, which was a new thing. The procession of the inhabitants... was ... exceeded in beauty by that of the Thracians' (Platon. *Repub.* i.).

Thrake, which contained Phoenician colonies, such as Abdera[1] and Oisyme, besides the adjoining island of Thasos, is illustrated in part by the presence of a Semitic divinity. (4) The vine-growing character of Thrake, and the notorious drinking habits of the Thrakians,[2] are in perfect accordance with the prevalence of the Dionysiak cult, especially in its important vinal phase. The more purely Semitic features of the Wine-god would naturally become comparatively obscured in non-Semitic Thrake as in non-Semitic Hellas, whilst his riotous and orgiastic character would harmonise with the savage carousals of the Thrakian tribes. An important appendage of Thrake is the island of Samothrake, the Thrakian Samos of Homeros, and which lies about thirty-five miles from the mouth of the Hebros, a river 'frequently mentioned in connection with the worship of Dionysos,' and on the banks of which Orpheus, according to mythic legend, was torn in pieces by the Thrakian Bakchai.[3] Now Samothrake was the head-quarters of the mysterious worship of the Semitic Kabeiroi,[4] one of whom was the Axiokersos or Worthy-horned-god who, as we have seen, is identical with Dionysos Taurokeros.[5] Here again we see Dionysos firmly planted in Thrakian regions. But Herodotos says that the Kabeirik worship was Pelasgik,[6] and this is undoubtedly true, but not the whole truth. The Pelasgoi, who have given so much trouble to the investigators of early Hellenik history, 'formed apparently the first wave in the flood of Indo-European emigration, which, passing from the Asiatic continent, broke upon the islands and the coasts of Greece.'[7] At an exceedingly remote

---

[1] The Teian colonisation of this place was a refoundation. Cf. Herod. i. 168. Dr. Wm. Smith, *Ancient Atlas*: *Greek and Phoenician Colonies*.

[2] Cf. Hor. *Car.* i. 27, ii. 7.

[3] Cf. Ovid. *Metam.* xi. 50.

[4] Cf. Herod. ii. 57; *sup.* IV. i. 3, iii. 2, *inf.* X. i.

[5] Vide *inf.* IX. iii.

[6] 'The Samothracians received these mysteries from the Pelasgi' (Herod. ii. 51).

[7] Rawlinson, *Herodotus*, i. 547.

period this Aryan element coalesced with the contiguous Semitic element; and Nature-worship, combining with monotheistic traditions and remnants, and with a more spiritual, although perhaps not really higher, view of the visible kosmogony, produced a strange, hybrid, esoteric, and highly mysterious, cult, which aided by the superstitious reticence of the pious ancients, has, even to the present, to a great extent defied investigation. But the task of analyzing these thoughts and theories of the earlier children of the earth is not only by no means hopeless, but becomes ever more and more within the reach of effort, as linguistic and historical research with increasing penetrative power probe the *intima regna* of the Past and, aided by philosophy, reveal and illustrate alike the inner and outer histories of the human race. It is possible that the Turanian element also was represented, to some extent, in the cult of Samothrake; since 'the *first* wave of population which passed into Europe was, beyond a doubt, Scythic or Turanian.'[1] Another passage[2] illustrates the connection between Dionysos and Thrake. Khshayarsha,[3] passing Maroneia[4] and Abdera, marches through the country of various Thrakian tribes, including the Homerik Kikones, the Edonoi,[5] and the Satrai. These latter 'are the Thracians who have an oracle of Bacchus in their country which is situated upon their highest mountain range,' *i.e.*, the Rhodopeian chain, which formed one side of the valley of the Nestos, as the Pangaion hills, similarly specially dedicated to the joint cult of Dionysos and Lykourgos, constituted the other. 'The Bessi, a Satrian race, deliver the oracles; but the prophet, as at Delphoi, is a woman; and her answers are not harder to read.'[6] The name Bessoi, as Canon Rawlinson

---

[1] Rawlinson, *Herodotus*, iii. 430.
[2] Herod. vii. 109–11.
[3] Xerxes.
[4] *Sup.* IV. iii. 4.
[5] *Sup.* IV. i. 2.
[6] As to the prophetic Dionysos, cf. IV. iii. 2.

notes, 'is probably connected with the title Bassareus'[1] ascribed to the Thrakian Dionysos as clad in the 'Edonian faun-skins.' Bassareus is itself connected with one or more of the Semitic words, *basar*, ' flesh,' especially in its sensuous and sensual aspect; *basar*, the 'unripe grape'; and *batzar*, ' to fortify,' possibly with all of them, for, as I have observed elsewhere, 'Occult symbolism has frequently availed itself, either of two words of similar sound, or of one word of manifold meaning.'[2] Here, for instance, we have a perfect plenitude of idea comprised in the epithet Bassareus. For, to take only one of the three Semitic words above mentioned, *basar*, ' flesh.' The root-idea of the word appears to be, ' that which is spread abroad,' Dionysos the all-pervading material Demiurge. It then comes to mean flesh, as distinguished from bones, blood, and skin, and hence is peculiarly appropriate to Dionysos the Earth-spirit. By an easy transition it signifies fleshly appetite, and so is again pre-eminently suitable to a sensuous divinity; and, lastly, it has a peculiar phallic meaning, the appropriateness of which in the connection needs on illustration. The term Bassara is actually used by Lykophron[3] for a courtezan. But this latter word, as I noticed before, is said, and doubtless truly, to have been the Thrakian equivalent of the Hellenik *alopex*, and the connection is probably as follows;—the root-idea of *basar*, ' that which is spread abroad,' becomes connected with the enfolding, all-covering spotted garments of the Bakchik devotees, whether made of leopard, jackal, faun, fox, or any other spotted skins, according to the various countries in which the cult obtained. This spotted skin, as we have seen,[4] represented the starry host spread out over the earth; and as Bassareus is the demiurgic divinity clad in

---

[1] Rawlinson, *Herodotus*, iv. 79; cf. Hor. *Car.* i. 18, 'Candido Bassareu;' Tibullus, III. vi. 1, 'Candide Liber.' *Sup.* IV. i. 2.

[2] *Poseidon*, xxiv.
[3] V. 771.
[4] *Sup.* IV. i. 2.

his spotted starry robe, so Bassara, not unnaturally, comes to be used as the name of one of the local animals connected with that robe.[1] The jackal, like the goat, was a vine-injuring animal.[2]

SECTION II.

DIONYSOS IN THE NORTH.

The Hellenik colonists of the shores of the Pontos Euxeinos diffused the Great Dionysiak Myth, to a considerable extent, among the regions of the remote North. Thus, in the country of the Boudinoi, a Skythik race, who inhabited the region now occupied by the Don Cossacks, was a 'city called Gelonus. Here are temples built in honour of the Grecian gods, and adorned, after the Greek fashion, with images, altars, and shrines, all in wood. There is even a festival, held every third year in honour of Bacchus; at which the natives fall into the Bacchic fury. For the fact is, that the Geloni were anciently Greeks, who, being driven out of the factories along the coast, fled to the Budini and took up their abode with them. They still speak a language half Greek, half Scythian.'[3] But the Skythai themselves appear on the whole to have had a deep abhorrence of Hellenik innovation, and so Anacharsis the Skythian, who introduced the sacred rites of the Mother of the gods from Kyzikos on the Propontis into ' the district called the Woodland, which lies opposite ' the Course of Achilles,' that is, immediately to the west of the Taurik Chersonesos, was slain with an arrow by the Skythik king Saulios,[4] and another innovator, Skylas, although the king of the country, fared no better. 'Aria-

---

[1] Vide *inf.* VIII. ii. *Spots.*
[2] Cf. *Cant.* ii. 15, 'The little foxes that spoil the vines.'
[3] Herod. iv. 108.
[4] Ibid. 76.

pithes, the Scythian king, had several sons, among them this Scylas, who was the child not of a native Scyth, but of a woman of Istria,' a Milesian colony situated at the mouth of the Ister.[1] 'Now when Scylas found himself king of Scythia, as he disliked the Scythic mode of life, and was attached, by his bringing up, to the manners of the Greeks, he made it his usual practice, whenever he came with his army to the town of the Borysthenites, —who, according to their own account, are colonists of the Milesians—to leave the army before the city, and having entered within the walls by himself, and carefully closed the gates, to exchange his Scythian dress for Grecian garments. The Borysthenites kept watch at the gates, that no Scythian might see the king thus apparelled. Scylas, meanwhile, lived exactly as the Greeks, and even offered sacrifices to the gods according to the Grecian rites.' But his doom approached. 'He wanted to be initiated in the Bacchic mysteries, and was on the point of obtaining admission to the rites, when,' what Herodotos calls 'a most strange prodigy' happened, namely, 'his house was struck by lightning from on high, and burnt to the ground. Scylas, nevertheless, went on and received the initiation. Now the Scythians are wont to reproach the Greeks with their Bacchanal rage, and to say that it is not reasonable to imagine there is a god who impels men to madness.' When Skylas was under the Bakchik influence, a Borysthenite, eager to vindicate his creed, privately from a tower in the city showed the chiefs of the Skythai their king ' with the band of revellers, raving like the rest.' A revolt against the innovating monarch at once followed; he took refuge with Sitalkes of Thrake, but was given up by the latter to the Skythai, and at once beheaded.[2] The 'town of the Borysthenites' was

---

[1] 'The Danaw' (Milton).   [2] Herod. iv. 78-80.

situate near the mouth of the Hypanis,[1] not very far from Odessa, and was proudly called by the inhabitants Olbia,[2] the 'Prosperous.' It was also known as Borysthenis, Miletopolis, as being a colony from Miletos in Ionia, and lastly as Sabia or Sauïa.[3] Hence Canon Rawlinson conjectures with great probability that the cult introduced by the Milesian colonists was that of the 'Phrygian Bacchus,' the horned Sabazios or Sabos, who stands by Dionysos as Jupiter by Zeus, representing the same being or concept as regarded by two different nations. To suppose that the Hellenik Dionysos was derived from the Phrygian Sabazios would be as reasonable as to imagine that the Latin Jupiter was the son of the Hellenik Zeus. The two are in each case identical, alike in origin and practically in cult. At some remote period the phallic, horned, solar, serpent-crowned, nocturnal, kosmogonic, dying, and reviving, divinity, known in Phrygia as Sabazios, was introduced there from regions more purely Semitic, in the same way that Dionysos appeared in Hellas as a stranger from the Outer-world. Sabazios was said to have first yoked oxen, and hence to have been represented with horns; his sacreds were performed in secret and at night.[4] In comparatively late times his cult, as that of a distinct divinity, was introduced at Athenai, but was always profligate and discreditable.[5] Bunsen says Sabazios is 'the god Sbat,' the seventh planet, Hadal or Saturn,[6] connected with the horned Kronos or Karnos;[7] and Lydus, when speaking of Dionysos, observes 'The Chaldeans call God Iao,[8] and in the Phoenician language he is often called Sabaoth.'[9] Iao,

---

[1] Boug.
[2] Herod. iv. 18.
[3] Rawlinson, *Herodotus*, iii. 58, Note 1.
[4] Diod. iv. 4.
[5] Cf. Aristoph. *Sphekes*, 10, *Lysist.* 388, *Ornith.* 875; Cic. *De Legibus*, ii. 15.
[6] *Egypt's Place*, iv. 201-208.
[7] Vide *inf.* IX. iii.
[8] *Sup.* II. iii. 2.
[9] *Peri Menôn*, iv. 38.

as we have seen, is identical with Dionysos, and Sbat, Sabaoth, or Tsebaoth the 'Lord of Hosts,' or Sabazios, is the same being, the two together forming the divinity 'Jehovah Sabaw, Iao Sabao,'[1] the Abraxas, or rather Abrasax, of the Gnostics.[2] 'Serpents,' remarks the Rev. G. W. Cox, 'played a prominent part in the rites of Zeus Sabazios, whose worship was practically identical with that of the Syrian Tammuz or Adonis. (The epithet Sabazios, which, like the words Adonai and Melkarth,[3] was imported into Greek mythology, is applied not less to Dionysos than to Zeus.'[4]) The reason of the confusion in idea between Zeus and Sabazios is extremely simple. Each, in his own Pantheon, is the protagonistic divinity and king of the gods; hence, according to the easy logic of antiquity, which in one point of view is correct, they are regarded as identical. But Dionysos, Sabazios,[5] Iao, Tammuz, and Adonis, are in reality identical; being not merely similar and corresponding divinities, but actually various phases of the same concept. The root of the name Sabazios has also been said to be a Persian word *sebs*, signifying *omnia viriditate induens*;[6] this meaning agrees remarkably well with Dionysos as the Spirit of Kosmic Life, but whether there is a real connection between the two words I am unaware.[7]

---

[1] Cooper, *Serpent Myths. of Anct. Egypt*, 17.
[2] C. W. King, *The Gnostics and their remains*, 81.
[3] Vide *inf.* VI. i. 2.
[4] *Mythol. of the Aryan Nations*, ii. 128, Note.
[5] A surname of Dionysos (Hesych. in voc. *Sabazios*. He calls *Sabos* 'Bakchik phrensy').
[6] Vide Hickie's *Aristophanes*, i. 183.
[7] Vide *inf.* VIII. i. *Sabazios*.

SECTION III.

DIONYSOS IN HELLAS.

The following singular story is a remarkable illustration of the Eleusinian cult of Dionysos. 'Dicaeus, the son of Theocyeds, an Athenian, declared, that after the army of Xerxes had, in the absence of the Athenians, wasted Attica, he chanced to be with Demaratus the Lacedaemonian in the Thriasian plain, and that while there he saw a cloud of dust advancing from Eleusis, such as a host of 30,000 men might raise. As he and his companion were wondering who the men, from whom the dust arose, could possibly be, a sound of voices reached his ear, and he thought that he recognized the mystic hymn to Bacchus. Now Demaratus was unacquainted with the rites of Eleusis, and so he enquired of Dicaeus what the voices were saying. Dicaeus made answer—" O, Demaratus! beyond a doubt some mighty calamity is about to befall the king's army! For it is manifest, inasmuch as Attica is deserted by its inhabitants, that the sound which we have heard is an unearthly one, and is now upon its way from Eleusis to aid the Athenians and their confederates. Every year the Athenians celebrate this feast to the Mother and the Daughter; and all who wish, whether they be Athenians or any other Greeks, are initiated. The sound thou hearest is the Bacchic song, which is wont to be sung at that festival." They looked, and saw the dust, from which the sound arose, become a cloud, and the cloud rise up into the air and sail away to Salamis, making for the station of the Grecian fleet. Then they knew that it was the fleet of Xerxes which would suffer destruction.'¹ Such was the tale told by Dicaeus the son of Theocydes; and he appealed for its truth to Demaratus and other eye-witnesses.'² Here Dionysos as the Associate of Demeter and Persephone, assists in the overthrow of the non-hero-worshipping Persians, across whose sun-stricken plains Euripides erroneously asserted that he had come. As a divinity of Semitic origin, he is appropriately opposed to the godless Aryan invaders who plundered and burnt temples and sacred shrines.

Another allusion of Herodotos to the Hellenik cult of Dionysos I have had already occasion to refer to, namely, the conduct of Kleisthenes despot of Sikyon, who abolished the rites performed in honour of Adrastos the Argeian hero, transferring his ritual to Melanippos, with the exception of the tragic choruses, which he assigned to Dionysos.³

The Dionysiak cult was, according to Herodotos, introduced into Hellas by the wise and famous Melampous son of Amytheon, a contemporary of Proitos, the fourteenth in the line of the mythic kings of Argos. 'He it was who introduced into Greece the name of Bacchus, the ceremonial of his worship, and the procession of the phallus. He did not, however, so completely apprehend the whole doctrine as to be able to communicate it entirely, but various sages since his time have carried out his teaching to greater perfection. Still it is certain that Melampous introduced the phallus, and that the Greeks learnt from him the ceremonies which they now practise. For I can by no means allow that it is by mere coincidence that the Bacchic ceremonies in Greece are so nearly the same as the Egyptian—they would then have been more Greek in their character, and less recent in their origin. Much less

---

¹ 'The Athenians assert in their songs that they were assisted by the gods in the battles of Salamis and Marathon' (Paus. viii. 10).
² Herod. viii. 65.
³ Ibid. v. 67; *sup.* III. i. 2.

can I admit that the Egyptians borrowed these customs or any other from the Greeks. My belief is that Melampous got his knowledge of them from Cadmus the Tyrian, and the followers whom he brought from Phoenicia into the country which is now called Boeotia.'[1] Again he says, 'The Greeks regard Hercules, Bacchus, and Pan[2] as the youngest of the gods.'[3] 'To me it is quite manifest that the names of these gods became known to the Greeks after those of their other deities, and that they *count their birth from the time when they first acquired a knowledge of them.*'[4] In these very important passages the great Father of History asserts, in perfect harmony with the Theologers and the Lyric and Tragic Poets, the non-Hellenik or foreign nature of the Dionysiak cult, and its comparatively recent introduction into Hellas. It is perfectly immaterial to the general argument whether such a personage as Melampous ever existed or not, and what amount of confidence is to be placed in the chronology of Herodotos; the main fact remains beyond all question that the latter, like all other Hellenik writers on the subject, believed that Dionysos and his cult came into Hellas from the Outer-world, *i.e.* was Barbarian in origin. Nor was this belief, in the case of Herodotos, merely an inherited tradition; actual researches in the East confirmed and established it to his mind beyond all doubt. His observations that had the Bakchik ceremonies been of Hellenik origin they would have been more Hellenik in character and less recent in their rise, and that the Hellenes counted the birth of gods from the time when they first acquired a knowledge of them, exhibit a far higher critical acumen and more judicious insight into

---

[1] Herod. ii. 40.
[2] The Homerik Hymn to Pan, the son of Hermes, quite confirms this statement of Herodotos. Probably Pan was so considered because his cult was in earlier times chiefly confined to Arkadia; cf. Paus. viii. 36, 54; Herod. vi. 105-6. *Inf.* VII. ii.
[3] Herod. ii. 145. [4] Ibid. 146.

THE DIONYSOS OF HERODOTOS. 175

the subject than has been possessed by a vast number of moderns. It is a perfect vindication, from an Hellenik standpoint, of the method which I have pursued when dealing with the mythic histories of divinities. Thus, in the Homerik Episode of Lykourgos, I noticed that Dionysos is represented as acting as if he were a child, in consequence of his cult being yet of recent introduction, and that in the Episode of the Tyrsenian Pirates, when he has been somewhat longer in Hellenik regions, he is described as a youth. And so, conversely, the practice of Homeros is an illustration and justification of the principle of Herodotos. The reader will observe his opinion that Melampous got his knowledge of the Dionysiak ritual from '*Cadmus the Tyrian, and the followers whom he brought from Phoenicia into Boeotia.*' As he nowhere asserts or implies that the Phoenician ritual was borrowed from Kam, he evidently was not of opinion that the worship of Dionysos originally arose in that country; but I shall have occasion to refer to his views on the question when considering the general connection between Dionysos and Uasar.[1]

SECTION IV.

DIONYSOS AND NYSA.

The usual connection between Dionysos and the mysterious Nysa appears in Herodotos, as in the other authorities whose works have been examined. 'Bacchus, according to the Greek tradition, was no sooner born than he was sewn up in Jupiter's thigh, and carried off to Nysa, above Egypt, in Ethiopia.'[2] Again, he notices

[1] Vide *inf.* sec. v.   [2] Herod. ii. 146.

that 'the Ethiopians bordering upon Egypt, who were reduced by Cambyses, and who dwelt about the sacred city of Nysa, have festivals in honour of Bacchus.'[1] Again, he relates that the sticks of cinnamon are said to come 'from the country in which Bacchus was brought up,'[2] apparently meaning Aithiopia. The Herodotean Nysa is thus deep in the Outer-world.[3] There were evidently very many Hellenik traditions about the situation of Nysa, but, wherever it was supposed to be, it was invariably connected with the Dionysiak cult.[4]

SECTION V.

DIONYSOS AND UASAR.

Subsection I.—Theory of Herodotos on the historic connection between the Divinities of Hellas and Kam.

According to Herodotos, all the Hellenik divinities were 'derived from a foreign source.' The Pelasgoi supplied Here, Hestia, Themis, the Charites, the Nereïdes, and the Dioskouroi, Kastor and Polydeukes. The Libyans introduced Poseidon, and the 'other gods have been known from time immemorial in Egypt.'[5] The principal divinities in his opinion thus common to both Kam and Hellas are Zeus,[6] Artemis,[7] Apollon,[8] Demeter,[9] Athene,[10] Diony-

---

[1] Herod. iii. 97.
[2] Ibid. iii. 111.
[3] Vide IV. ii. 1; VIII. i. *Nysios.* IX. viii.
[4] Vide *inf.* sec. vi.
[5] Herod. ii. 50.
[6] Amen, *Hellenikôs* Ammon.
[7] Sekhet or Pasht, *Hellenikôs* Bubastis.
[8] Har, *Hellenikôs* Horos.
[9] Uasi or Hesi, *Hellenikôs* Isis.
[10] Neith. Cf. Platon. *Timaios.* 'She is called in the Egyptian tongue Neith, and is asserted to be the same whom the Hellenes call Athene.' Bunsen inclined to this view, remarking:—'Athena, *i.e.* Athenaia, may probably be Annith with a second reduplication at the beginning, and the Egyptian N T pro-

sós,[1] Hephaistos,[2] Epaphos,[3] Pan or Mendes,[4] Leto or Bouto,[5] Ares,[6] Hermes,[7] and Herakles.[8] Such is the theory of Herodotos, a most intelligent observer, but ignorant of the ethnic and philological affinities which modern research has established. We are now aware that the Hellenik Pantheon is essentially Aryan, and therefore we should as soon suppose that the Hellenik language was derived from that of Kam as that the Homerik divinities, or even the majority of them, were importations from the Black Country.[9] The following Hellenik personages may be regarded as undoubtedly Aryan in origin and character:—Zeus, Here, Demeter, Athene, Apollon, Artemis, Ares,[10] Persephone,[11] Hermes, Pan, and Herakles.[12] But Poseidon, Dionysos, Hephaistos, Aphrodite, are non-Aryan importations. The effort to prove the entire Hellenik and Homerik Pantheons to be of Aryan origin is an undue extension of the Natural Phenomena Theory, an error which is itself a reaction from, and a result of, the opposite mistakes of former times. The theory, then, of the *absolute* identity of Zeus and Amen, for instance, may be unhesitatingly rejected; but, though distinct concepts, they correspond with one another, each in his respective Pantheon being 'the King of the Gods,' and therefore, in

---

nounced Ne-ith, may represent the most simple and therefore oldest form of it,' (*Egypt's Place*, iv. 272). But he notices 'the claims of the Aryans,' which are doubtless correct, upon the name. Vide Professor Max Müller's beautiful analysis of the epithets of the Dawn-queen. Athene is the Vedic Ahana the Morning.

[1]. Uasar, Heshar, Hesiri (Bunsen), or Asari (P. le Page Renouf, *Egyptian Grammar*, 50), *Hellenikôs* Osiris. In the present Work I have adopted the first of these forms. (Vide Dr. Birch, *Names of the Principal Deities* in Bunsen's *Egypt's Place*, v. 582.)

[2] Ptah.
[3] Hapi, *Hellenikôs* Apis.
[4] Khem.
[5] Maut.
[6] Mandou.
[7] Thoth or Tet.
[8] Khons.
[9] Besides Kam or Khemi, the Black Country, whence Chemistry or the Black Art, Egypt was called Nahai or Sycamore-land and Tameri.
[10] *Sup.* sec. i.
[11] Vide *inf.* VI. ii.
[12] For detailed proof of this the reader is referred to the works of Aryan comparative mythologists.

a sense, they are practically identical. But it is difficult to see even a resemblance between some of the pairs of divinities unified by Herodotos, *e.g.* between Artemis and the cat-headed Pasht.[1] Rejecting, then, the proposed identifications of Zeus with Amen, Artemis with Pasht, Apollon with Har, Demeter with Uasi, Athene with Neith, Pan with Khem, Ares with Mandou, Hermes with Tet, and Herakles with Khons, it will naturally be asked Why is the identity of Dionysos and Uasar to be accepted? If Herodotos admittedly errs in so many instances, is it not probable that here too he is wrong? To this highly proper enquiry, I reply that, in the abstract, it was almost certain from their relative geographical positions the non-Aryan East would exercise an important influence on Hellas; that the requirements of abstract probability are satisfied by the allotment of the far greater number of the personages of Hellenik mythology to Aryan sources; that an analysis of the histories and cult of some Hellenik divinities, *e.g.* Poseidon, Hephaistos, Aphrodite, and Dionysos, exhibits and illustrates a distinctly non-Aryan influence; that the whole course of the enquiry into the Dionysiak cult tends, in a great variety of ways, to show its Semitic character and foreign origin; and lastly, that a comparison between the Dionysiak and Uasarian myths will evidence not only a resemblance, as if they were merely corresponding members of two distinct Pantheons, but from its minute and singular agreement, and that often in obscure and curious points and phases, will necessitate an identity of origin.[2] Thus, two nations may possess a solar cult, and, in the abstract, each may have

---

[1] As to the singular manner in which the Hellenes bestowed the name of Artemis on most dissimilar divinities, vide *inf.* VI. i. 1. No personage is better represented in the British Museum than Ailouros, or 'Le Dieu Chat,' as Montfaucon calls her. Cf. Herod. ii. 66.

[2] Cf. the previously quoted remark of Herodotos, 'I can by no means allow that it is by mere coincidence that the Bacchic ceremonies in Greece are so nearly the same as the Egyptian.'

received and practised it entirely independently of the other. Both see the sun, and both are naturally inclined to adore or reverence it in some way. But if each community honoured it with similar rites and ceremonies, in themselves unique and peculiar, we should unhesitatingly assert that there must have been some contact between them. To deny this would be an outrage upon all probability. And, having these considerations before us, we shall neither rashly say, on the one hand, that the theory of Herodotos respecting the gods of Kam and Hellas is correct as a whole; nor shall we assert, on the other, that the Hellenes being Aryans must have had divinities purely Aryan in origin and none others, and so conclude that any apparent resemblance between Dionysos and Uasar is only illusory, and merely supported by 'the impudent assertions of Egyptian priests'; but, avoiding all excesses produced by the revenges of the whirligig of time, let us rather proceed to dissect patiently the complicated personage before us, knowing that however curious his structure and composition, he will nevertheless, like some strange and hitherto unknown beast or bird, ultimately fall into his place in the natural history of man, and so perhaps supply a link hitherto wanting in the chain of ideas.[1]

Subsection II.—Dionysos considered by Herodotos as identical with Uasar, but the Dionysiak cult not supposed by him to be derived from the Uasarian.

Dionysos, then, is identified by Herodotos with Uasar. 'Osiris, whom they [the Egyptians] say is the Grecian Bacchus.'[2] 'Osiris is named Dionysos by the Greeks.'[3]

---

[1] The view of the identity of Dionysos and Uasar is of course no novelty; but, in its usual presentation, it is nothing more than a correct guess. Satisfactory illustration of the fact is what I shall endeavour to supply.
[2] Herod. ii. 142. [3] Ibid. 144.

But, although the Egyptians and Herodotos affirm the identity of the two divinities, yet the latter nowhere asserts that the Hellenik Dionysiak cult was directly borrowed from the Kamic. For, admitting the identity of the personages, their ritual may, in the abstract, have been severally derived from a third source common to both. Thus, assuming for the sake of argument, that it had a starting point in Kaldea, the cult may have passed in a Dionysiak form into Hellas, and in a Uasarian form into Kam. And this assumption, so far as historic circumstances are at present known, is in substantial accordance with the facts of the case, for there is no evidence of any direct introduction of the Dionysiak cult into Hellas from Kam, and it is generally admitted that the religion and civilization of the Nile Valley were posterior to, and derived from or developed out of, the earlier systems of Western Asia.[1] The fact that this same great cult had a South-western or Kamic branch, and a North-western or Phrygio-Hellenik branch, which includes its developements in Asia Minor, also at once accounts for the differences as well as the similarities of worship of Dionysos and Uasar. As Zeus and Dyaus, although identical, severally bear the stamp of West and East, so Dionysos and Uasar, similarly identical, severally bear the stamp of Hellenik and Kamic adjuncts and associations. But it may possibly be asked, Does not Herodotos represent the Bakchik cult as being directly derived from the Uasarian; does he not say ' Almost all the names of the gods came into Greece from Egypt? My enquiries prove that they were all derived from a foreign source, and my opinion is that Egypt furnished the greater number.'[2] True, but he clearly does not directly derive the Bakchik cult from the Uasarian, for he says that Melampous ' introduced into

---

[1] Vide subsec. v. [2] Herod. ii. 50.

Greece the name of Bacchus, the ceremonial of his worship, and the procession of the phallus,'[1] and adds, as noticed, ' my belief is that Melampous got his knowledge of them *from Cadmus the Tyrian, and the followers whom he brought* from Phoenicia into the country which is now called Boeotia.'[2] Melampous, therefore, according to Herodotos, had not been to Kam, but was the first Hellene to adopt the Bakchik rites practised by the immigrant inhabitants of the Kadmeis. But Herodotos was well aware that Kadmos was not a Kamite, but a Phoenician,[3] and so plainly asserts that the Bakchik cult was common both to Phoenicia and Kam, that in the latter country it took the Uasarian form, but that it was introduced into Hellas from the former through the medium of Kadmos, the great founder of Thebai, ' mother-city of the Bakchai.'[4] Again, he states that originally the Pelasgoi had no distinct names or appellations for the gods, but that ' after a long lapse of time the names of the gods came to Greece from Egypt, and the Pelasgi learnt them, only as yet they *knew nothing of Bacchus*, of whom they first heard at a much later date.'[5] That is, the Pelasgoi did not receive the Dionysiak cult together with that of the other divinities from Kam, but at another time, and through Phoenician agency;[6] and he then relates a fabulous story how two sacred women were carried away by Phoenicians from the Kamic Thebai, and that one of them was sold into Hellas and founded the oracle of Dodona, a tale illustrative of Phoenician influence in the West. As to the existence of an individual Kadmos, let it be remembered that any leader of an Oriental colony into Hellas would be pre-eminently a Kadmos or Man-of-

---

[1] Cf. Diod. i. 97.
[2] Herod. ii. 49.
[3] Ibid. iv. 147; v. 57–8; vii. 91.
[4] Vide *inf*. X. ii, *Kadmos and Thebai*.
[5] Herod. ii. 52.
[6] Cf. *inf*. X. i.

the-East. Homeros, the Poet, personifies the divinity of the Strangers, and relates his adventures; Herodotos, the Historian, naturally describes his cult as introduced by the leader of the colony. Both are in exact agreement with each other, and with every other writer whose works have been examined in the course of the enquiry. Dionysos, it may be observed, was not the only divinity considered by Herodotos to be common both to Kam and Phoenicia. A Herakles,[1] distinct from the son of Alkmene, is described by him as being worshipped in both countries,[2] and he was also well aware of the wide-spread cult of Hephaistos, the Kamic Ptah.[3]

Subsection III.—Outline of the Uasarian Myth.

The great Uasarian myth as exhibited not merely in the comparatively scanty notices of the Egyptologists of antiquity, but also in the results of the researches of those of modern times, presents perhaps one of the most intricate and obscure subjects of investigation which can possibly engage the attention. The enquirer into the nature and character of Uasar may be perplexed with apparently absolutely conflicting statements, that he was a man, a god, a man-god, a husbandman, a warrior, a king, a martyr, the judge of the dead, the Nile, the sun, the principle of reproduction, the world, the Kosmos, and thus on. We may, therefore, well say with the Stranger in Platon's *Sophistes*, 'The object of our enquiry is no trivial thing, but a very various and complicated one. This is a various and very questionable animal—one not to be caught with the left hand, as the saying is.'[4] But I think it will not fail to occur to the reader that any one

---

[1] *I.e.* Melqarth. Vide *inf.* XI. i. 2.
[2] Herod. ii. 43–4.
[3] Cf. Ibid. ii. 51. with iii. 37. *Inf.* X. i.
[4] Mackay's Translation.

cognizant of the nature and character of Dionysos, or even of only such part of it as has been illustrated in the previous course of the present enquiry, possesses great advantages for the study of the Uasarian myth; in fact, that the two divinities, intricate and obscure as they are, mutually explain and illustrate each other, that each is to be studied in the light afforded by the other, and is, in fact, a master-key to the solution of the difficulties which they mutually create. For instance, it is perfectly simple to the Dionysiak student that Dionysos is not simply the sun, and yet that, at the same time, he has an exceedingly important solar phase. In the same way Uasar was identified with the sun,[1] of which, ' on a hieroglyphical tablet in the Louvre, he is stated to be the soul and body.'[2] But to suppose that he is merely the solar god would be as erroneous as to entertain such a theory respecting the developed Hellenik Dionysos, as *e.g.* in the tablet just referred to ' Osiris is also identified with Atum, the presiding deity of the air, and the judge and chastiser of souls.' Noticing, then, the various and apparently contradictory aspects and manifestations of Uasar, how shall we ascertain what he really is, or represents? Let us proceed philosophically to compare the opinions, ' to set aside as more or less discrediting one another those various special and concrete elements in which such opinions disagree; to observe what remains after the discordant constituents' have been eliminated; and to find for this remaining constituent that abstract expression which holds true throughout its divergent modifications.'[3] Thus, as the greater includes the less, What concept of Uasar will include all other narrower and derivative concepts, and hold true throughout their divergent modifications? And here Dionysos promptly steps in to our assistance, for as

---

[1] Diod. i. 11; Plout. *Peri Is.* lii. *Place,* i. 438.
[2] Dr. Birch in Bunsen's *Egypt's*
[3] H. Spencer, *First Principles,* ii.

we have seen,[1] he is Phanes, the spirit of material visibility, a Kyklops giant of the universe with one bright solar eye, the growth-power of the world, the all-pervading animism of things, son of Semele, 'the beginnings of nature,' and Harmonia, the starry universe existing 'in a wonderful order.'[2] And Uasar is no less. I noticed[3] that Dionysos and Adonis were brought forth from chests in which they had been concealed or preserved, and that these mythic chests were arks or kosmic eggs from which the powers of growth, heat, and life-beauty, come forth in the procession of existence; and so, similarly, Uasar is described as the egg-born.[4] He is the egg-sprung Eros of Aristophanes,[5] whose creative energy brings all things into existence; the Demiurge who made and animates the world, a being who is a sort of personification of Amen the Invisible God, as Dionysos is a link between mankind and the Zeus Hypsistos. Uasi or Isis is merely the female reflection of Uasar;[6] 'the two deities are always inseparable,'[7] and 'Isis and Osiris, alone and united, and Isis, Osiris, and Horus combined, can be shewn to comprise in themselves the whole system of Egyptian mythology, with the exception perhaps of Ammon and Kneph.'[8] Uasi is the sister, the wife, the daughter, the mother, of Uasar, who is her brother, husband, son, or sire. This is merely the creating, energising, and vital force of nature, conceived under the natural idea of a male and female dualism. Dionysos, also, had

---

[1] *Sup.* II. iii. 3.
[2] Vide *inf.* X. ii.
[3] *Sup.* III. i. 1.
[4] Diod. i. 27.
[5] *Ornith.* 695 *et seq.* Cf. Plout. *Peri Is.* lvii.
[6] Her address to the votary in Apuleius is very fine:—'I am nature, the parent of all things, the mistress of all the elements, the primordial offspring of time, the supreme among divinities, the queen of departed spirits, the first of the celestials, and the uniform manifestation of the gods and goddesses; who govern by my nod the luminous heights of heaven, the salubrious breezes of the ocean, and the anguished silent realms of the shades below: whose one sole divinity the whole orb of the earth venerates under a manifold form, with different rites, and under a variety of appellations' (Apul. *De Asino Aureo,* xi.).
[7] *Egypt's Place,* i. 431.
[8] *Ibid.* 427.

his attendant Uasi in the person of the Axiokerse of Samothrake, who in another phase appears as 'the Phoenician Athene, Onga, Onka, who was also worshipped by the Thebans and Gephyreans;'[1] but on Hellenik ground she became incorrectly identified with the great daughter of Zeus, and it is Demeter, the Earth-mother, of whom as we have seen Dionysos became the Associate, who in the Hellenik Pantheon corresponds, although she is not identical, with Uasi. This broad deep concept of Uasar will include all 'special and concrete elements' in the myth, and hold 'true throughout its divergent modifications.' Does he represent the growth-power in nature? then derivatively, he easily becomes a phallic personage, the all-fertilising Nile, the Sun, as the great vivifying and procreative power of the world, and Euemeristically, a nurturing king, who fosters arts, sciences, and civilization generally, developing them out of pre-existing barbarism. Are the principles of change and decay, death and resurrection, good and evil, rewards and punishments, mirrored and reflected alike on the face of nature and in the heart of man? Uasar answers in character to all these analogies and beliefs.[2] He dies to live again; he wars with aggressive evil, is slain on account of it, and finally overcomes it. He as god, and as the good god, according to the principles of eternal justice which are reflected from the Unseen in the mirror of the human soul, rewards virtue and punishes vice, for Amen, the Invisible Father, has committed all judgment to him the suffering and triumphant son. And this judgment is necessarily placed as occurring in the invisible world, where Uasar, in resurrection splendour, possessed of the keys of Death and Kerneter,[3] as Rhotamenti or

---

[1] *Egypt's Place* 303; cf. Ais. *Hept. epi The.* 152. 496. Schol. in Pind. *Ol.* ii. 30. 48; Schol. in Eur. *Phoi.* 1069; Tzetzes in Lykoph. 1225; Paus. ix. 12. 'Onga is Athena at Thebai' (Hesych. in voc. *Onga*).

[2] The reader should study in this connection the names and titles of Uasar (*Funereal Ritual*, cxlii.).

[3] Hades.

King-of-the-Under-world, the Rhadamanthos of the Hellenes, rewards every man according to his works, and permits to see his face, makes like, or even in some mysterious way incorporates with, himself, those who, like him, overcome the snares, seductions and opposition of the Great Serpent, adversary and accuser of the brethren, and the powers of evil, and appear at last as just men made perfect, weighed in the balance by Har and Anupu,[1] and not found wanting. This is he who makes numerous captives, whose majority or multitude[2] is continually increasing, the chthonian Dionysos, Ra the Sun, at times identified with the primal Amen, Helios shining in the Under-world,[3] Zagreus, 'the many-guest-receiving Zeus of the Dead.'[4] Thus the Uasarian cult is no mere observation of, and childlike deductions from, the external phenomena of nature; the sun is not simply regarded as a bright being who is born each morning of the darkness, and is slain each evening by the arrow of night. The spiritual and psychical element is everywhere predominant. God and the soul both exist; God not only is, but he is also a rewarder of them that diligently seek him; eternal life is no phantom, the resurrection of the dead is both probable and credible.[5] 'Osiris is the Sun-god, without ceasing to be the real Lord, the Self-created, the God of the human Soul.'[6] Thus, although essentially kosmogonic in development, he is far more than a mere pantheistic spirit of nature. Through all the elaborations and corruptions of Kamic mythology, through all the apparent intricacy of idea involved in the union and connection of, and in the distinction between, the shadowy

---

[1] 'The dog Anubis' (Milton).
[2] Cf. *Dan.* xii. 2.
[3] Cf. *Od.* xii. 383.
[4] Ais. *Iket.* 146.
[5] As to the Kamic belief in the resurrection of the body, cf. Bunsen, *Egypt's Place,* iv. 641; Lenormant, *Anct. Hist. of the East,* i. 322–3. No opponent of the doctrine has ever been able to answer S. Paul's subtle question, What is the abstract probability against it? (Acts xxvi. 8.)
[6] *Egypt's Place,* iv. 325.

groups of indistinct and oftentimes grotesque divinities of Kam, we may learn their belief that life, however developed, is greater and more glorious than inanimation, that 'mind is first and reigns for ever,' that all things come from God and go to God, that probation will in the case of the righteous be followed in due time by perfection, and that whatever is, exists for ' the glorification of God in time.' Solar, astral, phallic, kosmogonic, chthonian, and psychical, Uasar links together in one the various elements of nature and of religious idea. He stands between man and the far-off Primal Cause; and when the history of his worship shall be fully known, its various phases thoroughly understood, and its marvellous similarities with the teachings of our own Sacred Books duly appreciated, we shall unhesitatingly assert, with the philosophic Apostle, that ' the invisible things of God become distinctly visible when studied in the things that He hath made.'[1]

Subsection IV.—Identity of the Uasarian and Dionysiak Myths.

That the Uasarian and Dionysiak myths were, at a certain period, identified is beyond all contradiction; but on the fact whether they were originally identical or not, practically depends the important question, Is Dionysos non-Aryan in origin, or is he merely a simple Aryan divinity overlaid with Semitic incrustations? I will therefore notice various features and points of similarity which constitute the parallel between, and identity of, the two personages, and consider the deductions which may be legitimately drawn from these facts. The identity of Dionysos and Usar is illustrated by the following circumstances:—

I. *The consensus of ancient Authors.*—Herodotos, as

[1] For further considerations on this subject, vide *inf.* XII. i. 3.

we have seen,[1] identifies the two, and considers that the Uasarian or Dionysiak cult was introduced into Hellas, through the instrumentality of Phoenicians, by Melampous *many hundred years before his time.* The deliberate conclusion of the great historian and investigator on this last point, the time of the introduction of the cult into Hellas, is deserving of the greatest weight, and must, I think, carry conviction to an unprejudiced mind that the Bakchik worship was brought into Hellenik regions long anterior to the era of Onomakritos and the Peisistratids, to the reign of Psammetik the Great, when Kam was first partially thrown open by law to Hellenes, to the Olympiad of Koroibos, that wonderful epoch when, according to some moderns, by virtue of a mysterious *fiat lux* we pass at a bound from fiction to history,[2] and to the Herodotean era of Homeros and Hesiodos, some 400 years before his own time. Sir G. Wilkinson ingeniously suggests that if Melampous 'be an imaginary personage,' his name, 'Blackfoot,' was invented to show the origin of the rites he was said to have introduced as coming from Kam, the 'Black Land.'[3]

Diodorus is equally clear on the point. He states[4] that the first men in Aigyptos thought that there were two eternal gods, the Sun, Osiris, and the Moon, Isis;[5] and that some ancient Hellenik mythologists call Osiris Dionysos, and quotes verses from Eumolpos and Orpheus in illustration of this.[6] Again, he says that Osiris was explained to be Dionysos, and Isis, Demeter;[7] and, when alluding to the numerous opinions about the gods, he declares that 'Osiris was named by some Sarapis [*i.e.*

---

[1] *Sup.* Subsec. ii.
[2] Even the exact date of this *annus mirabilis* is far from certain. (Vide *The Olympiads in connection with the Golden Age of Greece*, W. R. A. Boyle in *Trans. of the Society of Biblical Archaeology*, ii. 289).
[3] Rawlinson, *Herodotus*, ii. 77, note.
[4] Diod. i. 11.
[5] Cf. Diog. Laert. *Introduction*, vii.
[6] *Sup.* II. i. 6.
[7] Diod. i. 13, iv. 1.

Osiri-Hapi, the deceased and canonised Bull of Memphis], by others Dionysos, by others Plouton [as the Lord of the Under-world], by others Ammon [*i.e.* Am'en the Invisible God, and Primal Cause, with whom he was at times indirectly identified], by some Zeus [as the great and universally-worshipped and Ammon-connected divinity], and by many Pan,'[1] [as the kosmogonic spirit of all nature.[2]] These apparently contradictory opinions will not, I think, perplex the judicious reader, who will observe that Uasar was, of course, absolutely distinct from the three Aryan divinities Zeus, Plouton, and Pan, and will further notice the special reasons which led to their being identified with him. The non-identity of, but the connection between, Sarapis, Ammon, and Uasar, especially through the solar and psychical links, is sufficiently known to all acquainted with Kamic mythology. Diodoros paid especial attention to the Dionysiak myth,[3] and although much confused by an absurdly extended principle of Euemerism, and believing that there were several Dionysoi, yet on the whole he appears to have quite admitted the identity of Dionysos and Uasar.

Plutarchos, who in his special work on the Uasar-Uasi myth, which is the gem of his writings, displays both considerable knowledge and ability, is quite clear on the point, remarking that 'it is better to identify Osiris with Dionysos, and Sarapis with Osiris.'[4] He had before him when writing Manethon's mythological Work on Uasi and Uasar,[5] so that he may be fairly considered to represent the views of that most distinguished of ancient Egyptologists on the matter. Later writers agree.[6]

---

[1] Diod. i. 25.
[2] *Sup.* IV. iii. 2.
[3] Cf. *sup.* 1.
[4] *Peri Is.* xxviii; cf. *Ibid.* xxxv.
[5] Cf. Euseb. *Euan Apod. Propar. Prooim.* ii; Theodoret. *Serm.* ii. *De Therapeut.*
[6] Cf. Nonnos, iv. 269-70.

II. *Uasar and Dionysos are both represented as great warriors and conquerors, especially in the East.*[1]

III. *They are both connected with Nysa.*—'Osiris was brought up in Nysa in Arabia Felix, the son of Zeus, and named from his father and the place Dio-nysos.'[2]

IV. *They are both pre-eminently suffering divinities.*—This is one of the most important links between them. Uasar is slain, and his body cut in pieces by the wicked Set.[3] Dionysos similarly is torn in pieces by the Titanes.[4] Adonis who, as we have seen, is identical with Dionysos, is also a suffering, dying, and yet immortal, divinity.[5]

V. *They are both of Asiatic origin.*—It will be almost universally admitted that the civilisation of the Nile is derived from Western Asia. 'The myth of Osiris is Asiatic.'[6] 'Osiris and Isis are sometimes represented as Egyptians; sometimes Isis comes from Phoenicia.'[7] 'Osiris seems to be the purely Egyptian form of an early Asiatic idea of the Deity.'[8] 'It is a well-known fact, and universally admitted, that the fundamental ideas of the worship and sacred ceremonies of Adonis and Osiris were identical.'[9] 'All the Phoenician names of Adonis-Osiris can be fully explained, both as to meaning and etymology, in that language.'[10] 'The Egyptians were a branch of the race of Ham. They came from Asia, through the desert of Syria, to settle in the valley of the Nile. This is a fact clearly established by science, and

---

[1] Cf. Diod. i. 19 with ii. 38, iii. 63, 65, 73, 74; Plout. *Peri Is.* xiii. xxii. xxix.; *inf.* IX. vii. *Indoletes.*

[2] Diod. i. 15; cf. Herod. ii. 146; Diod. i. 19; iii. 64-6, 70; iv. 2; *sup.* IV. ii. 1; *inf.* VIII. i; *Nysios,* IX. viii.

[3] Typhon. Diod. i. 21. 97; iv. 6; Plout. *Peri Is.* xiii. xviii.; cf. Herod. ii. 156, 171; Paus. x. 32; Vide 'The Lamentations of Isis and Nephthys,' translated by P. J. de Horrack (*Records of the Past,* ii. 117 *et seq.*), and '*The Book of Respirations*' (Ibid. iv. 119 *et seq.*).

[4] Paus. viii. 37; Non. vi. 165 *et seq.*; *sup.* IV. iii. 3, *inf.* IX. vi. *Zagreus.*

[5] Cf. Bunsen, *Egypt's Place,* i. 457; iv. 231, 347; *sup.* II. iii. 5; IV. iii. 3.

[6] Bunsen, *Egypt's Place,* iv. 325.

[7] Ibid. 331.

[8] Ibid. 332.

[9] Ibid. 347.

[10] Ibid. 348.

entirely confirms the statements of the Book of Genesis.'[1] 'The Egyptians were a people who immigrated from Asia into the valley of the Nile. The whole valley was peopled from Asia; and to this day the inhabitants bear the evident marks of an Asiatic and Caucasian origin.'[2] Whether Dionysos is a Semitic and Asiatic divinity is the chief question of the present enquiry, and the reader will draw his own conclusions from the whole of the evidence offered, remembering especially the connection between the god and Adonis. It will also be recollected that he was of Semitic origin, according to the Lydian theory of Euripides, who especially calls the Bakchai Asiatic.[3]

VI. *They are both many-named and manifold in nature.*—Thus Diodoros notes that Uasar is called Dionysos, Seirios, Phanetes,[4] Sarapis, Plouton, Ammon, Zeus, and Pan; and that Uasi is called Demeter, Thesmophoros, Selene, Here, etc.;[5] while Ploutarchos calls her Myrionymos,[6] the goddess of a thousand names, which, as we have seen, is most appropriately an epithet of Dionysos.[7] 'The prayers of the dead contain a countless multitude of names by which Osiris is invoked.'[8] Similarly sings the Roman poet:—

> Bacchumque vocant, Bromiumque, Lyaeumque,
> Ignigenamque, satumque iterum, solumque Bimatrem.
> Additur his Nysaeus indetonsusque Thyoneus.
> Nycteliusque Eleleusque parens et Iacchus et Euan.
> Et quae praeterea per Graias plurima gentes
> Nomina, Liber, habes.[9]

They are also both almost infinitely manifold in nature, being solar, astral, phallic, kosmogonic, chthonian, and

---

[1] Lenormant, *Ancient History of the East*, i. 202.
[2] Sir G. Wilkinson in Rawlinson's *Herodotus*, ii. 280.
[3] *Bak.* 1172.
[4] Diod. i. 11.
[5] Ibid. 25.
[6] *Peri, Is.* liii.
[7] Soph. *Antig.* 1115; cf. Diod. iv. 5; *inf.* VIII. i.
[8] Bunsen, *Egypt's Place*, i. 420. Vide the *Funereal Ritual*, cxlii.
[9] Ovid. *Metam.* iv. 11-17.

psychical; in fact, two such highly complex and intricate concepts, and yet so wonderfully similar and corresponding, that their independent evolution is an improbability amounting almost to an impossibility. The only question fairly remaining for discussion is whether the one is derived from the other, or whether they are both elaborated from a common original.

VII. *They are both chested.*—Uasar, according to the story in Ploutarchos, got into the coffin or chest which the wicked Typhon had prepared for him, to see if it would fit him, on which Typhon and the other conspirators nailed down the lid, poured hot lead over it, and threw it into the river, from whence it was carried down into the sea, and was ultimately washed ashore near Byblos in Phoenicia.[1] Thus Uasar, like that great Kamic minister Yousaiph,[2] was 'chested' or 'put in a coffin in Egypt.'[3] This history of Adonis is similar. 'The beautiful babe was placed in a chest and put in the hands of Persephone, the queen of the Under-world.'[4] So Semele and the infant Dionysos were said to have been enclosed by Kadmos in a chest, which, being thrown into the sea, was washed up on the Argolik coast.[5] These chests are another form of the mythic egg, sire of Uasar and Dionysos,[6] and of all things,[7] that mystic egg which appears in most theogonies,[8] and which, as Creuzer and Bunsen have demonstrated, 'was not laid by the Neo-Platonists.'[9] An Egyptian inscription at Philae, of the time of the Romans, speaks of 'the father of the begin-

---

[1] *Peri Is.* xiii.-xviii.
[2] Joseph.
[3] Cf. the following passages from the *Funereal Ritual*:—'Thou mayest approach, borne, oh Sun! in his chest' (cxxxiii.). 'Hail, oh thou Sun! in his ark' (cxxxiv.). 'Well is the Great One who is in the chest, so is Osiris' (clxii.).
[4] *Mythol. of the Aryan Nations,* ii. 7.
[5] *Sup.* III. i. 1.
[6] Cf. subsec. iii.
[7] Cf. Hyginus. *Fab.* cxcvii.; Paus. iii. 16; Damaskios. *Extract* iv. in Bunsen's *Egypt's Place,* v. 850; *Poseidon,* xxxvi.
[8] Cf. Bunsen, *Egypt's Place,* iv. 149-159.
[9] *Ibid.* 311.

nings, creating the egg of the sun and moon, first of the gods of the Upper-world.'[1] And the egg was known and revered far and wide, for even 'Finn cosmogonists believed the earth and heaven to be made out of a severed egg, the upper concave shell representing heaven, the yolk earth, and the crystal surrounding fluid the circumambient ocean.'[2] This mysterious kosmic egg is frequently alluded to in the Kamic *Funereal Ritual*. 'Oh Tum [the Creator] give me the delicious breath of thy nostril.[3] I am the Egg of the Great Cackler [Seb, the father of Uasar; his emblem was the goose.][4] I have watched this great egg which Seb prepared for the earth. I grow, it grows in turn; I live, it lives in turn, stimulating the breath.'[5] 'I live, it lives; I breathe air, it breathes air, in Kerneter.'[6] That is, the justified and perfected Uasarian is ultimately identified with, and becomes part of, all kosmic life, yet occultly retaining a personal potency. 'I have been made a Lord of the Age, who has no limit, for I am an Eternal Substance. I am Tum, made for ever.'[7] And so, according to the Orphik Poet, Protogonos the First-born is Oögenes the Egg-sprung;[8] and, as Ploutarchos informs us, a symbolical egg was consecrated in the Orgies of Dionysos as a representation of self-contained generation.[9] This egg, ark, chest, or coffin, also appears as the mystic ship or boat, Argo, connected alike with the cult of Uasi, of Athene, of a divinity of the rude German tribes,[10] 'identified by Grimm with a goddess Ziza,'[11] and of various other personages. It 're-appears in the shell of Aphrodite, and in the ship borne in solemn procession to the Parthenon on the great Pana-

---

[1] *Egypt's Place*, i. 396.
[2] S. B. Gould, *Curious Myths*, 415.
[3] Cf. *Gen.* ii. 7.
[4] Cf. *Herod.* ii. 72.
[5] *Funereal Ritual*, liv.
[6] *Ibid.* lvi.; cf. Caps. xvii. xxii. xlii. lix.
[7] *Ibid.* lxii.
[8] *Orph. Hymn*, vi. 2.
[9] *Sympos.* ii. 636.
[10] Tac. *Germ.* ix.
[11] S. B. Gould, *Curious Myths*, 331.

thenaic festival, as the phallos was carried before the god in the great feasts of Dionysos.'[1] The symbolism is sufficiently obvious, both in its anthropomorphic and in its kosmical connection. The ship is the boat of the sun, which in the Kamic *Funereal Ritual* contains the gods, and is almost overturned by the terrific struggles of Apepi, the great serpent of evil; but which ultimately 'attains the extreme limit of the horizon, and disappears in the heavenly region of Amenti.'[2] Apuleius,[3] in describing the procession of Uasi, states that one of the priests held 'a golden lamp of a boat-like form,' and that 'the chief priest dedicated to the goddess a very skilfully built ship, pictured all over with the curious hieroglyphics of the Egyptians, after having most carefully purified it with a lighted torch, an egg, and sulphur.' Nor was the mystic chest absent, for 'another priest carried a chest containing the secret utensils of this stupendous mystery.' 'Some of the sacred boats or arks contained the emblems of life and stability, which, when the veil was drawn aside, were partially seen;'[4] and, as Mr. Cox well notes, 'these ships, chests, or boats, are the *kistai mustikai* of the Mysteries,'[5] and we see them in the chest or coffin of Osiris.'[6] One suggested derivation of the name Thebai is *tebah*, a box or chest, the name given to Noah's ark, the Kibotos of the LXX.; so that in this connection the Phoenician city, whose kosmogonic character has already been alluded to,[7] becomes 'an image of the mighty world,' of the kosmic egg itself, and is thus a suitable abode for the cult of the manifold and all-animating Dionysos. But whether presented in the form and under the symbol of chest or coffin, ark or egg, ship or

---

[1] *Mythol. of the Aryan Nations*, ii. 118.
[2] Cooper, *Serpent Myths of Ancient Egypt*, 41; Cf. *Funereal Ritual*, xcviii.
[3] *De Asino Aureo*, lib. xi.
[4] Sir G. Wilkinson in Rawlinson's *Herodotus*, ii. 86.
[5] Vide *inf.* VI. i. 1.
[6] *Mythol. of the Aryan Nations*, ii. 110, Note.
[7] *Sup.* IV. iii. 1.

boat, and whether in connection with a male or female divinity, the idea is one and the same. Uasar or Dionysos, as Erikepeios the vital force and life-heat of the vast visible world, acted upon by the infinite creating power, burst the egg of darkness and chaos, and produced in grand procession the generation of heaven and earth and all things animate and inanimate. Darkly, and indeed sensuously, the myth throughout all its concealments and obscurity endeavours confusedly to set forth the sublime truth that 'In the beginning God created the heavens and the earth. And the Spirit of God moved upon the face of the waters,' that is, brooded dove-like over them,[1] the simile being taken from a bird in the state of incubation.[2] ' The terms used depicting the attitude convey to us, with the most vivid delineation and colouring, that Godlike love was the motive power,'[3] that Love, or Heavenly Eros, which, ' rejoices in its works.'[4] There is yet another symbol of this multiform chest, *i.e.* the mystic Kalathos, or Basket of Demeter the All-mother,[5] which was carried in the Eleusinian Mysteries, and which reappears in the hands of Assyrian divinities.[6]

VIII. *They are both connected with ivy.*—As the gods of life and immortality, Uasar and Dionysos are connected with ' ivy never sere.'[7] Ivy, Diodoros tells us, is called in the Egyptian language ' Osiris plant.'[8] But it is to be observed that ' ivy is not a plant of the Nile,' and Sir G. Wilkinson remarks that ' wreaths and festoons of ivy, or rather of the wild convolvulus or of the *Periploca secamone*, often appear at Egyptian fêtes.'[9] The connection between Dionysos and ivy has been already sufficiently noticed.

---

[1] Cf. Milton, *Par. Lost*, i. 20.
[2] Cf. Rev. R. G. S. Browne, *The Mosaic Cosmogony*, 25.
[3] *Ibid.* 26.
[4] Cf. *Ps.* civ. 31.
[5] Cf. Kallim. *Hymnos eis Dem.*
[6] Vide *inf.* VIII. ii. *Jar.*
[7] The shape of the leaf, in which some discern a phallic emblem, has been suggested as another link between them and the plant.
[8] Diod. i. 17; cf. Plout. *Peri Is.* xxxvii.
[9] Rawlinson, *Herodotus*, ii. 74.

IX. *They are both the youngest of the gods.*—According to the legend in Diodoros, the inscription on a stele of Uasar ran, 'My father is Kronos [Seb], the youngest of all the gods, and I am Osiris the king.'[1] 'The Greeks regard Hercules, Bacchus, and Pan as the youngest of the gods.'[2] Uasar is the head of the third and last Order of Kamic divinities, and his son Har is represented as the last god-king of Kam.

X. *They are both peculiarly connected with spotted animals and garments.*—Diodoros, as already noticed, mentions that the spotted faun-skin of Uasar was considered to be symbolical of the stars.[3] He also says that the second Dionysos was said to have worn a panther's skin.[4] 'The thyrsus,' remarks Sir G. Wilkinson, 'is shown by Plutarch to be the staff, often bound by a fillet, to which the spotted skin of a leopard is suspended near the figure of Osiris; for it is the same that the high priest, clad in the leopard-skin dress, carries in the processions.'[5] Similarly the shrines of the gods, when in procession 'were attended by the chief priest, or prophet, clad in the leopard-skin.'[6] The divine bull Hapi[7] appears also to have been at times represented as spotted.[8] The spots, their astral connection, and association with suffering, point to an origin in the Mesopotamian Valley, where we find a representation of a divinity bearing the Bakchik branch and the spotted faun,[9] whose tearing in pieces was symbolical of the rending asunder of Uasar.[10]

XI. *They are both vinal divinities.*—Thus Uasar is said to have introduced and nurtured the vine,[11] as 'the

---

[1] Diod. i. 27.
[2] Herod. ii. 145; cf. c. 52.
[3] Diod. i. 11; cf. *sup.* II. iii. 3; Plout. *Peri Is.* xxxv.
[4] Diod. iv. 4.
[5] Rawlinson, *Herodotus,* ii. 74; cf. Wilkinson, *Ancient Egyptians,* iv. 341, 353.
[6] Rawlinson, *Herodotus,* ii. 85.
[7] Apis.
[8] Cf. Kitto, *Bib. Cyclop.,* i. 308.
[9] Brit. Mus. Nimroud Gallery.
[10] *Sup.* IV. iii. 3; vide *inf.* VIII. ii. *Spots.*
[11] Diod. i. 15.

offspring of Semele discovered the liquid stream of the grape.'[1] Wine, it may be observed, has several aspects in a Dionysiak connection. Thus it has a phallic aspect, as a stimulant; and a kosmogonic and pantheistic aspect, as connected with blood the life and life-power of the world. Ploutarchos[2] notices a strange Kamic legend that the vine sprang from the blood of some who had fought against the gods, and that intoxication rendered men confused and irrational because they were thereby filled with the blood of their ancestors. Wine becomes a fitting sacrifice to Dionysos the martyr divinity of life-heat, whose blood was shed to benefit the world. Thus it by no means follows that even the Wine-god should be only a patron of innocent, or boisterous and unmeaning, rustic merriment.[3]

XII. *They are both tauric divinities.*—Uasar and Uasi being inseparable and even identical, as male and female symbols of the same idea, the characteristics and adjuncts of the one in reality appertain equally to the other. As Uasi is habitually represented with horns, we should from that circumstance alone be justified in regarding this form as connected with Uasar, and in fact he is at times thus pourtrayed.[4] Again, Uasar is a tauric god on account of his connection with the sacred bull Hapi, who ' was born of a cow mysteriously impregnated by lightning descending from heaven. The divine bull was not allowed to live more than a determined number of years, and at the end of that time if he did not die a natural death he was killed. The dead Apis was embalmed and deposited in the magnificent caves of the temple called by the Greeks "the Serapeum." He then became the object of a new worship. By the very fact of his death, he had become

---

[1] Eur. *Bak.* 278.
[2] *Peri Is.* vi.
[3] Vide *inf.* IX. ii. *Theoinos.*
[4] Bunson, *Egypt's Place*, i. pl. 5, fig. 4.

assimilated with Osiris, the god of the Lower-world, and received the name of Osir Hapi, converted by the Greeks into Serapis.'[1] 'The living Apis was called the Hapi-anch or "Living Apis;" he was the second life or incarnation of the god Ptah supposed to be visibly present in Egypt. At his death he was canonised, and became the Osor-Hapi or "Osirian," that is deceased Apis. This word the Greeks made Serapis, but the types of the Greek and Egyptian deities were always distinct, Serapis being represented in the form and with the attributes of Pluto or Hades;[2] Osor-Hapi was figured either as a bull or *a man with a bull's head.*'[3] Another remarkable figure in the tauric group of the Kamic Pantheon is Hat-har,[4] 'ei-t-Hor, Horus' mundane habitation, often substituted for Isis.'[5] 'She ordinarily appears with the cow's head, wearing the sun's disk between the horns. Even when represented in the human form she is rarely without the sun and horns.'[6] Hat-har and Uasi are in reality identical.[7] Each of them is the mother of Her-her, Arueris or Horos the Strong,[8] and also of Har, Horos the Younger, Her-pa-chrut, Harpokrates, or Horos the Child; each of them is the cow-horned, kosmic, goddess mistress of Amenti, the Lower-world, and each of them is called *par excellence* Maut, the Mother.[9] The primitive Kamites, according to a legend preserved in Diodoros, thought that there were two eternal divinities the Sun, Osiris or Dionysos, and the Moon, Isis, who accordingly is repre-

---

[1] Lenormant, *Anct. Hist. of the East,* i. 320.
[2] Cf. Plout. *Peri Is.* xxviii.
[3] Dr. Birch in Bunsen's *Egypt's Place,* i. 445. 'The solemnities at the burial of Apis were entirely Bacchic. It is true that the priests did not wear the deer-skin (*nebris*), but they wore the panther-skin, carried staves like thyrsus-staves, and cried out and convulsed themselves like the Bacchantes' (*Ibid.* 446).
[4] Athor.
[5] Sir G. Wilkinson in Rawlinson's *Herodotus,* ii. 247.
[6] Bunsen, *Egypt's Place,* i. 413.
[7] Cf. *Peri Is.* lvi. lxix.; Bunsen, *Egypt's Place,* i. 433.
[8] *Ibid.* 430.
[9] Cf. Sharpe, *Egyptian Mythology,* 6.

sented as horned, and also because the ox was sacred to her.[1] According to the legend preserved by Ploutarchos, when Horos, enraged with his mother, tore the crown from her head, Hermes[2] placed an ox-headed helm on her brow.[3] The moon was called by the Kamites 'Mother of the Kosmos,'[4] an excellent illustration of the kosmogonic character of Uasi. 'But according to the monuments the Egyptian moon[5] is always masculine.'[6] But the kosmic Uasi, identical with the male Uasar, is like Adonis 'male and female,' a 'two-natured Iakchos' or Dionysos.[7] Uasi and Hat-har as kosmogonic goddesses might therefore be connected with the moon, as the kosmogonic Uasar is with the sun, without interfering with or unduly impinging on Ra-Helios, the Sun-god, or the mysterious Aah, the Moon-god, who seems to be connected with Tet.[8] Uasar thus stands at the head of a complete group of tauric Kamic divinities, all most closely connected with him and with each other. Another important horned, but non-taurik member of the Kamik Pantheon is Khnum, the ram-headed god of Apt, Tape, Thaba, Thebai, the 'Head' or 'Capital,'[9] No-Ammon, or Thebes. The Hellenes and Romans confounded together the two primal gods of Apt,[10] Amen and Khnum, considering each of them as Zeus, Jupiter, and the combined divinity is the 'contortis cornibus Ammon.' Horned serpents were kept in what Herodotos calls the temple of Zeus at Apt, and were buried in it, being sacred to the god.[11] According to a Euemeristic legend preserved in Diodoros, Ammon was a king of Libye and the sire of

[1] Diod. i. 11.
[2] Tet-Thoth.
[3] *Peri Is.* xix.; cf. *ibid.* lii.
[4] *Ibid.* xliii.
[5] Like the Phrygian Mên, and the Kaldean Moon-god, Sin or Hurki, and the lunar divinities of various savage tribes. Cf. Tylor, *Primitive Culture*, ii. 271 *et seq.*
[6] Bunsen, *Egypt's Place*, i. 420.
[7] *Sup.* II. iii. 5.
[8] Cf. Bunsen, *Egypt's Place*, i. 407.
[9] Rawlinson, *Herodotus*, ii. 3.
[10] Cf. Herod. ii. 42.
[11] *Ibid.* ii. 74.

Dionysos.[1] The horned divinities are thus brought into contact. Diodoros also notices that Sabazios, whom he calls a more ancient Dionysos, and the son of Zeus and Persephone, and who, as we have seen,[2] is identical with Dionysos, and whose sacreds and sacrifices were in secret and at night, yoked oxen, and was therefore represented with horns.[3] The horned and tauric Dionysos has already been referred to.[4] He sometimes appears on coins with the horns of a bull or ram.[5] The general subject of horned divinities will be subsequently noticed when considering the special phase of Dionysos as Taurokeros.[6]

XIII. *They are both solar divinities.*—According to a legend of the primitive Kamites there were two eternal gods, Uasar the Sun, and Uasi the Moon, and Diodoros tells us that ' some of the ancient Hellenik mythologists named Osiris Dionysos, and by a slight change of name Seirios,'[7] the Hot-one, *i.e.* the Sun,[8] not ' Kuôn Seirios,'[9] Sothis the Dog-star. According to the tale in Ploutarchos,[10] Uasar was the son of Helios, or Ra the Sun. ' An esoterical explanation' of his character ' has been discovered on a hieroglyphical tablet in the Louvre. On this Osiris is associated with the Sun, of which he is stated to be the soul and body, the soul residing in the solar disk, the body reposing in the region of Suten-khen,'[11] or Bubastis. Sol Inferus, the ' Subterranean Sun, especially took the name of Osiris.'[12] ' The Sun, personified by Osiris, was the foundation of the Egyptian Metempsychosis. From a god who gave and preserved life, he had become a retributive and saving god.'[13] Uasar, as the Sun of the

---

[1] Diod. iii. 68.
[2] *Sup.* sec. ii.
[3] Diod. iv. 4.
[4] *Sup.* IV. iii.; Plout. *Peri Is.* xxxv.
[5] *Inf.* VII. iii.
[6] *Inf.* IX. iii.
[7] Cf. Plout. *Peri Is.* lii.
[8] Cf. Hes. *Erg. kai Hem.*, 415; 'Seirios Astêr,' Archil. *Frag.* xlii.
[9] Ais. *Ag.* 967.
[10] *Peri Is.* xii.
[11] Dr. Birch in *Egypt's Place,* i. 438.
[12] Lenormant, *Anct. Hist. of the East,* i. 320.
[13] *Ibid.* 322.

Under-world, is inseparably connected with his office as the Judge of the Dead, a point of contact between the two divinities which remains to be noticed. The *Funereal Ritual*[1] describes how the Soul of the Uasarian, having passed through the gates of Kerneter,[2] is filled with wonder and delight by the majestic apparition of the subterranean Sun, and exclaims, 'Hail! Sun, Lord of the sunbeams, Lord of eternity! Hail! O Sun, Creator, self-created! Perfect is thy light in the horizon, illuminating the world with thy rays! All the gods rejoice when they see the King of Heaven.' The solar phase or aspect of Dionysos has been already frequently referred to, and is witnessed and illustrated by his many solar epithets.'[3]

XIV. *They are both chthonian and telluric divinities.*—As regards Uasar, several distinct ideas combine to produce this phase of character. He is chthonian (1) as the sinking sun traversing and illuminating the Under-world during the hours of darkness; (2) as the germ-power of life and vitality buried in the earth, his mystic chest or coffin, from which the vegetation of the world springs according to the ordinary resurrection of nature;[4] (3) as Rhot-Amenti, King of the Under-world, and Judge of the Dead who people the subterranean Amenti, Sheoul, Hades;[5] (4) as the representative of the psychical element, that soul of the world and of individual things which is hidden and enclosed in the 'visible mantle' of materiality, as man's soul is in his body. And although the similar prerogatives of Dionysos are, to a great extent, usurped or rather obscured by other and Aryan divinities, such as father Zeus, the far-darting Apollon, Aïdoneus, and the shadowy Rhadamanthos, this latter personage

---

[1] Cap. xv.
[2] Hades.
[3] *Sup.* II. iii. 2; *inf.* VIII. i., IX. iv. *Chrysopes.*
[4] Cf. Plout. *Peri Is.* xv.; 1 *Cor.* xv. 36–38.
[5] Cf. *Is.* xiv. 9, 10; *Ez.* xxxii. 18–32.

being an Hellenik reflection of the great Kamic god, yet he too, on analysis, appears as a chthonian and telluric divinity for reasons similar to those which cause and illustrate this aspect of Uasar. Dionysos, as Erikepeios the soul of kosmic life, is buried and concealed in the embrace of the Earth-mother. As Adonis he is the Sun sinking to Amenti, the chthonian region of the West, and when there, he is 'Zagreus the many-guest-receiving Zeus of the dead,' before whose awful tribunal, as before that of Uasar, the trembling mortal who has entered the regions of Kerneter, must stand, that the 'highest of all gods,' the natural Associate of 'Venerable Earth' the Demeter or Uasi-power, may pronounce on his doom.[1]

Such, then, being some of the principal points of resemblance between the two divinities, it is sufficiently evident that they are too closely alike in character and in cult to have developed independently as distinct concepts. Either therefore one was borrowed from the other, or they both must have originated from the same common source. But it would be preposterous, as Herodotos was well aware, to suppose that Kam was a borrower in the transaction. Hellas, therefore, obtained her Dionysiak Ritual, or its more remarkable features, either from Kam, or from some other foreign region; and if she imported it from Kam, it was obtained either, according to the opinion of Herodotos, many hundred years before his time, or in a comparatively modern age subsequently to the period when Psammetik the Great first, to some extent, threw open the country to foreigners. That many of its most remarkable features were introduced into Hellenik regions in comparatively modern times is the opinion of the greatest English historian of Greece. Grote, after alluding to the obscurity of the subject, observes, 'We see enough to satisfy us of the general fact,

---

[1] *Inf.* IX. vi. *Zagreus.*

that during the century and a half which elapsed between the opening of Egypt to the Greeks and the commencement of their struggle with the Persian kings, 'the old religion *was largely adulterated by importations from Egypt*, Asia Minor, and Thrake.'[1] During this period there may have been, and doubtless were, some religious importations into Hellas from Asia Minor, and Thrake, but what were those from Kam? What Kamic divinity, or what portion of the elaborate Kamic Ritual, was introduced into Hellas by the rude and semi-barbarous Karian and Ionian mercenaries who, somewhere about the year B.C. 660, enabled Psammetik to overthrow the Dodekarchy? What single Kamic story or myth was carried back across the Great Sea by the Hellenik citizens of Naukratis, which was founded, or perhaps rather refounded, or enlarged,[2] cir. B.C. 550, during the prosperous reign of the Philhellene Aahmes,[3] and which was for many years the only place in the country where Hellenes were allowed to reside and trade? 'Amasis,' says Herodotos, 'was partial to the Greeks, and among other favours which he granted them, gave to such as liked to settle in Egypt the city of Naukratis for their residence.'[4] 'In ancient times there was no factory but Naukratis in the whole of Egypt; and if a person entered one of the other mouths of the Nile, he was obliged to swear that he had not come there of his own free will,'[5] and take his goods to Naukratis, 'which had an exclusive privilege.' Grote well observes: 'It is the general tendency of Herodotos to apply the theory of derivation from Egypt

---

[1] *Hist. of Greece*, i. 28.
[2] Cf. Bunsen, *Egypt's Place*, iii. 611, 620. Bunsen considers that there was an Old Naukratis on the coast and a New Naukratis inland. I do not see sufficient proof of this, and it is evident that the Naukratis of the time of Herodotos was very near the coast. Cf. Herod ii. 97, 170. Sir G. Wilkinson observes, 'The exact position of Naukratis is unknown.'
[3] Amasis.
[4] Herod. ii. 178.
[5] Ibid. 170.

far too extensively to Grecian institutions: *the orgies of Dionysos were not originally borrowed from thence*, though they *may have been* much modified by connexion with Egypt.'[1] First, we are told that, during the period in question, 'the old religion,' including, it is presumed, the cult of Dionysos '*was* largely adulterated by importations from Egypt;' and next, we learn that the Dionysiak Ritual, though not Kamic in origin, '*may have been* modified by connexion with Egypt.' Of course, in the abstract, it may have been so modified, but, as a fact, was it? One Dionysiak myth only is distinctly asserted by Grote, following Lobeck, to have been borrowed from Nilotic regions. 'The remarkable mythe *composed* by Onomakritus respecting the dismemberment of Zagreus was founded upon an Egyptian tale very similar respecting the body of Osiris, who was supposed to be identical with Dionysus.'[2] 'It is distinctly stated by Pausanias that Onomakritus was himself the *author* of the most remarkable and characteristic mythe of the Orphic Theogony—the discerption of Zagreus by the Titans, and his resurrection as Dionysus.'[3] Let us examine this statement. Onomakritos the Athenian, B.C. 520-485, collected and arranged or, as we should say, *edited*, certain ancient verses traditionally attributed to Orpheus, Mousaios, and others; and tradition also states, rightly or wrongly, that he to some extent tampered with and made additions to them, or to some of them. The statement of Pausanias to which Grote refers is as follows: 'Homeros first introduced the Titanes in his Poems. And Onomakritos having received from Homeros the name of the Titanes combined [*i.e.*, put together in orderly manner] the Dionysiak Ritual, and made out the Titanes to be the authors of the sufferings of Dionysos.'[4]

---

[1] *Hist. of Greece,* i. 32.   [2] *Ibid.*   [3] *Ibid.* 21.   [4] Paus. viii. 37.

Here the innovation of Onomakritos is evident. He did not *compose*, in the sense of inventing, the Dionysiak Ritual, which had been in existence centuries before; nor did he invent the story of the sufferings of the god which, as noticed,[1] was sung at Sikyon more than a century at least before his time. But he, according to the assertion of Pausanias which may or may not be correct, first introduced the Titanes, who names had been handed down from the time of Homeros,[2] into the myth, and described them as the murderers of Zagreus. Another passage from Pausanias will further illustrate this subject. 'Methapos was an Athenian, an arranger [*Sunthetes*, as opposed to *Poietes*, a maker or author] of the celebration of mysteries and of secret rites of all kinds. The same man *arranged* for the Thebans the Ritual of the Kabeiroi.'[3] Methapos, like Onomakritos, was or pretended to be an ecclesiastical expert; and he was retained by the Thebans to codify and set in order the foreign Kabeirik Ritual of which they were ignorant.'[4] No one would venture to assert that the obscure Methapos *invented* that wonderful Kabeirik cult which was wide-spread along the shores of the Eastern Mediterranean ages before his time. Such was the office and position of men like Onomakritos and Methapos; they were simply rearrangers and re-modellers, not inventors or even introducers, of great dogmas and mystic rituals. Their tamperings (if any) with the relics of antiquity were for political, not religious, purposes. Thus it is both possible and probable that Onomakritos, who was an adherent of the Peisistratids, may have forged an oracle or two to induce the Persian king the more eagerly to invade continental Hellas;[5] but that he was 'a setter forth of strange gods,' or of new

---

[1] *Sup.* IV. iii. 3.
[2] Cf. *Il.* xiv. 279.
[3] Paus. iv. 1.
[4] Vide *inf.* X. i.
[5] Cf. Herod. vii. 6.

and startling theories about the gods, there is absolutely no evidence whatever. Herodotos was firmly persuaded, and with good reason, of the identity of Dionysos and Uasar, and of the great antiquity of the Dionysiak cult in Hellas. He was, moreover, well acquainted with the sufferings of Uasar; and also, both of necessity and as appears from his notice of Kleisthenes and otherwise, with those of Dionysos, for if Dionysos had never endured sufferings he could not have been identical with Uasar. Speaking of the circular lake at Sa,[1] the god-*fearing* historian writes: 'On this lake it is that the Egyptians represent by night his sufferings whose name I refrain from mentioning, and this representation they call their Mysteries. I know well the whole course of the proceedings in these ceremonies, but they shall not pass my lips.'[2] Is it to be believed for a moment that the notion of the sufferings of Dionysos Zagreus had been introduced into Hellas from Kam little more than fifty years before the time of the visit of Herodotos? If such had been the case, must he not have known of it, and how could this most careful and truthful of historians have described as having existed for centuries, *i.e.*, since the remote era of the mythical Melampous, that cult which, if sprung from Onomakritos, would have been to him the child of yesterday? Again, what connection is shown to have existed between Onomakritos and Kamic regions? Was he ever there, and when, and what did he learn there? The priests told but very little to strangers.[3] It is palpably evident that Herodotos, with all his painstaking and advantages derived from being on the spot, knew but very little and far less even than he supposed. But it is

---

[1] Sais.
[2] Herod. ii. 171.
[3] At the close of the *Funereal Ritual* is written, 'This Book is the greatest of mysteries; do not let the eye of any one see it; that is detestable. Learn it, hide it.'

unnecessary to pursue the subject further. The only specific myth or portion of Dionysiak Ritual which is stated by Grote to have been introduced into Hellas from Kam during the period in question, *i.e.*, from the era of Psammetik the Great to the visit of Herodotos, proves on examination to have not been thus introduced; and it is idle to embarrass ourselves with attempts to support a negative proposition such as, No religious rite was introduced during this time. The theory, therefore, that the Ritual or all its more remarkable features (for what is left when the Semitic element is removed?) was borrowed from Kamic regions since the era of Psammetik, falls to the ground for want of evidence in its favour, and as being contrary to existing evidence.[1] We are reduced, therefore, to fall back upon the only two other possible suppositions, either the Ritual was obtained from Kam in very early, almost in prehistoric times, or it was obtained elsewhere. What evidence is there for the first of these two possibilities? None at all. Herodotos did not believe it, for he, as we have seen, was of opinion that the Dionysiak cult was introduced by Phoenicians. Grote did not, for he says 'the orgies of Dionysus were not originally borrowed from Egypt.' No one at present, so far as I am aware, accepts this view. There seems to have been an early connection between Hellas and Kam, but this part of ancient history is still almost as obscure as interesting; and their intercourse was chiefly of a hostile character, and so altogether unsuitable to the propagation of the religion of either party, as neither of them fully subdued the other.[2] The early Hellenes possessed

---

[1] For further examination of the question, vide *inf.* IX. vi. *Zagreus*.

[2] As to the early connection between Hellas and Kam, vide Hom. *Il.* ix. 381-4; *Od.* iv. 81-5, 351-483, 581-5; xiv. 245-86; xvii. 423-43; Lenormant, *Ancient History of the East*, 259-01; Bunsen, *Egypt's Place*, i. 112-15; iii. 603-39; Lauth, *Homer und Aegypten*; Gladstone, *Juventus Mundi*, 144-8: *Homeric Synchronism*, in which the latest discoveries in Egyptology are most ably and acutely discussed in their bear-

some knowledge of Aigyptos, and they were to some extent acquainted with Uasar as Rhadamanthos-Rhotamenti, a being naturally localized in Krete, an island not unaffected by the influence of the Nile Valley.[1] But the very fact that Uasar reached Krete as Rhadamanthos, shows us that he did not reach it as Dionysos, and so negatives any idea of the early introduction of the Dionysiak Ritual from Kam. The admitted connection between Uasar and Rhadamanthos lends great interest to the latter who, otherwise, like many adoptions, is a very colourless personage, in fact merely a kind of duplicate of his Phoenician brother Minos.[2] According to Homeros, 'godlike Rhadamanthos,' is the son of Zeus and the daughter of Phoinix.[3] He dwells on the Elysian Plain at the ends of the earth where no snow, or winter, or storms disturb the happy region, but where life is most pleasant,[4] 'where the ocean breezes blow around the blessed islands, and golden flowers burn on their bright trees for evermore.'[5] His usual Homerik epithet is 'Golden-haired,' a solar appellation corresponding to Dionysos Chrysokomes.[6] It would be interesting, but somewhat beside the point immediately in question, to trace and illustrate in detail his identity with Uasar, and his mysterious journey in the ships of the Phaiakes to see Tityos in Euboia. Being identical with Uasar, he is of course in fact identical with Dionysos, but not in Hellenik idea. Rhadamanthos is an importation from Kam; Dionysos is not, for we shall necessarily be compelled to adopt the

ings on Homer's place in history; Schliemann, *Troy and its Remains*, 228, 270; *Records of the Past*, iv. 37 *et seq.*: 'The invasion of Egypt by the Greeks, under the nineteenth Dynasty.'

[1] I have elsewhere attempted to illustrate the early connection between Krete, Kam, and Purusata Philistia), vide *Poseidon*, xix. xxx.-xxxiv.

[2] Cf. Grote. *Hist. of Greece*, i. 212-13.

[3] *Il.* xiv. 322.

[4] *Od.* iv. 563-8.

[5] Ruskin, *Queen of the Air*, i. 50; cf. Pind. *Ol.* ii.

[6] Cf. *Od.* iv. 564; vii. 323.

last supposition mentioned, namely, that the Dionysiak Ritual, having been neither derived from Kam in earlier or in later times but yet being foreign in character, was introduced, as Herodotos conjectured, from some other Semitic region, and that region the whole enquiry tends to show was Phoenicia.

Subsection V.—*Basis and Starting-point of the Uasario-Dionysiak Cult.*

It has been mentioned that the religion and civilization of the Hapi,[1] were admittedly posterior to and derived from or developed out of the early systems of Western Asia.[2] 'Egypt was colonised from the North, by way of Palestine, by Asiatics, who brought their language and gods with them.'[3] It being admitted, then, that the Kamic religion was originally the product of Western Asia, we have next to consider in what part of that region it probably arose. Nor is this enquiry at all a wide one, for the countries to which our choice is necessarily limited are Western Aram or Syria, including Palestine,[4] and Phoenicia, Eastern Aram, Aram-Naharaim, *i.e.* Aram-of-the-two-rivers, or Mesopotamia, and Kaldea, which included great part of Eastern Aram. Assur is admittedly the daughter of Kaldea,[5] and the same remark applies to Elam, *i.e.* Kissia or Susiana,[6] which latter also lies further off from Kam. Syria and Kaldea alone remain, and as the former must be crossed on the overland route between Kam and the latter, it is towards Syria that our attention must, in the first instance, be especially directed. The principal inhabitants of Syria in

---

[1] Neilos.
[2] *Sup.* subsec. iv.
[3] *Egypt's Place,* iv. 327.
[4] Cf. Herod. iii. 5; vii. 89.
[5] Cf. *Gen.* x. 10, 11; Rawlinson, *Anct. Mons.* ii. 52-3.
[6] *Gen.* xiv. *Anct. Mons.* i. 26; ii. 435.

early times were (1) the Rephoeem, Aimeem, Anokeem, and other ancient tribes, alluded to in the Pentateuch [1] as being almost extinct in the time of Moses, and collectively known to the Kamites under the appellation of Sati: [2] (2) The Kanaanites, including the Khitas or Hittites, and the Phoenicians, for, notwithstanding Canon Rawlinson's arguments,[3] I cannot but agree with Bochart, Kenrick, Lenormant, and others, that the Phoenicians were a branch or branches of the Kanaanites: [4] and (3) the North-Eastern Aramean population, known to the Kamites as the Rotennu,[5] and who are described in a Theban sepulchral inscription of the time of Thothmes III. as dwelling in the 'northern lands behind the Great Sea.' The Israelites and Philistines were comparatively modern nations, and Pharaoh, 'the son of ancient kings,'[6] could have truly said, 'Before Abraham was, I am.' Whatever religious connection may have existed at any time between the Sati and Rotennu, and Kam, and there was doubtless much, for probably the chief goddess of the former was the celebrated Ashtoreth Karnaim,[7] whom we meet with in Kam as Astarta, it is evident, by reference to certain Kamic divinities admittedly foreign in origin, that Phoenicia and the neighbouring region was the immediate quarter whence many of the important basis-elements of the Kamic religion were derived, a circumstance which forms the historical foundation for the statement that the Phoenician personage called by Philon Kronos, 'visiting the country of the South, gave the whole of Aigyptos to the god Taautos,[8] that it might be

---

[1] Cf. *Gen.* xiv. 5; xv. 19, 20. *Deut.* ii.
[2] *Anct. Hist. of the East*, ii. 147.
[3] *Herodotus*, iv. 196-202.
[4] Cf. Kenrick, *Phoenicia*, cap. iii.; Gesenius, *Script. Ling. Phoe.* 338, the Articles in Dr. Smith's *Geographical Dictionary* and Kitto's *Biblical Cyclopaedia*.
[5] *Anct. Hist. of the East*, i. 227; cf. Bunsen, *Egypt's Place*, iii. 133.
[6] *Is.* xix. 11.
[7] Cf. *sup.* IV. iii. 2.
[8] Thoth-Tet.

his kingdom.'[1] Thus, to take a familiar instance, 'the name Astartā, the celebrated Ashtaroth of the Bible, or Astarte of the Greek authors, occurs in the papyrus Anastasi II. In an historical monument of the time of the great Ramses where this name occurs she is called 'the goddess of the Cheta,'[2] or Khitas the Northern Hittites.'[3] Again, the important divinity Set or Sutekh, called by the Hellenes Typhon, the opposer of Uasar, is undoubtedly a Syrian importation. Thus, M. Lenormant remarks, 'Evil was personified by one particular god, Set, or Sutekh, sometimes also called Baal, who was the supreme god of neighbouring Asiatic nations, and in later times, that of the Shepherds.'[4] He was afterwards identified with Apepi or Apap, the great serpent of evil,[5] but was originally distinct, and considered to be a beneficent god.[6] His worship, as the tutelary god of Lower Egypt, dates from a very early period,[7] but 'the earliest traces of the existence of Set are in Palestine and Aramaea.'[8] 'Sutech is identified with Baal in numerous inscriptions, and is represented specially as the chief deity of the Cheta.' 'If we accept the probable tradition of Porphery,[9] that Aahmes I. suppressed human sacrifices offered under the Shepherd kings at Heliopolis, the form of worship must have been Typhonian, and in all probability of Phoenician origin.'[10] Porphyrios wrote with Manethon's work on *Archaeology and Devotion* before him, and as the authority of the latter writer is constantly increasing[11], we may feel fairly satisfied that the tradition

---

[1] Sanchou. i. 8.
[2] *Egypt's Place*, i. 425-6.
[3] As to the foreign divinities Anta and Renpa or Ranpo, introduced into the Kamic Pantheon, Vide *Egypt's Place*, i. 423-6; Rawlinson, *Herodotus*, ii. 248, 453.
[4] *Anct. Hist. of the East*, i. 320.
[5] Cf. Plout. *Peri Is.* xxxvi.
[6] Cf. *Egypt's Place*, iv. 310.
[7] Cf. De Rougé, *Recherches*, 0, 45.
[8] *Egypt's Place*, iv. 319.
[9] *Peri Apok. Emps.* ii. 55.
[10] Canon Cook, *Essay on the Bearings of Egyptian History upon the Pentateuch*, Speaker's Commentary, i. 449.
[11] Cf. *Anct. Hist. of the East*, i. 96.

is correct in substance. Bunsen considers Set to be 'the primeval name of God in Asia.'[1] Whether this be so or not, the Asiatic origin of the divinity is evident. Again, as regards the Kamic Pantheon generally, Sir G. Wilkinson, while observing that 'it is not certain that the great gods were limited to eight,' notices that 'the eight gods' of Herodotos,[2] 'who existed before the rest,' agree 'with the eight Cabiri (*i.e.* "great" gods) of the Phoenicians.'[3] Ptah, the idea of the creative power or personified Demiurge, the god of Mennefer,[4] is another Kamic divinity evidently Phoenician in origin. Speaking of his representations, Bunsen observes, 'Sometimes the feet are turned quite inwards, and in the Ritual Ptah is twice represented as bow-legged; such may or may not [this is cautious] assimilate with the lame Hephaistos.'[5] It is difficult, after considering the force of the combined evidence, to doubt the assimilation, and so Sir G. Wilkinson observes, 'the deformed figure of the Pthah of Memphis *doubtless* gave rise to the fable of the lameness of the Greek Hephaestus or Vulcan.'[6] Kambatt,[7] Herodotos tells us, when in Kam, 'went into the temple of Vulcan [Ptah] and made great sport of the image. For the image of Vulcan is very like the Pataeci of the Phoenicians, wherewith they ornament the prows of their ships of war.[8] If persons have not seen these, I will explain in a different way—it is a figure resembling that of a pigmy. He also went into the temple of the Cabiri, and not only made sport of the images but even burnt them. They are made like the statue of Vulcan, who is

---

[1] *Egypt's Place*, iv. 333.
[2] Herod. ii. 145.
[3] Rawlinson, *Herodotus*, ii. 242; cf. Sanchon. i. 8.
[4] Memphis.
[5] *Egypt's Place*, i. 395.
[6] Rawlinson, *Herodotus*, ii. 302.
[7] Kambyses.
[8] Cf. Eur. *Iph. in Aul.* 253-8: 'The armament of the Boiotoi fifty sea-traversing ships I beheld, equipped with figure-heads, and their sign was Kadmos holding a golden dragon around the lofty beaks of the ships.'

said to have been their father.'[1] 'The eight great gods of the Phoenicians, the offspring of one great father, Sydik, the "just," were called Cabiri.'[2] Ptah, as his name denotes, being derived from an old Kamic word *ptah*, 'to open,' akin to the Hebrew *patakh*,[3] is the father of the Phoenician Pataikoi, Openers, Expanders, Revealers. He thus takes his place in the Pantheon of Phoenicia.[4] Again, Anouke,[5] 'the third person of the triad at the first cataract, has the title of Ank;' and Neith, also the goddess of Sa, 'is sometimes called Neit-Ank or Onk.'[6] *Ankh* signifying 'life,' 'living,' 'the oil of life,'[7] the goddess Ank or Onk is the 'Living-one,' *i.e.* the possessor of inherent vitality, and the hieroglyph is naturally the *crux ansata*,[8] or handled cross, which phallically represents the combined Linga and Yoni. In Onk ' we recognise Onka, the name given to the Boeotian Minerva, according to Plutarch, and confirmed by Æschylus, who calls her Onka Pallas, and speaks of a gate at Thebes, called Oncaean, after her. It is also called Oncaean by Apollodorus.[9] The Scholiast on Æschylus says Cadmus founded a temple there to the Egyptian Minerva, who was called Oncaea. This temple and name are also mentioned by the Schol. Pind. *Ol.* ii., who says the name is Phoenician. Pausanias also calls it Phoenician, and uses it as an argument to prove Cadmus was a Phoenician and not an Egyptian, as some supposed.'[10] The supposition that the founder of the Boiotik Thebai was a Kamite is utterly groundless and untenable. Founded by Phoenicians, the city retained to a late age

---

[1] Herod. iii. 37.
[2] Sir G. Wilkinson in Rawlinson's *Herodotus*, ii. 80.
[3] Dr. Birch in *Egypt's Place*, i. 395.
[4] Vide *inf.* X. i. As to the Phoenician character of Hephaistos, vide Gladstone, *Juv. Mun.* 289-94, 529, *Poseidon*, xiv.
[5] Anukis.
[6] Rawlinson, *Herodotus*, ii. 90.
[7] Birch, *Dictionary of Hieroglyphics*, in voc.
[8] Cf. Cooper, *Serpent Myths of Ancient Egypt*, 45.
[9] *Bib.* iii. 6.
[10] Sir G. Wilkinson in Rawlinson's *Herodotus*, ii. 90.

the traditional and correct name of one of the divinities of the founders, the Kamitico-Phoenician goddess Onka.[1] Nonnos assigns the Onkaian gate of Thebai to 'the blue-eyed Mene.'[2] Isaiah speaks of the idolatrous Jews as 'furnishing the drink-offering unto Meni,'[3] whom Bunsen calls a 'Babylono-Kanaanitish' goddess, 'the Fortuna of the Semites,'[4] the female reflection of the Phrygian Moon-god Mên. It is to be observed that the name of the first king of Kam, Mena,[5] appears to be derived from the root *men*, to 'establish' or 'found,' 'and the interpretation " the eternal," given by Eratosthenes, is probably very correct.'[6] The blue-eyed Meni, the Eternal One, is doubtless the Kamic Anouke, who appears as a 'primeval goddess,' and the Phoenician Onka, the Ever-living. Were the constant heaven and the deathless morning mirrored in her deep blue eyes, as in those of the lovely Aryan dawn-goddess with whom she was doubtless not unnaturally confounded?[7] These specimen divinities Astarta, Baal-Sutekh, Ptah, and his Seven Sons, the Kabeiroi, and Onk or Onka, like other members of the Kamic Pantheon that could be instanced, are Phoenician in derivation. But did they absolutely originate in Phoenicia? No more than the Phoenicians themselves, who at an early period left Kaldea, as Herodotos tells us, and having 'formerly dwelt on the shores of the Erythraean sea,' or Persian Gulf, 'migrated to the Mediterranean.'[8] From the plain of the two rivers came the Kamic Astarta, the Hellenik Astarte, the Hebrew Ashtoreth, the Phoenician Astart, and the Assyrian Ishtar.[9] From the same

[1] Cf. *Sup.* subsec. iii.
[2] Non. v. 70.
[3] Is. lxv. 11.
[4] *Egypt's Place*, iv. 252, Note.
[5] Menes.
[6] *Egypt's Place*, ii. 54.
[7] As to Athene Onka, *vide* also Rawlinson, *Herodotus*, ii. 78; Leake, *Travels in Northern Greece*, ii. 234, 241; iv. 578; Kenrick, *Phoenicia*, 100; *inf.* IX. iii.
[8] Herod. i. 1; vii. 89.
[9] 'The name Istar, or Ishtar, meaning " goddess," is applied to any female divinity' (Geo. Smith, *Chaldean Account of Genesis*, 58).

THE DIONYSOS OF HERODOTOS.

locality came Bilu, Bel, or Baal, the Demiurge, and the Kabeiroi or Great Gods. The 'Song of the Seven Spirits' in Assyrian runs:—

> They are seven! they are seven!
> In the depths of Ocean they are seven!
> In the heights of heaven they are seven!
> Male they are not! Female they are not!

Like the 'two-natured Iakchos,' the combined Uasar-Uasi.

> Wives they have not! Children are not born to them!
> They are seven! and they are seven!
> Twice over they are seven![1]

Nor is it to be supposed that Uasar or Dionysos affords any illustration of an exception to the foregoing rule of derivation. He, like the divinities lastly referred to, entered Kam from Kaldea by way of Phoenicia. In Kam he appears under the Uasarian aspect, in Asia Minor as Sabazios; in Hellas as Dionysos, a name which, as we shall see in the sequel, was known in Assur centuries before. From the same Aramean basis his cult in varying shades spreads Northwestward and Southwestward, and Aram in her turn received him from the Kaldean cradle of art, religion and civilization.[2] An objection of Mr. Kenrick to the theory of a Phoenician Dionysos may here be noticed. He remarks, 'The connection of the history of Bacchus and the introduction of his worship, with the history of Cadmus, point to a migration of the Phoenicians from Thrace to Boeotia rather than immediately from Phoenicia. For the oldest mention of the Dionysiak worship in Grecian literature represents Bacchus as in conflict with Lycurgus, king of the Edones, and he had no

---

[1] Translated by H. F. Talbot in *Trans. Soc. Bib. Archaeol.* ii. 58.
[2] Vide *inf.* XII.

original or special connection with the Phoenician mythology (?). Thrace was the immediate, Lydia and Phrygia the remoter source from which it [*i.e.* the Dionysiak cult] came into Greece, and Thebes the first place in Southern Greece in which it gained a footing.'[1] On this it may be remarked, (1) That there is nothing in the Episode of Lykourgos, which has been already considered, to show that Dionysos was a Thrakian divinity, but the myth fully demonstrates his foreign character; (2) That there is no reliable evidence that Kadmos colonized Thebai from Thrake, but the contrary; (3) That, when considering the *Bakchai*, we found good reason to reject with Herodotos the theory of Euripides of the Lydian and Phrygian origin of the god; (4) That even at the present time our knowledge of the Phoenician Pantheon, although it has considerably increased, is still exceedingly incomplete; so that even had we no positive information on the subject to the contrary, we should be unable to say that Dionysos was entirely unconnected with the mythology of the Syrian sea-board; (5) The general tenor of the evidence, both already adduced, and also to be subsequently referred to, is contrary to Mr. Kenrick's supposition. Thus, *e.g.*, I presume that, according to this view, Dionysos and Uasar are distinct divinities. It cannot be shown that any mythology or divinity originated in Asia Minor, which was colonized by successive waves of Eastern immigrants, who brought their religion and ritual with them. Mr. Kenrick, after remarking the apparently Semitic character and derivation of certain Bakchik words, such as Evoe, Saboe, Bassareus, Brisaeus, etc., observes, 'As Lydia, however, *had a Semitic population*, we cannot argue from these coincidences the Phoenician origin of the Dionysiak rites.'[2] So, it is presumed, if Lydia had possessed a *non*-Semitic population, such an argument would

---

[1] *Phoenicia*, 99. [2] *Ibid.* 100, Note.

have been valid. But after all, modern research, notwithstanding the opposite opinion of many great names, inclines to the view that the Lydians were a non-Semitic and Indo-European race,[1] and, at all events, the question to which of the great Families they belong is a very doubtful one. Should it therefore appear that the Lydians were not Semites, I presume Mr. Kenrick would be willing to admit the Phoenician connection of the Dionysiak ritual, which latter fact is the simple and only explanation of the circumstance, otherwise incomprehensible, that Kadmos, who, Mr. Kenrick admits, is a representative of Phoenician influence in the West,[2] should have been an introducer and ardent supporter of the worship of the god.

SECTION VI.

DIONYSOS IN ARABIA.

'The Arabs,' says Herodotos, 'plight faith with the forms following. When two men would swear a friendship, they stand on each side of a third: he with a sharp stone makes a cut on the inside of the hand of each, near the middle finger, and taking a piece of their dress, dips it in the blood of each, and moistens therewith seven stones lying in the midst, calling the while on Bacchus and Urania. They have but these two gods; and they

---

[1] Cf. Rawlinson, *Herodotus*, i. 541, 548.
[2] 'Cadmus landed in Rhodes on his search for Europa, which is the mythical explanation of the traces of the Phoenicians in various parts of Asia and Greece' (*Phoenicia*, 80; cf. 84).

say that in their mode of cutting the hair they follow Bacchus. Now their practice is to cut it in a ring, away from the temples. Bacchus they call in their language Orotal, and Urania, Alilat.'[1] Does Herodotos here arbitrarily and erroneously identify Dionysos and the Arabian divinity whom he calls Orotal,—or is he correct in his supposition? It may assist us in arriving at a conclusion to consider the other divinity referred to, Ouranie-Alilat. Ouranie, the Heavenly-one, has a threefold aspect in Hellenik mythology. She is (1) the Mistress of the starry heavens, or, more familiarly, the Muse of Astronomy; (2) the 'goddess-like' daughter of Okeanos and Tethys;[2] and (3) a personification of heavenly love which produced and sustains all things, as distinguished from Aphrodite Pandemos, earthly or common love.[3] The heavenly-one, daughter of all-sustaining Ocean, and personified as god-like love, was early and naturally identified by the Hellenes with the Great Goddess Mother of the East. So Pausanias speaks of the temple of the latter at Athenai—'The temple of Aphrodite Ouranie, and Ouranie was first worshipped *by the Assyrians;* and after these by the Paphians of Kypros and by the Phoinikians who dwelt in Askalon, in Palestine: and the Kythereans worshipped her, having learnt her ritual from the Phoinikians.'[4] He places the introduction of her worship into Attike in the remote era of the mythical king Aigeus, who, he states, introduced her cult because he had no children; and she, as we shall see, was the representative of production and mother of all. In another passage[5] he speaks of exceedingly ancient wooden statues of Aphrodite possessed by the Thebans, and one of which was called the statue of Aphrodite Ouranie.

---

[1] Herod. iii. 8.
[2] Hesiod. *Theog.* 350.
[3] Cf. Platon. *Phaidros,* 259.
[4] Paus. i. 14.
[5] Ibid. ix. 16.

THE DIONYSOS OF HERODOTOS. 219

They were said to have been dedicated by Harmonia, and to have been made from the beaks of the ships of Kadmos, a remarkable tradition, and in exact accordance with the Phoenician custom.[1] These valuable traditions, of course incorrect in their literal details from a Euemeristic point of view, aptly illustrate the way by which the cult of the Great Goddess was introduced into Hellas. To consider her history and ritual further would be foreign to the subject of this investigation; suffice it to say that she is the Artemis of Ephesos, the Kybele of Phrygia, the armed Aphrodite of Sparta, the Atargatis or Derketo of Askalon, the Uasi of Kam, the Here of the Syrian Hierapolis,[2] the Anait of Persia and Armenia, the Astart of the Phoenicians, the Ashtoreth of the Rephoeem, the Ishtar of the Assyrians, the Mylitta of the Babylonians,[3] the Alala of the Akkadians,[4] and the Alitta,[5] or Alilat of the Arabians. This last name signifies 'to bear children,' and, according to Canon Rawlinson, Alitta 'is the Semitic root El, "God," with the feminine suffix added.'[6] Some learned readers may possibly be inclined to doubt the identity of the various phases of the Great Goddess Mother above mentioned; but accurate investigation will deduce them from a common origin, although by degrees they become distinct concepts, like the personified attributes of the Deity.'[7]

The Great Goddess, then, being the only, or at all events the protagonistic, female divinity worshipped by the Arabians, and they having also only one or one chief

---

[1] Cf. Herod. iii. 37; *sup*. sec. v. 5.
[2] Vide Loukianos. *Peri tes Syries Theou*.
[3] Cf. Herod. i. 131, 199.
[4] *Trans. Soc. Bib. Archaeol.* iii. 163.
[5] Herod. i. 131.
[6] Rawlinson, *Herodotus*, i. 217.
[7] As to the Great Goddess, vide Apuleius, *De Asino Aureo*, lib. xi. Sir G. Wilkinson, in Rawlinson's *Herodotus*, ii. 445 *et seq*. A great Goddess-mother exists in almost every human religious system, as a natural result of anthropomorphic thought. The Aryan Demeter, it may be observed, is a perfectly distinct concept from the Semitic Goddess-mother, although inevitably identified with her when the two came into contact.

male divinity, this latter must of necessity have been the Great God. And who is this Being? I shall not at this point of the enquiry consider Dionysos in his primal home; but it is evident that the Great God is the mighty Demiurge, and all-animating, all-sustaining Being, the husband of the Great Goddess, the Baal of Ashtoreth, the Sabazios of Kybele, the Uasar of Uasi, and thus on, like the Great Goddess many-named, one and yet many, 'Zagreus, highest of all gods,' Iao who changes with the seasons, but still 'One Zeus, one Aïdes, one Helios, ONE DIONYSOS.' The grand old oracle of Apollon Klarios rings true through all the changes of time and locality; and Herodotos, who, as we have seen, displays in his consideration of Dionysos a critical acumen that makes the wild Euemeristic stories of a writer like Diodoros Sikelos seem mere imbecility, spoke most advisedly when he identified Dionysos and Orotal. Can it then be pretended that Herodotos regarded the Dionysos of his countrymen as being only a simple rustic Wine-god? As regards the name Orotal, Sir G. Wilkinson observes, 'Urotal has been supposed to be "Allah-taal," the same name as now used by the Arabs for the Deity, signifying "God the exalted,"'[1] like Zeus the Most High, and Zagreus the Highest. And after alluding to the opinion of Scaliger and Selden that Alilat was the moon,[2]—a view undoubtedly correct in itself, though not containing an exhaustive explanation of the nature of the goddess—he remarks: 'If so, Urotal should be referred to the day, or [rather to] the sun, the *Aor* "light" of Hebrew.' Sir Henry Rawlinson, when speaking of the Kaldean divinity who is the god of the atmosphere, and whose name has not yet been satisfactorily deciphered,[3] observes, 'If we looked

---

[1] Rawlinson, *Herodotus,* ii. 336.
[2] Cf. *De Dis Syris,* 253, edit. 1688.
[3] This personage has been called Vul, Iva, Yem, Ao, Hu, Bin, etc.

to mere local tradition, a more probable reading would seem to be *Air*, or *Aür*, well-known gods in the Mendaean Pantheon, who presided over the firmament;' and we might then further explain the Orotal of Herodotus, as a compound term [*i.e. Ur* and *Tal*], including the male and female divinities of the material heaven,'[1] in fact, as being a sort of 'two-natured Iakchos.' Orotal is thus a god of light, of sun-light, and of the air; and the Sun himself, the 'one Helios' of the oracle, Hyperion the Climber, or Most High, in Akkadian and Hamitic Kaldean called San the Bright-one, whilst his Semitic name is Shamas, Shemesh, Chemosh, the Servitor, the exact opposite of Baal, Molekh, or Malek, the Lord, is undoubtedly the divinity referred to, or at all events the most remarkable phase of that divinity. Mr. King, alluding to the leontokephalic man on Gnostic talismans, remarks, 'May not this figure be the great god of the ancient Arabians, Ourotal, God of Light, whom Herodotus takes for Dionysos, and thus again equivalent to the later Pater Bromius?'[2] Similarly, the solar phase is the most remarkable feature in the concept of Uasar; and when Dionysos is traced to his origin, the same fact will also appear with respect to him;[3] although in his adopted Hellenik home this aspect may not, perhaps, at first sight, be particularly prominent. But the solar character of Orotal is susceptible of further illustration; for, as Mr. Fox Talbot observes, 'It is certain that the Arabians worshipped the Sun, and the Assyrian records confirm this by saying that tribute was brought by the Queen of the Arabians, who used to worship the sun.'[4] But Orotal is said to have been the only god whom the Arabians worshipped: therefore, Orotal and the Sun are identical. The Arabian cult was

---

[1] Rawlinson, *Herodotus*, i. 498.
[2] *The Gnostics*, 118.
[3] Vide *inf*. XII.
[4] *Trans. Soc. Bib. Archaeol.* ii. 33.

certainly of a Tsabaistic or star-worshipping nature, and among all star-worshippers 'that nebulous star we call the Sun' would naturally and necessarily have the first place. 'The astral character of the old Arabian idolatry,' observes Canon Rawlinson, 'is indubitable. The Bacchus and Urania of Herodotus are therefore with reason taken to represent the Sun and the Moon.'[1] So M. Lenormant, when speaking of the ancient religion of Yemen, remarks, 'Bil, Rahman ["the merciful"], Yathaa ["the Saviour"[2]], Haubas ["the Shining"], Samah ["the Elevated"], Simidan ["the Powerful"], Dhamar ["the Protector"], all represent the Sun under different points of view.'[3] But we notice, moreover, that the Arabian votary of the solar Orotal, on plighting his faith, like the Syrian votary of the solar Baal, cuts himself till the blood gushes out upon him,[4] and this savage custom obtained over the whole of Western Asia. Thus we find on an Assyrian tablet:—

> He who stabs his flesh in honour of Ishtar, the goddess unrivalled.
> Like the stars of heaven he shall shine;[5] like the river of night he shall flow![6]

'By "the river of night,"' says Mr. Fox Talbot, with great ingenuity and probability, 'I understand the Milky Way.' Here, then, the Tsabaist, or worshipper of the host of heaven, is encouraged to self-wounding by the prospect of shining with a glory equal to that of his divinities. Let the reader compare with this strange and fierce ritual the stern and ruthless side of the Dionysiak cult.[7] The Arabian next proceeded to moisten with his blood 'seven stones lying in the midst,' which would

---

[1] Rawlinson, *Herodotus*, ii. 336.
[2] Cf. Dionysos Soter.
[3] *Anct. Hist. of the East*, ii. 324.
[4] Cf. 1 *Kings*, xviii. 28.
[5] Cf. *Dan.* xii. 3.
[6] *Trans. Soc. Bib. Archaeol.* ii. 53.
[7] *Sup.* IV. iii. 2, 3.

THE DIONYSOS OF HERODOTOS: 223

appear to have formed a kind of rude altar; their number being significant and symbolical, as the twelve stones which formed the rude extempore altar of Elijah represented the twelve tribes of Israel.[1] Here the symbolism is evident; the Tsabaist worships in his oath the sacred seven planets, whose cult reappears in the seven gates of the city of Thebai. I have already quoted an extract from the Assyrian version of the Song of the Seven Spirits, and their connection with the seven sons of Ptah is sufficiently obvious; not, however, that the Kabeiroi were merely the planets or planetary influences, but the astral, kosmogonic, and psychical phases and ideas are as usual intermixed in their concept.[2] The last noticeable feature in the account of Herodotos further illustrates the solar character of Orotal. He describes the Arabians as saying that they follow or imitate their divinity in their mode of cutting the hair, which, from his account, they appear to have cut or shaved in a circular form; in fact, they seem to have worn a kind of tonsure, a practice particularly forbidden to the priests of Israel,[3] but followed by those of Uasar,[4] a being who, according to Macrobius, is 'nothing else but the Sun.' The Skythai, whose oaths were accompanied by similar mutilations, seem also to have cut their hair in a similar manner.[5] And, agreeably, we find that the ceremony of tonsure 'was an old practice of the priests of Mithra, who in their tonsures imitated the solar disk.'[6] Mr. C. W. King remarks that the devotees of Uasi 'carried into the new priesthood the former badges of their profession, the obligation to celibacy, the tonsure, etc. The sacred image still moves in procession, as when

---

[1] 1 *Kings*, xviii. 31-2.
[2] As to the number 7, cf. Mr. Fox Talbot in. *Trans. Soc. Bib. Archaeol.* ii. 58-60. Vide *inf.* X. 1.
[3] *Lev.* xxi. 5.
[4] Macrob. i. 21.
[5] Cf. Herod. iv. 70-1.
[6] Maurice, *Indian Antics.* vii. 851. Vide *inf.* XII. i. 4.

Juvenal laughed at it, escorted by the tonsured train.'[1] The solar significance of the tonsure is undoubted.

In illustration of the connection between Dionysos and Arabia,[2] may lastly be noticed the opinion of the poet Antimachos and others already referred to,[3] that Lykourgos was king of Arabia, and that Nysa was there situate. Euripides, too, as we have seen, describes Dionysos as having come to Thebai from Arabia the Happy. Later writers frequently place Nysa in Arabia, or in Asia, or in both.[4] Mr. Sharpe remarks that the birthplace of Uasar 'was Mount Sinai, called by the Egyptians Mount Nissa.'[5] These various mythic legends illustrate the ancient connection between Arabia and the solar cult of Dionysos-Orotal.

SECTION VII.

EIKON OF THE DIONYSOS OF HERODOTOS.

The Dionysos of Herodotos is a divinity of widespread and extended sway. In Kam, he appears as Uasar; in Arabia, as Orotal; in Asia Minor, as Sabazios; while he is found alike in Phoenicia, Skythia, Thrake, and Hellas. His mysteries and sufferings are similarly commemorated on the circular lake of Sa, in the tragic choruses of Sikyon, and at the sacred shrine of Eleusis. Nysa, far in the Outer-world, is his early home; and Kadmos and his Phoenician companions first introduced the Dionysiak cult into continental Hellas, where it was adopted by the illustrious seer Melampous. As

---

[1] *The Gnostics*, 71.
[2] Called in Hebrew Arab, in Assyrian Arabu, and in Egyptian Punt.
[3] *Sup.* IV. ii. 1.
[4] Cf. Apollod. i. 6, iii. 4; Diod. i. 19, iii. 64.
[5] *Egyptian Mythology*, 10.

Orotal and Uasar, Dionysos is a solar divinity, judge of the dead, and chief of the gods, but the superstitious reticence of the historian prevents the recital of his esoteric history, and the explanation of its meaning. Although, however, his cult is so widely spread, yet it never appears as indigenous in any non-Semitic regions. It is a novelty and an innovation alike in Skythia, Thrake, and Hellas, and Kam herself is but the debtor of Asia in the matter. First Phoenicians, and subsequently Hellenes, spread the worship; and the Phoenicians themselves are emigrants from Kaldea. The connection between the god and the vine, which, according to many, is all important, and actually the sum and substance of the whole matter, is so comparatively insignificant in the opinion of Herodotos, that he never once refers to it. Of all the writers who have been examined, none have given clearer or more important testimony to the true nature and origin of Dionysos; and though Herodotos, wiser on the point from actual knowledge and research than Euripides, avoids the error of the Lydian theory of the latter, yet this is a mere point of detail, and there is a substantial agreement between the historian and the author of the *Bakchai*. Herodotos, therefore, joins the cloud of witnesses who, from Homeros downwards, testify in tones of perhaps varying distinctness, yet with one mind and one mouth, that the Zeus of Nysa and son of Semele is a wandering and wondrous stranger, the child of the distant and glowing regions of the Semitic East. With Herodotos closes the line of early Hellenik writers who have treated of the Great Dionysiak Myth. Later authors, from Apollodoros to Nonnos, are in the main either copyists and compilers, who re-echo traditions and legends which in their time had become unmeaning, or else crude Euemerists, like Diodoros Sikelos, whose system compels them to run riot in all manner of absurdities. Their works, often highly valuable for reference and for the illustration of particular points, are, as a whole, undeserving of separate examination. The god-like Elders of Hellenik song, the poets, epic, lyric, and tragic, have given their testimony, which has been crowned and completed by that of the great Father of History. We shall now, therefore, turn from individual authorities to contemplate Dionysos as he appears in the ordinary life of Hellenik cities, and in the enduring triumphs of Hellenik art.

CHAPTER VI.

THE HELLENIK CULT OF DIONYSOS.

SECTION I.

THE FESTIVALS OF DIONYSOS.

Subsection I.—The Attik Cult.

WE have now to notice the Dionysiak cult and ritual as they obtained amongst the Hellenes of the great historical ages; and here the Festivals of the god, of which there were some five-and-twenty, claim especial attention. The four principal Attik Dionysiak festivals were (1) the Dionysia Mikra, the Lesser or Rural Dionysia; (2) the Dionysia Lenaia; (3) the Anthesteria; and (4) the Dionysia Megala, the Greater or City Dionysia. The Rural Dionysia, celebrated yearly in the month Posideon (December-January) throughout the various townships of Attike, was presided over by the demarch or mayor. The celebration occasioned a kind of rustic carnival, distinguished like almost all Bakchik festivals, by gross intemperance and licentiousness, and during which slaves enjoyed a temporary freedom, with licence to insult their superiors, and behave in a boisterous and disorderly manner. It is brought vividly before us in the *Acharnes* of Aristophanes, which was produced early in B.C. 425, the sixth year of the Peloponnesian War. In this Play Dikaiopolis, the Upright Citizen[1] and advocate of peace

---

[1] Cf. Orthagoras, Aristoph. *Ek.* 916.

at any price, influenced doubtless by the peculiarly exposed situation of the town of Acharnai, concludes a separate treaty on his own account with the Spartans and their allies—a felicitous arrangement which enables him to spend his time in Bakchik revelry and devotion. Having commenced with the Rural Dionysia, the Upright Citizen is left when the Play closes apparently celebrating the Anthesteria. Peace being concluded, he exclaims, 'O Dionysia! I freed from war and ills will go within and celebrate the Rural Dionysia.'[1] The scene then represents him engaged in the celebration, assisted by his wife, daughter, and slaves.

> *Di.* Speak words of good omen! Speak words of good omen!
> Let the Basket-bearer come forward a little:
> Xanthias set up the phallos erect.
>
> . . . .
>
> You two must hold the phallos erect behind the Basket-bearer,
> And I following will chant the phallic-hymn.
> O Phales, companion of Bakchos,
> Fellow-reveller, nightly-rambler-around,
> Seducer, youth-lover.[2]

Here we have the simple phallic cult of the personified Priapos, son of Dionysos and Aphrodite,[3] both Oriental divinities, and which, as we have seen, Herodotos states that Melampous obtained from Kadmos the Tyrian. It is remarkable that throughout the whole Play goddesses are never introduced into the licentious ritual of the Upright Citizen. It is to Dionysos alone that he sacrifices, and yet even here amongst the rustics, in the very place of all others where the simple wine-god, if such he were, should stand clearly before us, the vinal

---

[1] Vs. 201-2.
[2] A fragment of a phallic song, which, however, calls for no particular comment, is also given in Athen. xiv.
Vide Bergk. *Poet. Ly. Grac. Car. Pop.* Frag. viii.
[3] Cf. Diod. iv. 6.

phase is found to be altogether secondary, and it is as a phallic divinity that Dionysos appears on the stage. The highly important phallic element in religious mythology is now at length receiving full recognition, which indeed, in accordance with the customary movements of the human pendulum,[1] ere long promises to be somewhat too ample. Some ardent followers of Payne Knight in the present day appear to hold that phallicism is the key to all mysteries, the explanation of all rude stone monuments, and of an infinity of remains less barbarous, and the illustration and basis of all occult symbolism and mysterious practice. But we may be sure of this, that *one key will never open all locks*; one fact, however wide in influence and prevading in effect, will never explain in an entirety the whole of the intricate combinations of religious mythology. As previously observed,[2] if we rely solely in our investigations on the explanation afforded by a single principle, we shall inevitably be at fault in numerous instances, and be compelled sooner or later either to abandon the theory or to overstrain it. The thing itself to be dealt with, is complex and diverse in character; so, therefore, must be the elements which form the system of explanation. A judicious combination of principles and methods of treatment, not the arbitrary exclusion of any one of them, will ultimately cut the Gordian knot; for the problem is not insoluble, and the materials requisite for its solution are constantly increasing. The phallic character of Dionysiak worship was, from the nature of the god, inevitable. The essence and power of all kosmic vitality, Erikepeios is, necessarily, when anthropomorphically regarded, a phallic divinity. The religions of the world are, as a matter of course,

---

[1] 'The law of rhythm in its social applications implies that alternations of opinion will be violent in proportion as opinions are extreme' (II. Spencer. *The Principles of Sociology*, Number 40, Appendix A.)

[2] *Sup.* I.

developed in accordance with human nature, and hence their success; it is easy to be religious when that is only another name for 'fulfilling the desires of the flesh and of the mind.' Nor must it be forgotten that the Dionysiak worshipper, Eastern or Western, was often most religious when most depraved; for if religion is depravity, then frequently depravity is religion. Dikaiopolis is represented as being a very religious man, *i.e.* as replete with veneration for his divinity. His pretty little daughter is the Basket-bearer on the occasion. This mystic basket has been alluded to when considering the Uasario-Dionysiak symbols of chest, coffin, ark, egg, ship, boat, etc.,[1] and will be again mentioned in its place in the Eleusinian Ritual.[2] Speaking of the Palladion or sacred statue of Pallas Athene,[3] Mr. Cox observes, 'The word denotes simply a figure of Pallas, and Pallas is but another form of Phallos. To the same class belong the names of Pales, the Latin god of flocks and shepherds, and of the Sicilian Palikoi.'[4] It is possible, but highly improbable, that Pallas, the stainless virgin goddess, may be one of this phallic group. There are, as Mr. Cox notices, traditions which link her with a giant Pallas who, according to one legend, was said to have been her father, a statement which requires no explanation; but there is ever a contest between the two, and so Athene, in the war between the Giants and the Gods, which is said to have taken place near Pall-ene,[5] slays Pallas, who is always an earth-power. The characteristics of the earth-giant and of the queen of the air are so diametrically opposite that I cannot but regard the name of the latter as given in allusion to her vibratory power.[6] Phales, to whom Dikaiopolis addresses his pious hymn, appears

---

[1] *Sup.* V. v. 4.
[2] *Inf.* sec. ii. 3.
[3] Cf. Herod. iv. 189.
[4] *Mythol. of the Aryan Nations,* ii. 114, Note; cf. *Ibid.* i. 442.
[5] Diod. iv. 15; v. 71; Paus. i. 25.
[6] Cf. Ruskin, *Queen of the Air,* i. 43.

to be undoubtedly identical with the Latin Pales, an Aryan Erikepeios of doubtful sex, or of both sexes, like the 'two-natured Iakchos,' whose festival, the Palilia, celebrated yearly on the supposed birthday of Roma, partly solemn and partly joyous, and always accompanied in the country by riotous mirth and copious potations, presents a remarkable analogy to the Acharnian cult. Similar also are the Latin divinities Lupercus and Luperca, the latter apparently identical, or at all events identified, with the mythic shewolf which suckled Romulus and Remus.[1] The festival of Pales, the sire, is appropriately celebrated on the birthday of the Commonwealth. Phallos is sometimes rendered in Latin by 'oscillum.'[2] The oscilla or 'little mouths,' were small heads or faces of Bacchus,[3] 'fictiles imagunculus,' which hung from trees in and near the vineyards; and, whirled about by the breeze, were supposed to produce fertility in every direction they faced, and thus appropriately represented Phales-Erikepeios. So Virgil sings, 'Thee, O Bacchus, they invoke in joyful hymns and to thee they hang the benignant oscilla from the lofty pine.'[4] Phallic divinities are, as a matter of course, found amongst all races of mankind, although their cult is far more prominent in some special localities. It is sometimes difficult to draw the line between a licentious and an honestly religious use.

The Dionysia Lenaia, celebrated yearly in the month Gamelion, called among the Ionians Lenaion, from *lenos*, a wine-press, was presided over by the Archon Basileus, the second of the Nine Rulers of Athenai, and the representative in historic times of the ancient king in his priestly or sacerdotal aspect, for originally the king was,

---

[1] Cf. Mr. F. A. Paley on *Il.* vi. 134.
[2] Vide Aristoph. Edit. Ludolph Kusteri, 1710. 'A very beautiful edition,' (Moss, *Manual of Classical Bibliography*, i. 04).
[3] I use the Latin form when speaking of the god in Italia.
[4] *Geor.* ii. 388-0.

like Melchisedek, ' a priest upon his throne.'¹ Thus similarly at Roma there was a Rex Sacrificulus or Rex Sacrorum. The festival was held at the Lenaion or temple of Dionysos Limnaios the Marshy, where the first wine-press was said to have been erected, and which stood in a swampy quarter of Athenai, not far from the south side of the Akropolis.² Thus in the *Batrachoi* the Chorus of Frogs exclaim, ' Brekekekex koax koax. Marshy children of the fountains, let us loudly utter a harmonious sound of hymns, my sweet-sounding song koax koax, which around the Nyseian Dionysos son of Zeus in Limnai we cried lustily, when the rambling-revelling crowd of people passed through my glebe on the sacred Pitcher-feast.'³ The Dionysiak procession walked to the temple, where a goat⁴ was sacrificed, and the Chorus sang around the altar the dithyrambic ode in honour of the god. Both tragedies and comedies, but especially the latter, formed an important feature at the Lenaia.

The Anthesteria or Feast of Flowers, celebrated yearly in the month Anthesterion (February-March), formed a link between Dionysos and the Mother and the Daughter, whose Festival of the Anthesphoria or Flower-gathering very closely corresponds with it. Both these flower-festivals were, as of course, held in springtime, when the earth awakes from the sleep and arises from the death of winter to bloom in renewed beauty and restored vitality. The celebration lasted for three days, the first of which was called Pithoigia or Tap-barrel-day, on which they opened the casks and tried the wine of the previous year. The day was spent in merriment, and it is noticeable that in Boiotia, the Hellenik birthplace of the Dionysiak cult, it was called the Day of the Good Daemon, or favouring

---

[1] *Zech.* vi. 13.
[2] Thoukyd. ii. 15.
[3] Vs. 210-19; cf. *Achar.* 1,000, 1202.
[4] Cf. *Sup.* IV. iii. 2.

heavenly power who fills men's hearts with food and gladness, giving them of the fatness of the earth beneath, no mere wine-god, for as Donaldson well observes, ' this was not a vintage festival.'[1] The type, however, of this glad earth-life was wine; and so we find that ' in the Bacchian Mysteries a consecrated cup of wine handed round after supper, called the cup of the Agathodaemon, was received with much shouting.'[2] The second day of the Festival was called Choes the Pitcher-feast, when every toper had his own cup and vessel, and he who first drained his jug received a prize. Thus the Herald in the *Acharnes* proclaims, ' Hear ye people: according to ancient custom the pitchers must be emptied at the sound of the trumpet; and whoever shall have emptied his pitcher the first, shall receive—the wine-skin of Ktesiphon,'[3] a man ridiculed by the Poet, according to the Scholiast, for being thick-witted and pot-bellied. Thoukydides similarly calls the Anthesteria the more ancient festival of Dionysos,[4] and this is an important circumstance when we notice the mystic symbolism concealed beneath these apparently simple revellings. Orestes, according to one legend, when fresh from the pollution of the murder of his mother Klytemnestra, arrived at Athenai during the celebration of this Festival; and as no one could drink with him, Demophoon the son of Theseus, who then reigned over the Athenians, in order to spare the feelings of his guest, made every man drink out of his own cup, and hence the legendary origin of the custom. From this day Dionysos had the name of Choöpotes or Deep-drinker, and he who could take the most wine was honoured by a crown of leaves, the crown being an ornament which, as noticed, Dionysos was said to have

---

[1] *Theatre of the Greeks*, 212.
[2] Nicola, *De Ritu Bacch. apud* Gronovius, vii. 186.
[3] Vs. 1000-2; cf. vs. 1070-1234.
[4] Thoukyd. ii. 15.

invented. The third day of the Festival was called Chytroi or Pot-sacrifice-day, as on it the votaries offered sacred pots filled with seeds to Dionysos and Hermes in his character of Chthonios or the Infernal, and after sunset either on this or on the preceding day the peculiar sacreds of Dionysos Nyktelios or the Nightly-one were celebrated. Slaves enjoyed a temporary freedom during the Festival. Comedies appear to have been then represented, and it is probable that ' the Tragedians read to a select audience the Tragedies which they had composed for the festival in the following month.'[1]

Next, as to the mystic symbolism of the Anthesterian Ritual. The connection between Dionysos and that wonderful concept the Awful Damsel, ' the Maid whom none may name,'[2] I shall have to notice when considering the Eleusinian Mysteries;[3] suffice it at present to remark that both divinities descend from the Upper- to the Underworld, are both lost and sought for and at length found, and alike exhibit every phase from the mildest and most attractive beauty and gentleness up to the most awe-inspiring majesty and dread shadowy grandeur. At present all that need be remembered is that Dionysos represents (1) the Sun which rises, sinks, disappears, and rises again; and (2) the Earth-life, which, in the form of vegetation and otherwise, springs from the ground, fades, dies, and rises again. Remembering this, we next notice that the Wine-pitcher and the Seed-pot are in reality identical; that both alike, with slightly varied symbolism, represent the same great idea. The jar, pitcher, amphoreus, vase, or pot, in which the seeds of vitality and the wine, ' that animating principle which, infused into the various parts of the creation, gave life and support to the

---

[1] *Theatre of the Greeks*, 213. [2] Eur. *Alex.* Frag. xxii. [3] *Inf.* sec. ii.

whole,'[1] were placed, is only the kosmic ark, chest, or egg with which we are familiar.[2] Wine in the Dionysiak cult, as in the Christian religion, represents that blood which in different senses, is the life of the world. Seeds and fruits, such as the pomegranate and apple, were similarly used at Eleusis. Lastly, must be noticed the secret Dionysiak ritual performed at the Anthesteria with its meaning. The votaries entered the temple of Dionysos Nyktelios at nightfall with lighted torches, whilst cups of wine were placed around, as libations of the symbolised life-power to the great life-divinity. At Pellene in Eastern Achaia, where the Bakchik ritual was almost exactly similar, the god was worshipped as Dionysos Lampter or the Light,[3] a circumstance which further illustrates the symbolism. The god is the light as order, form, and life-vigour, emerging in visible and apparent procession from the kosmic egg of night and chaos; and again, he is pre-eminently *the* light, *i.e.* the sun. But the Egg-sprung is the Night-born, darkness precedes light, and chaos order; and again, the dread and mysterious Being, whose cult is only intelligible to the initiated few and to them but dimly, who sinks to the Under-world, and whose light and meaning is hidden, as the soul, of which the lamp-flame was a symbol, is in the body, is at once the son, the lord, the victim, and the conqueror of darkness. Thus the mystic title Nyktelios Lampter presents no real contradiction, but illustrates the manifold nature of the multiform divinity. Dionysos, 'leader of the chorus of fire-breathing stars,' the mystic torches of the infinite, brings light and life, physical, psychical, spiritual, and mental.[4] Another temple of Dionysos Nyktelios was situated in Megaris, not very far from Eleusis.[5]

On the second day of the festival there was also a

---

[1] Christie, *Disquisitions upon the Greek Painted Vases,* 45.
[2] Vide *inf.* VIII. ii. *Jar.*
[3] Paus. vii. 27.
[4] *Sup.* IV. ii. 2.
[5] Paus. i. 40.

special secret Dionysiak celebration, called the Dodekate, because it fell on the twelfth of the month, at the temple of Dionysos Limnaios before mentioned, under the control of the wife of the Archon-King, who appointed fourteen noble women free from all ceremonial pollution, and called Gerarai the Venerables, to assist on the occasion. 'The Anthesteria,' remarks Donaldson, ' was accompanied by mystic solemnities, pointing at once to this ideal [*i.e.* as a phallic divinity in the widest sense] of the religion of Dionysos, *and to its Semitic origin.* At this festival the mysteries were entrusted to the wife of the king Archon, and to fourteen priestesses, whose number is that of the victims sent to the Minotaur, and is obviously Semitic.[1] As the representative of the state, and as symbolizing the virgin daughter of Demeter, who returned to the earth in the spring, the king Archon's wife was solemnly espoused to Dionysos, just as conversely the Venetian Doge annually married the sea, and she alone was admitted to gaze on the mysterious emblems of the god's worship, on which the welfare of the state was supposed to depend, namely, the sacred serpent and the Phallus.'[2] The symbolism, in its widest signification, is nothing less than indicative of the marriage of heaven and earth, of mind and matter, of soul and body, of active and passive principles, and of that union and unity of effort whence and by means of which are all things. Thus, the most ancient Dionysiak Festival of the god brings him before us as the phallic, serpent-girt, life-bestowing, fire-breathing, solar, kosmic, and also tauric, divinity, whose pristine home is in the Oriental cradle of mankind.

The Dionysia Megala, the Greater or City Dionysia, celebrated yearly in the month Elaphebolion (March-April), was presided over by the Archon Eponymos, so

---

[1] As to the Minotauros, vide *inf.* IX. iii.

[2] *Theatre of the Greeks,* 19; cf. *Ibid.* 55, 212-3; Herod. ii. 48-9.

called because the year was registered in his name,[1] and who was the first of the Nine. The order of the solemnities was as follows:—

I. *The great public procession.*—This appears to have consisted of,—

1. A motley crowd of dancing, shouting votaries, adorned with the leaves and with crowns of Bakchik trees and plants, such as ivy, vine, pine, and fir; beating drums, and playing on various musical instruments, some dressed in fawn- or goat-skins.

2. The bearers of the sacred vessels or mystic jars, one of which was filled with water, humidity being necessary to life and growth; and moisture or fluid matter having existed previously to the dry land, water, the Homerik all-fostering ocean-stream, being thus in one sense and aspect a kind of sire of all.[2]

3. The Kanephoroi or Basket-bearers, noble maidens who carried the mystic golden baskets filled with fruit, and also at times containing serpents.[3] So the Chorus of Women in the *Lysistrate*, when enumerating the religious festivals which the Athenian maids took part in, conclude, 'And at length I bore the basket being a beautiful girl, having a string of dried figs.'[4] These basket-bearers also appeared in the processions of Athene and Demeter.[5] The Kaneon is identical in signification with the Kalathos, both words meaning primarily a wicker-basket.[6]

---

[1] The Assyrian practice was similar. Vide George Smith, *The Assyrian Eponym Canon.*

[2] Cf. *Gen.* i. 2, 6–10; Sanchou. i. 1; Berosos, *Chaldaika*, i. Frag. 1; Pindar, *Ol.* i. 1. 'It is evident that, according to the notion of the Babylonians, the sea was the origin of all things . . . a watery chaos preceded the creation and formed the origin and groundwork of the universe' (George Smith, *Chaldean Account of Genesis*, 64–5).

[3] 'The token of the Sabazian mysteries to the initiated is the deity gliding over the breast—the deity being this serpent crawling over the breasts of the initiated' (Clem. Alex. *Protrept.* i. 2).

[4] *Lysist.* 646–7.

[5] Cf. Kallim, *Hymn. eis Dem.*; Ovid, *Fasti.* 420–450; Hesych, in voc. *Kanephoroi.*

[6] As to the Kalathos and its mystic significance, vide *inf.* sec. ii. 3.

4. The Phallophoroi,[1] crowned with violets and ivy, and carrying wooden representations of the Linga.

5. The Ithyphalloi, dressed as women, thus representing the androgynous or two-natured divinity. They reeled along as if intoxicated, crowned with flowers.

6. The Liknophoroi, who carried the Liknon, or sacred fan of Dionysos Liknites,[2] the 'mystic fan of Iakchos,' which was an essential implement at the sacreds of the god, being typical of purgation and purification.[3] Liknon signifies (1) an osier winnowing-fan; (2) a shallow basket for fruits and offerings, and so becomes identical with the Kaneon and the Kalathos; and (3) a cradle.[4]

II. *The Chorus of Youths.*

III. *The Komos,* or band of Dionysiak revellers, whose ritual is best illustrated in Milton's exquisite poem.[5] And

IV. *The representation of Comedy and Tragedy,* for at Athenai the stage was religion and the theatre a temple. At the time of this great Festival the capital was filled with rustics from the country townships, and strangers from all parts of Hellas and the Outer-world, including the numerous naval allies of the Athenians, who would doubtless be suitably impressed, by the elaboration of the ritual, with a sense of the power of the great city both in things human and divine. Such was the character of, and the general procedure observed at, the four great Attik Festivals of Dionysos, and it cannot be truly affirmed that they merely illustrate the cult of a wine-god. We are not here concerned with Hellenik antiquities generally, but only in so far as they illustrate the intricate nature and concept of this elastic and Proteus-like divinity.

---

[1] Phallic Dionysiak processions appear to have been common in the majority of Hellenik cities. Cf. Aristot. *Peri Poiet.* iv.; Müller, *Doric Race,* i. 419; Donaldson, *Theatre of the Greeks,* 72.
[2] Vide *inf.* VIII. ii. *Liknites.*
[3] Cf. *S. Matt.* iii. 12.
[4] Cf. Hom. *Hymn. eis Herm.* 20.
[5] *Sup.* IV. iii. 1.

Three other Dionysiak Festivals peculiar to Attike require notice: the Askolia, the Brauronia, and the Oschophoria. The first was observed by the Attik husbandmen who, after the sacrifice of a he-goat,[1] made a bottle of the skin, filled it with oil and wine, and then played at the sport called Askoliasmos, which consisted in leaping on the leathern bottle *askos*, and endeavouring to stand with one foot upon it, the victor receiving the bottle as his prize.[2] Here the bottle corresponds with the mystic jar of the city festivals, and is in fact a kosmic Askidian.

The Dionysia Brauronia was celebrated once in five years at the Attik town of Brauron, situate near the sea coast almost due east from Athenai, and which, in the fifth century B.C., with the exception of the capital and Eleusis, was the most important place in Attike. The Festival was marked by the wildest and most dissolute Bakchik revelry, and Brauron on the occasion became a noted trysting-place for doubtful characters of both sexes.[3] It, however, is chiefly remarkable in a Dionysiak connection, as having been a point of contact between two similar divinities, Dionysos Taurokeros, the Bull-horned, and Artemis Taurike, the Bovine. Even a tyro in the study of mythology will at once see that Artemis Orthia, the Phallic, called Taurike, and also by the mysterious name Tauropolos,[4] is in reality, like Artemis Ephesia Polymastos, the Many-breasted, a being perfectly distinct in origin from the simple Dorik huntress-goddess, sister of

---

[1] Vide *inf.* VIII. ii. *Goat.*
[2] 'A simple Ascidian' is, according to some, the venerable grandsire of the human race.

'When Bacchus' feasts came duly round,
Athenian peasants beat the ground;
And danced and leapt, to ease their toil,
Mid leather bottles smeared with oil;
From which they slid, with broad grimace,
And falling, filled with mirth the place:
And so they owned and honoured well
Their great grand-sire—the leather bottel.—*Blackwood*, May 1871.

[3] Cf. Aristoph. *Eirene*, 874, et Schol.; Souidas. in voc *Brauron*.
[4] Vide *inf.* IX. iii.

the great Aryan sun-god Apollon. Nothing is more singular than the way in which the Hellenes apparently identified their innocent and beautiful concept of Artemis with such creations as Taurike of Brauron, Polymastos the Great Mother of Ephesos, or the Kamic Pasht. K. O. Müller, who is anything but clear in his view of the matter, is nevertheless constrained to remark that the image of the Ephesian Artemis 'is not connected by any visible bond,' nor indeed by any invisible bond, 'with the Hellenic notions of Artemis,' and mentions other forms of the goddess in Asia Minor, 'still more rude and unsightly. Altogether, Asia Minor was full of strange and peculiar representations of this deity' [of the Great Goddess Mother he should have said], 'which come nearer to the Anaitis of the East than to the Grecian Artemis.'[1] Doubtless; and all such representations, moreover, transgress the Hellenik anthropomorphic canon which I venture to lay down.[2] The name of Artemis may, therefore, be at once dismissed as being only calculated to create confusion of idea, and I will call the goddess Taurike. It must have been remarked that the Uasar of Hellas appears to have no Uasi, but we here find her at Brauron; and her connection with the Bull-horned Dionysos will become very apparent in the sequel. Her Brauronik festival, like that of Dionysos, was quinquennial, the first noticeable point of agreement between them; and was presided over by ten Hieropoioi, or Managers-of-sacred-rites, whose special function it was to see that the victims were without blemish. A goat was sacrificed, and rhapsodic recitations from Homerik Poems took place on the occasion.[3] But the most interesting feature in the ceremonial was a procession of little girls, all under ten years of age, dressed in saffron-coloured garments, and

---

[1] *Ancient Art and its Remains,* 456–7.
[2] Vide *inf.* VII. *Dionysos in Art.*
[3] Hesych. in voc. *Brauroniois.*

THE HELLENIK CULT OF DIONYSOS. 241

known by the singular appellation of Arktoi, Bears.[1] So the Chorus of Women in the *Lysistrate*, when recounting the part they had taken in various festivals, says, 'And when I was ten years of age I prepared the meal for the sacred cakes for the Fundatrix,'[2] *i.e.*, of Brauron, 'and then I was Bear at the Brauronia, wearing the saffron-coloured robe.'[3] The little maids seem to have imitated bears, and of course a story was easily invented in explanation of the rite. A tame bear enraged with an Attik maiden killed her, and was killed by her brothers, on which Artemis visited the land with a pestilence, and was appeased by the institution of the Brauronik ritual. Why the goddess of the chase should be supposed to object to the deeds of hunters, her special votaries, does not appear; nor need we enquire, for the legend is merely a confused afterthought, invented to explain a custom the origin and meaning of which were then unknown or forgotten. A far more interesting and important tradition represents the goddess—to whom it will be observed Aristophanes ascribes the founding of the town, for it cannot be supposed that the peculiar title Archegetis is used merely as an equivalent for Artemis—as a bear calling for human blood.[4]

The Oschophoria was an annual Attik Festival in honour of Dionysos and Athene, said to have been established by Theseus,[5] after the slaughter of the Minotauros. The legend ran that the hero on his return from Krete forgot to hang out the white sail which was the signal agreed upon between him and King Aigeus to denote his success, and that Aigeus, supposing Theseus had

---

[1] Souidas, in voc. *Arktos*; Ioul. Polydeuk. viii. 9.

[2] Archegetis; cf. Pind. *Pyth.* v. 80, where the epithet is applied, as frequently elsewhere, to Apollon.

[3] Vs. 644-5. In v. 447 the goddess is called Tauropolos.

[4] Apostolius, viii. 19. For full explanation of the nature and ritual of the goddess, vide *inf.* IX. iii. *Artemis-Orthia-Taurike*.

[5] Plout. *Theseus*.

R

been slain, in despair threw himself from a rock into the sea and so perished. The herald who entered the city brought the good news of the hero's safe return, and hung the garlands with which the people wished to crown him upon his herald's staff, and so returned to Theseus, who was sacrificing at the Port Phaleron; from which circumstance it was customary at this Festival to crown the herald's staff and not the herald, and at the sacrifice mingled cries of triumph and of woe, Iou and Eleleu, were raised commemoratively even in the time of Ploutarchos, who thus describes another singular circumstance connected with the celebration:—'Theseus took not with him the full number of virgins, which were chosen by lots to be carried away [to Krete], but selected two youths, of fair and womanish faces, but of manly and courageous spirits, and having by frequent bathings, and avoiding the heat and scorching of the sun, with a constant use of all the ointments, washes, and dresses, that serve to adorn the head, smooth the skin, or improve the complexion, changed them, in a manner, from what they were before; and having taught them to counterfeit the very voice, gesture, and gait of virgins, so that there could not be the least difference perceived, he, undiscovered by any, put them into the number of the Athenian maids designed for Krete. At his return, he and these two youths led up a solemn procession, with boughs and vine-branches in their hands, in the same habit that is now worn at the celebration of the Oschophoria; these branches they carried in honour of Bakchos and Ariadne.' The Festival derives its name from *oschos*, a vine-branch-with-grapes. The episode of Theseus and the Minotauros, and the peculiar position occupied by the great Attik hero with respect to various foreign oppressors, will be noticed subsequently,[1] suffice it to observe here, a peaceful

---

[1] Vide *inf.* IX. iii. *The Minotauros*, X. iv.

celebration of the Dionysiak cult in honour of the stranger god and the foreign Ariadne. The womanish youths illustrate the god as Dimorphos the Two-formed and Thelymorphos the Androgynously-effeminate, the familiar 'two-natured Iakchos.'[1] The Demiurge, fountain of the luxuriant productiveness of the world typified by the grape-laden vine-branch, contains within himself both male and female principles. The Festival was concluded by a race to the temple of Athene at Phaleron; the runners carried branches, and the victor was rewarded with a 'miscellaneous potion' of wine, honey, cheese, meal, and oil, appropriately called Pentaple the Fivefold, like our modern Punch.[2]

Subsection II.—The Boiotik Cult.

In Boiotia we find a singular cluster of Dionysiak Festivals, consisting of the Agrionia, the Omophagia, and the Trieterika; which were all somewhat similar in character, and distinguished by the un-Hellenik nature of their ritual. The Agrionia was celebrated at Orchomenos in honour of Dionysos Agrionios, or the Savage, a name given him, as Ploutarchos truly says, on account of his cruelty, *i.e.*, of the savage nature of his cult.[3] In earlier ages human sacrifices were offered at it, and even in the time of Ploutarchos, Zoilos, a Bakchik priest of Chaironeia, slew a maiden on the occasion, but died shortly after we are told of a mysterious disease, and subsequently such excesses were absolutely prohibited. In illustration of the extent to which human sacrifices at one time prevailed in Hellas, we find that Themistokles at the

---

[1] Vide *inf.* VIII. ii. *Misc.*
[2] 'The well-known beverage called Punch is said to be derived from the Hindostani *punch* = 5; it means a mixture of five ingredients,' (Graham, *A Book about Words*, 235).
[3] Vide *inf.* VIII. ii. *Agrionios*.

crisis at Salamis was compelled to assent to the sacrifice of three Persian captives to Dionysos Omestes,[1] the Raw-flesh-eater; but Hellenik feeling generally is most strongly opposed to such horrors, and more innocent victims are substituted, as in the case of Iphigenaia and others. The substitution of the sacrifice of a goat for that of a boy at the temple of Dionysos Aigobolos, or the Goat-piercer, near Potniai, a little to the south of Thebai, has been already referred to.[2]

Another curious custom at the Agrionia was the formal search for the lost god. 'Among us,' says Plout-archos, 'at the Agrionia the women seek for Dionysos as if he had forsaken them, and at length they cease and say that he has fled and concealed himself with the Muses.'[3] This is the search of Uasi for Uasar, and that of Demeter for Persephone is very, but not exactly, similar; the life-spirit of nature has departed in the wintry cold, and again, in the solar aspect, Helios has left us and is gone to shine amongst the dead.[4] And this is a feeling which of necessity is Aryan as well as Semitic, for all see the sun, only the Aryan idea is far simpler and free from the mysterious elements of the Semitic. 'When we hear the people saying, "Our friend the Sun is dead. Will he rise? Will the Dawn come back again?" we see the death of Herakles, and the weary waiting while Leto struggles with the birth of Phoibos. When on the return of day

---

[1] 'As Themistokles was sacrificing on the deck of the chief galley, three captives were brought to him of uncommon beauty. Euphrantides, the soothsayer, casting his eye on them, and at the same time observing that *a bright flame blazed out from the victims*, took Themistokles by the hand, and ordered that the three youths should be consecrated and sacrificed to Dionysos Omestes; for by this means the Hellenes might be assured not only of safety but of victory. Themistokles was astonished at the strangeness and cruelty of the order; but the multitude, who, in pressing difficulties trust rather to absurd than rational methods, invoked the god with one voice; and leading the captives to the altar, insisted on their being offered up, as the soothsayer had directed' (Plout. *Themist.* xiii.)

[2] *Sup.* IV. iii. 2.
[3] *Symp.* viii. Proöim.
[4] Cf. Lobeck, *Aglaoph.* 678.

we hear the cry—" Rise! our life, our spirit is come back, the darkness is gone, the light draws near!" we are carried at once to the Homeric hymn, and we hear the joyous shout of all the gods when Phoibos springs to light and life on Delos.'[1] 'Of gods,' says Pausanias, 'the Eleans especially revere Dionysos,'[2] and then he tells how that at the Elean Dionysiak Festival of the Thyia three empty vessels are brought into the temple of the god and left there; and though all the doors are made fast and sealed, yet, wonderful to say, the vessels are found next day filled with wine. This remarkable fact he had from very respectable persons who knew it of their own knowledge (for unfortunately he was unable to be present personally on the occasion), and we may well believe it, but the symbolism is exceedingly interesting. Elis, where Dionysos was especially revered, was, as noticed,[3] the locality where he was invoked as the Axiotauros or Worthy Bull, the Axiokersos or Worthy-horned-god of Samothrake. The Kabeiroi or Great Ones of Samothrake were three in number,[4] and if the Worthy-horned-god had an empty bowl left in his shrine, it is only natural to suppose that his female 'reflection,' as the Assyrian Inscriptions would have called her, namely, Axiokerse the Worthy-horned-goddess, was honoured with another, and Axieros the Worthy-lord, with the third.[5] Axiokerse we have just seen at Brauron as Artemis Taurike the Goddess-of-the-bull, for this epithet has in reality no connection with the Taurik Chersonesos;[6] and we find her in Sparta as Orthia the Phallic, to whom men were sacrificed, until Lykourgos introduced instead the custom of scourging, which was carried out with great severity.[7] The wine vessels in the Elean temple correspond in the

[1] *Mythol. of the Aryan Nations*, i. 103.
[2] Paus. vi. 26.
[3] *Sup.* IV. iii. 2.
[4] *Aglaoph.* 1221.
[5] Vide *inf.* X. i.
[6] Vide *inf.* IX. iii.
[7] Cf. Paus. iii. 16.

mystic symbolism with the missing god; but at length, unseen and unnoticed, he returns to earth; nature arises from the death of winter, and blooms again with ever-fresh luxuriance, and the vessels in the temple, itself an image of the kosmic house of the universe, become filled with wine or the life-blood of the world.

Orchomenos, where the Agrionia was celebrated, is the scene of the mythic childhood of Dionysos when brought up by Athamas and Ino,[1] and fortunately we are able, by the aid of the light thrown by the present upon the underlying significance of Hellenik mythology, to observe the earlier stages of the Dionysiak ritual, if not its actual introduction there. The mythic Athamas, a son of Aiolos, ruled Orchomenos, and a portion of the Athamantik legend is thus related by Herodotos:—On the arrival of Khshayarsha [2] 'at Alus in Achaea, his guides, told him the tale known to the dwellers in these parts concerning the temple of the Laphystian Jupiter,[3] how that Athamas the son of Aeolus took counsel with Ino and plotted the death of Phrixus; and how that afterwards the Achaeans, warned by an oracle, laid a forfeit upon his posterity, forbidding the eldest of the race ever to enter into the court-house. If one comes within the doors, he can never go out again, except to be sacrificed. Further, they told him, how that many persons, when on the point of being slain, are seized with such fear that they flee away and take refuge in some other country; and that these, if they come back long afterwards, and are found to be the persons who entered the court-house, are led forth, covered with chaplets, and in a grand procession, and are sacrificed.'[4] The children of the race of Athamas, or a portion of them, were thus devoted to Zeus the Glutton, so called on account of the human sacrifices

---

[1] Apollod. iii. 4.
[2] Xerxes.
[3] Zeus Laphystios, or the Glutton.
[4] Herod. vii. 197.

offered to him;[1] and this Being, who as a matter of course has no connection with Zeus the great Aryan Allfather,[2] like Kronos or Saturnus, in accordance with the Molekh-ritual, devours his own offspring.

Let us next consider the place of Athamas in mythic genealogy, and here, as the Aryan element is largely represented in the story, the Natural Phenomena Theory, in the able hands of Mr. Cox, affords great assistance. Athamas, a son of Aiolos and king of Orchomenos, at the command of Here, marries Nephele, and from this union spring two children, Phrixos and Helle; but he also loves Ino daughter of Kadmos, who becomes the mother of Learchos and Melikertes. The injured Nephele leaves the faithless king, and the angry Here strikes him with madness, in which state he slays Learchos, while Phrixos and Helle, who were to have been sacrificed through the intrigues of Ino, escape through the air upon a golden-fleeced ram, the gift of Hermes. Ino with her remaining child leaps into the sea, where their names and natures ' suffer a sea change,' Ino becoming Leukotheë and Melikertes Palaimon. The deserted Athamas, driven from his home, is told that he must wander until he reaches some place where wild beasts receive him hospitably. At length at Alos he finds a place where wolves, *lykoi*, having slain a sheep, leave the flesh for him, and there he rests and founds a new dwelling-place. Perhaps in no legend in which the Semitic and Aryan elements are intermingled can they be more clearly distinguished, and their respective underlying significance more plainly revealed; and as every part of the myth is full of interest both in a general and also in a Dionysiak point of view, I shall examine it in detail. First, let us take the Aryan portion of the tale, which the Natural Phenomena Theory makes

---

[1] Cf. Müller, *Eumen.* lv.
[2] Cf. Paus. i. 24; where Laphystios is alluded to as an obscure and foreign divinity.

perfectly lucid. Athamas, at the command of Here the Gleaming Heaven,[1] a peculiarly national divinity,[2] and hence opposed to strangers and strange gods, marries Nephele the Cloud; and becomes the father of Phrixos, the Unsunlit-ether, and Helle, the air or ether when lighted up by Helios the Sun. But the Phoenician Ino, daughter of Kadmos the Oriental, and whom Athamas prefers to his Aryan consort Nephele, is hostile to the children of her rival; and they are rescued from her devices through the instrumentality of Hermes the lord of cloud and breeze,[3] who sends the golden-fleeced ram or shaggy sunlit cloud, upon whose back they flee away; until the wearied Helle, deprived of her sun-strength, falls exhausted at sunset into the Hellespontos, while the colder and more vigorous Phrixos escapes to the far dwelling of the Kolchian king. Driven mad by the angry Here, the raging Athamas, like Herakles Mainomenos, slays his eldest Kadmeian child Learchos,[4] for whose name no Aryan derivation is suggested, and Ino, to escape him, leaps into the sea with her remaining infant Melikertes. Who then is Athamas, and what does he represent? Evidently the Sun. As Mr. Cox observes, he is 'a being on whose nature some light is thrown by the fact that he is the brother of Sisyphos, the sun condemned, like Ixion, to an endless and fruitless toil.' He slays Learchos; and this action which, in the Semitic phase, implies amongst other things that human sacrifices were offered to him as to Zeus the Glutton,[5] according to

---

[1] Cf. Preller, *Griechische Mythologie*, i. 124; Cox, *Mythol. of the Aryan Nations*, ii. 10.

[2] *Juventus Mundi*, 234 et seq.

[3] Cf. Hom. Hymn, *Eis Herm.*; Ruskin, *Queen of the Air*, i. 25-9; *Mythol. of the Aryan Nations*, ii. 224 et seq.

[4] Le-ar-chos may possibly be only a varient of I-ak-chos. His being slain, and his general place in the story, would exactly suit this connection.

[5] 'There was an ancient worship of Zeus in the land of the Minyans, which required human sacrifices, and that, too, from none other than the sacerdotal race of Athamas . . . . the whole mythus sprang from the worship, and not the worship from the mythus' (K. O. Müller, *Introduction to a Scientific System of Mythology*, 175).

the innocent Aryan symbolism, only signifies drought and the burning up by the scorching summer sun of his children the fruits of the earth, whom his genial beams have produced. The name Athamas, like Learchos or Melikertes, is not susceptible of an Hellenik explanation; and who then is this Athamas, ' in Ionic Tammas,'[1] who scorches the earth and slays his children? Who but Tammuz, whose name has been explained as signifying the ' Strong one,' or the ' Consumer-who-makes-perfect,' *i.e.* by fiery purgation, but who is the Kaldean ' Tamzi, the Sun-of-life,'[2] ' the glowing and triumphant sun,' whose title is connected with the fierce summer heats of June and July?[3] And Tammuz, like Dionysos with whom he is identical, for, as we have seen, Tammuz, Adonis, Iao, Sabazios, and Dionysos, are all one, is hated by the Aryan Here,[4] and, like Dionysos, is a wanderer. In this point, as in almost every circumstance in the myth, the distinct and double symbolism, Aryan and Semitic, is clearly visible. In his Aryan aspect, the Sun wanders across heaven; in his Semitic, also over earth as the fierce Molekh-cult is carried along the shores of the Midland Sea. But the exiled Athamas or Tammuz is here wandering in an Aryan region, and so Aryan mythology enwraps him in its misty mantle. Wolves welcome him, but wolves, *Lukoi*, are other than they seem; like the *Arktoi*, or Bears of the Brauronia, they are but light-children sprung from Leukos the Brilliant, and so welcome the resplendent Athamas.[5] At last the fugitive settles at

---

[1] K. O. Müller, *Orchomenos und die Minyer*, 156.
[2] Vide *inf*. XI. iv.
[3] Cf. Donaldson, *Theatre of the Greeks*, 18; Norris, *Assyrian Dict.* 50. The Jewish month Tammuz is derived from the Assyrian month Duzu. As to Tammuz, vide also *inf.* XII. i. 1.
[4] Cf. *sup*. IV. iii. 4.
[5] As to the mythic confusion between *leukos*, brilliant, and *lukos*, a wolf, vide *Mythol. of the Aryan Nations*, ii. 232-3; cf. Ais. *Hept epi The.*, 145; where the Chorus, playing on the words, pray that Apollon Lykeios the Light-king, may be fierce as a wolf to the enemy. According to the mystic principle of using a word of manifold meaning, or

Alos, the Place of Wandering, like Bellerophon in the Aleian Field;[1] but it is observable that in the neighbourhood of the historic Alos stood another Thebai, an important town in that district of Thessalia which in the time of Herodotos was still known as Achaïa. So closely is the Euemeristic undercurrent of history connected with the aërial aspect of the myth.

Athamas, again, is a son of Aiolos, and Mr. Gladstone, who has investigated the position of the mythic Aiolos and his descendants with that searching analysis and rare mastery of multitudinous detail which is so marked a feature of his genius, observes that 'everything combines to raise the presumption thus obtained, about the Phoenicianism of the Aiolids, to the rank of a rational conclusion;' and adds, that 'the historical question, which under the legendary veil invites investigation, is one of extreme interest: it is the question of the amount, the nature, and the channels of the earliest powerful Semitic influence upon an Aryan or Japhetic people.'[2] Mr. Gladstone does not refer to Athamas, doubtless because the latter is not mentioned in the Homerik Poems, and so would be beyond the immediate scope of his subject; but our conclusions respecting the Orchomenian king will tend in some degree to confirm the theory of the Phoenician connection of the Aiolids. Tammuz is, and must have been, a Phoenician; although even in Phoenicia he is not an autochthon, but an immigrant from Kaldea.

Lastly, we have the escape of Ino and her child Melikertes, and the change in their nature. The latter is

---

two or more words of the same or of similar sound, the Wolf becomes a symbol of the Light-king, as at Lykopolis in Kam, where Athamas the Austere, or Burning Sun (cf. *S. Luke*, xix. 21) was represented as a wolf (Macrob. i. 17); 'and on the medals of Cartha he is surrounded with rays, which plainly proves that he is there meant as a symbol of the sun' (R. P. Knight, *Worship of Priapus*, 81.)

[1] As to the myth of Bellerophon, vide Professor Max Müller, *Chips*, ii. Essay xix.

[2] Vide *Juventus Mundi*, cap. v.

universally admitted to have been a Semitic importation, he being the Phoenician Melqarth, the Melek-kartha or Astyanax, king of the enclosed space or city, the 'rex urbis,'[1] the divinity frequently alluded to as the Tyrian Herakles. But Melek is merely Molekh or Molokh the King,[2] so here we at once meet with this sanguinary Phoenician divinity on Boiotik ground, in the same way that we find Poseidon, Tammuz, and Onka, denizens of the Kadmeis. This point is fully admitted by Aryan advocates such as Mr. Cox, and as confessions from him in the matter are peculiarly valuable, I would call particular attention both to the admission itself and also to what it fairly involves. Thus, after alluding to the word Kadmos and its connection with the Semitic Kedem the East, he observes: 'This word, together with the occurrence of Banna as the Boiotian word for daughter, seem to satisfy Niebuhr as to the fact of this Phoenician settlement. We must add to the list of such words the epithet of Palaimon, Melikertes, the Syrian Melkarth or Moloch.'[3] Again, he notices that the few stories related of Palaimon or the Wrestler,[4] which was the name given to Melikertes when Ino received that of Leukotheë, 'have no importance, but his name is more significant. It is clearly that of the Semitic Melkarth, and thus the sacrifices of children in his honour, and the horrid nature of his cultus generally, are at once explained. It becomes, therefore, the more probable that Kadmos is but a Greek form of the Semitic Kedem, the East; and thus the Boiotian mythology presents us with at least two undoubted Phoenician

---

[1] Gesenius, *Script. Ling. Phoen.* 410; cf. Kartha-hadtha or Karchedon-Carthago, the 'New Town;' the numerous Kirjaths of Syria; Karthaia, a town of Keos; Karthada, the ancient name of a suburb of Palermo; Kartein (Tartessos), and numbers of other similar names on the shores of the Mediterranean.

[2] Cf. Melchisedek, Melchior, A-drammelekh, Anammelekh, Abdalmalek, Malchos, &c.

[3] *Mythol. of the Aryan Nations*, ii. 80, note; cf. *ibid.* i. 401.

[4] Vide *inf.* X. ii.

or Semitic names, *whatever be the conclusion to which they point.*'[1] The judicious reader will not, I think, doubt much what is the conclusion to which they point. The particular question with which we commenced was the consideration of the Boiotik and Dionysiak Festival of the Agrionia, and at every step of the way we find the country teeming with the Semitic associations and recollections of that wonderful people, so ill-succeeded by the dull Boiotian of historic times. Every spade of earth we turn over in the Kadmeis seems partly formed from the dust of some Phoeniko-Hellenik hero who had played his part on that great battle-stage which extends from Thermopylai to Kithairon, and which the ancients called the Orchestra of Ares, when Plateia and Chaironeia were yet ages in the future. 'In the island of Tenedos it is said that children were sacrificed to Palaemon,[2] and the whole worship seems to have had something gloomy about it.'[3] It had indeed. Tenedos, as noticed,[4] was one of the localities where human sacrifices were offered to Dionysos Omadios: for as Dionysos is Athamas, so is he Melikertes, the King of Phoenician cities. At Korinthos was a remarkable temple of Palaimon-Melikertes, which was near a sacred place with a subterranean entrance where he was said to be concealed,[5] like the Monster in the Kretan Labyrinth;[6] and his statue represented him sitting on a dolphin,[7] a circumstance which illustrates his solar aspect and foreign origin, and connects him with Apollon-Delphinios, the Fish-Sun.[8] According to one legend, Palaimon was carried on a dolphin from the rock Molyris, from which his mother

---

[1] *Mythol. of the Aryan Nations,* ii. 265.
[2] Cf. K. O. Müller, *Orchomenos,* 170.
[3] Smith, *Classical Dict. Palaemon.*
[4] *Sup.* IV. iii. 2.
[5] Paus. ii. 2; Leake, *Travels in the Morea,* iii. 201.
[6] Vide *inf.* IX. iii.
[7] Paus. ii. 3.
[8] Cf. *Mythol. of the Aryan Nations,* ii. 25; *Queen of the Air,* i. 39.

threw herself into the sea, to the harbour of Korinthos.[1]

Of this group of mysterious personages there remains Ino, the daughter of Kadmos, the beloved of Athamas, the mother of Melikertes, and whose name was changed to that of Leukotheë, the White-goddess. Of her and her son it may said nothing of them 'doth fade, but doth suffer a sea change into something rich and strange;' for their natures seem, in the legends, to be improved by the transformation. The appearance of the same personages in different aspects and relationships to each other, is almost a necessity of thought; sun, moon, stars, day, night, life, death, good, evil, light, darkness, dawn, stand, when anthropomorphically considered, in almost every possible relationship and connection with each other. So Donaldson observes, 'As Semele represents the earth, Dionysos appears not only as her son, but also as her husband;' and he well adds, 'these oscillations in the persons of the sacred allegory need not create any difficulty, for the free play of fancy has combined and re-combined the elements of the picture, like the changing figures of a kaleidoscope.'[2] Thus, as Dionysos is the husband and son of Semele, so, here, as Athamas and Melikertes, he is the husband and son of another of the Kadmeian sisters. Who or what then is Ino? The Neo-Platonists had some glimpses of the kosmogonical character of the family of Kadmos, and their utterances on the point, if incorrect, are at least intelligible. Thus, according to Olympiodoros, the four daughters of Kadmos represented the four (so-called) elements. 'They consider the four elements of a Dionysiacal nature: Semele is fire; Agaue the earth, which tears to pieces her own offspring; Ino is water, being marine; and Autonoe is the

[1] *Paus.* i. 44.   [2] *Theatre of the Greeks,* 20.

air.'¹ These statements, like nineteen-twentieths of Neo-Platonik theories, are perfectly arbitrary and groundless, but yet in this particular case show some faint appreciation of the depth of the myth. It will be at once admitted that Ino in the story represents some natural phenomenon or influence; and bearing this in mind, we find from Pausanias that on the western coast of Lakonike, at no great distance from the Phoenician settlement in Kythera,² was ' a temple and oracle of Ino. They prophesy when asleep, since the goddess answers those who consult her by dreams. Bronze statues stand in the uncovered part of the temple, one of Paphie and the other of Helios. Water, too, pleasant to drink, flows from a sacred fount, and they call it the Fount of the Moon.³ Paphie is not a divinity of the country.'⁴ Here we have a Semitic temple dedicated to the Sun, Moon, and Paphie, who, as Pausanias truly observes, is not a native divinity, but Kyprogenes, the Kypros-born; and as Aphrodite Anadyomene, Venus Rising-from-the-sea,⁵ has landed, like Dionysos, a stranger in Aryan regions.⁶ Ino, the dream-giving goddess, stands in this temple, as in the myth we have been considering, by the side of Helios-Athamas. The Moon as the queen of night, and especially in her phase as Hekate-Selene, presides over dreams; and the ill effects of evil dreams were not unnaturally supposed to be dispelled by the sun. Thus Klytemnestra is represented as relating her terrible dream to Helios, in his character of Apotropaios, the Averter-of-evil;⁷ and it is noticeable that the Homerik 'people of dreams' live near

---

[1] MS. Commentary on the *Phaidon*.
[2] Cf. Paus. i. 14.
[3] Cf. Account of the Lake of Ino, Paus. iii. 23.
[4] Paus. iii. 26.
[5] Cf. Paus. ii. 1.
[6] As to the Semitic character of Aphrodite, who is pressed into the service of the Natural Phenomena Theory as one of its innumerous Dawn-goddesses, vide *Juventus Mundi*, 311-17.
[7] Soph. *Elekt.* 424.

the flowings of Ocean and the Leukadian, or White Rock,[1] which may have some connection with Leukotheë, the White-goddess. The sacred fount still connects Ino, who as the moon rules the sea, with water and she takes refuge with her horrid child in the deep, in the same way as Dionysos when flying from the wrath of Lykourgos; for all these Semitic divinities, Dionysos, Poseidon, Aphrodite, Hephaistos, and the rest, are connected with water, as having come across it to Hellas from the East. So, similarly, Europe, the 'broad-faced moon,'[2] and sister of Kadmos, and who is another phase of Ino, is borne over the sea on the back of the mystic bull. Again, Ino, as the moon and moon influence, is naturally hostile to Helle the bright nymph whose life is only sustained by the light of Helios. Thus the Natural Phenomena Theory, though to a far less extent, enters into and illustrates Semitic Mythology as well as Aryan; but here it is generally mixed with a subtle and delicate underlying Euemerism, which speaks of the clash of creeds and the contests of the human race, as well as of the movements and characteristics of the ever-varying phenomena of nature. Again, Ino with the infant Melikertes is a representative of the Mother and Child; but this is too wide a field of mythology to enter on here, suffice it to remark, that the Moon-queen of night is the mother of the young sun of the coming day, and was represented in this character as a crescent forming part of a circle. Creuzer, who has noticed the phase of Ino as a fostering mother, for in illustration of this and of the identity of Melikertes and Dionysos, it was Ino who in the mythic legend nurtured the latter when an infant after his mother's death,[3] compares her with Juno, Juno Matuta, the matronly dawn-goddess, and remarks that she is the mother of the

---

[1] *Od.* xxiv. 11.   [2] *Theatre of the Greeks*, 10.
[3] Apollod. iii. 4; *sup.* III. i. 1.

morning light.[1] In this case the name Ino will be Aryan, as Juno undoubtedly is, and appears to be connected with Zeus and many other familiar appellations.[2] Ino has been hastily identified with Io,[3] but this, though tempting, as their lunar characters are so harmonious, is doubtless incorrect. Creuzer well observes that most of the ideas connected with these lunar divinities spring from 'the Phoenician colony in Boiotia.'[4]

One last glimpse of Ino shall pourtray her in her most favourable phase.[5] We have seen how she becomes Leukotheë the White-goddess, as the Semitic moon is Lebanah the Pale-shiner, as distinguished from the burning golden Tammuz. Whilst the tempest-tossed, much-enduring, Odysseus is driven wearily on his raft through the raging seas, the gentle Ino, once mortal but now a partaker of the honour of the gods, beholds and pities him. He had recently seen in the far distance the shadowy mountains of the happy Phaiakian land, rising like a shield from the dark sea. But Poseidon, on his return from Aithiopia, spies the injurer of his savage son the Kyklops, and with his trident stirs up the latent fury of the waves, covers earth and heaven with gloomy clouds, and lets loose the winds. Then, as the Poet particularly notices, 'Night started from heaven,' *i.e.* she sprang from the vast black mass of clouds above, that rained down darkness on the deep. The distant mountains disappear in the vortex of gloom, the raft is carried hither and thither, and Odysseus is hurled from it into the sea: painfully he rises and clings to it again, but, as in the storm in Adria, hope has fled; all the bright lights of heaven are darkened over him, no star is visible; when

---

[1] *Symbolik und Mythologie,* x. 586; cf. *ibid.* iv. 259; vii. 494; *Gen.* xxxiii. 14, 'The precious things put forth by the moon.'
[2] Cf. *Mythol. of the Aryan Nations,* i. 354.
[3] Clem. Alex. *Strom.* i. 21, and many moderns.
[4] *Symb.* iv. 236.
[5] *Od.* v. 333-53.

suddenly the silver arrow of Artemis pierces the gloom, 'from one lonely cloud the Moon rains out her beams, and heaven is overflowed.' 'The White-goddess, daughter of Kadmos, Ino, with-beautiful-ankle,[1] saw him.' As the rising moon 'she came up from the deep,' according to mythic tradition near the coast of Messenia,[2] 'and sat on the raft,' *i.e.* illumined it with her rays.[3] Her appearing and disappearing above the sea and through the darkness is compared to the flight of a gannet or some other kind of sea-bird, and the simile shows that the goddess was imagined by the poet as a being generally above water, although closely connected with the sea. The friendly Ino foretells the escape of Odysseus, for, as we have seen, she is possessed of prophetic power,[4] urges him to leave the raft and escape by swimming; and, lastly, makes him a present of her 'immortal *kredemnon*' to spread under his breast, wearing which he cannot perish. 'Thus having spoken, the goddess gave him [Milton says she has "lovely hands,"] the *kredemnon*, and she back again into the billowing sea sank,' the term employed is used of the setting sun or stars, 'like a gannet; and the black wave concealed her.' It is to be remembered that to Odysseus on the raft the Moon would appear to sink in the sea when the waves dashing up high around and joining the dark above concealed her from him. Fearing treachery on the part of the goddess, he clings to the raft, which is at length broken in pieces by the waves, and Odysseus, after having been two nights and two days in the deep, at length, by the assistance of Athene and the *kredemnon*, gains the friendly shore. What, then, was the

---

[1] Cf. *Job*, xxxi. 26, 'The moon walking in brightness.'
[2] Paus. iv. 34.
[3] Cf. 'How sweet the moonlight sleeps upon this bank.' 'The chaste Dian, bright with beauty and delight, lay listening on the mountains.'
[4] As the moon is connected with the changes of many natural phenomena which her phases foretell. Vide Babylonian lunar portents, *Trans. Soc. Bib. Archaeol.* iii. 210 *et seq.*

gift of Leukotheë? The Kredemnon, or Headband, was a kind of scarf or flowing veil which was fastened to any covering for the head and descended over the shoulders. It would naturally be unsuitable for violent exercise, and so Nausicaa and her maidens lay aside their *kredemna* when about to play at ball.[1] Several distinct ideas appear to unite in this incident of the story. Thus, the moon-scarf which Ino throws to Odysseus is the line of waving light across the waters coming from around her face, and by means of which he may find his way to land. But her crescent horns of light are the peculiar ornament of the Moon as a female goddess, and this emblem of Io-Ino is connected with the mystic boat or ship of the horned Uasi, which brings us round again to the coffin of Uasar, and the chests of the Mysteries.[2] It would be too far a departure from the immediate subject to analyse these various ideas as connected with the lunar goddess, suffice it to say, that as a fostering mother, Juno-Matuta, her mystic life-boat preserves all, as somewhat similarly the Kamic divinities sail over the mysterious ocean in the boat of the Sun, which the struggles of the wicked serpent Apap threaten to overturn.[3] Euripides wrote a tragedy entitled *Ino*, of which Stobaios, who seems to have been particularly partial to his writings, has preserved some fragments. Nonnos also, that diligent student of Dionysiak legends, has treated of her and Athamas at length.[4]

The Omophagia was celebrated in honour of Dionysos as Omophagos, Omadios, or Omestes, the Raw-flesh-eater, Zeus the Glutton, and possibly was rather an important part of the Agrionia and similar celebrations than a distinct festival. In earlier times men were torn in pieces at it; in later ages, goats, whose entrails were devoured by the

---

[1] *Od.* vi. 100.
[2] Cf. *sup.* V. v. 4.
[3] Cooper, *Serpent Myths of Ancient Egypt*, 40.
[4] *Nonnos*, v. 198, ix. x. xxxix. 104, etc.

phrensied worshippers. When speaking of the myth of Zagreus,[1] I shall have occasion to refer to this discerption and its mystic significance. 'In the Mystéries,' says Clemens Alexandrinus, ' the Bakchik votaries perform orgies in honour of the phrensied Dionysos, exciting their sacred madness with the eating of raw flesh.'[2] Euripides, as noticed, describes Dionysos as ' hunting for the blood of goat-slaughter, a raw-eaten delight,'[3] and in another place, speaks of the mystics as ' fulfilling the life of the night-wandering Zagreus and the raw-flesh-eating feasts.'[4]

The Trieterika was a Triennial Festival in honour of the god ' and one legend stated that he instituted it on his return from India, his expedition thither having occupied three years.'[5] A similar festival was held in honour of his fellow Semitic divinity, Poseidon,[6] who was also almost equally conspicuous for his raw-flesh-eating propensities.[7] Euripides speaks of ' the raving Satyrs ' as having ' added the dances of the Triennial Festivals in which Dionysos rejoices ;'[8] and Virgilius says of the deceived Dido, ' she rages with reason overthrown, and inflamed wanders wildly (*bacchatur*) through the whole city : as a Thyiad[9] aroused by the celebration of the sacred rites, when the Triennial Orgies spur her on as she hears the cry of Bacchus and Cithaeron at night calls her with uproar.'[10] This Festival appears to have obtained widely through Hellas, and was even carried into Skythia by Hellenik colonists.[11] It took place in winter, when Dionysos Antheus, the Blooming, is dead and the earth is stripped of its luxuriant vegetation.[12] As the fierce wind tears off the withering leaves, the frantic votaries can wildly

---

[1] *Inf.* IX. vi.
[2] *Protrept.* ii. 12.
[3] *Bak.* 139.
[4] *Sup.* IV. iii. 5.
[5] Vide *inf.* IX. vii. *Indoletes.*
[6] Pind. *Nem.* vi. 00.
[7] Cf. Diod. xi. 21 ; xiii. 80.
[8] *Sup.* IV. iii. 2.
[9] Cf. Ais. *Hept. epi The.* 493 ; Hippomedon 'raves for fight like a Thyiad.'
[10] *Aen.* iv. 300-3.
[11] Herod. iv. 108.
[12] Cf. Creuzer, *Symbolik,* iv. 187.

lament for the temporary suppression of that base earth-life which the Apostle styles *psychikos*.[1] A Bakchik devotee, either of the past or of the present, would rather enter into swine[2] than be altogether divorced from matter.[3]

Subsection III.—*Other Festivals of the God.*

The ceremonies in honour of Dionysos Lampter at the Athenian Anthesteria have already been noticed, and a similar ritual prevailed in Sikyonia. During the Festival of the Lampteria at Pellene the torch-bearing votaries entered the temple at night and placed bowls of wine throughout the city.[4] At Sikyon itself there was a magnificent statue of the god, of ivory and gold, and near it statues of Bakchai of white stone. The Sikyonians had also other mysterious statues, evidently Kabeirik, which on the eve of the annual festival of Dionysos Lampter, they used to carry into his temple with lighted torches, singing hymns. The chief of the procession of statues was called Bakcheios, the Exciter-to-phrensy. 'Androdamas the son of Phlias dedicated this, and a statue called Lysios follows, which Phanes the Theban, at the bidding of the Pythia, brought from Thebai.'[5] Phlias, we are told, was the 'son of Dionysos.'[6] All this is history, though not exactly in the simple sense in which good Pausanias received it.[7] Phlias, son of Dionysos, is merely Dionysos in his phase as Phleon or Phloios, the

---

[1] Jude, 19.
[2] Cf. *inf.* VIII. i. *Choiropsalas*.
[3] Vide *inf.* VIII. i. *Trieterikos*.
[4] Paus. vii. 27.
[5] Ibid. ii. 7.   [6] Ibid. 6.
[7] 'After belief in classic legends as entirely true, there comes repudiation of them as entirely false: now prized as historical fact, they are now thrown aside as nothing but fiction. Both of these judgments are likely to prove erroneous. Being sure that the momentum of reaction will carry opinion too far, we may conclude that these legends are neither wholly true nor wholly untrue,' (H. Spencer, *The Principles of Sociology*, No. 40, Appendix).

fullness or overflowing of the life or generative powers of the world; for Dionysos, as Pindaros notes, 'is 'lord and first cause of the whole humid nature.'[1] So K. O. Müller observes, 'Phlias is nothing else than the country [a part of Arkadia] personified, the name being derived from *phles* or *phlidas*, and signifying "damp," or "abounding in springs," which appellation was full merited by the nature of the spot. Hence Phlias was with more reason called the son of Bacchus.'[2] Androdamas, the Man-slayer, or Man-subduer, is either another phase of the god, who as we have seen was truly a man-slaying divinity, or a personification of the power which first introduced the Bakchik ritual into Sikyonia. Androdamas, we are told, dedicated the statue of Dionysos as the Exciter-to-phrensy, and Phanes the Theban brought from Thebai another statue of the god in his opposite phase, Lysios the Soothing, or Delivering-from-care, the Latin Liber. Phanes the Theban is only Dionysos again in his familiar phase, as Phanes the Spirit-of-the-apparent; and the whole account resolves itself into a relation of the introduction of the Dionysiak cult from Thebai, 'mother-city of the Bakchai.' Bakcheios, Lysios, Phlias, Androdamas, Phanes, are all phases of the plastic and Protean Dionysos; and thus understood, the story is true history, and affords a good instance of that finer kind of Euemerism against which no valid objection can be raised. The symbolism of these Festivals has been already illustrated, and the Dionysiak tragic choruses of Sikyon have also been noticed.[3] The Bakchik ritual at Korinthos was very similar, and there was also a special festival of the god at Patrai.[4]

In Ellis, as noticed,[5] Dionysos was especially revered,

---

[1] *Sup.* III. i. 1.
[2] *Doric Race*, i. 92.
[3] *Sup.* III. i. 2.
[4] Paus. vii. 19.
[5] *Sup.* subsec. ii.

and I have already referred to the Elean Dionysiak Festival of the Thyia, when empty wine-vessels were mysteriously filled, and also to the Elean worship of Dionysos as Axiokersos.

Arkadia, also, had several special Bakchik Festivals, one of the most remarkable of which was that held at Kynaitha, when men, anointed with fat, carried on their shoulders to his temple a bull, which Dionysos himself was supposed to inspire them to select.[1] The bull apparently was a type of the god himself, whose tauric connection is everywhere conspicuous. The inhabitants of Kynaitha were noted for their wild and dissolute character.[2] At Alea, in north-eastern Arkadia, was celebrated a Dionysiak Festival at which women were scourged in the same manner as the Spartan youths suffered in honour of Artemis Orthia.[3] The cult of these two savage divinities thus exactly corresponded. There were also the Dionysia Arkadika, when the Arkadian youth yearly celebrated the god with dances and games, and songs chiefly taken from the two great dithyrambic bards Philoxenos of Kythera, B.C. 435-380, and Timotheos of Miletos, B.C. 446-357. The Festival was held in the theatre at Megalopolis, which was the largest in Hellas;[4] and our chief authority on the subject is the historian Polybios, who was a native of the place,[5] and whose statue stood on a pillar in the forum.[6] The Festival is uninteresting in the present connection, since possessing no great antiquity, it is not illustrative of the nature and origin of the god. The two favourite Megalopolitan Poets are comparatively modern, and the place itself is almost the youngest of ancient Hellenik cities.[7]

Argolis, the stronghold of the Aryan Here, the bitter

[1] Paus. viii. 18.
[2] Polyb. iv. 3.
[3] Paus. viii. 23.
[4] Ibid. ii. 28; viii. 32.
[5] Polyb. iv. 3.
[6] Paus. viii. 30.
[7] Cf. Ibid. viii. 27.

enemy of Dionysos as noticed, for a long time wholly abstained from his worship.[1] The contest between the rival cults is displayed in a lively manner in the mythic history. Here smites Dionysos with madness,[2] on which he similarly afflicts the Argeian women for neglect of his rites, according to Hesiodos.[3] They are at length cured by the wise seer Melampous, who, as we have seen, learnt the Phoenician ritual of the god from Kadmos and his companions;[4] and who in the legend drives the frantic Bakchik votaries over the border as far as Sikyon,[5] which, as has been just noticed, was a great Dionysiak centre. Dionysos, who had similarly smitten Antiope at Thebai for being connected with the punishment of his votary Dirke,[6] emerges from the contest completely triumphant, and his hierophant Melampous succeeds to a third of the realm; and so, in later times, the cult is found firmly implanted in the country. Thus at Lerne near Argos, famous as having been the scene of the mythic contest between Herakles and the Hydra, was a celebrated Festival called the Lernaia, in honour of Demeter, Persephone, and Dionysos, whose connected worship I shall notice subsequently.[7] The mythical poet Philammon, who was said to have lived before the time of Homeros, according to tradition first instituted the Lernaian Mysteries, but they had been remodelled in comparatively modern times. In the neighbourhood was the Alkyonian, or Kingfisher's, Pool, through which, according to Argeian local tradition, Dionysos descended to Hades, to bring up Semele.[8] The habits of the kingfisher seem to be connected with the idea: the beautiful little bird sits watching the surface of the water, until 'at length, attracted by a floating insect, a fish rises to take

[1] *Sup.* IV. iii. 4.
[2] Apollod. iii. 5.
[3] Apud Apollod. ii. 2.
[4] *Sup.* V. v. 2.
[5] Cf. Paus. ii. 18.
[6] Paus. ix. 17.
[7] *Inf.* sec. ii.
[8] Cf. Apollod. iii. 5.

the prize; at that instant, like a shot, down descends the glittering bird, the crystal water scarcely bubbling with its plunge; the next moment it re-appears, bearing its victim in its beak.'[1] There may, however, be other allusions in the name which is also connected with the Pleiad Alkyone, beloved by the Phoenician Poseidon. This mysterious pool was about seventy feet in diameter, and apparently circular in form; it was reported to be bottomless, Nero having in vain attempted to gauge the depth, and to have an undercurrent which drew down swimmers. Pausanias concludes his account of it by remarking, 'But of the Dionysiak rites which are yearly performed by it at night it is not lawful for me to write to all.'[2] Ploutarchos is less reticent, and seems to allude to the Bakchik ritual of this mysterious lake in the remarkable passage where he says, 'Among the Argeioi the god is known by the name of the Ox-sprung Dionysos, and they summon him by trumpet from the water, while they throw down a lamb into the abyss to the Gate-keeper,' *i.e.* Kerberos, or Aïdoneus, as Pylartes Guardian-of-the-gate, like Poseidon Pylaochos, 'and they conceal the trumpets in thrysos-staves.'[3] The whole circumstance forms an exact and singular parallel to the account of Herodotos of the similar Kamic ritual. 'Here, in this precinct of Minerva [Neith] at Sais, is the burial-place of one whom I think it not right to mention in such a connection. There are also some large stone obelisks in the enclosure, and there is a lake near them adorned with an edging of stone. In form it is circular, and in size, as it seems to me, about equal to the lake in Delos called "the Hoop." On this lake it is that the Egyptians represent by night his sufferings whose name I refrain from mentioning, and this representation they call their Mysteries.

[1] Martin, *Pict. Museum*, i. 297; Gosse, *Nat. Hist.* ii. 49.
[2] Paus. ii. 37.
[3] *Peri Is.* xxxv.

I know well the whole course of the proceedings in these ceremonies, but they shall not pass my lips. The daughters of Danaus brought these rites from Egypt, and taught them to the Pelasgic women of the Peloponnese. Afterwards when the inhabitants of the peninsula were driven from their homes by the Dorians, the rites perished. Only in Arcadia, where the natives remained, and were not compelled to migrate, their observance continued.'[1] It is just possible, but very highly improbable, that the Dionysiak ritual of lake Alkyone was copied in late historic times from the Kamic ceremonial at Sa : we have, however, no reason to suppose that this was the case, and Pausanias would doubtless have mentioned such a remarkable adoption ; but, on the contrary, the whole context implies that the connection between the god, the lake, and the locality generally, had existed from ancient times. The Peloponnesos, according to Herodotos, was impregnated before the Dorik invasion with Kamic and Phoenician rites, and the former ritual after this event perished, except in Arkadia. But this statement must evidently be accepted with some modification, for even admitting the historical character of the invasion, it could in the nature of things have only produced a partial, not an absolute, alteration in religious observances. This particular district of the Peloponnesos, it is to be observed, was peculiarly connected with Danaos, and not far distant was a spot called the Landing-place, which was traditionally the exact locality where Danaos landed with his children.[2] Now we have seen that there are no sufficient reasons for believing that Hellas received the Dionysiak ritual from Kam in very early times,[3] but there is no real difficulty in the matter, for, as Mr. Gladstone observes, 'There is every reason to

[1] Herod. ii. 170-1.   [2] Paus. ii. 38.
[3] *Sup.* V. v. 4.

suppose that Danaos was a Phoenician. That in the later tradition he stands for an Egyptian is not to be wondered at, when we consider how the two countries melted into one another, in the view of the early Greeks, like a concave line of bays upon a coast trending towards a distant horizon; and while Phoenician vessels were the channel of communication, Phoenicia itself was, before the time of the Troïca, deeply charged with Egyptian elements. M. Renan has found a district in the neighbourhood of Tripoli called Danniè or Dyanniyeh. Again, Pausanias tells us that there stood at the reputed landing-place of Danaos, on the Argive coast, a temple of Poseidon Genesios, an association which at once assigns to that personage a Phoenician origin.'[1] This exact accordance between the ritual of Argolis and Kam, the circular lakes, the annual nightly celebration in honour of the suffering god, its occult nature, and the pious reticence of Herodotos and Pausanias, necessitates the identity of the two worships. Either the one was a copy of the other, or both came from a common source; but it would be ridiculous to suppose that Sa copied Alkyone, and there is not the least reason to imagine that Alkyone copied Sa. This very ritual, Herodotos tells us, was introduced by the daughters of Danaos centuries before his time; and was celebrated, says Pausanias, near the exact spot where Danaos was said to have landed, and lastly Danaos himself proves to be a Phoenician. Whether there ever really was any particular Phoenician immigrant of the name is utterly unimportant; the historical fact which the legend implies is the truly important matter, and here as everywhere we find fresh proof of the Oriental character and of the identity of the various phases of this suffering and mysterious divinity. The nature of his sufferings has already been partly illustrated, and this

[1] *Juventus Mundi*, 136.

portion of the myth will be again referred to.[1] At Larymna in Boiotia was a temple of the god near a somewhat similar lake.[2]

At Hermione in Eastern Argolis was 'a shrine of Dionysos Melanaigis. To this divinity musical contests are yearly celebrated, and swimming and sailing matches with prizes are established. And there is a temple of Artemis surnamed Iphigenaia, and a bronze Poseidon having one foot upon a dolphin.'[3] There was a tale connected with the Attik Festival of the Apatourea, so called from *apate*, 'deceit,' that King Melanthos, who succeeded Thymoites the last of the line of Theseus, when about to engage in single combat with Xanthos, king of Boiotia, pretended to see behind the latter a man clad in a black goat-skin, *melanaigis*, and when Xanthos turned round to look, treacherously slew him. The epithet is also used by Ploutarchos when describing dark red wine, and is thus doubly connected with the god as relating both to the wine and the wine-skin, and the Bakchik goat. But from the somewhat singular circumstance that aquatic contests took place in honour of Dionysos, we may also understand the term in the Aischylian sense as meaning Wrapped-in-dark-storms.[4] Dionysos seldom appears as a distinctly marine divinity, except when regarded as a stranger who has come to Hellas over the sea, but perhaps we have here a representation of the sun above the sea shrouded or surrounded with shaggy storm clouds, a lurid Melikarthos,[5] to whom the sailor sacrifices with trembling heart. The sportive aquatic contests of Hermione, changed in nature and associations, may embody the last recollections of the great western explorations of

---

[1] *Inf.* IX. vi.
[2] Paus. IX. 23.
[3] Ibid. ii. 35.
[4] Cf. *Hept. epi The.* 600; 'Melanaigis Erinys,' the Vedic Saranyu; Paus. I. 28; also Ais. *Choe.* 592; where *aigis* is equivalent to storm-blast.
[5] Cf. Sanchou. ii. 15.

the Phoenician Sun-god and his followers;[1] and it will be noticed that when the Herakles of Hellas was identified with the Herakles of Tzur, the son of Alkmene was made to travel over the regions of Phoenician exploration,[2] and so naturally came to be considered by the later Pagans as a solar divinity whose Twelve Labours indicated his passage through the zodiacal signs. Hard by the shrine of Dionysos Melanaigis, stands the temple of his grim consort Artemis Taurike, and also a third Oriental divinity Poseidon, connected like Melikertes with the dolphin. According to one legend, among other opponents of the Dionysiak cult in Argolis was the great Argeian hero Perseus. This may at first sight seem singular, inasmuch as he was the son of Danae, but similarly Pentheus was the grandson of Kadmos, and as will readily be acknowledged, it is very rarely that all the members of a large family agree in their religious opinions. If Perseus be a phase of the Aryan Sun-god,[3] the myth still more clearly resolves itself into a contest between the supporters of rival divinities. The Bakchik host arrived in Argos, 'from the islands of the Aigaion,' and this invasion is distinct from that in the time of Melampous before noticed, and which occurred about a generation earlier according to mythic chronology. A battle ensued, in which Dionysos was defeated, and many of the Bakchai, including Ariadne, were slain. But this victory was, like the ill-omened success of Lykourgos, ultimately followed by the complete triumph of the Dionysiak cult. Near Argos was 'the shrine of Dionysos of Krete,' the country of the Minotauros. 'They say that after he had warred with Perseus, and had laid aside his hostility, he was greatly honoured by the Argeians, and

---

[1] Vide *inf.* XI. i.
[2] Vide George Smith, *The Cassiterides.*
[3] 'Perseus, the Sun' (Schol. in Lykophron).

that this selected glebe was assigned to him. And it was afterwards named the glebe of Kresios [the Kretan], because he here buried Ariadne when she died. Near the shrine of Dionysos is that of Aphrodite Ouranie.'[1] Dionysos is here again in close proximity to the Great Goddess, Mother of the East, of whom Artemis Orthia, who also had a temple in the neighbourhood,[2] is only a special phase.[3] Another peculiar Argeian Festival in honour of the god was called Turbe, Disorder;[4] and its character was similar to those Attik celebrations which have been referred to.

In Lakonike 'nothing is known of any sumptuous or regular ceremonies in honour of Bacchus,'[5] but his worship, though in a minor degree, prevailed throughout the country, and he had in the mythical period driven the women frantic for resisting his cult.[6] Thus everywhere in Hellas we meet with records of a similar struggle on the introduction of the Dionysiak ritual, always or almost always resulting in its ultimate triumph. On Mount Larision, near Gythion, in early spring, a festival was celebrated to Dionysos, doubtless as Antheus the Blooming, the returning beauty and budding vigour of the world. There was a tradition that the celebration was instituted in consequence of a ripe grape having been found on the mountain.[7] At Sparta was a shrine of Dionysos Kolonatas; his priestesses the Dionysiades had a special ritual, and virgins ran a race in his honour.[8]

No special Bakchic festival obtained in Messenia, but various Dionysiak associations are connected with the country. Thus at Korone was a temple and statue of the

---

[1] Paus. ii. 23; *sup.* V. vi.
[2] Paus. ii. 24.
[3] Vide *inf.* IX. iii. *Table of Horned Divinities of the Phoenician Pantheon.*
[4] Paus. ii. 24; Müller, *Doric Race*, i. 418.
[5] Müller, *Doric Race*, i. 418.
[6] Ælianus, *Poikile Historia*, iii. 42; Schol. in Aristoph, *Orn.* 963; *Eir.* 1071.
[7] Paus. iii. 22.
[8] Ibid. iii. 13; Hesych. in voc. *Dionysiades.*

god,[1] and at Kyparissia was a fountain which sprang from the ground when Dionysos struck the place with the thyrsos.[2]

Connected with the Dionysiak cult were the two Naxian Festivals, called Ariadneia, both in honour of Ariadne, and representing her in that Janus-character which, as we have seen, constantly appears in Dionysos. One of these, in memory of her happiness, was lively and cheerful; the other, in memory of her woes, solemn and mournful. She was also said to have died at Amathousios in Kypros, where was a celebrated temple of Aphrodite, and was there called 'Aphrodite Ariadne,' circumstances illustrative of her Semitic character.[3] The connection between Dionysos and Naxos has already been noticed.[4]

At Lesbos, special ceremonies were performed in honour of Dionysos Kephallen, or Of-the-head. 'A face made of olive wood was drawn up from the sea in the nets of the fishermen in Methymne: this appeared to bear some resemblance to the divine, *but was foreign and not in accordance with Hellenik divinities*. Wherefore the Methymnaians asked the Pythia, of which of the gods or heroes is the likeness; and she commanded them to revere Dionysos Kephallen. On this account the Methymnaians keep among them the carved head from the sea, and honour it with sacrifices and prayers.'[5]

In Sikelia was celebrated a nocturnal Dionysiak Festival called Agrypnis, Sleepless, because the votaries watched all night long.[6] This is the Naxian cult of Dionysos Nyktelios, the Nightly, alluded to by Sophokles.

There was also a Dionysiak Festival called the Semeleia, already noticed.[7]

Other Festivals of the god were the Theoinia, to him

---

[1] Paus. iv. 34.
[2] Ibid. 36.
[3] Plout. *Theseus*.
[4] *Sup.* II. i. 3.
[5] Paus. x. 19.
[6] Hesych. in voc. *Agrypnis*.
[7] *Sup.* III. i. 1.

as the Wine-god; the Neoinia, when the new wine was tasted; the Iobacheia, which appears to have formed part of the Eleusinian Ritual; the Haloa, or Festival of the Threshing-floor, a kind of Harvest Thanksgiving to Demeter and Dionysos, as bestowers of the autumn-plenty;[1] and the Ambrosia, which was celebrated in the month Lenaion in many parts of Hellas.[2] Ambrosia, the principle of immortality, is in Homeros the food of the gods, and in later writers their drink. The Festival may have merely honoured Dionysos as the Wine-god, but it probably possessed a deeper significance, and his votaries would doubtless adore him as the principle and lord of vitality, Karpios, Antheus, and Erikepeios. There was also a grand yearly Dionysiak Festival with games in Ionia.[3]

Lastly, the annual Bakchik Festival at Parnassos, the connection between which place and Dionysos has been already referred to,[4] must be noticed. 'I was not able to understand,' says Pausanias, 'on what account Homeros calls Panopeus,' an ancient town near the Boiotik frontier of Phokis, 'Kallichoros,[5] until I was informed by those Attik women who are called Thyiades. The Thyiades are Attik women who roam wildly about at Parnassos yearly, and they and the Delphik women hold orgies to Dionysos; and it is customary for these Thyiades, along the road from Athenai and elsewhere, and among the Panopeans, to perform circling dances; and the appellation of Homeros for Panopeus seems to have reference to the choric[6] dance of the Thyiades.'[7] 'Kallichoros,' Famed-for-the-beautiful-dance, in the Homerik passage

---

[1] It is, however, to be observed that *halos* also means the disk of the sun or moon, and the festival may have had a solar or lunar significance. Ais. *Hept. epi The.* 484, uses the term of the vast round shield of Hippomedon.

[2] Schol. in Hes. *Erg. kai Hem.*
[3] Strabo, xiv. 1.
[4] *Sup.* IV. iii. 2.
[5] *Od.* xi. 581.
[6] Or 'circling.'
[7] Paus. x. 4.

in question, has been considered merely an Epik form for *kallichôros*, having-beautiful-places, like *eurychoros*, 'spacious,' an Homerik epithet of great cities, for *eurychôros*. This may be so, but the term was not so understood by Pausanias, himself a profound student of Homeros, and the circumstance he mentions throws a singular light on the passage. There is nothing at all unnatural in the supposition that dances in honour of Apollon or Dionysos, or both, may have been celebrated along the road from Thebai, sufficiently early to be noticed by the author of the *Odysseia*. The sacred spring of Demeter at Eleusis was called Kallichoros,[1] the Fount-of-the-beauteous-dance, and it is quite possible that the passage may contain a distinct Homerik allusion to the Dionysiak cult. 'The peaks of Parnassos are above the clouds, and on them the Thyiades rave to Dionysos and Apollon;'[2] as Euripides says, 'You shall see Dionysos on the Delphik rocks bounding with torches upon the double-peaked hill top, brandishing and shaking the Bakchik branch, and mighty in Hellas.'[3]

Such were the principal non-theatrical Festivals of Dionysos in Hellas, and their combined significance cannot be mistaken. They were in honour of no simple Wine-god, and represented no mere rustic merriment, but almost all exhibit more or less strongly a Semitic character, and thus harmonise with the portraiture of the son of Semele left us by the Theologers, the Lyric and Tragic Poets, and Herodotos. We will next view the god as he appears in other phases of the home life of his adopted country.

[1] Hom. *Hymn. eis Dem.* 273; Paus. 38.
[2] Paus. x. 32.¹
[3] *Bak.* 306-9.

* Grote, when speaking of the Dionysiak ritual, strangely says, 'It deserves to be remarked that *the Athenian women never practised these periodical mountain excursions*, so common among the rest of the Greeks.' (*Hist. of Greece*, i. 30).

SECTION II.

DIONYSOS AT ELEUSIS.

Subsection 1.—The Legend of the Homerik Hymn.

Having noticed the more remarkable of the Dionysiak Festivals of ancient Hellas, we come next to the consideration of the place which the god occupies in the mystical Eleusinian cult of Demeter and Persephone, the Mother and the Daughter, its meaning and significance, and the causes which led to the union of the ritual of the three divinities. Let us first inspect the legend of the Two Goddesses, as presented with beautiful simplicity in the ancient Homerik Hymn. The rites of Eleusis have been the mystery of mysteries, and the *crux* of investigators, who, by various illogical suppositions, have infinitely added to the difficulties which necessarily beset the subject; but, be it remembered, that if we fairly grasp the meaning of the concepts, Demeter, Persephone, and Dionysos, we can have no serious difficulty in comprehending the character of their cults, considered either separately or in union. As the Christian religion stands revealed in its Founder, so the ritual of Eleusis is but an illustration of the nature of the Eleusinian divinities, for the supposition that the votaries there initiated in earlier times, whilst they were supposed to worship the powers of the place in reality adored something else, *e.g.* the one merely God, may be permanently set aside as being not only in itself intrinsically improbable, but also entirely unsupported by any real evidence.[1] We may not be able

---

[1] Vide the searching examination of Lobeck, *Aglaophamus,* in voc. *Eleusinia.* According to Payne Knight, 'the initiate was admitted into the inmost recesses of the temple, and made acquainted with the first principles of religion, as the knowledge of the God of Nature, the first, the supreme, the

to see all that the Epopts saw, we may be ignorant of certain questions addressed to them, we may even doubt as to the meaning of the celebrated words of dismissal, Konx Om Pax ; but as to the main gist and significance of the spectacle of Eleusis we need entertain no uncertainty whatever. It will be remembered that the Eleusinian Mysteries are only noticed here so far as is necessary to explain and illustrate the part which Dionysos bears in them.

The Homerik Hymn tells how Persephone, the daughter of Zeus and Demeter, was gathering flowers with the daughters of Okeanos in the pleasant *Nysian Meadow near the Ocean-stream*,[1] when the earth clave asunder, and Aïdes Polydegmon, the Many-receiving, bore her away in his chariot to the unseen Under-world; while she shrieked in vain to Zeus for aid. Her mother, Hekate, daughter of Perses, and Helios, heard her cry, and the latter told the sorrowing Demeter of the fate and destiny of her child, whom for nine long days she sought o'er land and sea with lighted torches in her hands. At last the Goddess came to Eleusis, and being wearied, sat by the well, to which the fair daughters of Keleos came to draw water. They spoke kindly to her, and she went with them to their father's house, where she remained many days, and nursed his infant son Demophoon, and soothed her mind with the jests of Iambe. At last she revealed her divinity, and ordered the Eleusinians to build her a mighty temple near the well Kallichoros, promising to teach them secret sites.[2] But the still-grieving Goddess sat down apart from the blessed gods, and restrained the

---

intellectual.' Creuzer and De Sacy thought that he beheld symbolic representations of the Kosmogony, origin of things, wanderings and purifications of the soul, destiny of the world and of man, 'the origin and progress of agriculture and the Hellenik civilization,' &c. This last feature was doubtless brought forward, and all the others may have been *in later times.*

[1] Vide *inf.* IX. viii.
[2] Orgia.

fruitfulness of earth, so that it gave forth no seed, and mankind were in danger of perishing. In vain Zeus sent all the gods, one after another, to summon Demeter to Olympos to soften her anger by gifts; and so at last he ordered Hermes to seek the Under-world, and induce Aïdoneus to permit his bride Persephone to return to the upper air. Nor did the King of the Dead disobey, but summoned the chariot, and Hermes drove the daughter to her mother; but ere she went Polydegmon gave her secretly the seed of a pomegranate, which she ate, a deed which compelled her to return to the dark kingdom.[1] Demeter threw her arms around her recovered child, and Zeus granted that Persephone should spend two-thirds of the revolving year with her mother and the other immortals, and but a third in the gloom of the Under-world. And happy Demeter made the wide earth bring forth abundantly, till it was weighed down with leaves and flowers, and she showed Keleos, and Triptolemos, and Eumolpos, and others her Eleusinians, her sacred rites, 'which it is in no wise lawful either to neglect or to enquire into or to utter, for mighty religious awe of the gods restrains the voice. Happy is he whosoever of mortal men has seen these things; he who is uninitiated in the sacreds, and he who is a partaker of them, have by no means the like fate, when dead, beneath the dreary darkness.'[2] These lines sound somewhat like additions to the original Hymn, but at all events their sentiment undoubtedly belongs to an early period; for Pindaros,[3] when speaking of the Eleusinian Mysteries, exclaims:—

> Happy who these rites hath kenned
> Ere beneath the ground he goeth;
> Well he knoweth of life's end;
> Well it's god-given source he knoweth.[4]

[1] Vide inf. VIII. ii. Pomegranate.
[2] Verses 478–82.
[3] Threnoi, Frag. vii. apud Clem. Alex. Strom. III. 3.
[4] Conington.

Such being the simple and beautiful story of the ancient Hymn,[1] let us briefly consider the nature of the Two Goddesses as indicated in it.

I. *Demeter.*—Ge-Meter, or the Earth-Mother, represents, as already noticed,[2] the earth in a state of comparative order and civilisation, Kosmos as opposed to Chaos, and as such is Thesmophoros, the Law-giver, the establisher of agriculture, marriage, and the ordinary arts of life. As such, she is opposed to Gaia, the Earth in the abstract, but also, especially, as comparatively chaotic and of colossal size, the Assyrian Anatu. The earlier and more shadowy divinities are generally of huge size, as corresponding with the natural phenomena and principles of ontology which they represent. Such are the god-conquered Giants and Titanes, nine-acre-covering Tityos, and others.[3] In honour of Demeter Thesmophoros was celebrated in various parts of Hellas, and especially at Athenai, the great Festival of the Thesmophoria, which lasted for three days, and was commenced by a procession of women carrying on their heads the sacred laws of Demeter, and various symbols of civilised life, from Athenai to Eleusis, where they spent the night in the celebration of the secret rites. The second day they mourned and fasted around the statue of the Goddess, and on the third day made merry and rejoiced. The whole ritual typified the advent of Demeter to Eleusis, her melancholy and the institution of mystic ceremonies, then the success of Iambe in soothing and amusing the Goddess, and the joyful conclusion of the rape of Persephone. The

---

[1] Another and somewhat similar account of the grief and wanderings of Demeter is given in a probably spurious and corrupt Chorus of the *Helene* of Euripides, vv. 1301-68. Vide *inf.* XII. i. 1, the legend of Ishtar descending to Hades.

[2] *Sup.* III. i. 3.

[3] Cf. Paus. x. 4. The worthy Pausanias occasionally displays a traveller's appetite for the marvellous. He quotes with great respect a story of one Kleon who *had seen* near Gadeira (Gades) the body of a marine man-monster, more than 500 feet long.

legendary teaching of Demeter, then, comprised the regulation of agriculture a great basis of civilisation, marriage, and those arts universally admitted in all communities which have risen above a low savage state; and this being so, it is evident that the mysteries of the Goddess would necessarily and naturally have special relation to these matters. But it is also evident that the initiated were supposed to obtain certain peculiar advantages after death; for the immense majority of mankind have ever believed that death was not annihilation. These advantages the pious Epopts and Mystics hoped to enjoy by virtue of their godliness, or conformity to the will of the gods; the godliness which has promise of the life to come as well as of that which now is, for it is a most legitimate deduction that if the god-fearer is specially blessed in this life, he will also be specially blessed hereafter. The initiated, therefore, as peculiarly confiding in the power, submitting to the will, and endeavouring to draw near to the presence of divinity, were by themselves, and by the god-fearing generally, considered as truly happy, and as entitled to look forward with confidence to their future lot either in this world or another. This knowledge and state of mind was undoubtedly that of the pious votaries of Eleusis, for the idea that high and occult dogmas and esoteric truths relating to the origin of nature and earlier history of the world, and also to man's future destiny and the fate of all things, had been handed down from age to age, precious relics of primeval wisdom, has to a great extent crumbled away under a severe investigation.[1]

---

[1] 'Bishop Thirlwall is contented to express a doubt whether the Greek Mysteries were ever used for the exposition of theological doctrines differing from the popular creed. Mr. Grote's conclusion is more definite. In his judgment it is to the last degree improbable that any recondite doctrine, religious or philosophical, was attached to the Mysteries, or contained in the holy stories of any priesthood of the ancient world. If by this recondite teaching be meant doctrines relating to the nature of God and the Divine government of the world, their judgments may per-

Marriage, involving as it does the ideas and mystery of sexual difference and of reproduction, formed a second important element in the cult of Eleusis; while agriculture, especially the operations of sowing and reaping, the disappearance and death of the grain, and its reappearance in a new and beautiful form, bearing testimony to the triumph of life over decay, supplied the third. These three ideas or principles, (1) the innocent and cheering victory of life in the material world around, (2) marriage, with its adjuncts and suggestions, and (3) reverence for the will of the gods, producing order in this life and good hope for the future, *i.e.*, a hope of the ultimate peaceful triumph of the soul or Ego, include all the original phases and subsequent developments of the innocent Eleusinian cult of the Earth-mother, and comprise the materials for her orgies or secret rites. Her particular phase, as representing the orderly and cultivated earth, is indicated with a subtle beauty by the epithets Euplokamos Having-goodly-locks, and Kallistephanos Beautifully-crowned, and that this alludes to the ripe and waving yellow corn we know, for the Goddess is also Xanthe the Golden-haired.[1]

II. *Persephone.*—The second personage in the story, the Daughter, or the Awful Damsel, is a far more occult and mysterious concept than her Mother. And first, as to her name and its meaning; it appears in many forms, as Persephoneia in the Homerik Poems, Per- or Phersephassa or -phatta, Proserpina, etc., and the ordinary etymology which was accepted by the Hellenes themselves, and which explained the name as signifying Deathbringer, is utterly inappropriate and inadmissible.[2] It is

haps be in accordance with fact.' (*Mythology of the Aryan Nations*, ii. 126).
[1] Cf. *Juv. Mundi*, 262.
[2] The following is a specimen of the *Kratylos*:—'Phersephone means only that the goddess is wise (σοφή); for seeing that all things in the world are in motion (φερομένων), that principle which embraces and touches and

quite possible, but not perhaps very probable, that the word may be an adaptation from a foreign language; and numerous interpretations have been suggested, none of which seem entitled to acceptance.[1] Mythology will be found to give considerable assistance in the matter. Thus, with respect to the first part of the name, Perse is the wife of Helios and the daughter of Okeanos;[2] Perseis is a name of Hekate, as the daughter of the Titan Perses, husband of Asteria, the Starry-heaven; Perseus is the solar hero, son of Zeus, in the form of a gleaming golden shower, and his son Perses is the mythic sire of the Persians,[3] the lords of the sun-stricken plains of the East.[4] It is evident, therefore, that the name is connected with heavenly and solar brightness and splendour, all the personages, male and female, who bear it being found in this association. Phatta or Phassa reminds us of Euryphassa, the Widely-shining-one,[5] or the Widely-apparent-one;[6] and similarly Phone or Phoneia seems akin to Phanes, the Spirit-of-the-apparent, and a well-known epithet of Dionysos. The name Persephone would therefore seem to signify the Apparent-Brilliance, that is, the visible beauty-splendour of the material world. Let us see how this interpretation harmonises with the position of the Daughter in the Myth. She is the child of Zeus, the All-father and broad, bright heaven, and Demeter, the beautiful earth, in orderly cultivation, and is playing with her companions, the daughters of Okeanos, in the

is able to follow them, is Wisdom. And therefore the Goddess may be truly called Pherepaphe, or something of that sort, because she touches that which is in motion, &c.' This way Neo-platonik madness lies. According to Varro, 'Proserpine signifies the fecundity of seeds, from *proserpere*, to creep forth, to spring. Many things are taught in the Mysteries of Ceres which only refer to the discovery of fruits,' (apud S. Augustin, *De Civ. Dei*, vii. 20).

[1] Cf. Heindorf, Plato, *Kratyl.*, 404; Creuzer, *Symbolik*, iv. 333 *et seq.*
[2] *Od.* x. 139.
[3] Herod. vii. 61, 150.
[4] Cf. *Juv. Mund.* 310.
[5] Cf. *Mythol. of the Aryan Nations*, i. 417; ii. 38.
[6] Cf. *Phasma*, that which appears, hence an apparition.

pleasant meadow of Nysa, that wonderful Nysa that meets us everywhere in the Dionysiak myth, when she is snatched to the Under-world by Aïdoneus Polydegmon, the Many-receiver. Aïdoneus is a perfectly distinct concept from Zagreus, the Many-guest-receiving Zeus of the dead, but the idea is precisely the same in both cases; each is King of the Under-world, and as such each receives into his dark domains the falling leaf, the sinking splendour, and the 'multitude of them that sleep in the dust of the earth,' called euphemistically 'the greater number.' And who are the daughters of the all-fostering Okeanos, 'source of Deities?'[1] for if people's characters are to be determined to a great extent by the company they keep, should we succeed in ascertaining who are the playmates of Persephone, we shall derive material assistance respecting Persephone herself. Twenty-one names are given, for the line which represents Pallas and Artemis as being of the party may be unhesitatingly rejected. Among them we find Leukippe, White-horse-rider, an epithet of Persephone herself;[2] Phaino, the Apparent;[3] Elektre, Beaming-female-sun;[4] Ianthe, Violet-coloured; Melite, Sweet-one; Iakche, apparently a female reflection of the 'two-natured Iakchos;' Rodeia, Rosy; Kalliroe, Sweet-flowing; Okyroe, Swift-flowing; Chryseis, Golden; Ouranie, Heavenly-one; and Galaxure, nymph of the Galaxy, or Milky-way, the Assyrian 'river of night;' and the whole band, with the exception perhaps of Iakche and Tyche or Fortuna, the mysterious power that appears to govern human affairs, a purely mental concept, introduced here[5] to complete the happy picture, represent the brilliant, beaming, flowing, pleasing, grateful, colour-splendours of

---

[1] *Il.* xiv. 201.
[2] Pindar. *Ol.* vi. 160.
[3] Cf. Phanes.
[4] Cf. Eliktor.
[5] 'Homeros was the first,' says Pausanias, quoting this passage, 'as far as I am aware, to make mention of Tyche' (Paus. iv. 30). She is generally Good Fortune, and so Sôtêr, the Saviour (Ais. *Ag.* 664).

earth beneath and heaven above, children of the light, and, with one or two exceptions, of the day, for it is dark Night that robs the world of colour, and even she is conquered by 'lovely Galaxure.' It will now be evident that Persephone or Apparent-Brilliance is the protagonist of the lovely Chorus, being their combination or epitome, and as such, she, and she only, is snatched away by the dark king; in taking her he took them all. From the happy fertile earth and the beautiful benignant heaven, the bestower of bright sunshine and the refreshing rain, springs the green earth-mantle, chequered with the hues and perfumed with the odours of all flowers, expanding smilingly beneath the bright beams of Phoibos Apollon, 'a thing of beauty and a joy for ever,' for Persephone is the glad light and life of the apparent world around, that bursts forth, and dies, and rises in immortal being and glory, no mere Phanes or earthly spirit of material visibility, but a concept infinitely higher and purer, nobler far and more spiritual, and as such is pictured as a beautiful maiden, stainless, innocent, and gladsome. Of all the truth-spangled legends which our earlier brethren of mankind have left us, I know of none more exquisite, and in its sequel more august, than this. To thoughtful minds at Eleusis or elsewhere, the mythic history must have seemed replete with hope for the future; to the acceptor of Christianity it will ever appear as a revelation of the Gospel, or glad-tidings of the Invisible God, written in indelible characters upon that world which is His own; for He has not left Himself without witness, and the rain from heaven and the fruitful seasons that fill our hearts with food and gladness,[1] the yellow-haired Demeter and the bright Persephone, speak to the godly of that Zeus Hypsistos who has prepared still better things for

---

[1] *Acts*, iv. 17.

them that love Him. The Founder of the Christian religion did not disdain to use the simile of the buried and dying grain in illustration of His course and purpose, and the greatest of His followers in that mighty exhortation to the Church of God at Korinthos, which we still read by every open grave in token of belief in our ultimate triumph over all the chthonian powers of the Under-world, uses language and illustrations which to the Korinthians, accustomed as they were to the neighbouring ritual of Eleusis, must have seemed at once familiar in themselves, and yet new in a strange and splendid application. No trace of Persephone as the Awful Damsel appears in the Homerik Hymn; even when she returns from the Underworld her girlish delight at again meeting her Mother is the most prominent feature in the representation: but, as a matter of necessity, the bride of Aïdoneus must partake of his nature and be in harmony with his domain. The sombre change which steals over her is felicitously expressed by a modern poetess:—

> The eyelids droop with light oppressed,
>   And sunny wafts that round her stir,
> Her cheek upon her mother's breast,
>   Demeter's kisses comfort her.
> Calm Queen of Hades, art thou she
> Who stepped so lightly on the lea,
> Persephone, Persephone?
>
> The greater world may near the less,
>   And draw it thro' her weltering shade,
> But not one biding trace impress
>   Of all the darkness that she made;
> The greater soul that draweth thee
> Hath left his shadow plain to see
> On thy fair face, Persephone!

And so in the Homerik Poems she becomes Hagne the Severely-pure, Agaue the Majestic, and Epaine the Terrible, and bears equal sway with her husband in the Underworld. 'She is represented,' says Mr. Gladstone, 'as ruling together with Aïdoneus, and by no means merely as his wife. Introduced together with him into the legend of Phœnix by his father, and also by Althaia, she seems even to be charged in chief with the sovereignty. She gathers the women-shades for Odysseus, and she disperses them. It is she who, as he fears, may send forth the head of Gorgo should he tarry over long; who may have deluded him with an Eidolon or shadow in lieu of a substance, who endows Teiresias with the functions of a seer. Notwithstanding the high rank of Aïdoneus, as the brother of Zeus, she is the principal, and he is the secondary, figure in the weird scenery of the Eleventh Odyssey.'[1] 'The goddess who represents the teeming earth,' says Donaldson, 'weds her daughter to Plutus, or Pluto, the owner of the treasures hidden below the surface of the ground, either actually, as metallic riches, or potentially, as the germs of vegetable growth.'[2] This connection between concealed wealth and the Two Goddesses is very clearly brought out at the close of the Hymn. 'Highly happy is he, whomsoever of men on the earth they readily love. For immediately they send Ploutos as a sojourner to his noble dwelling place, who gives wealth to mortal men.' Thus in the Hesiodik Theogony Demeter is said to be the mother of Ploutos.[3] One or two other points in the Hymn require special note. It will be observed that Dionysos Iakchos, at all events *eo nomine*, does not appear on the scene in it, although his reflection, the nymph Iakche, is found among the train of Persephone. According to the later legend, Iakchos assisted Demeter in her search, and carried a flaming torch, kindled at

[1] *Juv. Mundi*, 300-10.
[2] *Theatre of the Greeks*, 19; cf. *Mythol. of the Aryan Nations*, ii. 206 et seq.
[3] *Theog.* 969.

Mount Aetna, and in the Temple of Demeter at Athenai his statue, holding a torch, was placed by that of the Two Goddesses.[1] But in the Hymn it is as Helios, the Sun who sees and knows all things, or in his solar phase, that the god appears as the friend and assistant of the Mother. This is interesting as showing the connection and even identity of the 'one Helios, one Dionysos.' The treatment of the various personages in the Hymn is thoroughly simple and un-Semitic, but Helios is not identical with the Aryan Apollon, and as Mr. Gladstone has shown, is a being of Semitic proclivities.[2] The introduction of Helios Dionysos into the Eleusinian ritual will be noticed subsequently.[3]

Persephone, while in the Under-world, eats of the seed of the mystic pomegranate, Rhoia, a name closely resembling that of the Goddess-Mother Rhea. This fruit, in Hebrew Rimmon, both from its shape and the multiplicity of its seeds, was an emblem of the fruitful female, while one derivation connects it also with the Linga. It stands, therefore, anthropomorphically speaking, as a euphemism for the reproductive powers, and in the myth signifies that the Apparent-brightness of the world when buried in the earth becomes associated with the reproductive powers of nature, and so must share with them their concealment in the Under-world. Thus the statue of Here, the Matron-goddess, in her great temple near Mykene, held a pomegranate in one hand,[4] and the fruit was a usual symbol in the Mysteries.[5]

The rape of Persephone being viewed Euemeristically, great differences not unnaturally arose as to the locality where it occurred. The author of the *Argonautika* says,

---

[1] Paus. i. 2.
[2] *Juv. Mundi*, 321 *et seq.*
[3] Subsec. ii.
[4] Paus. ii. 17.
[5] Clem. Alex. *Protrepts.* ii. 22. Vide VIII. ii. *Pomegranate.* Pausanias noticed that the Arkadians brought all fruits, except the pomegranate, into the temple of Despoina, the Mistress, an epithet specially applied by them to Persephone (Paus. viii. 37).

on an isle in the ocean.¹ Some stated she was snatched away from a plain in Sikelia, and this version was afterwards followed by the Roman poets: Bakchylides placed the scene in Krete; Phanodemos, whose age is uncertain, and who was the author of a work on Attik antiquities, preferred Attike. Others showed the very spot, which was near Eleusis, and was called Kaprifikos; but the Argeioi stoutly contended that it was near Lerne, and to prevent mistake, marked it out by a stone inclosure.² Hesiodos mentions no particular locality;³ nor did the writer, whose verses were attributed to the mythic Pamphos,⁴ who was said to have composed the most ancient Hymns of the Athenians.⁵ The Orphik Poet held, with the author of the Homerik Hymn, that it was by the Ocean marge, in what the latter calls the Nysian Meadow, the pleasant abode of beauty and flowers.⁶

Subsection II.—The Union of the Cults.

The origin of the Eleusinian cult is lost in the mists of ages: in one form or other it was doubtless coeval with the dawn of order and civilisation. Some have argued from the silence respecting it in the Homerik Poems that it arose in comparatively recent times. The argument from silence, on which far too great stress is constantly laid, is very frequently of the slightest weight, and it must be remembered that the Poems do not profess to give a general history of Early Hellas, but confine themselves almost jealously to their own particular subjects; and again, that the few scattered notices of Demeter and Persephone in them are in perfect accordance with the

---

[1] V. 1195.
[2] Cf. Schol. *Theog.* 914; Paus. i. 38, ii. 36; Lobeck, *Aglaoph.* 546.
[3] *Theog.* 913.
[4] Paus. ix. 31.
[5] Ibid. 29.
[6] Vide *inf.* VIII. i. *Nysios.*

Eleusinian legend. Thus the latter appears to be the unnamed child of Zeus and Demeter, whose loves are noticed.[1] The Mysteries of Eleusis, a name which signifies 'Coming,' and is said to have been given on account of the arrival of Demeter there, having thus been established probably for some ages, a new personage, Dionysos, was at length introduced on the scene as the Assistant and Associate of the Two Goddesses. No connection between Dionysos and the more ancient divinities of Eleusis appears in Homeros, or in the Hesiodik Theogony, but his installation at the Mysteries had taken place considerably earlier than the time of Pindaros. I have already noticed some of the passages which introduce and illustrate the part of Dionysos at Eleusis, which is in exact parallel to his position by the side of Apollon at Delphoi. Thus he is 'the Associate of bronze-rattling Demeter,'[2] whom Euripides frequently, but incorrectly, treats as being absolutely identical with Kybele. The Chorus in the *Antigoné*, addressing the god, exclaimed, 'Thou rulest over the Eleusinian rites of Deo in the vales common to all.'[3] The last word seems to imply that the ceremonies of initiation were for the people at large, not for any particular persons or classes. Thus Herodotos says, 'Every year the Athenians celebrate this feast to the Mother and the Daughter, and all who wish, whether they be Athenians or any other Greeks, are initiated.'[4] The Fragment quoted[5] from the *Triptolemos* of Sophokles is very valuable in this connection. Triptolemos, 'the law-administering King,' appears in the Homerik Hymn as one of those to whom Demeter unfolded her mysteries; and as already noticed, his patroness gave him a winged or dragon-drawn chariot, in which he was carried over the earth,

---

[1] *Il.* xiv. 326; cf. *Juv. Mundi*, 261.
[2] Pind. *Isth.* vi. 3.
[3] Soph. *Antig.* 119–21.
[4] Herod. viii. 65.
[5] *Sup.* IV. ii. 1.

distributing wheat-seeds to mankind.' 'I beheld,' Triptolemos himself is probably the speaker, 'the famed Nysa, the abode of Bakchik fury, which the Ox-horned Iakchos inhabits as his best beloved retreat.' Triptolemos, in the course of his journeyings over the earth, arrives at the mystic Nysa, the very place whence Persephone was snatched away, and at Nysa, of course, meets with Dionysos, the taurik god of the East, who, it will be observed, is called by the special name under which he was known in the Eleusinian mysteries, Iakchos. The absolute identity of the taurik Dionysos and the ox-horned Iakchos of Nysa comes out with great clearness. A singular statement of Grote on this point may here be noticed:—' Bacchus or Dionysos are in the Attic Tragedians constantly *confounded* with the Demetrian Iacchos *originally so different*—a personification of the mystic word shouted by the Eleusinian communicants.'[1] 'The greater part of the Hellenes,' says Strabo, 'attribute to Bakchos, Apollon, Hekate, the Muses, and Demeter everything connected with orgies and Bakchanalian rites, dances, and the mysteries attendant upon initiation. They also call Bakchos Dionysos, and the chief Daemon of the mysteries of Demeter.'[2] So that not only 'the Attic Tragedians,' but also 'the greater part of the Hellenes,' were, according to Grote, entirely in error on this simple point. All these, many of whom had actually been initiated, believed that Dionysos was an important personage at Eleusis, when in reality he was never worshipped there at all. How comes it that the modern historian knows these facts so much better than the persons who made the history which he has recorded? This is not a point on which information has increased: Dionysos was either worshipped at Eleusis, or he was not, and of this

---

[1] *Hist. of Greece*, i. 86, Note.   [2] Strabo, x. 3.

fact, those who took part in the ritual of the place are, according to all laws of evidence, the best judges. But if he was worshipped there at all, it was as Iakchos. Again, who is Iakchos? and if he were not Dionysos, how came he to be confounded with him? But Iakchos is said to be the personification of a mystic word, and so for that matter is Dionysos also. Donaldson very properly alludes to Iakchos as the 'synonym' of Bakchos, and explains the name in the usual way, *i.e.*, as 'referring to the outcries attending' the worship of the god.[1] The observations of Ouvaroff on this subtle question are well worthy of attention:—'The third Bacchus is the Iacchus of Eleusis, who seems to have been imagined only that he might consecrate, in some degree, the alliance between the recent worship of Bacchus and that of Ceres, to which all the mysteries tended. Iacchus is the symbol of this association: his only destination having been already fulfilled by his birth, the myth has remained imperfect; it is the most vague of all.' The sixth day of the Eleusinian mysteries 'consecrated to Iacchus was the most solemn of all. But it requires very little reflection to perceive that this procession, subsequently so famous, was at first only an addition, foreign to the mysteries of Eleusis. It had not, in fact, any relation with the basis of the mysteries, but reveals incontestably the association of the secret worship of Bacchus to the mysteries of Ceres. Several mythographers have endeavoured to distinguish between Bacchus and Iacchus; but this attempt has been useless. There is in the employment of Iacchus, so distinct from the basis of the Eleusinian Mysteries, something which rather bespeaks a later association than a perfect identity.'[2] A passage in the *Iôn* of Euripides, which I have already illustrated,[3] represents Dionysos as hastening to Eleusis, in

[1] *Theatre of the Greeks*, 17.
[2] *Essay on the Eleusinian Mysteries*, vi.   [3] *Sup.* IV. iii. 1.

order to appear there on the sixth day of the mysteries as Protagonist in the universal nature-dance in honour of the Mother ànd the Daughter.[1] In the *Kretes*, Frag. II.,[2] the office of Iakchos as torch-bearer is alluded to. The mystic imitates the life of 'the night-wandering Zagreus,' by 'holding up torches to the Mountain-mother,' *i.e.*, Kybele, who, according to Euripides, is identical with Demeter. Thus the god in all his phases as Zagreus-Dionysos-Iakchos is represented as the Attendant, Associate, and chief Torch-bearer to the Great Goddesses of Eleusis. So in the Orphik Hymn Demeter is called the 'hearth-sharer of Bromios,'[3] which, although incorrectly expressed, aptly illustrates their connection. The writer should have styled Dionysos the hearth-sharer of Demeter; he is the second, not the first. So, again, Persephone is said to be 'the Mother of Eubouleus, the Wise-counselling-One, *i.e.*, Dionysos,[4] an easy transition, as Dionysos, the Earth-spirit, is naturally the son of all the great telluric and chthonian goddesses. Kallimachos forcibly illustrates the union of their nature and cult when he says that the same acts enrage Demeter and Dionysos,[5] and the mythological itinerary of Pausanias frequently affords illustrations of the close connection between them. The introduction of Dionysos to the mysteries is also illustrated in the *Batrachoi* of Aristophanes, where Herakles first explains to him the state of the initiated;[6] and then, having crossed the Styx, he is terrified by a dreadful spectre called the Empousa, which was covered with bloody pustules,[7] and constantly, Proteus-like, changed its shape.[8] This having disappeared, he hears the Chorus of Mystics calling on Iakchos to lead the sacred dance in the

[1] Cf. Eur. *Hel.* 1301-68.
[2] Noticed *sup.* IV. iii. 5.
[3] Hymn xl. 10.
[4] Hymn xxix. 8, with xxx. 6.
[5] *Hymn. eis Dem.* 71.
[6] *Bat.* 154-8.
[7] Cf. *Ekkle.* 1000.
[8] *Bat.* 288-305.

meadow, torch in hand, on which the god exclaims, 'I will go with the damsels and the women where they by night celebrate the festival of the goddess, bearing the sacred torch.'[1] Thus was Dionysos installed as the Dadouchos, or Torch-bearer, at the Mysteries.

Such being the connection between Dionysos and the Goddesses of Eleusis, we have next to consider the reason of it, why Dionysos more than any other divinity should have been introduced into the ritual which was in itself complete without him.[2] The answer is supplied at once, and completely, by the nature of these several personages. The terrestrial Earth-mother and her chthonian and telluric Daughter exactly harmonise and accord, alike and yet how different, with Dionysos, the spirit of kosmic life. The one idea in origin was simple, innocent, and Aryan; the other, although corresponding, more psychical, involved, mysterious, and Semitic. Dionysos appears as a stranger in Hellas; his worship becomes eminently popular, as both appealing directly to the lower nature, and yet at the same time attempting to satisfy some of the higher aspirations of the soul. Many of his more remarkable and repulsive Phoenician phases become altered and obscured; the glowing Sun-god loses much of his fierce heat and high dignity; he sinks to an inferior, an assistant and associate, and although his rays for a time are partly shorn, he still bravely bears his torch, and, ere long, again reaches high honour and mysterious dignity. Nations are not in the habit of changing their gods that are no gods, and so Demeter and her Daughter are not forsaken for the brilliant stranger; but the entrance to the

---

[1] *Bat.* 444-5.

[2] Canon Rawlinson remarks, 'Bochart believes that the Phœnicians introduced the worship of Ceres [Demeter,] into Greece. Certainly the Eleusinian mysteries appear to have been thoroughly oriental in their character' (*Herodotus*, iii. 217). Bochart's conjecture cannot be allowed, Demeter being a purely Aryan goddess. I trust I have indicated as clearly as the subject allows, the respective amounts of Aryan and Semitic influence at Eleusis.

Pantheon is wide enough to admit him and many others, and he may thus seat himself by their side. In the first place, he is 'the son of a Kadmeian mother,' a fact of unmistakeable significance, but afterwards, when his general character and kosmogonico-solar affinities are duly appreciated, he naturally becomes the son of Persephone. But he is never represented as the son of Aïdes, whom I regard as a thoroughly Aryan concept, for as the subterranean sun, and also as the chthonian earth-god, he is himself an Aïdes, but, like his other self Uasar, a Semitic Pluto. His mother Semele, as we have seen, is but a special and peculiar phase of the Gaia-Demeter, and he is appropriately found as an attendant upon the furious and orgiastic Kybele, the Phrygian phase of the great Goddess-mother of the East. Apparent fluctuations in the details of the myth in reality but indicate the breadth of its basis and the unity of its primal ideas, as the Dawn is with equal propriety the mother, sister, and bride of the Sun, who himself may be regarded as either the son or sire of the Day. And the root-idea is this, that alike in Semitic and Aryan concept, there is a great Goddess-mother, a many-breasted nurturer of heroes and of all things, whose glowing life-beauty is pictured in a beautiful and blooming child, Persephone, or Dionysos-Antheus. On the shores of Hellas these ideas touch, mingle, and are united; and it was in this attractive form, and shorn of his savage and repulsive features, that Dionysos entered the shrine of Eleusis, and became the chief Daemon of the Goddesses. Our difficulties in dealing with divinities mainly arise from ignorance of their real nature, but when this is once revealed it is easy to understand their mythic harmony or opposition. The Great Dionysiak Myth is vastly wider than that fragment of it which was crystallised into tangibility at Eleusis; but the Eleusinian union, so far as it extends, simply typifies the harmony between a group of somewhat similar concepts, all illustrating in a pleasing and attractive form, the varied changes of the earth-life, and a mass of human reflection, hope, and imagination inseparably linked therewith.

Subsection III.—*The Eleusinian Ritual.*

As this Section would be somewhat incomplete without a notice of the Ritual of Eleusis, I subjoin a brief account of the ceremony as it obtained during the most prominent period of Hellenik history. The principal symbols connected with the Mysteries are referred to separately.[1]

1. *The Lesser Mysteries.*—The Mikra Musteria, or Lesser Mysteries, were celebrated annually on the banks of the Ilisos, close by Athenai, in the month Anthisterion—February-March. They were a prior step to the Greater Mysteries, and as such were called Prokatharsis, or Preliminary Purification. The participants were purified by an Hydranos, or Water-priest, and sacrificed a sow, a fitting type of the earth-life and a corn-injuring animal, to the Earth-mother. They then took an oath of secrecy, which was administered by the Mystagogos, or Leader-of-the-Initiated, and thereupon themselves became Mustai, Mystics. They were then in a position to obtain the higher initiation at the Greater Mysteries in the following year, and also received such instruction as enabled them to comprehend more or less the underlying significance of the latter ceremonial. The division of the Mysteries into Lesser and Greater seems an artificial alteration of a comparatively late age.

2. *The Greater Mysteries.*—These, generally called The Mysteries simply, were celebrated annually during the month Boedromion—September-October, the ceremonial taking place partly at Athenai and partly at

[1] Vide *inf.* VIII. ii.

Eleusis, and lasting nine days, the period of the unsuccessful search of Demeter.[1]

First Day.—Agyrmos, or The Assembling. The Mystics met at the Temple of Demeter at Athenai, which was called the Eleusinion, and stood a little to the east of the Akropolis, with which there appears to have been a subterranean communication. This temple was strongly fortified and greatly revered, so that when at the commencement of the Peloponnesian war Athenai was crowded with all the north-western population of Attike, in addition to the ordinary inhabitants, and nearly all temples and shrines were used as dwelling-places, the Eleusinion, like the Akropolis, remained unoccupied through reverence for its sanctity.[2] Pausanias provokingly tells us that he had intended to relate the particulars about it, but was restrained from so doing by a dream.[3] The reticence of earlier writers respecting the Eleusinian Mysteries has been followed, according to what may be called the Principle of the Pendulum, by the copious revelations of very late, and many modern, scribes: but the former, unfortunately, knew and would not tell; while the latter did not know, but insisted on revealing, the secrets of the Earth-mother and her attendant train.

Second Day.—The March to the Sea. The Mystics went in procession from the Eleusinion to the sea shore, and were there further purified by a 'baptism in salt water.'

Third Day.—The Sacrifices. These consisted chiefly of a mullet and barley from the sacred field of Eleusis, called Rarion, where the grain was said to have been first sown. These oblations represented the combined offerings of sea and land to the Earth-mother, nurturer of heroes. The Mystics fasted during the day, an act in

---

[1] Hom. *Hymn. eis Dem.* 47.   [2] Thou. ii. 17.
[3] Paus. i. 14.

itself a sacrifice to the giver of food; for one important principle in sacrifices is the devoting to a divinity the gift which he is supposed peculiarly to confer; *e.g.* the Phrygian priests of the Great Mother sacrificed the reproductive principle in her honour. At even the Neophytes partook of a cake made of roasted and pounded sesame-seeds and honey. The symbolism of all seeds and seed-plants in the Mysteries is similar and obvious, as noticed in the case of the pomegranate; and agreeably with this, we find that the sesame cake was an Attik wedding delicacy.[1]

Fourth Day.—The Basket Procession. The Kalathos, or mystic hand-basket of Demeter, containing pomegranates and poppy seeds, was carried in procession in the sacred ox-drawn cart. The accompanying crowds shouted 'Hail Demeter!' whilst behind walked the Kistophoroi, each bearing a small box or chest, *kiste, cista,* which contained salt, wool, pomegranate-seeds, ivy, and little round cakes.[2] Ptolemaios Philadelphos introduced the Eleusinian ritual into Alexandreia, on which occasion Kallimachos composed his famous *Hymn to the Basket.* The symbols represented, somewhat protoplasmically, the germs of things.

Fifth Day.—The Torch Procession. Towards night on this day there was a procession of the Mystics, bearing torches, and headed by the Dadouchos, or Torch-bearer, who was the first of the three assistants of the Hierophant, and symbolised the Sun, to the temple at Eleusis, where they passed the night. The ritual of the day is very interesting as showing the exact circumstances under which Dionysos was introduced to the Mysteries. In the Homeric Hymn, as was noticed, it was Dionysos

---

[1] Aristoph. *Eirēnē.* 869.
[2] One kind of these was called Ox-cake, made with little horns and dedicated to the Moon (Hesych. in voc. *Bous*), with whom Persephone became connected. (Cf. *Juv. Mundi,* 311). Souidas remarks, 'They call it Ox,' *boun*; In voc. *Boushebdomos.*) Is this our bun?

who, as Helios with his all-seeing eye of light, assisted the Goddess in her search by informing her who had carried away her Daughter. But in Hellas Dionysos is not at first conspicuous in a solar phase, as the place of the solar god was already well occupied by the Aryan Apollon, and therefore when, for the reasons and in manner above noticed, he was introduced into the drama of Eleusis, he appears as apparently unconnected with Helios. In this day's ritual neither Helios nor Iakchos is visible *eis nominibus*. The former has disappeared from the scene; the latter has not yet arrived on it: and so we have the Torch-bearer as the Protagonist. Now the Torch-bearer, as we have seen, is Dionysos himself, and of course it will be observed that this torch-procession was a representation of the night search of Demeter, assisted by Dionysos, leader of the igneo-starry choir, bearing the torch which he held up to the Mother on the mountains. Torches suggest the night, and the sun with still greater force the day, but both appear in the Homerik Hymn, and show that the search of the Goddess was continued without cessation. Both day and night are full of meaning in the symbolism; on the other hand, it is the cheering influence of the solar-torch, for day is only night kept at bay by the torch of Iakchos, which makes the earth bring forth and bud, and so assists in recovering Persephone, the lost beauty-splendour; and, on the other, Night is a mighty nurturer of all things, which, wrapped in the sable folds of her star-fringed mantle, can rest and increase in peace. The Sun, too, in some respects is a nocturnal as well as a diurnal divinity, and is busy in the Under-world until again, as Hyperion, the Climber, the Winged Disk of mysterious potency, he 'scales high heaven, exulting like a god,' or giant-athlete.[1] 'The nights,' says Hesiod, 'belong to the blessed gods; and the

---

[1] *Psalm*, xix. 5.

Orphik Poet calls night the source of all things, to denote that productive power, which, as I have been told, it really possesses; it being observed that plants and animals grow more by night than by day. The ancients extended this power much further, and supposed that not only the productions of the earth, but the luminaries of heaven were nourished and sustained by the benign influence of the night.'[1]

Sixth Day.—The Day of Iakchos. On this day, as noticed,[2] the statue of Dionysos-Iakchos, torch in hand and crowned with myrtle, was carried along the Hiera Hodos, or Sacred Way, from the Kerameikos, or Potter's Quarter, to Eleusis, accompanied by the Iakchogogoi, or Iakchos-leaders, also myrtle-crowned, who danced and sang and beat upon their *tympana*, or kettle-drums. They made a brief halt at a spot marked by an Hiera Syke, or Sacred Fig-tree, and then proceeding, entered Eleusis by the Mystike Eisodos, or Mystic Entry. On this day, the twentieth of Boedromion, the solemnity of the ritual reached its height; and Dionysos, as we saw in Euripides, hastens from Kastalia to lead the universal dance in honour of the golden-crowned Damsel and her awful Mother.[3] The starry-faced Ether and the Moon begin the dance, and all nature follows; and the starry-Ether is but Dionysos in his spotted starry robe, the 'pattern of things in the heavens.' And how does the dance honour the Two Goddesses of life? Because it exhibits, to use modern terminology, the rhythm and continuity of motion and the persistence of force, and is thus the great life-manifestation. Motion being a special manifestation of life, and dance, 'the poetry of motion,' of orderly and harmonious life, hence is derived the simple yet profound and beautiful symbolism by which all

---

[1] R. Payne Knight, *Worship of Priapus*, 106.
[2] *Sup.* IV. iii. 1.   [3] *Ion*, 1074 *et seq.*

things are said to dance in honour of the mighty embodiment of kosmic being. An ancient bronze, which in Payne Knight's time was at Strawberry Hill among the many curiosities and objects of art collected by Horace Walpole, represents in a remarkable manner the union and harmony of the Demetrian and Dionysiak cults. Demeter is seated with a cup in one hand, various fruits in the other, and a small bull in her lap. The Earth-mother, it will be observed, is thus herself possessed of wine and the grape, which she brings forth equally with other food for the service of man; while the tauromorphic Dionysos, emblem of productiveness and of the vigour of the natural life, nestles to her as his patroness and superior.[1] But the votaries of Eleusis have reached the entrance to the temple of Demeter, which was a square building of about 200 feet on each side, commenced by Iktinos, the architect of the Parthenon, and finished by Philon about B.C. 315. A herald thereupon dismissed the general crowd by solemn proclamation ('Procul, procul ite profani!'), and the Mystics were then admitted into the illumined interior of the shrine, a process termed Photagogia, or the Leading-to-the-light. They were next admonished to draw near 'with hearts sprinkled from an evil conscience and bodies washed with pure water,' and having repeated the solemn oath of secrecy, holy mysteries were read to them out of a sacred book called Petroma, because it consisted of two stones closely joined together. At Pheneos, in northern Arkadia, was a temple of Demeter Eleusinia, where the same mystic ceremonies were performed as at Eleusis;[2] and near the temple were two large stones closely joined together, and called Petroma, between which were preserved the mystic writings. These at the Greater Mysteries were taken out

---

[1] *Worship of Priapus*, 72. Pl. viii.   [2] Paus. viii. 14.

and read to the neophytes, and replaced at night. Oaths were usually sworn on the Petroma; and inside, besides the sacred writings, was kept a mask of Demeter Kidaria, which the priest having put on invoked the infernal powers by striking with rods upon the ground.[1] Pausanias is here unusually communicative about the mysteries, and the passage is of very considerable interest and importance, it being remembered that the ceremonies of Pheneos and Eleusis were similar, a fact of which Pausanias, himself an Epopt,[2] was well qualified to judge. The reading being finished, the Mystics severally confessed to the Hierophant, and were strictly examined by him on numerous matters, but especially with regard to fasting and chastity, both of which were indispensable prerequisites to initiation. Answers were given according to a set form, and this part of the ceremony having been duly observed, the Aspirants were admitted to the mystic Sekos, or Enclosure, which adjoined the temple, and was of considerable size, large enough indeed to contain the crowd of a theatre.[3] They were further prepared for the performance by partaking of a cup 'craftily qualified,' being an imitation of the celebrated 'Miscellaneous Potion' given to Demeter on her visit to Eleusis,[4] and called Kykeon, meaning primarily that-which-is-stirred-up, and hence the state of confusion produced by drinking. Such was the drugged preparation given by Kirke to the companions of Odysseus.[5] Poppies were an ingredient of it, and this 'presented to each mystic before the shows began, might have contributed more to that confusion of intellects than the awful appearance of the objects exhibited.'[6] Deeply excited and agitated by all they had

---

[1] Paus. viii. 15.
[2] Ibid. i. 37, 38.
[3] Strabo, ix. i.
[4] *Hymn. eis Dem.* 208.
[5] *Od.* x. 234 *et seq.*
[6] Christie, *Disquisitions upon the Painted Greek Vases*, 37.

gone through, ready to believe anything and everything, in that state of abstinence which is, or is supposed to be, most favourable to the reception of supernatural displays, with their minds more or less affected by drugs, and their whole being permeated with the impression and expectation of a revelation of the more-than-mortal, they were allowed TO SEE. This is the Autopsia or Personal Inspection, the Crown of Mysteries, the Epopteia or Divine Beholding, which was used as a synonym to express the highest earthly happiness, and he who had enjoyed it became an Epoptes, or Contemplator, beyond which this world could give him nothing. But what saw they? naturally exclaims the reader. Before attempting to give some answer to this question, let us for a moment consider this august phraseology irrespective of what the Epopts of old saw or thought they saw. The extraordinary suitability of the language of the Mysteries to the Christian religion is as evident as remarkable. The mind can conceive no higher idea than to behold the Invisible God in peace, a privilege which implies a likeness of nature; for the Apostle declares that those who will see Him as He is, *i.e.*, anthropomorphically displayed in His Eikon, or Personified Idea, will be like Him; and that this very hope stimulates them to aim at infinite purity and perfection.[1] There can be no more godlike aspiration than the desire of being like God. So could the delighted astronomer exclaim on making his great discoveries that he entered into the mind of the Creator and read His thoughts, which naturally are not as man's. 'All men,' says Homeros, 'yearn after the gods.' 'Thou hast made us for Thyself,' says S. Augustin, 'and we cannot rest till we rest in Thee.' The ancient Patriarch Job, in a noble and familiar declaration of faith, which certain moderns have vainly attempted to twist into something comparatively

---

[1] 1 John iii. 2, 3.

petty and meaningless, states his emphatic belief in the Autopsia: 'In my flesh I shall see God, Whom *I shall see for myself*, and mine eyes shall behold, and not another;' and this belief in a Zeus Soter, and in His ultimate epiphany or manifestation to His worshippers, is called 'the root of the matter.'[1] The anthropomorphic element and idea in religion is at present disparaged and attacked; people begin and end their creed with a Final Cause, a Great Unknown. But belief which contains no more than this is essentially valueless and unpractical. Amen, the Hidden God, will remain for ever hidden until anthropomorphically revealed. Gods who are only afar off are useless.

> The gods who haunt
> The lucid interspace of world and world,
> Where never creeps a cloud, or moves a wind,
> Nor ever falls the least white star of snow,
> Nor ever lowest roll of thunder moans,
> Nor sound of human sorrow mounts to mar
> Their sacred everlasting calm!

Such gods, or again a mere pantheistic Dionysos, 'everlastingly *within* creation[2] as its inmost life, omnipresent and omniactive,'[3] Erikepeios forsooth, Spring-time-garden-growth, are truely valueless; and no wonder that men should begin to doubt the propriety of praying to them. This vast subject cannot be further dealt with here. I merely mention it to illustrate the grandeur of the concepts to which the Eleusinian initiation naturally gives rise. Let us never be beguiled out of our faith in a

---

[1] Job xix. 26–8. I am well aware that in certain quarters the Book of Job is called a poetical allegory, and is said to have been composed in the time of Solomon or later. *Sed ei incumbit probatio qui dicit.* Vide Sir W. Drummond's sage treatment and explication of *Gen.* xiv. (*Œdipus Judaicus.* Dissert. Two). 'A man may say.'

[2] Instead of creation being within him. Vide *sup.* II. iii. 3.

[3] Rev. William Knight in *Contemporary Review*, Dec. 1873.

Personal Divinity, but, holding fast to the anthropomorphic principle, say with the 'divine Poet':[1]—

> That each, who seems a separate whole,
>   Should move his rounds and fusing all
>   The skirts of self again, should fall
> Remerging in the general Soul,
>
> Is faith as vague as all unsweet;
>   Eternal form shall still divide
>   The eternal soul from all beside;
> And I shall know Him when we meet.
>
> And we shall sit at endless feast,
>   Enjoying each the other's good;
>   What vaster dream can hit the mood
> Of Love on earth?

But to return to the Mysteries, and to the question, What was seen there? The priest at Pheneos, and also apparently at Eleusis, put on the mask of Demeter Kidaria. The *Kidaria* was an Oriental head-dress [2] distinguished by a peculiar peak or prominence in front, closely connected with and probably being a species of the horned head-dresses still worn as tokens of rank, wifehood, etc., in parts of Syria. Demeter being a purely Aryan divinity, is never, so far as I am aware, represented as horned; but in her phase as Kidaria, wearing the peaked or pointed head-dress, an Oriental addition to the goddess, she approaches as nearly to Artemis Tauropolos, or to Astarte, as the anthropomorphic principles of Hellas will allow. It seems, so to speak, to be the result of taking the Semitic bull in her lap. Kidaris is also the name of an Arkadian dance,[3] so that it is sufficiently

---

[1] A term applied by Mrs. Browning to the Laureate. Vide *Contemporary Review*, Dec. 1873, 160.

[2] In Hebrew *Keter* (Esth. vi. 8); in Kaldeo-Assyrian *Kudurri* (vide *Records of the Past*, v. 112).

[3] Athen. xiv. 7.

evident that at Pheneos the Demetrian votaries danced, in honour of the Mother and the Daughter, adorned with these peaked head-dresses. This reminds us of the dances of the Satyroi, the horned attendants of Dionysos.[1] Next, as to the mask, *prosopon*, or *prosopeion*. 'The tragedian was increased to a collossal stature by his mask, which not only represented a set of features much larger than those of any ordinary man, but was raised to a great height above the head by a sort of elevated frontlet or fore-top, rising in the shape of the letter Λ.'[2] This frontlet corresponds with the peak of the *kidaris*, and on the Attik stage was covered with the tire, or periwig. The Hierophantes, or Shower-of-sacred-things, being thus habited, he next invoked the Infernal, or Nether, Divinities, by striking with rods upon the ground, *i.e.* knocked at the door of their house, a most ancient and natural mode of invocation. Thus Althaia, the mother of Meleagros, called upon the rulers of the Under-world:—

> With her hands
> Beating the solid earth, the nether pow'rs,
> Pluto and awful Proserpine, implor'd.[3]

Sacred mysteries, as a matter of course, could only be shown through the eye or the ear, and the latter having already been filled with them by means of the reading from the Petroma, it remained to astonish the eye; this was to be effected by means of displays of a theatrical and illusory character. As of course, but at the same time a circumstance too generally unnoticed, the programme of the entertainment varied greatly in different ages; numerous novel ideas being imported in later times from Kam and the East, and the stage appliances by degrees becom-

---

[1] Amongst the North American Indians the 'Buffalo dance' was performed by horned votaries, (Catlin, *North American Indians*, ii. 128).

[2] *Theatre of the Greeks*, 248.

[3] *Il.* ix. 568, Earl of Derby's Translation.

ing more elaborate as the element of deception and unreality grew stronger. It is sufficiently evident that at the commencement of the Epopteia the nerves of the Mystics were tried, it may be severely, by more or less terrible appearances; which, as noticed, Aristophanes seems to refer to when he represents Dionysos as meeting with the spectral Empousa near the happy meadow where the initiated were dancing as in Arkadia. The Eleusinian dances were of two kinds, the public, which took place openly in the meadow near the well Kallichoros,[1] and the private, which apparently were performed within the Sekos adjoining the temple. Bearing in mind then, (1) that these were private dances, (2) performed before the votaries at initiation, (3) of a nerve-trying character, and (4) after the invocation of the Infernal Divinities, let us endeavour to realise to some extent what took place on the occasion.[2] We have noticed the invocation of Althaia as being exactly similar to that of the Hierophant, nor was it unheeded:—

> From the depths
> Of Erebus Erinnys heard her pray'r,
> Gloom-haunting goddess, dark and stern of heart.

The dread Erinyes or Furies, called euphemistically Eumenides the Appeased, and Semnai the Venerable, are said by Hesiodos to be the daughters of Gaia,[3] Earth; by Aischylos, of Night;[4] whilst Sophokles ascribes their

---

[1] St. Croix, *Recherches sur les Mystères*; Mitchell, in *Bat.* 325.

[2] The Tractate of Loukianos, *Peri Orcheseōs*, 'concerning the Dance,' contains several remarks worthy of notice. Thus he observes that 'no ancient initiation can be found where there is not dancing,' and that 'the imitative art is a certain knowledge, an exhibition, a showing of things arcane to the mental powers, and the expression of the living things which are occult.' 'The choral dance of the stars, the orderly concert of planets, their common union and harmony of motion, constitute the exhibition of the dance of the first-born.' Vide also R. P. Knight, *Symbolical Language of Ancient Art and Mythology*, sec. clxxxvii.; *sup*. IV. iii. 1.

[3] *Theog.* 185.

[4] *Eumen.* 394.

parentage to Earth and Darkness.¹ Thus, when appearing, they rise from the gloom of the Under-world, Phoberopes Of-terrific-aspects,² and Ophio-plokamoi³ Snaky-haired. 'Aischylos,' says Pausanias, 'was the first who [to his knowledge] represented them with snakes in their hair;'⁴ and he notices that neither their statues nor those of any of the Infernal Divinities were dreadful in appearance, a striking illustration of the Hellenik clinging to the anthropomorphic principle, which I have so frequently occasion to notice as an important rule in distinguishing the origin of divinities. Now Aischylos was accused of having divulged the secrets of the Mysteries, and of incorporating incidents from them in his Plays;⁵ he too provided masks and stage dresses, and is said to have himself inserted various peculiar choral-dances. He also wrote a play entitled *The Eleusinians*, which is supposed to have formed the third in the Trilogy of the *Thebais*, and to have been the sequel of the *Hepta epi Thebas*.' Almost every word of the Play is lost, but the subject would give tempting opportunities to an Epopt who was at all inclined to reveal the secrets of the Sekos. It is hardly necessary to allude in detail to his *Eumenides*; suffice it to remind the reader that he represented the Erinyes as black-bodied, blood-dripping beings, with snakes entwined in their hair, dwelling in evil darkness in Tartaros below the earth. He calls them 'wingless,'⁶ but Euripides more naturally represents them as 'wing-bearing,'⁷ and on the Vases they sometimes appear with wings and sometimes without. Again, they are torch-connected and torch-bearing powers, and so are described as being 'delighted with the blazing

---

¹ *Oid. epi Kolôn.* 40.
² *Orph. Hymn.* lxx. 10.
³ *Ibid.* lix. 12.
⁴ Paus. i. 28.
⁵ Aristot. *Ethik.* iii. 1; Aelian,
Poik. Hist. v. 10; Clem. Alex. *Strom.* ii. 14, 'Aischylos, who divulged the mysteries on the stage.'
⁶ *Eumen.* 51.
⁷ *Orestes*, 317.

torch,'[1] which is 'sunless,'[2] as being in the Under-world, and Athene promises to send torches to the lower regions,[3] apparently in their honour. Thus a Fury is represented on a Vase as bearing two spears in one hand and a large and fiercely blazing torch in the other;[4] and in another representation of the 'enthroned Persephone in Hades,' a Fury stands on her right hand, with two large torches.[5] So Ovid,

> Tristis Erinnys
> Praetulit infaustas sanguinolenta faces.

Lastly, the Furies had a terrible malignant dance, which they accompanied by a weird, mind-destroying hymn.[6] It is especially called an 'un-Bakchik dance,'[7] as being joyless and accompanied with groans and weeping, and their incantations, like those of the mediaeval witches, made healthy life wither away,[8] thus being the exact opposite to Dionysos Karpios or Erikepeios. Their forms, Empousa-like, appear to change. As it showed like an ox, a mule, a woman, or with a fire-blazing visage;[9] so they are winged and wingless, Gorgon-like and un-Gorgon-like, dog-faced[10] and woman-faced.[11] Speaking of the connection between the Furies and the Mysteries, Thomas Taylor observes: 'There is a passage in the *Cataplus* of Lucian which very much corroborates my opinion: "Tell me, Cynic, for you are initiated in the Eleusinian Mysteries, do not the present particulars appear to you similar to those which take place in the Mysteries? *Cyn.* Very much so. See then, here comes a certain torch-bearer, with a dreadful and threatening countenance. Is it, therefore, one of the Furies?" It is evident from

[1] *Eumen.* 994.
[2] *Ibid.* 365.
[3] *Ibid.* 974.
[4] Smith, *Class. Dict.* 272.
[5] Ibid. *Smaller Class. Dict.* 313.
[6] Ais. *Eumen.* 310 et seq.
[7] Eur. *Orestes*, 319.
[8] Ais. *Eumen.* 319.
[9] Aristoph. *Bat.* 288 et seq.
[10] Eur. *Orestes*, 260.
[11] Ais. *Eumen.* 47.

this passage that the Furies in the Mysteries were of a terrible appearance.'[1] The *Kataplous*, or Sailing-to-shore, like the *Batrachoi*, describes a voyage across the Styx. 'It is a circumstance remarkably singular, that the Pythagorean philosopher Numenius was, as well as Pausanias, deterred by a dream from disclosing the Eleusinian Mysteries. When *delusive faith* succeeded to *scientific theology*, and *divine* mystery was no more, it then became necessary to reveal this most holy and august institution. This was done by the later Platonists.'[2] Thus we are informed that 'in the most holy of the mysteries before the presence of the god certain *terrestrial* daemons are hurled forth,'[3] and that these spectres appeared in the shape of dogs,[4] like the dog-faced chthonian Furies in their uncouth hateful dance. 'The dog, in general, mythically represents all utterly senseless and carnal desires,' like Kerberos, the hell-hound, and Seirios, 'the dog-star of ruin . . . . . . the Greek notion of the dog being throughout confused between its serviceable fidelity, its watchfulness, its foul voracity, shamelessness, and deadly madness.'[5] St. Croix, following Dion Chrysostomos, A.D. 50-117, and others, speaks similarly, observing that the eyes of the Mystics were powerfully affected by alternate light and darkness, while a multiplicity of phantoms appeared before them having the figures of dogs and other monstrous forms, and that the sights and sounds were so terrible that Ploutarchos[6] compared initiation with death agony.[7] These forms are 'the fleet-hounds of raging madness,'[8] the tire-

---

[1] Taylor, *Pausanias*, iii. 221; vide also his remarks on *Orph. Hymn*, lxx. in his *Mystical Hymns of Orpheus*, 135 *et seq.*

[2] Taylor, *Pausanias*, iii. 200. Taylor's own views have been already alluded to. *Sup.* II. iii. 6.

[3] Proklos, Comment. on the *First Alkibiades*.

[4] Pletho, *On the Oracles*, apud Taylor, *Dissertation on the Eleusinian and Bacchic Mysteries.*

[5] Ruskin, *Queen of the Air*, i. 23.

[6] Frag. apud Lobeck, *Aglaoph*, i. 126.   [7] *Recherches*, 214.

[8] Eur. *Bak.* 977.

less ever-pursuing, fury-dogs,[1] prototypes of the hell-hounds and were-wolves of later ages. 'Material daemons actually appeared to the Initiated previous to the lucid visions of the Gods themselves.'[2] 'Sometimes terrible apparitions astonished the trembling spectators.'[3] As I am not writing a treatise on the Mysteries, but only alluding to them incidentally in connection with Dionysos, it is unnecessary to consider how the scenic apparatus was managed, and what was the amount of scientific knowledge of the stage manager and his assistants. It is now sufficiently recognised that the so-called supernatural is, in a great variety of instances,[4] merely the natural misunderstood; and the Mysteries of Eleusis, like the egg of Columbus, were doubtless very simple when once fully comprehended. Nor need I further refer to that part of the exhibition which related to the Two Goddesses, merely observing that, especially in earlier times, their whole legendary history was symbolically represented, and perhaps more or less acted, on the Eleusinian stage, as Clemens says, 'Deo[5] and Kore[6] are now become a mystic drama; and the wandering and the rape and their grief Eleusis shows by torchlight.'[7] But, confining ourselves to Dionysos and his share in the celebration, it is necessary to remember carefully the difference between the earlier and the later stages in the Mysteries, and especially in a Dionysiak connection. The entry of 'Dionysos the Mystic'[8] on the stage, and the

---

[1] Ais. *Eumen.* 127.
[2] Taylor, *Dissertation on the Eleusinian Mysteries*, 43.
[3] Potter, *Antiquities of Greece*, i. 448; and similarly, dread spectres were to be seen at times in the Hellenik temples of Uasi. (cf. Paus. x. 32).
[4] But not in all. A hasty and heedless logic argues that, *e.g.* because it is admitted that there have been many pseudo-miracles, therefore there have never been any real miracles; as if we were to say, perjury is often committed in courts of justice, therefore no true testimony is ever given in them.
[5] Dyâvâ-mâtar or Demeter.
[6] Persephone.
[7] *Protrept.* ii. 12.
[8] Paus. viii. 54.

reasons of it have already been referred to; and as the Vedic Hymns show us in a state of plastic and crystalline clearness the elements which subsequently hardened into the familiar forms of the later Hellenik Mythology, so the Homerik Hymn to Demeter shows us with equal clearness the root of the matter; while the solar, chthonian, kosmogonic, and altogether occult and mysterious character of the introduced divinity Iakchos, illustrates how, when the worships were brought into local proximity, 'like two meteors of expanding flame,' they touched, mingled, and were united. Dionysos assists Demeter with his torch, and this symbolical incident aptly illustrates the whole scope and phase of the earlier connection. But in later times, and especially when the intercourse with Kam, transmuted into Aigyptos, was permanently established on a broad basis, a change came o'er the spirit of the Eleusinian dream, which manifested itself chiefly in three particulars: (1), The simple, earlier idea of a settled, orderly, god-fearing life, with good hope for the future, fades away; while (2) there is a repetition of the old legends in forms coarser and more phallic, combined with less of reverence and more of superstition, the whole producing moral corruption and decay; and (3) new and elaborate psychical ideas relating to the soul, its destiny and pantheistic union with the divine nature, and theories of pseudo-purity are introduced. As a matter of course the actual machinery of the Mysteries became more perfect and extensive, as in the modern theatre, where scenery, dresses, and decorations frequently serve to sustain a piece otherwise intrinsically worthless. Looking at the simple legend of the lost Persephone, the reader will doubtless wonder how the idea of monstrous and fiendish beings could have first entered into the Mysteries. The singular history of the Furies is an answer and explanation. Comparative Mythologists have traced back the idea of the dread Erinys to its simple and innocent starting-point in the Vedic Saraṇyû, the Running-Light of morning. 'The Night,' says Professor Max Müller, 'was conceived by Hesiod as the mother of War, Strife, and Fraud, but she is likewise called the mother of Nemesis or Vengeance.' In a passage from the Veda 'the mischievous powers of Night are said to follow the sins of man. "The Dawn will find you out," was a saying but slightly tainted by mythology. "The Erinyes will haunt you," was a saying which not even Homer would have understood in its etymological sense.'[1] Professor Kuhn also, the advocate of the 'meteorological theory' of mythology, 'has identified Saraṇyû with the Greek Erinys.'[2] 'Hence, in spite of all the failure of memory, and of the fearful character which Erinys had assumed, the poet who tells the terrible tale of Oidipous could not but make him die in the sacred grove of beings who, however awful to others, were always benignant to him;'[3] *i.e.*, the Sun sinks to his rest surrounded with a pale light which corresponds with the dawn. Pausanias derives the name from an old Arkadian word *erinnuein*, signifying to be angry,[4] a derivation acquiesced in by Professor Blackie, who appears to be anything but partial to the comparative theory, at all events in its extension. Replying to his strictures, Professor Max Müller remarks: 'If, like other scholars, Professor Blackie had pointed out to me any cases where I might seem to him to have offended against Grimm's law, or other phonetic rules, I should have felt most grateful; but if he tells me that the Greek Erinys should not be derived from the Sanskrit *Saraṇyu*, but from the Greek verb ἐρινύειν, to be angry, he might as well derive *critic* from *to criticise*.'[5] We may

---

[1] *Lectures on the Science of Language*, ii. 564.
[2] *Ibid.* 530.
[3] *Mythol. of the Aryan Nations*, i. 423.
[4] Paus. viii. 25.
[5] *Contemporary Review*, Dec 1871, p. 119.

unhesitatingly agree with the great philologist. The Furies are Aryan personages, daughters of Night, inasmuch as the Dawn springs from the Night; then by easy transition daughters of Night as dwelling in gloom; next, terrible in character; and lastly, symbolically awful in form. Thus, man's coward, fear-haunted, guilt-conscious heart pollutes, but in idea only, God's most beautiful works, and turns the lovely Dawn, Daphne-Athene, with her rosy fingers and saffron mantle, into the vile, black, blood-dripping monsters that, like unclean and hateful birds, swarmed around the Delphik tripod of Apollon in pursuit of the wretched Orestes. If our thoughts and ideas are, like our sensations, founded upon realities, then there exists somewhere and somehow a vast and awful background of something terrible. It is vain to reply, that Aurora is a fact and the Furies are a fiction. Whence came the fiction? We can trace the process by which the Dawn-queen becomes a Fury, but what gives rise to such a mental concept, and renders it possible? Why are not the darkness and the light both alike to us? In a word, whence came horror? Has it no real foundation? I would as soon believe that thirst had none. There are two further points connected with the origin of the Furies which are of interest to the Comparative Mythologist. I noticed the remark of Pausanias that Aischylos first represented them with *dragons* in their hair. Now the dragon is primarily the keen-eyed creature.[1] 'The name dragon denotes simply any keen-sighted thing, and in its other form, Dorcas, is applied to a gazelle;'[2] and hence the head of Saraṇyu, the Running-light, is dragon-crowned, as her piercing eyes, like the great solar eyes, discover all things.[3] Again, in Arkadia, a district peculiarly con-

---

[1] Cf. Liddell and Scott, Lex. in voc. δέρκομαι.
[2] *Mythol. of the Aryan Nations*, i. 428.
[3] This consideration shows, as Taylor argued *aliter*, that Aischylos was doubtless only the first who *openly* represented the Furies as serpent-crowned, not the inventor of the idea.

servative of the relics of antiquity, Pausanias observes that when the inhabitants of a certain locality sacrificed to the Maniai or Ragers, another name for the Furies, they sacrificed at the same time to the Charites or Graces.[1] Now, who are the Charites? Again the Comparative Mythologist shall tell us: 'Though occasionally both the Sun and the Dawn are conceived by the Vedic poets as themselves horses, that is to say, as racers, it became a more familiar conception of theirs to speak of the Sun and the Dawn as drawn by horses. These horses are very naturally called *hari*, or *harit*, bright and brilliant. After a time the etymological meaning of these words was lost sight of, and hari and harit became traditional names for the horses which either represented the Dawn and the Sun, or were supposed to be yoked to their chariots. Even in the Veda, the Harits are not always represented as mere horses, but assume occasionally, like the Dawn, a more human aspect. Thus they are called the Seven Sisters, and in another passage they are represented with beautiful wings.'[2] He then shows how in Hellenik Mythology these beings became the Charites, the beautiful sister Graces, 'attendants of the bright gods,' and has successfully maintained the identity of the Harits and the Charites against severe criticism.[3] But these bright beings, personifications of the rays of the Sun and of the Dawnlight, are absolutely identical with Saraṇyu, the Runninglight of Morning. Well, therefore, might the Arkadians, though they knew not why, sacrifice at the same time to the Furies and the Graces, for wonderful to say, both can be traced to a common origin, and are actually identical. They are all winged sisters, alike, but how different, and truly marvellous is the plasticity of idea. A figure of an

---

[1] Paus. viii. 34.
[2] Prof. Max Müller, *Lectures on the Science of Language,* ii. 408.
[3] *Ibid.* 418; vide *Mythol. of the Aryan Nations,* i. 48.

archaic type given by Creuzer,[1] and which he calls 'Eris, or Adrastea-Nemesis,' appears aptly to illustrate the costume and general appearance of a stage Fury in the Mysteries. It is Gorgon-faced, and clad in a black mantle reaching to the ankles, which, like those of Hermes, are winged, and appears to be dancing or leaping uncouthly. It has four large wings, two on each side, the two upper extended as semi-volant, the two lower dependent as semi-close. Not very dissimilar figures occur in several Oriental Mythologies, but it would lead us from the subject in question to consider them, or Wing-symbolism in general; suffice it to quote an illustrative passage of Sanchouniathon, who says that the god Taautos[2] 'contrived for Cronus, the ensign of his royal power, . . . upon the shoulders four wings, two in the act of flying, and two reposing as at rest. And the symbol was . . . . with respect to the wings, that he was flying while he rested, yet rested while he flew,'[3] *i.e.*, was tireless, like the Fury-hounds. I have alluded to the colossal size and stature of the tragedian, which was attained by means of the mask, padding the figure, and the use of the thick-soled *kothornos* or tragic buskin, the 'learned sock' of Milton, which

> Ennobled hath the buskined stage;

the performers being thus supposed to arrive at the measure of the stature of the great men of former ages; and it is observable in this connection that many of the Demetrian statues were of large proportions, especially in Arkadia, where the Eleusinian cult greatly prevailed. Thus, in one temple were statues of Demeter, Persephone, and Dionysos, each seven feet high; in another was the statue of Demeter as Erinys the Searcher,[4] a torch in its

---

[1] *Symbolik*, iii. pl. 5, fig. 16.
[2] Thoth, Tet.
[3] Cory, *Ancient Fragments*, 15.
[4] An excellent illustration of the office of Saranyu. Vide *supra*.

right hand and the mystic kist in its left, about nine feet high.¹ In another sacred enclosure of the Great Goddesses were their statues fifteen feet high; and in another temple where their mysteries were performed, 'which were imitations of the things done at Eleusis,' was a statue about eight feet high.² Another ancient statue of Demeter was black,³ apparently because her mysteries were celebrated at night and in secrecy.⁴ Taking into consideration these circumstances and the practice of the stage, it may be fairly concluded that the weird figures which appeared at Eleusis before the trembling Mystics at initiation were of more than mortal stature, a circumstance which would increase the accompanying horror. Christie thought that these Eleusinian shows were at least in the main transparencies, and that the subjects of them are to be found on the Vases, and remarks: 'These scenes may be supposed to have consisted either of a dark superficies, in which transparent figures were placed, and hence their Vases with red figures on the black ground; or of opaque figures moved behind a transparent canvas, and hence their earlier Vases with black figures upon a red ground.'⁵ This may very likely have been one feature in the performance. The proper way to deal with spectres of this character is to laugh at them; and so we read that when that famous philosopher Apollonios Tyanensis and his friends were on their journey to India 'as they were going along in the bright moonshine, they [like Dionysos in the *Batrachoi*] fell in with an Empousa, who, now in this form, now in that, followed after them, until Apollonios, and at his instigation his companions, attacked it with scoffs and jeers, the only safeguard

---

¹ Paus. viii. 25.
² Ibid. 31.
³ Ibid. 5.
⁴ Cf. remarks of Paus. viii. 6, on Aphrodite Melanis.
⁵ *Disquisitions upon the Greek Painted Vases*, 37.

against it, and it fled away jabbering.'[1] But let us suppose that the 'terrestrial daemons,' with their masks, wings, black garments, and uncouth dreadful forms, have flitted away across the stage into the dark recesses of the Sekos. The agitated spirits of the Mystics are next to be soothed and refreshed by 'the lucid visions of the gods themselves.' And here let us note the introduction and influence of the psychical idea. How can man approach any nearer to Mother-Earth and her Daughter, and to Phanes-Iakchos, Spirit-of-the-Apparent and Growth-power of the Kosmos, than he is at first placed by nature? But when the divinities are regarded as anthropomorphic personages, with peculiar local habitations, then, though their dwelling be not with men, yet they may appear to mortals under special circumstances, and the latter may under certain conditions, especially at and after death, approach their abodes, and even in some mysterious way be united with them and made partakers of the divine nature. Peculiarly does this idea hold good with respect to such divinities as have once lived on earth, and still more so if they are supposed to have suffered there like mortals. The Uasar of Kam is the divinity who fulfils all these conditions in the highest degree; and, as noticed, he is identical, and was by the Hellenes regarded as being identical, with Dionysos. Their error lay in supposing that the Dionysiak rites were direct Kamic importations, and thus when in later times the Hellenik world acquired a general acquaintance with the Egyptian ritual, as a matter of course the ideas and ceremonial of Eleusis received a Uasarian colouring and hue; that is, the psychical element came into far greater prominence, the Earth-mother and her Daughter changed their simple phases, and became, like the Great Goddess of Apuleius, Pessinyntike, Athene,

---

[1] Priaulx, *Apollonius of Tyana*, 5.

Aphrodite, Diktynna, Here, Uasi, etc., in wild confusion; and Dionysos-Uasar, the Great God, appeared no longer merely as the assistant torch-bearer, but as one of the first and most important of divinities. In later times, too, it would seem, especially considering the confused and contradictory accounts and opinions of the Fathers on the subject, that the ritual of various festivals, once distinct, became, as Paganism faded slowly before Christianity, blended and intermingled. Dionysos wholly joining Demeter, the two great divinities grown greater still by being identified rightly or wrongly with almost all the leading gods of the nations, made a last desperate stand against the conquering Galilaean at Eleusis, and were not finally subdued until more than fifty years after the death of Constantinus. The researches of the present day have revealed the mysteries of Aigyptos in almost all their varied intricacies. We know that they were psychical to the core, and represented in endless detail the eventful journey of the soul towards the Great God, terminating in its triumphant union with him. This idea of the pilgrimage of the soul finds expression in the later ages of Eleusis. Thus Bunsen remarks, 'It is easy to prove that the meaning and aim of the symbols was to shadow forth in a pious and reverent manner the progress of the soul in her pilgrimage through the finite. The real element of the mysteries consisted in the relations of the universe to the soul, more especially after death.'[1] So the Neo-Platonik philosopher Sallustius, in his treatise *Peri Theôn kai Kosmou*, Concerning the Gods and the Existing State of Things, explains the rape of Persephone as signifying the descent of the soul; and we are informed that the Mysteries 'intimated obscurely by splendid visions the felicity of the soul here and hereafter when

---

[1] *God in History*, ii. 73.

purified from the defilements of a material nature,'[1] and adumbrated the future expansion of its 'splendid and winged powers.'[2] So, again, Sallustius, who was a friend of the Emperor Julianus, asserts that 'the intention of all mystic ceremonies is to conjoin us with the world and the gods.' This is the occult union of the purified and perfected Uasarian with Uasar. Leaving, therefore, the rest of the show, and referring the curious to the exposure of the ancient mysteries by Clemens,[3] Arnobius,[4] and others,[5] let us glance at the later mystic manifestations of Dionysos, who 'appears in splendour to mortals.' So Themistios, writing in the fourth century of the Christian era, 'illustrates his father's exposition of the Aristotelic philosophy by the priest throwing open the propylaea of the temple of Eleusis; whereupon the statue of the Goddess, under a burst of light, appeared in full splendour, and the gloom and utter darkness in which the spectators have been enveloped were dispelled.'[6] 'In all initiations and mysteries the gods exhibit many forms of themselves, and appear in a variety of shapes; and sometimes an unfigured light of themselves is thrown forth to the view; sometimes this light is shaped according to a human form, and sometimes it proceeds into a different shape.'[7] The approximation to divinity was only to be attained by a triumph over the carnal nature; and where this prevailed the soul was comparatively dead, and so Plotinos says that ' to be plunged in matter is to descend into Hades and then fall asleep.'[8] Dionysos, like Uasar, had suffered, and had also triumphed in and over his sufferings; and,

---

[1] Cf. the Sokratik considerations in the *Phaidon* on the desirability of death as a release from the body.
[2] Vide Taylor, *Dissertation on the Eleusinian and Bacchic Mysteries.*
[3] *Protrept.* cap. ii.
[4] *Adversus Gentes.*
[5] For Eleusinian details vide Meursius, *Eleusinia*, which has been a great storehouse for subsequent writers. Also Lenormant, *Monographie de la Voie sacrée eleusinienne.*
[6] Christie, *Disquisitions*, 59.
[7] Proklos, *Commentary* in Platon *Repub.*
[8] *Ennead.* i.; lib. viii.

like Uasar, he represented the Sun, and especially the nocturnal or subterranean Sun, Sol Inferus,[1] who in the blessed regions of the West sinks to the Under-world, sailing in his mystic boat,[2] the golden solar cup;[3] for 'his nightly journey from the West to the East is accomplished in a golden cup, wrought by Hephaistos.'[4] So Stesichoros, B.C. 632-552, sings how Halios [Helios], Hyperion's son, went down into his golden cup and sailed away o'er ocean to the deep realms of night, to visit his beloved ones in the sacred laurel grove.[5] And thus in the Kamic mysteries the soul of the Uasarian having descended into Kerneter, the Under-world, is struck with ecstasy at the magnificent appearance of the subterranean Sun, which he apostrophises in a long address: 'Hail, thou who hast come as the soul of souls reserved in the West! Hail, thou descending light formed in his disk! Thou hast traversed the heaven; thou hast followed above in yellow. The gods of the West give thee glory; they rejoice at thy perfections.'[6] And as the Mystic at Eleusis had to withstand the daemons and spectres, which in later times illustrated the difficulties besetting the soul in its approach to the gods, so the Uasarian had to repel or satisfy the mystic crocodiles, vipers, avenging assessors, daemons of the gate, and other dread beings whom he encountered in his trying passage through the valley of the shadow of death. But as at last the Uasarian penetrated, despite all opposition, to the secret presence of the divine Uasar, so the Eleusinian Mystic was permitted to behold his divinity, and to see 'holy phantoms,'[7] and 'awful but ravishing

---

[1] Cf. Macrob. *Sat.* i. 18; R. P. Knight, *Worship of Priapus*, 113; D'Hancarville, *Arts de la Grèce*, i. 233, 271-3.
[2] Vide Cooper, *Serpent Myths of Ancient Egypt*, 40-1.
[3] Apollod. ii. 5; Paus. iii. 16.
[4] *Mythol. of the Aryan Nations*, ii. 39.
[5] Apud Athen. xi. 4.
[6] *Funereal Ritual*, xv.
[7] St. Croix, *Recherches*, i. 215. Lobeck charges 'Sancrucius' 'quem omnes gregatim sequuntur,' with

spectacles,'[1] such as one of the last of the ancient philosophers described as follows: 'In a manifestation which must not be revealed, there is seen on the wall of the temple a mass of light, which appears at first at a very great distance. It is transformed, while unfolding itself, into a visage, evidently divine and supernatural, of an aspect severe, but with a touch of sweetness. Following the teachings of a mysterious religion, the Alexandrians honour it as Osiris or Adonis,'[2] both of which, as we have seen, are identical with Dionysos, and with each other. 'At the close of the scene,' says Bunsen, 'the victorious god (Dionysos) was displayed as the Lord of the Spirit. The predominating idea of these conceptions was that of the soul as a divine, vital force, held captive here on earth and sorely tried; but the initiated were further taught to look forward to a final redemption and blessedness for the good and pious, and eternal torments after death for the wicked and unjust.'[3] But this was a development; the original idea of Demeter, 'friend of the noble heroes of civilisation,'[4] is far simpler. The Mystics having arrived at a joyful conclusion, ' for the Mysteries, by the name of whatever god they might be called, were invariably of a mixed nature, beginning in sorrow and ending in joy;'[5] and having now become Epopts, were dismissed with a benediction and the words 'Konx Om Pax,' in the interpretation of which much ingenuity has been exercised.[6] The Dionysiak mysteries relating

---

drawing at times upon his own imagination for Eleusinian detail (*Aglaoph.* i. 182); but if St. Croix occasionally errs a little in this direction, Lobeck is liable to an opposite fault of unbelief.

[1] Christie, *Disquisitions*, 40.
[2] Damaskios, apud Photios, *Bibliotheka*, cod. 242.
[3] *God in History*, ii. 73.
[4] *Ibid.* 69.

[5] Faber, *Dissertation on the Cabiri*, ii. 337. A long exploded work, of great learning, absurd etymologies, and baseless theories.

[6] Wilford (*Asiatic Researches*, vol. v.) identified them with Canscha-Om-Pacsha, words with which the Brahmans close their services (vide Ouvaroff, *Essay on the Eleusinian Mysteries*, 28. Nork. i. 7, apud Rev. G. W. Cox, *Mythol. of the Aryan Na-*

to Zagreus and the Titanes, I shall notice subsequently.[1]

Seventh Day.—The Return. The initiated returned to Athenai, and merrily jested with those whom they met, especially at the bridge over the Kephissos. Sacred games also were held, the victors in which were rewarded with a measure of barley.

Eighth Day.—The Day of the Epidaurians. On which those who had been too late for the Greater Mysteries were initiated in the Lesser. It was so called from a tradition that Aisklepios once then arrived at Eleusis from Epidauros.

Ninth Day.—The Day of Earthen Vessels. Two large earthen vessels were filled with wine, type of the animating principle, and were then upset, the wine being thus offered as a libation to the Infernal Divinities. One of these jars 'was placed towards the east, the other to the west; and they were emptied while certain mystic words were uttered. These have been made known to us by Proclos in the Timaeus of Plato. They were, υἱὲ, τοκυῖε, while the first of these was pronounced, they looked up to heaven; and casting their eyes downward to the earth, they pronounced the latter. By thus accosting each Epopt as a son, υἱὲ might be implied the heavenly origin of man; by τοκυῖε might be denoted regeneration.'[2]

The four principal personages at Eleusis were the Hierophant, who is said by Eusebios to have been an impersonation of the Demiurge; the Dadouchos or Torchbearer, a type of the Sun or Helios-Dionysos; the Assistant at the Altar, who is said to have represented the Moon; and the Hierokerux or Sacred Herald, who was a type of Hermes. With respect to this last subtle-

tions, ii. 126). Pococke, in his romance asserts 'the language is Tibetian,' and signifies 'salutation to the Three Holy Ones.' (*India in Greece,* 273, vide Lobeck's remarks and collection of authorities, *Aglaoph.* 775 *et seq*). The subject does not concern a Dionysiak enquiry.
[1] *Inf.* IX. vi.
[2] Christie, *Disquisitions,* 33.

phased divinity, Professor Max Müller remarks; 'He is the herald of the gods; so is the twilight. He is the spy of the night, νυκτὸς ὀπωπτήρ; he sends sleep and dreams; the bird of the morning, the Cock, stands by his side. Lastly, he is the guide of travellers, and particularly of the souls who travel on their last journey; he is the Psychopompos.'[1] 'The officiating ministers at Eleusis,' observes Christie 'were four in number, in imitation of those in Samothrace.'[2] Without absolutely accepting this proposition, we may undoubtedly conclude that the two rituals were by no means unconnected; but it must be remembered that the Mysteries of Eleusis, however subsequently impregnated with Orientalism, were Aryan in origin, whilst those of Samothrake were Semitic. These latter I shall notice subsequently,[3] when speaking of the introduction of the Bakchic cult into Hellas, for the principles of the Dionysiak Myth are to be found in full vigour 'in the secret Phoenician worship of Lemnos and Samothrake.'[4]

SECTION III.

DIONYSOS AND THE DRAMA.

From the theatrical exhibitions of Eleusis we pass, by easy transition, to the stage of Athenai, and here again find Dionysos enthroned in the persons of his two daughters, Tragedy and Comedy, twin representations of his Janus character, and of the double aspect of life, either in the individual or in the abstract.[5] The Drama

---

[1] *Lectures on the Science of Language*, ii. 522; cf. *Od.* xxiv. i.; Ruskin, *Queen of the Air*, i. 25-9, where a subtle and elegant partial analysis of the concept of Hermes is given.
[2] *Disquisitions*, 94.
[3] *Inf.* X. i.

[4] Bunsen, *Egypt's Place*, iv. 235.
[5] It will be remembered that I am not speaking of the Hellenik Drama as such, critically, historically, or otherwise, but merely of it in its connection with the god from whose prolific being it sprung.

is That-which-is-done imitatively and representatively: a definition equally true when applied to the drama of life and existence, or to a stage-play; inasmuch as all our actions are imitative and unoriginal, and also representative; and that doubly so, first, because in doing them we aim consciously or unconsciously after an ideal model:[1] and secondly, because in acting we become representatives of other actors, and embody more or less accurately their feelings and circumstances. Thus, in this latter sense, the kings and queens of tragedy and comedy form a parliament selected to their state and dignity by the universal suffrages of mankind, and so chosen because the electors of the world see themselves, *i.e.*, their own feelings, aims, and possibilities reflected with surpassing merit in the individuals of their choice. Human feeling, using the expression in its widest sense as including the power of feeling after truth, makes man the astonishing creature that he is;[2] without it he would be a stone, or at best a plant, or as some have put it, 'a forked, straddling animal, with bandy legs.' The existence of this property of feeling alone renders the Drama specially so called possible, for plants and trees imitate nothing; we imitate them. And, therefore, the Drama is the expression of feeling in action; but feeling in action is Dionysos the kosmic Life-source, beaming, blushing, blooming, blowing, storming, raging, raving, bearing with him life and death. The Drama, then, in one aspect is but an anthropomorphic crystallisation of Dionysos the Wine-god, yes, the Wine-god, but his wine is not merely the typical juice of the grape, but rather the heat and life-blood that beats through all worlds. Well says Professor Ruskin,

---

[1] Cf. Emerson, *Essay* x. *Circles*. 'The flying Perfect, around which the hands of man can never meet, at once the inspirer and condemner of every success.'

[2] 'What a piece of work is man! How noble in reason! how infinite in faculty! In action, how like an angel! In apprehension, how like a god!' (*Hamlet*, II. ii.)

'Wine, the Greeks, in their Bacchus, made, rightly, the type of all passion,'[1] which noble word, including in its sweep a wide range of action from righteous anger to holy suffering, leads us to Tragedy, the eldest daughter of Dionysos, Lord of the Drama, herself often styled the Drama, inasmuch as in this world's history the tragic element is the stronger and prevailing one. Tragedy considered etymologically, and with reference to its historic origin, is a song accompanied by a satyrik dance, *i.e.*, one performed by persons in the garb of Satyrs, and these songs in early Hellas were the choric, dithyrambic odes in honour of Dionysos; and so Aristoteles tells us that, 'Tragedy originated in a rude and unpremeditated manner from the leaders in the dithyrambic hymns.'[2] The Chorus, who thus celebrated the god, 'bewailed the sorrows of Bacchus, or commemorated his wonderful birth, in spontaneous effusions, accompanied by suitable action, for which they trusted to the inspiration of the wine-cup.'[3] This Chorus at first 'was nothing more than a Comus, and one too of the wildest and most corybantic character. A crowd of worshippers, under the influence of wine, danced up to and around the blazing altar of Jupiter. They were probably led by a flute-player, and accompanied by the Phrygian tamborines and cymbals, which were used in the Cretan worship of Bacchus.'[4] Now it was as the kosmogonic Lord of life, and especially as the Sun-god, head of the animated creation and protagonistic principle of vitality, that Dionysos was honoured. Hence the changes and apparent sufferings both of Nature and of the Sun,[5] when imitated and viewed anthropomorphically as the joys and sorrows of Dionysos, occasioned the mixed nature of the dithyrambic celebration, which

[1] '*Unto this last*,' 124.
[2] *Poet.* iv.; vide *inf.* VIII. ii. Dithyramb.
[3] *Theatre of the Greeks*, 30.
[4] *Ibid.* 35.
[5] Vide *sup.* IV. iii. 3.

was tragedy and comedy combined. Such, then, was the germ and origin of what we now know as Tragedy; its cradle was a Dionysiak combination of satyr, goat, and psychico-solar life-heat worship. But what then is Tragedy, considered with reference to its familiar development? Aristoteles has given us a somewhat painfully elaborated definition, according to which it is ' an imitation of an action that is important, entire, and of a proper magnitude—by language embellished and rendered pleasurable, [*i.e.*, having rhythm, harmony, and melody], in the way of action—effecting, through pity and terror, the correction and refinement of such passions.'[1] This applies fairly enough to Attik tragedy during the brief period of its perfection, though Aristoteles, himself a schoolmaster, evidently regards the Stage as an important means of improvement for youth, and probably instructed his pupils to draw such moral lessons from the fate of heroes, as an industrious apprentice of the City of London may have deduced in olden days from the career of George Barnwell. But not to wander into suggestions which arise from this definition, Platon seems to me to speak far more deeply and satisfyingly, when he says that real Tragedy is an imitation of the noblest life, which is necessarily that of gods and heroes;[2] and this observation, though far from being in itself a complete definition, yet goes to the very root of the matter. Now a hero has been beautifully defined as 'a god-born soul true to its origin;' and so gods are great heroes, heroes, little gods. But heroes, from the necessity of things, must suffer, and that chiefly for others, and it is evident that voluntary suffering is far higher and nobler than compulsory What nobler concept then, than a voluntarily suffering

[1] *Poet.* v.
[2] 'We, according to our ability, are tragic poets, and our tragedy the best and noblest, for our whole state is an imitation of the best and noblest life, which we affirm to be indeed the very truth of tragedy' (*Laws,* vii.).

hero, except indeed a voluntarily suffering god? Hence the passion of gods and heroes, as connected and in divine agreement with the harmony of things, gives Tragedy her lofty theme. And in this delineation there must ever be an absence of two things,[1] (1) a record of crime as such, a *Titus-Andronicus*-like Newgate Calendar of horrors, which constitutes spurious or bastard Tragedy; and (2) all final triumph of the worser cause, of baseness, or evil, or by whatever name the inharmonious principle may be designated.

Next, as to Comedy, which, according to Platon, is the common name of all performances intended to cause laughter,[1] and which 'originated in a rude and unpremeditated manner from those who led off the phallic songs.'[2] Etymologically regarded, it is the song of the Komos, or band of revellers; and 'whatever may have been the birthplace of Greek Comedy, it was, in fact, the celebration of the vintage, when the country people went round from village to village, some in carts, others on foot, who bore aloft the phallic emblem, and invoked in songs Phales, the comrade of Bacchus,'[3] or personified Priapos. So sprang Comedy into existence, amidst Semitic vintage-shoutings,[4] in honour of the riotous and orgiastic god of earth-life; and thus from Oriental materials, moulded by a gifted family of an Aryan nation, sprang into their familiar forms Tragedy and Comedy. Syria and Egypt had rites and orgies many, but drama none. Yet even the West was, on the whole, scarcely more successful than the East; and in Hellas itself a single city almost monopolised dramatic genius, which could only be maintained in an exalted form, even in its peculiar home at Athenai, during a few brief years. The Drama

---

[1] *Laws*, vii.
[2] Aristot. *Poet.* iv.
[3] *Theatre of the Greeks*, 70.
[4] Cf. *Is.* xvi. 9, 'I will bewail the vine of Sibmah: I will water thee with my tears, O Heshbon, and Elealeh: for the shouting for thy summer fruits and for thy harvest is fallen.'

is thus Aryan and Hellenik; and is yet singularly connected in origin with the cult of a Semitic-divinity of the Outer-world, for had Dionysos remained what he once was, a stranger to the shores of the Aigaion, the theatre, whatever form it might have assumed, would never have known him as its patron. The question why the Drama became a fact in Hellas, and was almost unknown elsewhere, has often been considered; it depends on ethnic characteristics, and is not to our present purpose.

Thus was Dionysos the fountain alike of Tragedy and of Comedy; the Drama formed a part of his worship, and the Theatre was his temple. In this large stone Dionysiak shrine at Athenai, which was finished about B.C. 380, and stood a little south of the Akropolis, almost the entire population assembled to celebrate the dramatic cult of the god from dawn to dark on the occasion of the production of the new pieces at the Lenaia and the Dionysia Megala. The actors generally performed not in what we should consider appropriate costumes, but in 'modifications of the festal robes worn in the Dionysian procession,'[1] which were of bright and gaudy hues, the under garments having coloured stripes and the 'upper robes of purple or some other brilliant colour, with all sorts of gay trimmings and gold ornaments, the ordinary dress of Bacchic festal processions and choral dances;'[2] in fact, remnants of barbaric splendour and Oriental magnificence.[3] Euripides, who was a striver after a certain kind of reality, 'ventured to allow his tragic heroes to appear in rags, and he incurred by this departure from Bacchic magnificence the keenest ridicule of his comic contemporaries.'[4] The stage character of the tragic Dionysos has been already noticed. The Dionysos of Comedy is chiefly known to us from the *Batrachoi* of

---

[1] *Theatre of the Greeks*, 211.
[2] Müller, *Hist. Lit. Gr.*, i. 206.
[3] Vide *inf.* VIII. i. Aiolomorphos.
[4] *Theatre of the Greeks*, 254.

Aristophanes. He is cowardly and effeminate, but quick-witted, and a good judge of poetry; and, as the patron and lord of the Drama, is appropriately appointed arbiter by Aïdes of the great question whether Euripides should eject Aischylos from the tragic throne of the Under-world. His decision is in favour of the greater poet, and posterity, that highest court of appeal, has in its ultimate judgment confirmed the verdict. In illustration of the connection between Dionysos and the Drama, Aischylos is said to have written his tragedies at the command of the god, who appeared to him in a dream, and who is also said to have shown himself at the time of the death of Sophokles.[1]

To conclude, the Drama, like Dionysos, has two faces, one raised to heaven, the other bent ever upon the earth. The former reflects the blue eyes of Athene, the latter the fierce, gloating gaze of the Earth-god. And in life this last predominates. 'Greatly as the Greeks succeeded in the Beautiful, and even in the Moral, we can concede to their culture,' says Schlegel, 'no higher character than that of a refined and dignified sensuality.' Is our present condition very much superior? I do not undertake to answer the question; but let it be remembered that Dionysos, changed in the Middle Ages into S. Denys,[2] has ever ruled and reigned with undiminished sway in countless temples, whose Bakchik cults are infinitely lower than the grand ritual exhibited of old to the Athenians. No mightier engine for good than the Drama, properly applied, can well be imagined: its patrons should do their utmost to reform it altogether; to purge away those taints

---

[1] Paus. i. 21.
[2] Cf. S. Sabas, *i.e.* Sabazios, whose festival is on Dec. 5, S. Mithra of Arles, S. Amour, S. Ysis (Nov. 27), S. Saturnin (Nov. 29), S. Satur the Martyr (March 29), S. Bacchus the Martyr, S. Dionysius, S. Eleuther, and S. Rusticus (Oct. 9), *i.e.* 'Festum Dionysi Eleutherei (vide *inf.* VIII. i. *Eleuthereus*) *rusticum.*' At the triumph of Christianity 'the gods of Greece and Rome went into exile —either degraded into evil spirits or promoted into Christian saints' (Deutsch, *Literary Remains*, 182).

of the earth-life which have so long stained it that they falsely appear to be all but inseparable. The Athenians were wont to hear in solemn state the last great tragedy of the day, the purgation of Orestes, or the woes of Oidipous, as a message from the gods with whom alone dwells understanding, and who breathe into the divine poet his star-lit wisdom and aid his mortal harp to echo the eternal music. As for ourselves, unable to write tragedies, or indeed comedies either, it is at least left us to listen in a reverent spirit to the outpourings of vanished genius, and to support those who enable us to do so; and thus the Theatre of Dionysos will for us become not unhallowed ground.

CHAPTER VII.

DIONYSOS IN ART.

SECTION I.

VASES OF THE DIONYSIAK CYCLE.

The Hellenik Vases, beautiful and remarkable in themselves, and of high value as assistants to the artist, the historian, the archaeologist, and the mythologist, do not nevertheless present much independent illustration of the concept of the central figure of the Dionysiak Myth. The Dionysos of the Vases is supplementary to, and illustrative of, the Dionysos of the Poets and Historians; and though the god of moisture, of water, and of wine, is naturally the protagonist on liquid-holding vessels,[1] yet there is scarcely a feature in his character, or an incident in his life, illustrated or pourtrayed upon a Vase, which is otherwise unrecorded, and for acquaintance with which we are indebted to the potter alone. While the number of discovered Vases is immense,[2] and the treatment of the subjects represented almost infinite in its variety, the subjects themselves are comparatively few. The great myths, the Gigantomachia, the Amazonomachia, the Wars of Thebai and Troia; the most prominent divinities, Zeus, Aphrodite, Apollon, Artemis, Athene, Eros, Hermes, Nike; the

---

[1] Keramos, after whom the Kerameikos, or Potter's Quarter, was said to have been named, is called the son of Dionysos and Ariadne, *inf.* X. iii.

[2] 50,000, De Witte (*Etudes*, 4). 20,000 in collections, Birch (*Ancient Pottery*, 149).

Saviour-heroes, Herakles, Perseus, Theseus; and, more numerous and prominent than all, Dionysos and his train, appear again and again on the Vases, to the exclusion of an infinite number of subjects and personages deemed less worthy of delineation, and notably of scenes from actual history. Kroisos on the pyre; Homeros in the Samian pottery; Arkesilaos, king of Kyrene, weighing silphion; a love scene between Alkaios and Sappho; Anakreon the Reveller; and Dareios hunting; almost exhaust the undoubtedly historical subjects, and serve, by their introduction, to render the blank still more remarkable.

Although the Vases, the great majority of which belong to a comparatively late age, do not offer any very remarkable independent illustration of the origin and character of Dionysos, yet in as much and so far as their testimony extends, it is quite in accordance with that already adduced; and as Dionysiakal subjects form such an important feature in them, it would be improper to omit their notice from the enquiry. Here, as heretofore, it will be remembered that I am writing not of Art, but of Dionysos as he appears in it, and with special reference to his origin; and that, therefore, remarks upon the manufacture, classes, uses, and general history of the Vases, are in the main foreign to the present purpose. The Dionysiak Cycle forms the third of Millingen's well-known seven divisions of the Vases according to their subjects; and includes the History of Dionysos, the Satyroi, Seilenoi, Bakchai, Mainades, the Bakchik Thiasos, the ass Eraton, Dionysiak Festivals, processions, dances, mystic scenes, and general amusements. 'So numerous,' observes Dr. Birch, 'are the Vases upon which the subject of Dionysos and his train is depicted, that it is impossible to detail them all.'[1] 'On them we see depicted his birth, childhood,

---

[1] *Anct. Pottery*, 237.

education, all his exploits, his banquets, and his games; his habitual companions, his religious ceremonies, the Lampadophorae brandishing the long torches, the Dendrophorae raising branches of trees, adorned with garlands and tablets.'[1] To begin with the god himself, the following are the principal scenes and circumstances in which he appears on the Vases:—

I. *His birth from the thigh of Zeus*, who, seated on an altar, holds the new-born and long-haired infant in his arms. Poseidon, standing, near, extends his left hand to receive the child; a Vase of the finest style.[2] The birth of the god is also the subject of a fine Vase in the Vatican.[3] It is noticeable that at his birth the foreign Poseidon is represented as waiting to receive and cherish his brother divinity. Compare the reception and cherishing of the Oriental Hephaistos when an infant by Thetis and Eurynome.[4] Such legends are the last historic traces of the original local connection of divinities.[5]

II. *Dionysos in the Gigantomachia.*—The god attacks with his spear two giants, Eurytos and Rhoitos, one of whom has fallen; he is ivy-crowned, bearded, wears a panther's skin, and has buskins of the same; he holds a kanthar and two ivy branches in his left hand; his tunic is dotted: his panther assists him, and has fastened on the right shoulder of the fallen giant.[6] *The same subject.*—The god, overpowering the falling Eurytos, with his left hand seizes the giant's helmet and stabs him with the thyrsos-spear held in his right hand; his hair flows down in ringlets; he is bearded, wears spotted buskins, and is assisted by his spotted serpent, which coils around the giant's leg.[7]

[1] Westropp, *Handbook of Archaeology*, 257.
[2] Brit. Mus. *Vase Cat.* No. 724.
[3] Vide Birch, *Anct. Pottery*, 209.
[4] *Il.* xviii. 308.
[5] Cf. No. xxix.
[6] Brit. Mus. *Vase Cat.* No. 788.
[7] Millingen, *Anct. Uned. Mons.* Pl. xxv.

III. *Destroyed and resuscitated in a boiling cauldron.*[1] —The following are parallel myths : Thetis, wishing to make Achilleus immortal, concealed him, by night in fire to destroy the mortality inherited from his father, and anointed him with ambrosia ; but Peleus, discovering him, cried out in terror, and so frustrated the design of the goddess. An exactly similar legend is told of Demeter and Demophoön, son of Keleus of Eleusis ;[2] and Medeia, the sorceress, changes a ram into a lamb by boiling it in a cauldron, a scene depicted on three Vases in the British Museum.[3]

IV. *Introduced to Olympos.*[4]—The principal non-Aryan members of the Hellenik Pantheon are formally introduced into Olympos as being strangers. Thus Hephaistos when expelled is reintroduced by his fellow-divinity, Dionysos, in whom, according to Pausanias, he placed great confidence.[5]

V. *At the birth of Athene.*—Pallas stands on the head of Zeus, and behind several other figures stands Dionysos, holding the thyrsos, ivy-crowned, and with long hair and beard.[6]

VI. *Conveyed by Hermes to be brought up by the Nymphs of Nysa.*[7]

VII. *With the Tyrrhenian pirates,* who are changed into dolphins.[8]

VIII. *With the golden amphora, which he gave to Thetis.*[9]

IX. *Discovering Ariadne,* a constantly repeated sub-

---

[1] Gerhard, *Auserlesene Vasenbilder.* Pl. ccvi. Vide *inf.* IX. vi. *Zagreus.*
[2] Hom. *Hymn. eis Dem.* 228 *et seq.*
[3] *Vase Cat.* Nos. 406, 540, 717.
[4] Vide Birch. *Anct. Pottery,* 238.
[5] Paus. i. 20; cf. No. xxxi. As to the Homerik distinction between the habitual dwelling-place of Poseidon and that of the Aryan divinities, vide *Poseidon,* xxix.
[6] Brit. Museum, *Vase Cat.* No. 741.
[7] D'Hancarville, *Vases, Grecs.* iii. 105; vide *inf.* VIII. i. *Nysios.*
[8] Gerhard, *Auserl. Vasen.* Pl. xlix. Vide *inf.* VIII. ii. *Dolphin.*
[9] François Vase, Florence Museum ; cf. *Od.* xxiv. 74.

ject.' 'On the older Vases this incident is depicted in the most passionless way; but on those of a later style, Dionysos is introduced by Aphrodite and Eros to Ariadne, who throws herself into his arms in the most graceful manner.'[1]

X. *With Ariadne at Naxos.*[2]—Dionysos and Ariadne are sitting under a bower formed by the vine and grape-clusters; he holds a thyrsos and kanthar, and she the pearl-studded crown of gold, made by Hephaistos, given her by Theseus, and placed by Dionysos in the sky; a tympanon or tambourine hangs from the tree to be taken down at sunset; when, under the auspices of the allegorical Pannychis or personified Night-time, who herself appears on late Vases,[3] the Naxian dance can continue until Aos (Eos-Aurora) rises from the eastern sea with her dew-filled urns.[4] Dionysos appears 'as on all monuments of a late time, of a youthful form.' Eros flying, bears a fillet or girdle, 'emblem of nuptial and amorous concerns.'[5] The girdle, both plain and also dotted or spotted, very frequently appears on the Vases, and always in scenes more or less erotic.[6]

XI. *With Ariadne, in a deer-drawn chariot.*[7]

XII. *With Ariadne, in quadriga.*[8]

XIII. *As Dionysos Pelekys on winged car with axe.*[9] —The rare and singular representation of Dionysos on a winged car like that of Triptolemos, and armed with the sacred axe or hatchet, *pelekys*, is an occult illustration of the spirit of kosmic life in his grandest manifestation as the Storm-god; the axe is the thunderbolt, and the winged

---

[1] Birch, *Ancient Pottery*, 238.
[2] Millingen, *Anct. Uned. Mons.* Pl. xxvi.
[3] Birch, *Ancient Pottery*, 250.
[4] Vide Millingen, *Anct. Uned. Mons.* Pl. vi.; cf. Soph. *Antig.* 1152.
[5] Millingen, *Anct. Uned. Mons.* 67; cf. *Od.* xi. 245.
[6] Vide Millingen, *Anct. Uned. Mons.* Pls. xii. xxxv.; Christie, *Disquisitions upon the Painted Greek Vases.* cap. xiii.; *inf.* VIII. ii. *Spots.*
[7] Brongniart, *Traité Céramique.*
[8] Gerhard, *Auserl. Vasen.* Pl. lii.
[9] *Ibid.* Pl. xli.

car symbolizes its swift descent. Mr. Evans[1] has collected the facts and authorities in illustration of the ancient belief, 'semper, ubique, et ab omnibus,' that the celts and adzes or stone chisels were thunderbolts. Thus in the Rig-Veda we read: 'Whet, O strong Indra, the heavy red weapon against the enemies. May the axe [thunderbolt] appear with the light!' Thus, too, in various European countries the celts are called 'thunder-axes,' 'pierre de tonnerre,' 'tonderkiler,' 'tordensteen,' 'donnerkeile,' 'thorskeile,' 'donderbeitels,' or thunder chisels; and similar names prevail in Portugal, Brazil, Greece, Java, Burmah, West Africa, and various other countries. The Sioux, a tribe of North American Indians, 'among their varied fancies about thunder birds and the like, give unusually well a key to the great thunderbolt myth which recurs in so many lands. They consider the lightning entering the ground to scatter there in all directions thunderbolt stones, which are flints, etc., their reason for this notion being the very rational one, that these siliceous stones actually produce a flash when struck.'[2] Mr. F. C. Lukis[3] gives an instance of a flint celt having been found on the spot where a signal staff had been struck by lightning, and which was proved to have been the bolt, by its peculiar smell when broken.'[4] ' It was from a hatchet that, according to Plutarch, Jupiter Labrandeus received that title;[5] and M. de Longpérier has pointed out a passage, from which it appears that *Bacchus was*, in one instance, at all events, worshipped *under the form of a hatchet.*'[6] This circumstance also sufficiently appears from the Vase in question; and Mr. Evans notices that on a Kaldean cylinder an offering is made to the hatchet enthroned, and that the Kamic

---

[1] *Ancient Stone Implements of Great Britain*, 51 et seq.
[2] Tylor, *Primitive Cult.* ii. 238.
[3] *Reliquary*, viii. 208.
[4] *Ancient Stone Implements*, 51.
[5] 'The statue of Jupiter at Labranda in Caria held in his hand the battle-axe, instead of thunder' (R. P. Knight, *Worship of Priapus*, 58). See also, Coins of Tenedos and Thyatira.
[6] *Ancient Stone Implements*, 54.

hieroglyphic for god, Nouter,[1] is the figure of an axe. Mr. Evans and M. Lenormant consider that the flint-axes were venerated on account of their antiquity, the latter remarking, 'Aussi est-ce à la hache de pierre que se sont attachées, plus tard le plus grand nombre de superstitions, parce que son origine par le travail de l'homme était complètement oubliée.' Their high antiquity gives them a religious character with many nations. 'On les recueillait précieusement, et on leur attribuait mille propriétés merveilleuses et magiques, croyant qu'elles tombaient du ciel avec la foudre. Au témoignage de Pline on distinguait les *cerauniae*, qui, d'après sa description même sont des pointes de flèches, et les *betuli*, qui sont des haches.'[2] The stones were used as talismans, and were supposed to possess medicinal virtues; they were preservatives against lightning and sweated at storms. The fortunate owner would 'Fear no more the lightning's flash, nor the all-dreaded thunder-stone.' Nor does this use seem to be entirely discarded at the present time, for Mr. Halliwell notes that in West Cornwall 'rheumatism is attempted to be cured by a "boiled thunderbolt"; in other words, a boiled celt, supposed to be a thunderbolt. This is boiled for hours, and the water then dispensed to rheumatic patients.'[3] These 'living stones' appear in the Phoenician mythology of Sanchouniathon, and form the wall of the wondrous Thebai, mother-city of the Bakchai.[4] With the origin of the celt-betyls we are not concerned, but their connection with Dionysos shows at once the antiquity and Oriental character of his cult.

XIV. *Drawn by Gryphons*.[5]—I am not aware that any other Hellenik divinity except Dionysos is represented on the Vases as drawn by gryphons, 'the dogs of Zeus that

---

[1] Natr. Bunsen, *Egypt's Place*, v. 448.
[2] *Les Premières Civilisations*, i. 170-1.
[3] *Rambles in Western Cornwall*, 205.
[4] Paus. ix. 5, 17.
[5] Passeri, *Pict. Et.* Pl. clx.

never bark,'[1] which are a thoroughly Asiatic concept; and although Apollon appears riding on a gryphon,[2] it is only when his cult has been introduced by arbitrary fancy into the blessed regions of the Hyperboreans beyond the bitter north wind. Numerous Vases represent contests between the Amazons, who are said to have originally lived near the Kaukasos and migrated thence to the banks of the Thermodon in Western Pontos, and the Gryphons.[3] But their most famous legendary foes are the one-eyed Arimaspoi,[4] who tried to despoil them of the gold which they guarded, and who inhabited the north-east of the Herodotean world. So Milton writes,—

> As when a gryphon thro' the wilderness
> With winged course, o'er hill or moory dale,
> Pursues the Arimaspian, who by stealth
> Had from his wakeful custody purloin'd
> The hoarded gold; so eagerly the fiend.
> — *Par. Lost*, book ii.

The *Arimaspeia*, an epic poem attributed to Aristeas of Prokonnesos, a poet hidden in nebulous fable, 'treated in three books of the affairs of the Arimaspians, with the history and geography of the Griffins, guardians of the golden harvest, and of their wars against the Arimaspians, in defence of the sacred treasure.'[5] The Arimaspians were described as a race of Scytho-Cyclops, or one-eyed barbarians, covered with hair; the Griffins as lions in body, with the head and wings of eagles.'[6] 'The griffin has been found as an ornament in Scythian tombs, the drawing, however, being Greek. It was the special emblem of Panticapaeum [Kertch], and is often met with on the coins. The Greek griffin is curiously like the Perse-

---

[1] Ais. *Prom.* 803.
[2] Brit. Mus. *Vase Cat.* No. 934.
[3] Ibid. Nos. 1368, 1393-4.
[4] *Arima*, one, and *spu*, the eye, Herod. iv. 27.
[5] Cf. Herod. iii. 116; Paus. i. 24.
[6] Mure, *Hist. of Greek Literature*, ii. 470.

politan, and both are apparently derived from the winged lion of the Assyrians.'[1] In Kam the Asiatic god Set, who is represented amongst other forms as a gryphon, was called Nub, or Nubti, which 'means the "Golden" or "Gold God." It is curious, though not conclusive, to compare this Gryphon form of Set with the Hyperborean legends of gryphons which guarded the gold.'[2] The palace of Skylas, king of Skythia, was ornamented with gryphons carved in white marble;[3] and gryphons are said to have been spotted like leopards,[4] a further link between them and Dionysos. The contests of the Gryphons and Arimaspoi are also depicted on the Vases of Pantikapeion.[5] In Assyria the Gryphon appears at times to have been hostile to the gods, and Canon Rawlinson observes, 'We can scarcely be mistaken in regarding as either an evil genius, or a representation of the evil principle, the monster, half-lion half-eagle, which in the Nimrod sculptures retreats from the attacks of a god, who assails him with thunderbolts.'[6] The Gryphon thus belongs to the valleys of the Nile and the Euphrates, and to the mountains of Asia; and in the example before us the Eastern god is car-drawn by the Eastern monster, who, hostile no longer, is subdued by the thunderbolts of Dionysos Pelekys. The Gryphon plays a very important *rôle* in heraldry and in mediaeval myth. The Kaldean 'dragon of the sea' 'is generally conceived of as a griffin.'[7] 'The form of this creature, as given on the gems, is that of a griffin or dragon, generally with a head like a carnivorous animal, body covered with scales, legs terminating in claws, like an eagle, and wings on the back. Our own heraldic

---

[1] Rawlinson, *Herodotus*, iii. 20.
[2] Dr. Birch, in Bunsen's *Egypt's Place*, i. 430. Vide *inf.* VIII. ii. *Gryphon*.
[3] Herod. iv. 79.
[4] Paus. viii. 2.
[5] Birch, *Ancient Pottery*, 432.
[6] *Ancient Monarchies*, ii. 31. This scene is now known as Bel and the Dragon.
[7] Geo. Smith, *Chaldean Account of Genesis*, 87.

THE GRYPHON IN BURMAH.

griffins are so strikingly like the sculptures of this creature that we might almost suspect them to be copies from the Chaldean works.'[1] Sir John Mandeville reports of 'Bactrie, " In this Land are many Griffins, more than in other places, and some say they have the Body before as an Eagle, and behind as a Lion, and it is true, for they are made so: but the Griffin hath a body bigger than 8 Lions and stronger than 100 Eagles, for certainly he will bear to his nest flying a Horse and a Man upon his Back, or two Oxen yoked together as they go to plow, for he hath long nails upon his feet as great as horns of oxen, and of those they make Cups to drink with."'[2] Sportive Hellenik art manufactured gryphon-terminated drinking-cups.

XV. *On a Panther.*[3]

XVI. *On the ass Eraton.*[4]—The Dionysiak Ass Eraton, the Beloved, is another of the countless links between the god and the Semitic East, the animal having been in very early times unknown to the Aryans. 'It was introduced to the Aryans of Persia,' remarks M. Lenormant, 'by the Semites of Mesopotamia; thence it passed over into India, always retaining its Semitic name, proof whence it sprung. Among the Greeks the ass has been introduced by a nation speaking a Semitic tongue, probably by the Phoenicians.'[5] The Kamic gryphon-god Set was also the ass-god.[6]

XVII. *On a bull.*[7]

XVIII. *On a ram with Hermes.*[8]

[1] Geo. Smith, *Chaldean Account of Genesis*, 90.
[2] *Travels*, lxviii.
[3] Millin. v. i. 60.
[4] Tischbein, *Vases Grècs*. ii. 42. Another Vase represents Dionysos riding on the ass between two symbolical eyes (Brit. Mus. *Vase Cat.* No. 690).
[5] *Premières Civilisations*, i. 320.
[6] Vide *inf.* VIII. ii. *Ass.*
[7] Gerhard, *Auserl. Vasen*, Pl. xlvii. Vide *inf.* IX. iii. *Taurokeros.*
[8] Ibid. *Archäologische Zeitung.*

XIX. *On a camel, as the subduer of India.*[1]—His beard is long and dress spotted; attendant Mainads bear tambourines and male followers thyrsos-spears. 'At Mr. Beckford's sale the late Duke of Hamilton gave 200*l.* for a small Vase with the subject of the Indian Bacchus.'[2]

XX. *In orgiastic state, tearing a kid.*[3]—He holds the two halves of the kid he has just torn asunder: hair ivy-crowned and long, as is his beard; a panther-skin knotted around his neck.

XXI. *Dancing with a Backche.*—He is bearded, and both are clothed in the spotted *bassaris.*[4]

XXII. *Warring with the Indians.*[5]

XXIII. *At the marriage of Thetis.*[6]

XXIV. *Presenting the vine.*[7]

XXV. *Teaching Oinopion to make wine.*[8]—The god is long-haired, bearded, and ivy-crowned; in his right hand he gives the kanthar to Oinopion, and in his left holds four vine-branches.

XXVI. *Visiting Althaia.*—A comic scene.[9]

XXVII. *Received by Ikarios*, an Athenian, who, according to the myth, welcomed him on his first arrival in Attike.[10]

XXVIII. *As the inventor of Tragedy.*[11]—The god, as in later representations, is youthful and beardless, and holds in his left hand a tragic mask: Nike crowns him with a wreath, and behind her stands Pan, youthful, beardless, and with little horns on his forehead, caressing the Iÿnx or Wryneck. This mysterious bird of love was peculiarly

---

[1] Birch, *Ancient Pottery*, 438. Vide *inf.* IX. vii. *Indoletes.*
[2] *Ancient Pottery*, 437.
[3] Brit. Mus. *Vase Cat.* No. 788. Vide *inf.* IX. vi. *Zagreus.*
[4] Kirk, *Hamilton's Vases*, Pl. lvii.; cf. No. XLIX.
[5] *Revue Archéologique*, 1863, 348.
[6] Brit. Mus. *Vase Cat.* No. 811.
[7] Passeri, *Pict. Et.* Pl. cciv.
[8] Brit. Mus. *Vase Cat.* No. 554.
[9] Brit. Mus. *Vase Cat.* No. 1438.
[10] Ibid. Nos. 565, 577; cf. Paus. i. 23.
[11] Brit. Mus. *Vase Cat.* No. 1293.

connected with the Semitic Aphrodite and with Adonis. So Pindaros :—

> The Cyprian queen, whose hand
> Points the resistless arrow, from above
> Her mystic Iÿnx brought, the maddening Bird of Love.[1]

Iÿnx, according to one legend, was a daughter of Pan, who therefore is represented on the Vase in question as caressing her. She is also said to have been the daughter of Echo, or of Peitho (Persuasion), and to have been changed into a bird by Here, for having aided the loves of Zeus and Io.[2] Another Vase[3] represents Adonis holding out the Iÿnx in his right hand to Aphrodite, who is seated. The bird, which was so named from its cry, is described by the Scholiast as hairy, with a long neck and tongue, and possessing the power of rotating its head and neck. It is also said to have been tied to a wheel and whirled round to assist amorous incantations. 'There exists an ancient picture of the magic wheel, formed by fixing the bird by the extremities of its neck, tail, and two wings at equidistant points within a circle, of which it thus constitutes the spokes.'[4] Pindaros calls it 'pied,' an epithet which, as applied to birds, corresponds with 'spotted,' which is appropriate to beasts only, and this forms a link in its Dionysiak character. 'Damis,' records Philostratus, 'saw four Iÿnges suspended from the ceiling of the Parthian King Bardanes, which was covered with lapis-lazuli, embossed with figures of the gods in gold.'[5] Regarded in the Aryan aspect of the story, Iÿnx, daughter of Pan, the purifying Breeze, or of Echo, is the free lovelorn wind of night that shrouds Io the Moon from 'great Here's angry eyes,' while the Argicide slays the everwatchful guardian. But the wild bird of love, in Hellas

---

[1] *Pyth.* iv. 214.
[2] *Schol.* in Pind. *Nem.* iv.
[3] Brit. Mus. *Vase Cat.* No. 1356.
[4] King, *Antique Gems and Rings*, i. 381.
[5] Ibid.

identified with the wryneck, is also Semitically connected with the myth of Astarte-Semiramis of Askalon, the dove-nurtured [1] and voluptuous,[2] that Sammuramit who was changed into a dove, 'Semiramis in columbam,' [3] a bird sacred to Aphrodite, and whose nature was supposed to be shewn in its name; and hence belongs to the cycle of the Syrian Adonis,[4] who is identical with Dionysos. 'On a beautiful Etruscan gold ring, a winged Venus, seated upon a myrtle-twined altar, holds forth by the tip of its wings this wonder working-bird.' [5] Psyche Breath, is Anima the Soul, the true bride of Eros-Cupido; and the cluster of soul-words, *spiritus, animus* the mind, *anima* air, *thyella* storm wind, and *thymos* the soul, are from roots which in Sanskrit mean to blow, rush, and shake; [6] and Platon truly says, in the *Kratylos*, that the soul is so called 'from its raging and seething.' The soul, 'the seat of the passions,' is thus depicted as the disturbed air troubled by joy or sorrow; and the transition in idea to the bird, and thence to the soul-bird, and the bird of passion, is most easy if not necessary, for 'passionate music is wind music,' [7] and the bird 'is the air incarnate.' [8] So the soul and soul-passion are represented as a bird. In Kam, the Ba or Soul, 'for Bai is the Soul,' [9] was represented by a hawk with human head and arms; [10] and when in the Funereal Ritual the exhausted Uasarian recruits his failing energies with the water of life supplied by the goddess Nu, while he drinks his soul depicted as a human-headed bird, 'the usual emblem of the soul,' [11] drinks eagerly with him.[12] And the human soul-bird is

[1] Cf. Clem. *Protrept.* ii. 39; 'The Syrians who inhabit Phoenicia, of whom some revere doves.'
[2] Diod. ii. 4.
[3] Ovid. *Metam.* iv. 47.
[4] Apollod. *Frag.* xix.
[5] King, *Antique Gems*, 361.
[6] Cf. Cox, *Mythol. of the Aryan Nations*, i. 31.
[7] *Queen of the Air*, i. 41.
[8] *Ibid.* 43.
[9] Horapollon. i. 7.
[10] Bunsen, *Egypt's Place*, v. 135.
[11] Lenormant, *Ancient Hist. of the East*, i. 311.
[12] Cooper, *Serpent Myths of Ancient Egypt*, 43.

accompanied, in Kamic idea, through the Under-world by the divine soul-bird, the Bennu-Phoinix, who 'is Osiris,'[1] 'We see sometimes on a sarcophagus the soul figured by a human-headed hawk, holding in its claws the two ring symbols of eternity, and beneath, as an emblem of the new life reserved for the deceased, the rising sun,'[2] 'the great Bennu which is in Annu'[3] or Heliopolis, the City of the Sun. And the idea of the soul-bird is found equally in Hellas. Thus on a Vase[4] representing the death of Prokris, the departing soul hovers over the body in the form of a human-headed bird.[5] The soul flies in all religions. Thus the Assyrian prayer for a sick man is, 'May his soul fly up to heaven. Like a bird, may it fly to a lofty place.'[6] So the bird of passion held out by Adonis to Aphrodite is the infinitely-yearning soul, 'greatest of things created,'[7] eager to fly as a bird to its mountain; 'the soul of the turtle-dove,' as the Hebrew poet expresses it, longing to flee away, and be at rest with the beloved object, the all-conquering and all-persuading, Iÿnx, daughter of Peitho. In Neo-Platonism the Iÿnges are apparently regarded as being somewhat equivalent to the Platonik ideas, and we are informed that they constituted the first division of the 'Intellectual Triad.' The Pseudo-Zoroastres states that:—

The Iÿnges, objects of perception themselves, perceive from the Father,
Being moved by ineffable counsels so as to perceive.[8]

XXIX. *Allied with Poseidon.*[9]
XXX. *With the Eleusinian Goddesses*, Demeter and Kore.[10]

[1] *Funereal Ritual*, xvii.
[2] Lenormant, *Ancient Hist. of the East*, i. 321.
[3] *Funereal Ritual*, xvii.
[4] Brit. Mus. *Vase Cat.* No. 1260.
[5] Millingen, *Anc. Uned. Monuments*, Pl. xiv.
[6] *Trans. Soc. Bib. Archaeol.* ii. 20.
[7] *Funereal Ritual*, ix.
[8] Frag. liv. apud Cory.
[9] Lenormant and De Witte, *Elite des Monumens Céramographiques*, iii. 4.
[10] Birch, *Anct. Pottery*, 232. Vide sup. VI. ii. 2, 3.

XXXI. *With Hephaistos*, who ascends to heaven at his instigation.[1] Another Vase represents Hephaistos returning to heaven on the Dionysiak ass.[2]

XXXII. *As Iakchos.*[3]—'Sometimes he is presented under the form of Iacchos.'[4]

XXXIII. '*With Eumolpus and Iacchos.*'[5]—Millingen, incorrectly, states that the figure of the mystic Iakchos, whom he vainly attempts to distinguish from Dionysos, was unknown.[6]

XXXIV. *Pursuing Ariadne.*[7]

XXXV. *In a galley-shaped car.*[8]—Dionysos, seated in the centre of the car, holds an overshadowing vine; at each end of the car sits a satyr, playing on the double flute; the galley terminates at the prow with a boar's, and at the stern with a goose's, head. Dr. Birch remarks that 'the sacred ship of Dionysos' was one of the religious matters represented on the Vases.[9]

XXXVI. *Female offering a goat to Dionysos Stylos*, or the Pillar.[10]—'The most remarkable and evident [religious] incidents represented are the offerings to Aphrodite, sacrifices to Hermes, to Dionysos Stylos, Phallen, or Perikionios.'[11]

XXXVII. *Dionysos with Pan.*[12]—The god, seated in a chair, holds his thyrsos; Pan, with two goat's horns stands, before him, holding the two-handled cup.

XXXVIII. *With Briachos and Erophylle.*[13]—The ivy-crowned Dionysos stands in the centre, his long hair flowing down his back, and clustered in curls on the forehead in imitation of grape bunches, according to the fashion

---

[1] Birch, *Anct. Pottery*, 235.
[2] Brit. Mus. *Vase Cat.* No. 527.
[3] *Archäologische Zeitung*, 1848, 220.
[4] Birch, *Anct. Pottery*, 237.
[5] *Ibid.* 242.
[6] *Anct. Uned. Mons.* 5.
[7] Vide Birch, *Anct. Pottery*, 238.
[8] Brit. Mus. *Vase Cat.* No. 087.
[9] *Anct. Pottery*, 277. Vide *inf.* VIII. ii. *Boat.*
[10] Kirk, *Hamilton's Vases*, Pl. xv. Vide *inf. sec.* ii.
[11] Birch, *Anct. Pottery*, 277.
[12] Brit. Mus. *Vase Cat.* No. 1549.
[13] *Ibid.* No. 790.

bostrychoeides; his beard is long and pointed; he wears an embroidered *peplos* over a tunic, and holds the kanthar in his right hand: Erophylle advances towards him, holding in her right hand a snake with raised head and darting tongue, and in her left a branch: behind Dionysos is the Satyr Briachos, gathering grapes from the vine-branch on the god's shoulder.

XXXIX. *With Komos, Ariadne, and Tragoidia.*[1]

XL. *With the symbolical eyes.*[2]—The head of the god, with full face, long hair, beard, and vine branches appears between the two eyes, symbols of the nocturnal and diurnal sun, itself a type of the sentient soul of the world. In Kam the symbolic eye is sometimes represented as held by an ape.[3]

XLI. *With the spotted snake.*[4]—The god in the centre bounds along, brandishing in his right hand the spotted snake, and in his left the thyrsos; he is ivy-crowned, tunic-clad, with hair and beard in ringlets, and wears panther-skin buskins, *endromides*, reaching to the knee: the Mainad Oreithyia accompanies, a panther-skin depending from her shoulders.

XLII. *In the faun-skin.*[5]—The god stands between two Satyroi, and stretches out his arms, from each of which hangs a faun-skin; the skirt of his tunic is encircled with a row of dots.

Among other Vases relating to the Dionysiak Cycle are:—

XLIII. *A very fine kanthar from Melos*; subject a Bakche, with Oriental robes and thyrsos-spear, surrounded by the symbolical spotted girdles, and an elegant border of vine-leaves.[6]

XLIV. *Seilenos swinging a Bakche*, with the motto, 'Rise at pleasure.'[7]

[1] Birch, *Anct. Pottery*, 242.
[2] Brit. Mus. *Vase Cat.* No. 526.
[3] Bunsen, *Egypt's Place*, i. 528, Sign No. 340.
[4] Brit. Mus. *Vase Cat.* No. 816.
[5] Ibid. No. 817.
[6] Birch, *Anct. Pottery*, 300.
[7] Ibid. 318.

XLV. '*A group, often repeated, is that of a female seated upon a rock,* holding a basket, fillet, and bunch of grapes, and approached by a flying figure of Eros, holding similar objects.'[1]

XLVI. '*A common subject is Eros*, holding grapes, and flying alone through the air.' The flying, grape-holding Eros, is the representation of Kosmic Love, the Uniting Principle of Empedokles, which includes personal and all other kinds of sympathy and affection, as wine and the grape are the types of all passion. He is naturally represented as flying Iÿnx-like.[2]

Dr. Birch observes that the most remarkable feature in the Vase-treatment of Eros 'is his Dionysiac character, for he seems scarcely to be separated from the wine-god.'[3] What a testimony is this to the reality of the profoundness of the true concept of the latter!

XLVII. *The attendants of Dionysos*, Nymphs, Satyroi, etc., in erotic scenes, which need not be further noticed.

XLVIII. *Bakche*, with thyrsos-spear and snake-bound hair, holding up a small spotted panther in her left hand.[4]

XLIX. *Bakche*, arrayed in 'bassaride, a species of garment said to have been worn by the god in his expedition into India.'[5]

L. *The Bakchik Thiasos.*—An almost infinite number of examples of this favourite subject occur, *e.g.*, Dionysos, with embroidered tunic, holding the kanthar in his right hand and the ivy-branch in his left; in front, the Mainad Oreithyia, wearing a striped tunic, with the panther-skin over it, and playing the castanets; near her the Satyr

---

[1] Birch, *Anct. Pottery*, 213.
[2] 'The all-generating powers and genial heat
Of Nature, when she strikes
thro' the thick blood
Of cattle, and light is large, and lambs are glad
Nosing the mother's udder, and the bird
Makes his heart voice amid the blaze of flowers.'
Tennyson, *Lucretius*.
[3] *Anct. Pottery*, 246.
[4] Smith, *Class. Dict.* 225.
[5] Kirk, *Hamilton's Vases*, Pl. vii. Cf. *sup.* V. i.

DIONYSOS IN ART. 345

Dithyrambos, playing on the heptachord lyre; behind Dionysos, the Satyr Komos playing on the double flute: near him, a Mainad, carrying a fawn, and with a snake issuing from her garments; all have flowing hair, and are crowned with ivy or myrtle.[1]

LI. *The same.*—Dionysos, ivy-crowned, with flowing hair and long-pointed beard, in the centre, holding a kanthar in his right hand, and a vine-branch in his left. Oinos stands before him, holding the *askos* or wine-skin, with hair like a mane, and long and pointed beard; on each side of the god a necklace-wearing Mainad, with flowing hair, one advancing towards him, and the other looking back at him.[2]

LII. *The same.*—Dionysos, with the usual adjuncts, standing in a quadriga, holding the reins and goad, surrounded by Satyroi and Mainades, running and dancing, with castanets, panthers' skins, etc.[3]

LIII. *Dionysos, between the two symbolical eyes,* and stands opposite a Satyr: the reverse of the cup gives the same subject with slight variation, Dionysos offers the Satyr the wine-cup.[4]

LIV. *Bakchik Thiasos.*—Round the inside of the last-mentioned cup. Dionysos, as usual, with long hair and beard, Mainades and Satyroi dancing in grotesque attitudes behind him.[5] On the other side, the youthful, beardless Iakchos, on the ithyphallic ass, crowned with a diadem, and wearing an embroidered tunic, surrounded by Satyroi and Mainades, the latter with diadems, necklets, embroidered tunics and faun-skins.[6]

LV. *Dionysos, seated* on the kind of folding stool, called *okladias,* holding the *keras,* or drinking-horn,

---

[1] Brit. Mus. *Vase Cat.* No. 447.
[2] Ibid. No. 537.
[3] Ibid. No. 589.
[4] Ibid. No. 674; cf. No. XL.
[5] Cf. *Il.* xviii. 590–606, as to the grotesque and other dances in the Bakchik Isle of Krete connected with Ariadne.
[6] Brit. Mus. *Vase Cat.* No. 674.

which, with the *kantharos*, is his favourite vessel. The keramic art fitly commemorates the cult of the horned god. On the reverse of the same Vase he holds a *keras* in each hand, and another lies on the ground; and in the inside of the cup he is similarly represented, Satyroi and Mainades around.[1]

LVI. *Satyroi and Deer.*—A deer, standing between two Satyroi; the one in front running and waving his hands to drive it back. The reverse almost similar.[2]

LVII. *Ariadne-Nymphaia offering a libation to Dionysos.*—The god, ivy-tressed, and with long hair and beard, receives the libation in his kanthar, which he holds out in his right hand over an altar.[3] Ariadne, daughter of Pasiphae the All-shining and the Phoenician Minos, and granddaughter of Helios the Sun, is non-Aryan in origin, although the splendour of Hellenik beauty has been thrown over her. She is also described, and truly, as the daughter of the nymph Krete, a personification of the island, and, as might be anticipated of the bride of Dionysos, belongs to the Phoenician Cycle.

LVIII. *The Satyr Tyrbas*, the personification of Joyous-disturbance, pursuing the Mainad Oragie, who often appears in juxtaposition with him.[4]

LIX. *Bakchik Thiasos.*—In the centre Dionysos, with long hair and beard, clad as usual in tunic and robe, *peplos*, and holding the kanthar and ivy-branch. Behind him, a dancing Mainad, with diadem-bound tresses, waving her hands, and wearing tunic, robe, and panther's skin round the neck; over her head EVA. Behind her, a dancing Satyr, and behind him another dancing Mainad, playing on the castanets, her hair diademed with a snake, with forked tongue outstretched; in front of her face [E]VA. In front of Dionysos another Mainad, holding a

[1] Brit. Mus. *Vase Cat.* 675.
[2] Ibid. 692.
[3] Ibid. 808.
[4] Ibid. 813.

snake in both hands, and with a panther's skin hanging from her shoulders. Behind her an ithyphallic Satyr, with the keras in his right hand, and another dancing and castanet-playing Mainad.[1]

LX. *Seilenos and Bull.*—A crouching Seilenos, with outstretched hands, advances to meet a bull, which is rushing towards him.[2]

LXI. *The Mainad Opora*, the personification of the late summer-bloom, holding out a basket of fruit to another Mainad; a Satyr near, with keras.[3]

LXII. *Bakchik Thiasos.*—On a vine-shaded couch, over which is a panther's skin, recline Dionysos and Ploutos, the former with the thyrsos and usual adjuncts, the latter with a keras. On the right, a torch-bearing Seilenos leads forward Hephaistos staggering, as if intoxicated; on the left a Mainad and a Seilenos bring fruits to Dionysos, and a seated female beyond them holds a dish of fruit. Below the couch is Eros, playing with a swan. A faun-skin hangs from the arm of the Seilenos on the left, and the Seilenos on the right holds an axe, *pelekys*, in his left hand.[4] This instance of the Thiasos affords an excellent example of kosmic grouping. In the centre the demiurgic Dionysos, Soul-of-the-world, reclines on his spotted skin, accompanied by Ploutos, representative of the buried treasures of the earth which are in the power of the Demiurge. Both are covered by the o'ershadowing vine, the green earth-mantle of Dionysos Ernesipeplos. A torch-bearing Seilenos, representative of life-heat vigour, leads towards them the staggering flame-god,[5] maimed, limping, and deformed.[6] But this only deals with the Aryan aspect of Hephaistos, as the deformed

---

[1] Brit. Mus. *Vase Cat.* 815.
[2] Ibid. 960. [3] Ibid. 1298.
[4] Ibid. 1331.
[5] Cf. Paus. i. 20: 'Dionysus, on whom Hephaistos especially relied, intoxicated him, and led him heavenwards.'
[6] 'The fire at its birth is weak, and its flame puny' (*Mythol. of the Aryan Nations*, ii. 104).

god passed over into Hellas from Phoenicia[1], yet mighty and irresistible, the natural servant and ally of the solar Demiurge. Satyro-Seilenoi and Mainades, representatives of the male and female principles, Kain-like, bring the fruits of the earth as a fit offering for the Earth-king, and sportive Love plays before him. But, it may be asked, is it supposed that the artist in designing the group had such occult symbolism in mind? In all probability not, and so much the more valuable is his testimony as that of an unconscious witness who faithfully reproduced pre-existing ideas.

An infinite number of examples of Vase-illustrations of the Dionysiak Cycle might be cited in an almost exhaustless and varied monotony; but the above-mentioned are sufficient for the purpose, and show that the testimony of the Vases, like that of all other branches of Bakchik evidence, illustrate the Oriental and kosmogonico-solar character of the god. If we do not find the Mysteries of Eleusis fully depicted, the far more important mysteries of nature are freely pourtrayed.

A few specimens of grotesque Dionysiak Vase art may be instanced:—

LXIII. *Cup terminating in the heads of a Seilenos and Mainad*, placed back to back.—On it Dionysos, holding a bunch of grapes; and on the reverse, the androgynous Eros, also holding a grape-bunch.[2]

LXIV. *Lekythos* (oil-cruse), *in the form of a Satyrik head*, with mask-face, raised brows and wide open mouth.[3]

LXV. *Lekythos, in the form of a seated pigmy Seilenos*.[4]—Vases also occasionally occur in the shapes of wine-skins, ducks, human bodies and feet, fish, elephants, Gorgons' and negroes' heads, etc. The Janus-like cup

[1] Cf. Herod. iii. 37.
[2] Brit. Mus. *Vase Cat.* No. 1476.
[3] Ibid. 1479.
[4] Ibid. 1484.

symbolizes the character of the 'two-natured Iakchos,' attended by the sexless Eros. Among the recent Kypriot discoveries of General Cesnola are archaic Vases of various grotesque and fanciful forms. The grotesque is contrary to the indigenous Hellenik spirit, and is borrowed from the East, nor can it be found in any instance in early Hellas, except either within or under the influence of the Dionysiak Cycle.[1] Ancient art also ran riot in the forms of Lamps, which frequently are of Satyrik shapes, or have Dionysiak subjects pourtrayed on them, but which call for no special notice.

LXVI. *The celebrated karchesion, commonly called 'the two-handled cup of St. Denys.'*—Dr. Birch, after remarking that the shape of the karchesion is not very intelligible from the descriptions of early writers, observes 'as, however, it was the sort of cup held by Dionysos and his " wassail rout " in the Pageant of Ptolemy Philadelphus, it was probably a kind of kantharos.'[2] Some critics consider the cup to belong to the time of Nero, others place it earlier. 'It was presented, in the ninth century, to the Abbey of St. Denys, and was always used to hold the wine at the coronation of the Kings of France. Its sculptures represent masks, vases, and other Bacchic emblems.'[3]

Thus the general Vase attributes and adjuncts of Dionysos are his flowing locks, ivy-wreath, long tunic *peplos*, the vine, kanthar, keras, thyrsos, serpent, torn fawn, or goat, and long beard on the earlier Vases. Of animals, the panther, goat, bull and mule, or ass attend him. His train consists of Satyroi, Seilenoi, and Mainades; such as Oinos, Wine-personified; Hedyoinos, Sweet wine; Komos, Revel; Dithyrambos, the Dithyramb personified;

---

[1] Cf. Wright, *Hist. of Caricature and Grotesque in Literature and Art*, cap. I.
[2] *Anct. Pottery*, 380.
[3] Westropp, *Handbook of Archaeol.* 279.

Opora, Latter-summer-bloom; Oreithyia, the free fresh life of the hills;[1] Oragie, mountain wildness; Gelos, Laughter; Briachos, a form of Iakchos; Phanope, Bright-eyes; Xanthe, Golden-hair; Dorkis, Large-eyed; Klyto, Beauteous; Eros, Love; Himeros, Longing; Pothos, Desire; Simos, Flat-nosed; Tyrbas, Joyous-disturbance; Eudaimos, Luck-bringer; Euoia, a personification of the Bakchik cry Euoi; Kissos, Ivy; Nais, Water-nymph; Eirene, Peace; Galene, Calm; Chora, Dance-and-song; and similar concepts. They drink, dance, leap, feast, play with animals at games, and on kettle-drums and castanets, chase each other, form processions, and generally serve and attend upon the god.

As there is no mystery about anything we thoroughly understand, and the conjurer's trick when explained appears simplicity itself; so the varied figures and complicated incidents of the Great Dionysiak Myth easily resolve themselves into harmonious order when once the kosmico-solar and pantheistic character of the divinity is recognised and admitted. Around the Spirit of Material Existence, their proper centre, sport the manifestations of the forces of nature and of man; and life, heat, sound, motion, and passion, find their appropriate representatives and fitting symbolism in the Bakchik train.

SECTION II.

DIONYSIAK STATUARY.

The upright stone preceded the pillar, and the pillar, the statue. Dionysos, ancient god, is known as Stylos the Pillar, and Perikionios the Column-twiner;[2] and Pillar-

---

[1] Cf. Milton: 'The mountain nymph, sweet Liberty,' Oreithyia, not Oragie.

[2] Vide *inf.* VIII. i. *Perikionios.*

cult, Oriental in origin, is illustrated by the following instances, among others:—

Jacob sets up a pillar-stone, and pours oil on it.[1] A similar anointing was practised in the days of Theophrastos, B.C. 371-287,[2] and in those of Arnobius, A.D. 300.

Sets up a stone as a witness-pillar and boundary mark.[3]

Sets up a grave-pillar.[4]

The pillars of the doomed nations to be destroyed.[5]

The pillar of Shechem.[6]

Absalom's pillar.[7]

The two pillars in the porch of the Temple, Jachin and Boaz.[8]

The two pillars in the temple of the Tyrian Melqarth,[9] and his mythic and other pillars at the Straits of Gades.[10]

The god Ouranos makes Baitylia, or living stones.[11]

Inscribed pillars of Uasi and Uasar.[12]

Inscribed pillars of Sesostris (Sesortasen), with phallic emblems.[13]

Worship of the Ashera, or phallic rod, the thyrsos-staff of Dionysos, the grove-cult of the Old Testament, prototype of the maypole.

The monumental stones in the race-course before Troia.[14]

The monumental pillar of Sarpedon.[15]

Ancient round tower-pillars from India to Ireland.

The great pillars in front of the temple of Atargath at Bambyke in Syria, bearing the inscription, 'These phalloi Dionysos erected to his mother Here, *i.e.*, the goddess of the country who corresponded with the Aryan Here.[16] 'Phalloi,' says Loukianos, 'the Hellenes raised

---

[1] *Gen.* xxviii. 18.
[2] Theoph. *Charak.* xvi.
[3] *Gen.* xxxi. 45.
[4] *Ibid.* xxxv. 20.
[5] *Deut.* xii. 3; xvi. 22.
[6] *Judges* ix. 6.
[7] 2 *Sam.* xviii. 18.
[8] 1 *Kings* vii. 21.
[9] Herod. ii. 44. Vide *inf.* XI. ii.
[10] Cf. Sanchou. ii. 14.
[11] Ibid. i. 6.
[12] Diod. i. 27.
[13] Herod. ii. 102-106.
[14] *Il.* xxiii. 320.
[15] *Ibid.* xvi. 457.
[16] Loukianos, *Peri tes Sy. The.* xvi.

to Dionysos,'[1] and Uasi in legend had acted similarly to Uasar.[2]

Blocks of wood and stone were the earliest representations of the gods, for in old time 'the temples were without carved images,'[3] and Themistios affirms that until the time of Daidalos, *i.e.* the age when the sculptor's art was introduced into Hellas from the East, all Hellenik images were shapeless.[4] There are various notices of rude stone divinities in the mythological Itinerary of Pausanias. Thus at Pharai in Achaia were thirty square stones, each called after the name of a god, and venerated by the inhabitants; and Pausanias observes that all the Hellenes formerly reverenced rude stones, instead of statues.[5] Near Sikyon was a pyramidal statue of a divinity, who was called Zeus Meilichios (*i.e.* Melqarth) or the Appeased, as Hekate was euphemistically styled Meilione; and also a pillar-statue of Artemis Patroa, identical with the Taurik Artemis.[6] In Phoenician regions sacred stones occupied a most prominent place. Thus Tacitus describes the statue of the celebrated Aphrodite of Pappa (Paphos) as coniform;[7] and Lajard remarks, 'In all Cyprian coins, from Augustus to Macrinus, may be seen where we should expect to find a statue of the goddess, the form of a conical stone.'[8] Maximus Tyrius records, 'The Paphians worship Aphrodite, whose statue is like a white pyramid.'[9] Thus, again, a coin of Chalkis, bearing the head of the Phoenician Poseidon with his trident, has on the reverse a temple with two columns and a conical stone between them;[10] and 'Melkarth was adored in the great temple at Tyre, in the form of a

---

[1] Cf. Diod. iv. 6; 1 *Cor.* xii. 23.
[2] Diod. i. 22.
[3] Loukianos, *Peri tes Sy. The.* iii.
[4] Themist. *Orat.* xv.
[5] Paus. vii. 22; cf. Tylor, *Prim. Cult.* ii. 151.
[6] Paus. ii. 9.
[7] *Hist.* ii. 3.
[8] *Recherches sur la Culte de Vénus*, 30.
[9] *Dissert.* xxxviii.; cf. Servius in *Aen.* i. 720; Philostratus, *Vita Apollon.* iii. 58.
[10] Eckhel, *Doc. Num. Vet.* ii. 323.

luminous stone.'[1] These stones, like the 'thunder-axes' of Dionysos Pelekys, were generally supposed to be ouranopipt,[2] or heaven-fallen;[3] and so the inhabitants of the Hauran worshipped Katsiu, the Aërolite.[4]

To these instances may be added the prehistoric, megalithic, and other stone structures and erections, into the design of which it is unnecessary to enter further here. That many of them are connected with religious uses I do not doubt, for the fact that human remains have been found interred within stone circles in no way proves that these places were *only* used as burying grounds. We might as well contend, from the existence of graves in a ruined abbey, that the only services ever held in the building had been of a funereal character.

Let us examine some part of the symbolism and ideas connected with this Ebenezer or Stone-of-Strength. Amongst ourselves the letter I, the upright pillar, denotes the Ego, and also One, the first of numbers, the number sacred in monotheistic symbolism to the Deity. Now, as it is given to man alone 'to walk upright and to behold the heaven,' and as man can never practically conceive of God, except anthropomorphically, so the pillar and pillar-stone, on account (1) of its uprightness, a word of suggestive double meaning; (2) strength, both in substance and phallically considered; (3) as connected with the serpentine and aspiring flame; and (4) among lower races, through the principles of Fetishism, became even a divinity, or the supposed seat of supernatural influence.[5] In addition to these considerations, there is also to be taken into account (1) the curious and suggestive natural

---

[1] Lenormant, *Anct. Hist. of the East*, ii. 221.
[2] Cf. Rabelais, iv. 49.
[3] Cf. *Acts* xix. 35.
[4] Lenormant, *Anct. Hist. of the East*, ii. 221.

[5] 'The Dacotas would pick up a round boulder, paint it, and then, addressing it as grandfather, make offerings to it and pray to it to deliver them from danger.' (Tylor, *Primitive Culture*, ii. 147).

shapes of many stones and of specific stones. Thus Mr. Phené considers that the Sphinx before being sculptured into its present form had a human similitude, a circumstance which suggested the artistic effort.[1] (2) The value of certain kinds of stones, more especially of those called *precious*, and the medicinal and other virtues attributed to them; and (3) the belief in the aërolitic nature of many ancient stones and kinds of stones. In our own Sacred Books the similitude of the Deity to a stone is equally familiar to both Testaments. Thus He is 'the Shepherd, the Stone of Israel,'[2] the heavenly aërolite whose descent is to destroy the kingdoms of this world,[3] the 'Chief Corner Stone' in the mystic temple. The sacred stone belonged in idea to the three worlds; it fell from heaven,[4] was on earth, and, as in the case of the celts, was found under the earth. It was equally connected with life and the Upper-world, and death and the Under-world; being the symbol of life-vigour, and yet marking the place of the dead. In its character as a god, Terminus, its site was a place for treaty and agreement, for covenant and invocation of divinity. As man civilised makes his statue of Zeus after the fashion of a man and of a magnificent specimen of a man, for he can do no more ; so man, barbarous, having similar wants and feelings, gets him a statue of his Zeus, if statue it may be called, on which nature alone has worked,[5] for he can do no less, and by slow degrees makes it more like a god by making it more like a man.

These being some of the root-ideas connected with the sacred stone and the pillar, let us next notice the

[1] Vide *Paper read before the British Association at Belfast*, 1874.
[2] Gen. xlix. 24.
[3] Dan. ii. 34; S. Matt. xxi. 44.
[4] Thus near the temple of Dionysos at Orchomenos in Boiotia were certain revered stones said to have fallen from heaven' (Paus. ix. 38).
[5] 'The primitive memorial erected to a god did not even pretend to be an image, but was often nothing more than a pillar, a board, a shapeless stone or a post' (Grote, *Hist. of Greece*, iv. 132).

region whence the statuary's art emerged into Hellas; and this we find clearly indicated by a triple legendary myth in the stories of Hephaistos, Pygmalion, and Daidalos.

It is the Semitic Hephaistos, who formed self-moving, golden maidens to aid him in his forge,[1] and who made the wondrous dogs of Alkinoös.[2] It is the Kypriot King, Pohem-Elyon, or Pygmalion, who made the ivory maiden into whom at his prayer Aphrodite-Astarte breathed the breath of life, and by whom he became the father of Paphos, one of the myriad creatures representing a personified locality. Lastly, it is Daidalos, the Cunning Worker, the personification of the statuary's craft,[3] who in Phoenicia, Krete, and then subsequently westward, introduces a development of art hitherto unknown.[4] He, according to tradition,[5] first wrought his figures with separate feet, and so was credited with having, Hephaistos-like, made living statues.[6]

Some legends represent him as a Kretan,[7] others as an Athenian; nor is the latter view unjust, for the glory of sculpture belongs to the Hellenes, who soon outstripped their teachers. Krete was a great centre of Semitic influence in the West;[8] the labyrinth was Kamic in

---

[1] *Il.* xviii. 417.
[2] *Od.* vii. 92.
[3] Cf. the statement of Pausanias, that Daidalos received his name from the statues, not they from him (Paus. ix. 3).
[4] Clemens asserts that anciently the Skythians worshipped their swords, the Arabs stones, and the Persians rivers; and that some still more ancient races 'set up blocks of wood in conspicuous situations, and erected pillars of stone, which were called Xoana, from the carving of the material.' He mentions an Artemis of 'unwrought wood,' a Here 'merely a tree trunk;' another Here 'at first a plank;' and quotes Varro that Mars was first worshipped as a spear (*Protrept.* iv. 1).
[5] Themistios, *Orat.* xv.
[6] Palaiphatos, *Peri Apiston*. The Delians had a wooden statue of Aphrodite, which marks exactly the transition between the conical stone of Paphos and the finished work of later times. It was small, and terminated in a square block, instead of feet (Paus. ix. 40). There was a similar Hermes at Phigaleia (Ibid. viii. 30), and there is also a similar Aphrodite in the British Museum.
[7] As to early sculpture among the Kretans, vide Müller, *Doric Race*, i. 377.
[8] Vide *Poseidon*, xxx–xxxi.

design as in name,¹ and the monster it contained Phoenician.² In the time of Pausanias there were still four statues existing which were traditionally ascribed to Daidalos, a Britomartis, the Kretan Artemis, in Olos; and an Athene at Knosos in Krete; a statue of Herakles at Thebai; and another of Trophonios at Lebadeia in Boiotia.³ He was an assistant of the fair-haired Ariadne,⁴ and by degrees, *i.e.*, as the arts he typified extended, his fame was widely spread throughout all Sikelia and Italia.⁵ The ancient wooden statues of Hellas, and at one time probably all carved statues, were wooden,⁶ coloured, and covered with real drapery, were called after him Daidala;⁷ and there were also in Boiotia two Festivals of this name, the ritual of which aptly illustrates the legends of Daidalos and the introduction of the art of statue-making.⁸ Ploutarchos composed a treatise, fragments of which are preserved in Eusebios, on the greater Festival. The Lesser was held in the great oak-grove of Alalkomenai, where was a very ancient shrine of Athene,⁹ in ruins in the time of Pausanias.¹⁰ This goddess is not the Aryan daughter of Zeus, but the Phoenician divinity Athene-Onka, who dwelt in the suburbs of Thebai;¹¹ and the ancient Kretan statue of Athene attributed to Daidalos was probably a representation of this goddess. Pausanias remarks that the works of Daidalos, though rude and inelegant, yet appeared to have something divine about them.¹² Ancient statues were sometimes partly of wood and partly of stone. Thus at Megalopolis was a wooden Aphrodite, the hands, face, and extremities of the feet of which were of stone; also a Persephone, partly wooden and partly

---

¹ Bunsen, *Egypt's Place*, ii. 306.
² Vide *inf*. ix. iii.
³ Paus. ix. 40.
⁴ *Il.* xviii. 592.
⁵ Paus. vii. 4.
⁶ Ibid. ii. 19.
⁷ 'The name of Daedalus denotes the activity of the Attic and Cretan artists' (K. O. Müller, *Anct. Art.* 39).
⁸ Vide Paus. ix. 3.
⁹ Cf. *Il.* iv. 8.
¹⁰ Paus. ix. 33.
¹¹ *Sup.* V. v. 3, 5; *inf.* ix. iii.
¹² Paus. ii. 4.

stone.[1] We are not now dependent on statue-myths for our knowledge of the regions where the art flourished and whence it was introduced into Hellas. The statuary powers of Kam, Assur, and Kaldea, are revealed to us; and although the arts of the early inhabitants of Syria, Phoenicia and Asia Minor, are even at present more concealed, yet ample materials exist to confirm the significance of the legendary traditions. History when really known almost invariably corroborates all truly ancient myths, and the Natural Phenomena Theory is no exception to this rule, for its teachings are history in the highest sense.

Descending to the particular, we have next to notice the statues of Dionysos, and first those of the archaic period. 'The eldest Grecian world was satisfied in the repetition of this god of nature with a phallic herma,'[2] 'a mere piece of wood, a pillar turned with the narrowest end down, occasionally surmounted by a mark or head,'[3] a circumstance which brings us to the consideration of the apparent connection of the Aryan divinities Hermes,[4] and Apollon with Dionysos Stylos. The worship of Apollon as Agyieus was peculiar to the Dorians, and of great antiquity at Delphoi, a locality where, as has been noticed, the Dionysiak element was introduced in archaic times, from which place it was brought to Athenai at a very early period,[5] partly at the command of an oracle. His statue was erected in courtyards and before the doors of houses,[6] as a tutelary deity, and to avert evil. The symbol or image of the god was most simple, being a conical block of stone, a form manifestly Phoenician. 'The ancients knew not whether to consider it as an altar

[1] Paus. viii. 31.
[2] Müller, *Anct. Art.* 488.
[3] Murray, *Manual of Mythol.* 145.
[4] Vide Prof. Max Müller, *Lects. on the Science of Language*, ii. 521.
[5] 'The Athenians first worshipped mutilated Hermai' (Paus. i. 24).
[6] 'They worship Hermes as a god, and place Aguieus as a doorkeeper' (Clem. Alex. *Protrept.* iv. 5).

or statue. The Athenians represented their Hermes in a similar manner. This god, although distinct from Apollon, was by them invested with the same offices.[1] Both were represented by simple columnar statues.' A 'phallic form always distinguished the Mercuries of Athens.'[2] First, as to Hermes, a divinity incorrectly identified with the Latin Mercurius, the god of traffic.[3] M. Michel Bréal, in a letter to Professor Max Müller,[4] evidently approved by that high authority, well points out that there is no real connection, but only a verbal confusion, between the name of the god and 'le mot ἕρμα, qui désigne une pierre, une borne, une poteau.' To this Mr. Cox agrees,[5] and indeed there is a consensus of investigators. Hermes, the Morning Breeze, the cloud-divinity, the Psycho-pompos, or Soul-leader,[6] is not in origin a phallic god at all, and may be at once dismissed from the connection. Next, as to Apollon called Agyieus, supposed patron power of Aguia, the Way or Public Place, and whose image was a block of stone. Here we have another verbal error, for I doubt not that the name of this god was Agyïos, the Limbless, and it is to be noted that *guia* especially refers to the *lower* limbs, the feet or knees, and so the name would also be peculiarly appropriate to a terminal statue. We have, then, the same limbless and phallic divinity introduced from the direction of Delphoi both at Athenai and Sparta, at the former place incorrectly called Hermes, being in reality Dionysos for, as we have seen, the phallic herma was the first representation of the god; and at the latter place incorrectly called Apollon. But it was the same divinity in

---

[1] Cf. Thoukyd. vi. 27.
[2] Müller, *Doric Race*, i. 323.
[3] 'Mercurius possessed not a single attribute in common with the Hellenic Hermes; and the Fetiales persistently refused to admit their identity' (Cox, *Mythol. of the Aryan Nations*, ii. 237. Note).
[4] *Lects. on the Science of Language*, ii. 520.
[5] *Mythol. of the Aryan Nations*, ii. 237.
[6] *Sup.* VI. ii. 3.

both localities, for the supposed Hermes of Athenai was equally Agyieus and Agyïos, whose cult is especially noticed as obtaining at Acharnai,[1] and at Athenai this divinity was in fact Dionysos; therefore at Sparta it was Dionysos.[2] And this reasoning, in itself conclusive, is singularly confirmed by independent investigation into Dorik mythology. Apollon, the great Aryan Sun-god, and almost the chief of Dorik divinities, absorbed in himself, and covered with his name nearly all solar myths among the Dorians. But since the non-Aryan element was strong in many Dorik regions as elsewhere in Hellas, and for proof of this assertion let the invaluable *Itinerary* of Pausanias be carefully studied, so its developments became in many instances attributed to phases in the grand concept of the overshadowing Apollon. Now, it may be laid down as a general rule, numerous illustrations of which are to be met with in the present work, that Hellenik divinities whose shapes are grotesque, monstrous, or similarly unhuman, are invariably not indigenous.[3] Apparent exceptions to this canon, such, for instance, as the Horse-headed Demeter of Phigaleia,[4] or the Arkadian Pan,[5] on careful examination, serve only to confirm it.[6] Mr. Cox, having justly noticed that the Hellenik divinities have not the monstrous forms of the Hindû, finds an apparent exception in the case of 'the four-armed Lake-

---

[1] Paus. i. 81.

[2] 'Agyieus is represented by a pillar tapering to a point, which is placed by the gates; some say that they belong to Apollon, *and others to Dionysos, or to both alike*' (Souidas, in voc). "Aguieus, according to many, belonged to Dionysos' (Müller, *Anc. Art.* 36).

[3] Vide remarks *sup.* IV. iii. 2.

[4] Vide *inf.* sec. iv. No. XLV.

[5] Vide *inf.*

[6] Vide the excellent observations of Pausanias on the statue of a Derketo-mermaid, commonly but erroneously said to represent Artemis (Paus. viii. 41). He also remarks that the statues even of the Erinyes and of other chthonian divinities are not at all dreadful in appearance (Ibid. i. 28). Thus, again, at Argos was an ancient triple-eyed statue of Zeus, said to have stood in the palace of Priamos, and to have fallen to the lot of Sthenelos on the division of the spoils of Troia (Ibid. ii. 24), so that it was foreign in origin.

daimonian Apollon,[1]' at Amyklai, which was also four-eared, and called Kouridios,[2] the Wedded, a singular appellation for Apollon.[3] Symbolical ideas of omniscience and omnipotence represented by practical monstrosities properly belong to Kam and India, to Phoenicia and the Euphrates Valley, not to the soil of Hellas. Now the worship of Dionysos held a very prominent place at Amyklai,[4] where he was called Psilas the Winged, a solar epithet;[5] and perhaps this statue, with a double complement of arms and ears, and very likely of other members also, was that of a male and female joined together or wedded on the same principle as the Janus-like Bakchik cups above noticed,[6] and like them in this case would typify the 'two-natured Iakchos;' the androgynous Hindû Ardanari-Iswara, a figure male on the right side and female on the left, presents the same idea. Bardesanes, A.D. 220, author of a work called *Indika*, some fragments only of which are preserved, says, 'In a very high mountain in the middle of the earth there was a large natural cave, in which was to be seen a statue 10 or 12 cubits high, standing upright, with its hands folded crosswise; its whole right side was that of a man, its left that of a woman; and the indissoluble union of these two incongruous halves in one body struck all who saw the statue with wonder. On its right breast was engraved the sun, on its left the moon.'[7] On its arms were general representations of the phenomena of the Kosmos.[8] If, however, the Lakedaimonian statue represented a single figure it would doubtless symbolize Dionysos-Iakchos the Time-king, in his aspect as Lord of the four seasons,[9] with

---

[1] *Mythol. of the Aryan Nations*, i. 370.

[2] Hesych., in voc. *Kouridion*; Müller, *Doric Race*, i. 370.

[3] This curious statue appears to have been unknown to Pausanias.

[4] Paus. iii. 19.

[5] Vide *inf.* VIII. i. *Psilas*.

[6] *Sup.* sec. i. Vase, No. LXIII.

[7] Bardesanes, apud Priaulx, *Apollonius of Tyana*, 151-2.

[8] Vide a representation of the androgynous Demiurge noticed *infra*.

[9] Vide *sup.* II. iii. 2, 3.

DIONYSOS IN ART.

whom Movers[1] well compares the Four-faced Karthaginian Baal and the four-faced image of Zeus (Baal), which Manasseh is said to have set up in the House of the Lord.[2] Manasseh, the Minase of the Assyrian Inscriptions, was peculiarly devoted to the Baalic, sidereal and phallic-grove cults. The statement in Souidas is in exact accordance with those of the writers of the Books of Kings and Chronicles.[3] The king apparently introduced various monstrous gods, for his son 'sacrificed unto all the carved images which Manasseh his father had made.' This particular carved image 'receives the somewhat unusual name of *semel*, which some regard as a proper name, and compare with the Greek Semele.'[4] *Semel*, the Assyrian *Samulli* and Akkadian *Sir-gal*, means 'image.' It is quite possible that Semele may be really an Oriental name, to which, as in many other cases, an Hellenik derivation suitable in itself has been attached, and may mean 'the image of the sublunary world,' as a Neo-Platonist would say.

That this four-armed, four-eared Baalic image of the all-penetrating, all-hearing Sun should have had some connection with bovine symbolism or idea would seem very probable; and, without unduly anticipating any remark on this latter phase of the god,[5] I may notice a curious indication that the so-called Apollon and actual Dionysos was not unconnected with the Bakchik ox. Hesychios calls *kynakias* 'leather thongs; the four hands from the hide of the slaughtered victim; the prize of an ox devoted to Apollon.' The ox is an animal peculiarly

---

[1] *Phönizier*. i. 541.

[2] 'Having desecrated the House of the Lord, he set up the four-faced image of Zeus in it' (Souidas, in voc. *Manasses*). It is especially noticed that the Attik Hermes-statue was quadrangular (Paus. iv. 33).

[3] Cf. 2 *Kings*, xxi. 7: 'He set graven image of the grove that he had made *in the house*, of which the Lord said to David etc.' 2 *Chron*. xxxiii. 7: 'He set a carved image, the idol which he had made, in the house of God.'

[4] Canon Rawlinson in loc. *Speaker's Commentary*, iii. 360.

[5] Vide *inf*. IX. iii. *Taurokeros*.

sacred to the sun;[1] and the flayed-off hide with the four feet of the beast still attached to it apparently answered in symbolism to the four arms, ears, or faces of the images, so that the ox or bull thus devoted became a representation of the solar Time-king in his four changing seasons. Strange as it may seem, this monstrous fourfold divinity actually appears in Athenai itself, though still in the disguise and under the name of Hermes, in the exact Phoenician form in which Manasseh introduced him into the Temple. In the Kerameikos, at a place where three ways met, stood a four-headed Dionysiak statue, the work of the sculptor Telesarchides.[2] It has been frequently said that Hekate and Hermes derive their occasional triplicity,[3] and other unanthropomorphic adjuncts, from presiding over places where three roads met and the like. But although in later times these ideas were to some extent connected, and though the statue of a trikephalik or tetrakephalik divinity might indeed with much propriety be erected where three or four roads met; yet the previous supposed character of the personage would occasion the act, the idea of many heads would not spring from that of cross-roads. That the heads in origin were quite independent of the roads is well shown in the instance before us, in which the *four*-headed god presided where *three* ways met. Close to Amyklai was Brysiai, another Bakchik locality, where stood a temple of the god with statues in its arcane recesses, which the profane were not allowed to behold, possibly on account of their repulsive, *i.e.*, unanthropomorphic character. Behind the town rose the heights of Taÿgetos, on the highest peak of which, Taletos, sacred to Helios, horses were sacrificed to the Sun,[4] whose

---

[1] Vide *inf.* VIII. ii. *Bull.*
[2] Hesych. in voc. *Hermes Trikephalos*; Eustath. ad *Il.* xxiv. 333; Photios. *Lex.* in voc. *Hermes Tetrakephalos.*
[3] Thus Hekate is styled Triformis, Triceps, Tergeminus, etc. She is also Trioditis, Lat. Trivia, because the triple-formed goddess is fitted, like Hermes Trikephalos, to preside at three cross-roads.
[4] Paus. iii. 20; cf. 2 *Kings*,

statue stood in the open air by that of Paphia, *i.e.*, Astarte, near Oitylos, a place not far distant on the Messenian Gulf.[1] In Elis, too, their statues stood side by side; that of the Moon-Goddess or Astarte was horned, and that of the Sun had the 'caput radiatum,'[2] in fact, was Apollon Karneios, the Horned-sun, which, as we have already seen,[3] was another non-Aryan ·phase of the great Dorik solar divinity, another aspect of the multiform and ever-changing Iao. This horned and non-Aryan Sun-god appears at Tarsos, a kind of half-way house between Hellas and the East, in forms that yet further illustrate his real origin. Though still called Apollon he is here rayed and winged; in fact, is the winged Sun of Kam and the Orient. One fine radiate head 'Mr. Birch has recognised as the same as that upon the coins of Rhodes.[4] It is Helios, or the Sun, and a copy of the Colossus at Rhodes. This radiation was not usual with the Romans and Greeks; but in the present case it admits of an easy explanation. Tarsus, bordering upon Phoenicia, and having ready access to Egypt, would have its mythology tinted with that of its neighbours.' Another point about this so-called Apollon is very significant. 'There hangs upon the wing a cluster of grapes; grapes were used in the decoration of the great temple of Baalbec, and *on the images of Baal grapes are hung round the neck.* The grapes, therefore, show the Syrian cast of the mythology of Tarsus.'[5]

To recapitulate.—The following solar and kindred phases introduced from Thebai and Delphoi do not in

xxiii. 11. The reforming Josiah takes away the horses of the Sun, perhaps dedicated, but at all events used, by the four-faced-Baal-introducing Mannasseh, and burns the solar chariots. The dedication of solar horses, as Pausanias observes, was also a Persian custom. Vide Xen. *Kyrop.* viii. 3; *Anab.* iv. 5.
[1] Paus. iii. 26.
[2] Ibid. vi. 24.
[3] *Sup.* IV. iii. 2.
[4] Cf. *inf.* sec. iii. *Coins of Rhodos.*
[5] Barker, *Cilicia and its Governors*, 101-2.

reality belong to the Aryan, but to the Semitic, Sun-god, who is also a kosmogonical divinity:—(1) Agyieus, the Lord-of-the-Way, otherwise Agyïos, the Limbless; image, a block of stone: (2) Kouridios, the Wedded, or of-ripe-age; image, a four-armed, four-eared figure: and (3) Karneios, the Horned-sun; image, a human figure, with rays around the head.

The earliest Hellenik statues of Dionysos, then, were conical or columnar stones; then terminal pillars, with a head on the top; then busts, in which the human figure was represented sometimes as far as to the waist; and, lastly, the whole human form divine or statue proper: the entire series forming a chain of evolution in stone. This series, be it observed, is the Hellenik statue-treatment of the god, and does not include the symbolical and monstrous forms which he assumed under other hands. And with respect to these latter, it is most instructive to remark that, in accordance with the principle above laid down, the anthropomorphic feeling of the Hellenik sculptor *never* permits the Horned-god to appear as such [1] in his compositions, though Coins, more faithful to the truth and to his origin, constantly so exhibit him.[2] The following are instances of statuary representations of the god, showing the early ideas:—

I. *Female offering a goat in sacrifice to Dionysos Stylos*, represented as a column.[3]

II. *Dionysiak Festival.*—In the centre the terminal

---

[1] 'Ptolemy the Fourth was called Dionysos; and Mithridates of Pontus was also called Dionysos; and Alexander wished to be considered the son of Ammon, and to have his statue made horned by the sculptors—eager to disgrace the beauty of the human form by the addition of a horn' (Clem. Alex. *Protrept.* iv. 9). Cf. Spence, *Polymetis*, 129: 'There is one thing which the poets generally attribute to Bacchus, *which I am sur-prised not to find commonly in his statues*, and that is, his horns. Even these were little and pretty, and Ariadne, in Ovid, mentions them as one reason why she loved this god.'

[2] Vide *inf.* sec. iii. 'The bull-Dionysos naturally gave less occasion to the formative art than to the mystic ceremonies' (K. O. Müller, *Anct. Art.* 489).

[3] *Sup.* sec. i. No. XXXVI.

figure of the god clad in tunic and robe, with long and pointed beard, long curly hair bound with ivy and crowned with a diadem. Above him a mass of ivy, and before him a female figure making a libation from a kanthar: before her a tripod table, on which are round cakes and a piece of flesh: a thyrsos, with an ivy branch fastened to the narthex, leans against the table.[1]

III. *A terminal bearded Dionysos*, with flowing hair, the upper part of the column spotted.[2]

IV. *Dionysos was represented at Thebai as a column*, overgrown with ivy.[3]

V. *At Kyllene in Elis, as an upright Phallos.*[4]—This latter is called a statue of Hermes, but the mistake which connects that god with similar statues has been already noticed.[5]

VI. *The various phallic and other hermai*, which, in reality, are statues of Dionysos.—One Prokleides is said to have made an image of a trikephalik Hermes in Ankyle, an Attik village, which statue we are distinctly told was so formed for the express purpose of 'shewing the road, bearing a direction whither one way led and whither another.'[6] The idea of many-headed *hermai* having been once received, it is applied in purely Hellenik hands in the simplest manner possible, without any occult symbolism, or underlying meaning. No Hellene would ever reverence this image as a representation of divinity; it seems to have been an unique work, and as such to have attracted much notice.

VII. *Head of Dionysos Kephallen.*[7]

VIII. *Bearded head on pillar*: before it a large

---

[1] Brit. Mus. *Vase Cat.* No. 743.
[2] Christie, *Disquisitions*, 97.
[3] K. O. Müller, *Anct. Art.* 36.
[4] Paus. vi. 26.
[5] Cf. Clemens Alex. *Protrept.* iv. 16: 'Consecrating these pillars of shamelessness, as if they were the images of your gods.'
[6] Vide Philochoros, *Frag.* lxix.; Souidos, in voc. *Trikephalos*,
[7] Vide *sup.* VI. i. 3.

amphora, behind which, and fronting the pillar, a cock.[1] A very interesting representation, as illustrating the confusion in the mind of the artist between Hermes and Dionysos. The cock is the usual symbol of the former, and the wine-jar of the latter. The cock, however, is sometimes regarded as the solar herald.[2] Montfaucon asks 'Pourquoi ce Vase entre l'Herme et le coq? C'est ce qu'on ne peut savoir sans pénétrer dans la pensée de celui qui fit faire cette bague.' The beard, too, belongs rather to Dionysos Katapogon than to Hermes, although the latter appears occasionally as bearded on the Vases.

IX. *Terminal figure of the so-called Hermes*, bearded and ithyphallic, before which an altar, with blazing fire; over it a youth roasts part of a goat, other portions of which hang on the wall and the head lies under a table, where another figure is cutting up the rest of the animal.[3] A thoroughly Dionysiak concept, phallos, goat, beard, pillar.

X. *Terminal Dionysos*, to which a bull is about to be sacrificed.[4]

XI. *Terminal, bearded, ithyphallic Dionysos*, before him an altar, behind him the Bakchik tree.[5] At Naxos the heads of such statues were made of fig,[6] a tree which, according to Sosybios of Lakedaimon, B.C. 250, had been given to man by Dionysos,[7] so the Priapus of the Roman poet declares:—

'Olim truncas eram ficulnus, inutile lignum.'[8] The later and peculiar phallic connection of the fig-tree with the explanation of the occult phrase, 'a fig for you'[9] is

---

[1] Montfaucon, *Supplement* I. Pl. xxxviii. Fig. 5.
[2] Vide *inf.* sec. iii. *Karystos*. sec. iv. No. XXXIV.
[3] Brit. Mus. *Vase Cat.* No. 561.
[4] Vide *inf.* sec. iii. *Pergamos*.
[5] David, *Antiquités Grecques*, iii. Fig. 3.
[6] Ibid. 126.
[7] Athenaios, iii. 5.
[8] Hor. *Sat.* lib. I. viii. 1.
[9] Cf. 'A figo for thy friendship' (*Hen. V.* iii. 6).

given with much learning and research by the Editor of Payne Knight's *Worship of Priapus*.[1]

XII. *Two females presenting a mystic chest and casket to a column, symbol of Dionysos.*—One holds in her hand a staff, crowned with sesame;[2] bandelets (*i.e.* the girdle or zone, which is unbound by Eros) appear suspended, and also fastened to the column, on the top of which is a singularly shaped diota, and the Bakchik pine-cone.[3]

We next come to the statue proper or whole human figure, which, in the case of Dionysos, is divided into two classes: (1) the Elder or Bearded, and (2) the Younger or Beardless, god. The former class represents Dionysos in mature manhood with ' a stately and majestic form, with a magnificent luxuriance of curly hair restrained by the mitre, gently flowing beard, clear and blooming features, and the oriental richness of an almost feminine drapery, with usually the drinking cup, and a vine-shoot in his hand.'[4] Dionysos Katapogon or Barbatus is sometimes called the Indian Bakchos, from a legend that he was born in India where the men are bearded,[5] or that he vowed to let his beard grow during the three years of his Indian expedition.[6] On that ancient and celebrated work of art the Chest of Kypselos, who ruled at Corinthos, B.C. 655–625, the god is represented as bearded, and lying in a cavern holding a golden patern, *Stolatus*, or clad in a garment reaching to the feet, and surrounded with the vine, apples, and pomegranates.[7] There is a statue of Dionysos Pogonites, the Bearded, in the Vatican.

The last phase of the god in statuary is that of Dionysos Ephebos, the blooming and femininely shaded youth, who has arrived *epi* Hebe, at Pubertas. Hebe

---

[1] P. 149 *et seq.* Vide *inf.* VIII. ii. *Fig.*
[2] Vide *inf.* VIII. ii. *Sesame.*
[3] David, *Antiquités Grecques*, iii. Fig. 49.
[4] Westropp, *Handbook of Archaeol.* 184.
[5] Diod. iii. 63.
[6] Vide *inf.* IX. vii. *Indoletes.*
[7] Paus. v. 19.

herself, in later legend the goddess of youth, is in earlier the divine Cup-bearer,[1] who hands man the wine of life-vigour and enjoyment. These statues can never be better described than in the words of Winkelmann: 'In the most beautiful statues, he always appears with delicate, round limbs, and the full expanded hips of the female sex,[2] for according to the fable, he was brought up as a maiden.[3] The type of Bacchus is a lovely boy, who is treading the boundaries of the spring-time of life and adolescence, in whom emotions of voluptuousness, like the tender shoots of a plant, are budding, and who, as if between sleeping and waking, half in a dream of exquisite delight, is beginning to collect and verify the pictures of his fancy.' Of one of these statues Müller remarks 'the very femininely formed torso is remarkably beautiful.'[4] It was the genius of Praxiteles, B.C. 360, amongst whose creations were the exquisite Aphrodite of Knidos and the renowned Eros of Thespiai, an infinite advance on the ancient statue of the god there which was only a rough stone,[5] which chiefly delighted in delineating the androgynous softness of the two-natured Iakchos. The statues of the youthful Dionysos are comparatively numerous; amongst them is the marble group of Dionysos, Ampelos or the Vine personified, and tiger, now in the British Museum. Of this Payne Knight remarks, 'On one side is the Bacchus Diphues, or Creator, of both sexes, known by the effeminate mould of his limbs and countenance, and on the other, a tiger, leaping up, and devouring the grapes which spring from the body of the personified vine, the hands of which are employed in receiving another cluster from the Bacchus. This composition represents the vine between the creating and destroying

---

[1] *Il.* iv. 2.
[2] Vide *inf.* VIII. i. *Thelymorphos.*
[3] Apollod. iii. 4.
[4] *Ancient Art.* 491.
[5] Paus. ix. 27.

attributes of the god; the one giving it fruit, and the other devouring it when given. The tiger has a garland of ivy round his neck, to shew that the destroyer was co-essential with the creator, of whom ivy, as well as all other evergreens, was an emblem representing his perpetual youth and viridity.'[1] Dionysos is also represented as enthroned and surrounded by his train, reclining, lying down, staggering as intoxicated, carried by Hermes to the Nymphs, when a child, and overcoming Pentheus, Lykourgos, the Tyrrhenian pirates, and the Indians; also handing grapes to the panther, pouring out wine from a *karchesion* or drinking cup, etc.; but these delineations require no special notice, as they do not additionally illustrate the concept of the god. The *Itinerary* of Pausanias shows that in his time a multitude of Bakchik statues existed all over continental Hellas: amongst them was a torch-bearing Iakchos at Athenai, the work of Praxiteles[2]; a statue in the Odeion or concert-hall there;[3] a statue of Dionysos Eleuthereus the Liberator, yearly carried into a temple near the Akademeia,[4] brought from Eleutherai,[5] on the Boiotik border, and a place anciently included in Boiotia; a wooden statue at Korinthos, covered with gold-leaf, except the face, which was painted with vermilion; near it a statue of Artemis Ephesia similarly adorned[6]; a statue of ivory and gold in the god's temple at Sikyon, and near it statues of the Bakchai of white stone;[7] a statue at Argos said to have been brought from Euboia;[8] a bearded statue at Epidauros;[9] a wooden seated statue of Dionysos Soter, at Lerne;[10] a statue of Hermes, carrying the infant Dionysos at Sparta;[11] a bronze statue at Thebai, where

---

[1] *Worship of Priapus*, 75.
[2] Paus. i. 2.
[3] Ibid. 14.
[4] Ibid. 20.
[5] Ibid. 38.
[6] Ibid. ii. 2.
[7] Ibid. ii. 7.
[8] Ibid. 23.
[9] Ibid. 30.
[10] Ibid. 38.
[11] Ibid. iii. 11.

was a tradition that when Semele was slain a piece of wood fell from heaven which was adorned with bronze and called Kadmeian Dionysos;[1] the three Graces were often placed in the head of statues of the god;[2] a stone statue at Thelpouse in Arkadia, seven feet high, near similar statues of Demeter and Persephone;[3] a statue near Megalopolis, with buskins, holding a cup and a thyrsos;[4] a statue at Phigaleia, the lower parts of which were concealed in laurel and ivy leaves, and the upper rubbed with vermilion and thus made to shine.'[5] Legend told that, on the destruction of Troia the hero Eurypylos received as his share of the spoils a statue of Dionysos Aisymnetes, made by Hephaistos.[6] Macrobius tells us that 'Dionysos, who is Liber, is represented as an infant, a youth, of middle age, and as an aged man.'[7] 'By these were signified the four seasons of the year, the vine being dedicated to Sol, in whom they all exist.'[8] These are the four faces of Iakchos the Time-king, the Baal of Manasseh, and the Hermes Tetrakephalos of Athenai. With them we may compare the Latin Janus Quadrifrons.

The remaining subjects of Dionysiak Statuary are the various associates of the god and members of his train, 'the good-for-nothing and wanton Satyroi,'[9] Seilenoi, Mainades, Nymphs, and Pan and his Paniskoi. 'The natural life whose purest blossom we observe in Dionysos now appears in lower cycles.'[10] The Satyroi present powerful limbs, but not ennobled by gymnastics, snub-

---

[1] Paus. ix. 12.
[2] Ibid. 35.
[3] Ibid. viii. 25.
[4] Ibid. 31.
[5] Ibid. 39. Mr. King, after noticing that members of the Bakchik train were often depicted on 'the vermilion jasper,' observes 'The last stone by its colour manifested a kindred nature to the *rosy* god, whose rustic figures, like the primitive idols, continued to the last to be besmeared with red-ochre, according to the ancient practice' (*Antique Gems*, 263).
[6] Vide *inf.* VIII. i. *Aisymnetes.*
[7] *Sat.* i. 18.
[8] Salmon, *Polygraphice*, 1685, iv. 22.
[9] Hesiod. apud. Strabo, x. 3.
[10] Müller, *Anct. Art.* 496.

noses, ignoble countenances, pointed goat-like ears, bald foreheads, bristly hair, and sometimes a scanty tail.[1] This description includes the Seilenoi or older Satyroi. In the satyrik drama the bearded, hair-covered figures were called Pappo, or Down-covered Seilenoi. As regards the equable Seilenos himself, Müller observes, 'Yet is this happy daemon, in a deeper mode of thinking which was unfolded especially by the Orphici, full of a wisdom to which all the restless bustle of mankind appears folly; the plastic art also represents him in nobler and grander forms as the fosterer and instructor of the young Dionysos.'[2] Of the female figures Ariadne is the protagonist; she is represented as beautiful, ivy-crowned, and frequently richly draped. Female Satyroi very rarely occur; and the Mainades have their serpents, flying garments, torn fawns and thyrsos staves as usual. The whole Dionysiak Cycle in art as elsewhere is of the earth earthy; from Dionysos downwards all the concepts are the links in a descending scale from the most refined voluptuousness to the grossest lust. But little innocent hilarity is found amid the maddened revel; but little rural freshness in the turbulent excitement. According to Müller, 'Nature overpowering the mind, and hurrying it out of the repose of a clear self-consciousness, lies at the basis of all Dionysian creations.'[3] This is in a measure true; but yet is a very imperfect expression of the root-cause of these concepts. It is not so much Nature as human nature, the lower nature in man, which in the later developments of the Dionysiak Myth overpowers the higher and crushes down the aspirations towards infinite good, the grossest, *i.e.*, most patent, instance of this overpowering occurring in the case of abuse of wine.

Here may be noticed the Arkadian divinity Pan, who,

[1] Westropp, *Handbook of Archaeol.* 184.
[2] *Ancient Art.* 400.
[3] *Ibid.* 488.

although originally as unconnected with Dionysos as Hermes with the *hermai*, has been enrolled in the Bakchik train through accidental circumstances. The Panisks 'represent the secret pleasure and the dark horror of sylvan solitude. Here also there occurs, and that too in their native Arcadia, a human form which is only characterized as Pan by the shepherd's pipe, the pastoral crook, the disordered hair and also, *perhaps*, sprouting horns. This is the usual shape on coins and vase-paintings of the best period.'[1] So that even in the case of Pan, a mere local genius of flocks and herds, not a divinity of Olympos, the anthropomorphic principle was so strong in the best period of Hellenik art that little budding horns, and *perhaps* not even these, formed the only unnatural feature in the figure of the rustic daemon. I have already[2] endeavoured to point out that there is no real connection between Pan and Dionysos; but their points of apparent affinity and assimilation are chiefly the following: Each is a nature-god and a horned-god. It is the late Pan of the age of Praxiteles who appears fully horned, hook-nosed, and goat-legged. Each is a kosmogonic god; Dionysos is the animated universe, and through a false etymology Pan is made to represent the All, and consequently is thus addressed:—

> Strong pastoral Pan, with suppliant voice I call,
> Heaven, sea, and earth, the mighty queen of all,
> Immortal fire; for all the world is thine,
> And all are parts of thee, O power divine.
> —(*Orphik Hymn*, XI. Taylor's Translation.)

Pan, it will be observed, has nothing kosmogonic about him in origin; but the Orphiks fasten on the innocent country divinity all the dread, mystic and occult attributes and adjuncts of Dionysos, calling him the 'horned Zeus'

---

[1] *Ancient Art*, 501.   [2] *Sup.* IV. iii. 2.

and 'universal queen,' like Semele. 'Pan,' says Pausanias, 'in the same manner as the most powerful gods, consummates the prayers of men and punishes the wicked;' before this Pan a fire, which is never extinguished, burns.'[1] This is the later not the earlier cult of Pan; like Zagreus, he has become the equal of the highest gods, and is symbolized in accordance with the Orphik Hymn by ' immortal fire.' The fabled loud voice of Pan, another connecting link between him and Bromios the Noisy, is the mountain Echo whom he loved. His mythic parentage, again, as the son of Hermes, shows his Aryan character. His cult was not introduced into Attike until after the Persian Wars.[2] A noisy, horned, nature-god, whose name was supposed to signify 'all,' could not avoid being connected with Dionysos, and so the luckless Pan is thrown into the Dionysiak train, and thoroughly degraded as a goatish, ithyphallic, grotesque monster. 'It was the misapprehension of later times, which, however, was very wide spread, that first transformed the ancient god of pasture into a universal daemon, and his unpretending reed-piping into the harmony of the spheres.'[3] Mr. Boscawen[4] compares the Kaldean Heabani (*i.e.*, 'Hea makes') with Pan. Heabani ' is always drawn with the feet and tail of an ox, and with horns on his head.'[5] I should rather connect the friend of Izdubar with other tauromorphic personages of Semitic regions.

The following example, though not strictly an instance of Statuary, may be here appropriately noticed. The androgynous Demiurge, with female breasts, and holding a scarf or fillet in the right hand and a serpent in the left, stands by the Dionysiak column. The scarf is wrapped round the arm and one end held over the head.[6] This

---

[1] Paus. viii. 37.
[2] Herod. vi. 105.
[3] Müller, *Anct. Art.* 501.
[4] *Trans. Soc. Bib. Arch.* iv. 286.
[5] Geo. Smith, *Chaldean Account of Genesis*, 196.
[6] Montfaucon, *Supplement* v. Pl. 1. Fig. 2. Some sages of the past called it a Kleopatra!

scarf or *kredemnon*, in addition to a frequent meaning previously noticed,[1] here signifies the veiling of darkness, the Demiurge being concealed in the Under-world, the secret home of life-potency. This *kredemnon* of blackness, the exact opposite to that of Ino,[2] is well illustrated by a beautiful sable figure of Night,[3] with rays of darkness round her head, reversed torch, the flaming Sun having sunk to the Under-world, and holding a very large black scarf which surrounds the rays and is star-spotted, and thus equivalent to the kosmic Dionysiak panther-skin. Another similar figure[4] holds the scarf over her head with both hands, and without it are three eight-rayed stars. Europe, *i. e.* Ereb, the West,[5] as the region of night and darkness at times, appears on Kretan coins, holding this scarf over her head when carried away westwards by the Zeus-bull.

SECTION III.

DIONYSIAK COINS.

As in Statuary the shapeless block, often a supposed ouranopipt, preceded the carved figure; so in coinage, using that term in its widest sense, the familiar circular form was the last and highest development of the art, and the successor of other and ruder shapes; and further, as such forms in statuary were peculiarly connected with Dionysos, so were they in coinage. Ploutarchos writes that the money anciently in use at Sparta 'was of iron,

---

[1] *Sup.* sec. i. Nos. X., XLV.
[2] *Sup.* VI. i. 2.
[3] Montfaucon, i. Pt. ii. Pl. ccxiv. Fig. 1.
[4] Ibid. Fig. 2.
[5] The Homerik Erebos, which was in the West (*Od.* xii. 81); the Assyrian *eribu*, to 'descend, enter, or set,' as the sun (Rev. A. H. Sayce, *Assyrian Grammar*. Syllabary, No. 60). So Aïdes, as king of the Under-world, is called 'Hesperos Theos' (Soph. *Oid. Tyr.* 177), and a westward position was generally adopted when invoking infernal divinities (*Od.* x. 528. Cf. *Ibid.* xi. 37. Mitford, *History of Greece*, xxii. 2).

dipped in vinegar while it was red hot, to make it brittle and unmalleable, so that it might not be applied to any other use. Besides, it was heavy, and difficult of carriage, and a great quantity of it was but of little value. Perhaps all the ancient money was of this kind, and consisted either of pieces of iron or bronze, which, from their form, were called *obeliskoi*; whence we have still a quantity of small money called *oboloi*, six of which make a *drachme* or handful, that being as much as the hand can contain.'[1] To the same effect writes the learned Isidoros, Bishop of Hispalis (Seville), A.D. 600-636 :—' The obol was made formerly, from bronze, like an arrow, whence also it received the name Obel (Arrow) from the Greeks.'[2] *Obolos* and *Obelos* are only Ionik and Attik differences in pronunciation,[3] and *belos* is a glance, an arrow, or their effect. *Obeliskos*, the diminutive, is any small pointed instrument. Speaking of obelisks, Plinius remarks that 'monarchs have entered into a sort of rivalry with one another in forming the elongated blocks known as *obelisci* and consecrated to the divinity of the Sun. The blocks had this form given to them in resemblance to the rays of that luminary, which are so called in the Egyptian language. Mesphres, who reigned in the city of the Sun [Han, On, Heliopolis], was the first who erected one of these obelisks, being warned to do so in a dream.'[4] So Herodotos notes that the Kamic King whom he calls Pheron presented two stone obelisks to the temple of the Sun.[5] These obols or obelisks are identical with the sacred conical stones above referred to,[6] which formed the germ of statuary, and like them were frequently supposed to have been heaven-fallen thunderbolts,[7] and represent

---

[1] Plout. *Lysandros*, xvii.
[2] *Origin.* xvi. 23.
[3] Ioul. Pol. ix. 77.
[4] Plin. xxxvi. 14.
[5] Herod. ii. 111.
[6] *Sup.* sec. ii.
[7] Cf. D'Hancarville, *Arts de la Grèce*, i. 1.

the spears, rays, arrows, or golden-locks of the beaming sun; for, as Macrobius observes, 'Under the name of arrows the darting of the rays is shewn.'[1] By the Nile, Euphrates and in Syria, monetary transactions were anciently conducted by weighing the metals employed. Barter appears to have sufficed for the earlier Phoenicians, chiefly engaged in traffic with barbarous peoples, and it was reserved for the Lydians to originate a regular coinage.[2] Thus the solar disk was substituted for the solar rays. Pheidon of Argos, cir. B.C. 750, according to the Parian Chronicle, first introduced copper and silver coinage into Hellas from Asia, and at the same time deposited in the temple of Here a number of the ancient obeliscal arrows.[3] Aigina was then part of his dominions, and his coining is said to have been carried on in the island; hence the Aiginetan standard which prevailed generally in early times and in later was used throughout the Peloponnesos, except at Korinthos. Plinius says, 'the form of a sheep was the first figure impressed upon money, and to this fact it owes its name *pecunia*.'[4] He is speaking only of Roman history, but there is an Eastern parallel, for the 'shekel is, in the Book of Job, called *kesitah*, a lamb, the weight being possibly made in that form.'[5] Gesenius observes that 'most of the ancient interpreters understand by *kesitah* a lamb, a sense which has no support either from etymology or the kindred dialects;'[6] and Professor Jevons remarks, 'I am informed by my learned friend, Professor Theodores, that this translation probably arises from an accidental blunder, and that the original meaning of the word *kesitah* was that of

---

[1] *Sat.* i. 17.
[2] Vide Rawlinson's *Herodotus*, i. 563 *et seq.*, where the contrary opinion of Col. Leake is considered.
[3] *Etym. Magnum*, In voc. *Obeliskos*.
[4] Plin. xxxiii. 13.
[5] Humphrey, *The Coin Collector's Manual*, 8.
[6] Cf. Wilson, *Eng. and Heb. Lex.* In voc. *Money*.

APPENDIX L.

A TABLE SHOWING THE VARIETIES OF ORDER FOLLOWED IN THE NAMING OF THE TRIBES OF ISRAEL IN SCRIPTURE, AND IN THE PLACING OF THEIR STANDARD-BEARERS, AND IN THE NAMING OF THE CHERUBIC EMBLEMS[1]

Gen. xxix, xxx, xxxv.	Gen. xlvi.	Exod. i.	Exod. xxviii. 9.[2]	Num. i.	Num. ii, vi, vii, x.	Num. xiii.	Num. xxvi.	Num. xxxiv.	Deut. xxvii. 12, 13.	Deut. xxxiii.
IV. Reuben Simeon Levi	IV. Reuben Simeon Levi	IV. Reuben Simeon Levi	IV. Reuben Simeon Levi	IV. Reuben Simeon	II. Judah Issachar Zebulun	IV. Reuben Simeon	IV. Reuben Gad	II. Judah Simeon Benjamin	Simeon Levi	IV. Reuben Levi Benjamin
II. Judah Issachar Zebulun Gad Asher	II. Judah Zebulun Issachar	II. Judah Issachar Zebulun Benjamin	II. Judah Issachar Zebulun	II. Judah Issachar Zebulun	IV. Reuben Simeon Gad	II. Judah Issachar	II. Judah Issachar Zebulun Manasseh	III. Dan Manasseh	II. Judah Issachar	I. Ephraim Manasseh Zebulun Issachar
III. Dan Naphtali Gad Asher Issachar Zebulun	III. Dan Gad Asher Naphtali	III. Dan Naphtali Gad Asher	III. Dan Naphtali Gad Asher	I. Ephraim Manasseh Benjamin	I. Ephraim Manasseh Benjamin	I. Ephraim Benjamin Zebulun Manasseh	I. Ephraim Benjamin	I. Ephraim Zebulun Issachar Asher Naphtali	I. Joseph Benjamin IV. Reuben Gad Zebulun	Gad
I. Joseph Benjamin	I. Joseph Benjamin	I. Joseph	I. Joseph Benjamin	III. Dan Asher Gad Naphtali	III. Dan Asher Naphtali	III. Dan Asher Naphtali Gad	III. Dan Asher Naphtali	*Reuben and Gad were on the other side of Jordan*	III. Dan Naphtali	III. Dan Naphtali Asher *Simeon omitted*

Josh. xv–xvii.	Judg. v.	1 Chron. ii. 1, 2.	1 Chron. iv.–viii.	1 Chron. xii. 23–38.	1 Chron. xxvii.	Ezek. xlviii. 1–28.	Ezek. xlviii. 11–34.	Rev. vii. 5–8.	THE CHERUBIC EMBLEMS.	
									Ezek. i. 10.	Rev. iv. 7.
II. Judah	I. Ephraim Benjamin Manasseh Issachar	IV. Reuben Simeon Levi	II. Judah Simeon	II. Judah Simeon Levi Benjamin	IV. Reuben Simeon Levi	III. Dan Asher Naphtali Manasseh	IV. Reuben Judah Levi	II. Judah IV. Reuben Gad Asher Naphtali Manasseh Simeon Levi Issachar Zebulun	IV. Man	II. Man
I. Ephraim Manasseh Benjamin Simeon Zebulun Issachar Asher Naphtali	IV. Reuben	II. Judah Issachar Zebulun	IV. Reuben Gad Manasseh Levi Issachar Benjamin Naphtali	I. Ephraim Benjamin Zebulun Issachar	II. Judah Issachar Zebulun Naphtali	I. Ephraim Reuben Judah	II. Joseph Dan Simeon Issachar Zebulun Gad Asher Naphtali	I. Joseph Benjamin	II. Lion	I. Lion
III. Dan	III. Dan Asher Naphtali	III. Dan	III. Dan	III. Dan IV. Reuben Gad	I. Ephraim Manasseh Benjamin	IV. Reuben Judah II. Judah Benjamin			I. Ox	IV. Calf
IV. Reuben Gad	*Judah, Simeon, and Gad omitted*	I. Joseph Benjamin Naphtali Gad Asher	I. Ephraim Asher *Dan omitted*		III. Dan IV. Reuben Gad *Gad and Asher omitted*			*Dan omitted*	III. Eagle	III. Eagle

[1] The Jewish standard-bearers and the cherubic figures are numbered according to their emblems in the Zodiac.
[2] The traditional order of the names in the High Priest's breast-plate, as preserved by the Targumists (see Bishop Wordsworth on Exod. xxviii.).

To face p. 36.

"a certain weight," or "an exact quantity."[1] It is quite admitted that *kesitah* properly means 'something weighed out,' but how could this idea become confused with a lamb, and why should there be such unanimity in so singular a mistake?[2] There is nothing at all incredible in supposing either that the coin bore the rude figure of a sheep, or that being also a weight, it was actually in that form.[3] Lion-shaped weights, with ring handles on the back, have been found at Khorsabad; and 'on the tombs at Thebes there are representations of men weighing rings of gold, the weights having, like these, the form of some animal, as stags, *sheep*, and gazelles.'[4] With *kesitah* the English *cosset*, 'a lamb brought up without the dam,'[5] has been compared; but this latter word, though curiously resembling *kesitah*, means more properly 'pet lamb' or 'pet' generally, being connected with the Old English *cosse*, 'kiss.'[6]

Dionysiak Coins are such as illustrate the Dionysiak Myth; either directly, by bearing figures or symbols evidently Bakchik; or indirectly, by designs which, though not manifestly of this character, are found on examination to belong more or less to the same cycle of idea. It will be well to take the former class first, as all reasoning must be from the known, and their consideration will materially assist the further examination of the subject.

The Lists of Coins mentioned, though far from exhaustive are, it is believed, sufficient for the purpose.[7]

---

[1] *Money and the Mechanism of Exchange*, 80.
[2] Vide the *Chaldee Targum*, LXX. in *Job* xlii. 11. *amnada*; Vulgate, in loc. *ovem*.
[3] Vide Parkhurst, *Heb. Lex.* In voc. *Kesitah*.
[4] Bonomi, *Nineveh and its Palaces*, 337.
[5] Johnson, in voc.; cf. Bailey, *Eng. Dict.* 1724, in voc. *Cosset*.
[6] Vide Halliwell, *Dict of Archaic Words*, in voc. *Cosset*.
[7] Principal authorities:—Montfaucon, *L'Antiquité Expliquée*. Eckhel, *Doctrina Numorum Veterum*. Calmet, *Dict. of the Bible*, by Taylor, 1841. D'Hancarville, *Arts de la Grèce*. Leake, *Numismata Hellenica*. Humphrey, *Coin Collector's Manual*. Smith's *Classical Dict.* Gesenius, *Scripturae Linguaeque Phoeniciae*.

The following coins bear the head or the figure of Dionysos:—

Amisos. A city of Pontos. Head of Dionysos.—Reverse. Mystic kist of Dionysos and thyrsos. A late coin.

Andros. Ivy-crowned head.—Rev. Thyrsos, on panther.

Boiotia. Head of horned Dionysos, ivy-crowned.—Rev. Boiotik buckler.

Herakleia. In Bithynia. Head, ivy-crowned, with thyrsos behind.

Histiaia. In Euboia. Female head. The 'Bacchi foemineum caput,' crowned with grape-clusters.—Rev. A woman, sitting on the prow of a ship. Homeros calls the place 'rich in grapes,'[1] and Sophokles applies the same epithet to Euboia.[2]

Ios. Head of bearded Dionysos.—Rev. A palm tree.

Karthaia. In the island of Keos. Head, ivy-crowned.—Rev. Grape-cluster, under a star.

Korkyra. Dionysos, panther-carried.—Rev. Satyr, pouring drink from one *diota* or double-eared cup into another.

Kydonia. Head, crowned with ivy and clusters of ivy-berries.—Rev. A she-wolf, suckling a little boy.

Kyzikos. Head of Persephone.—Rev. Dionysos, tiger-carried.

Dionysos *stolatus*, holding a torch.

Lamia. In Thessalia. Head, ivy-crowned.

Lampsakos. The same.

Larymne. In Boiotia. The same.—Rev. Two-handled cup and grape-cluster.

Makedonia. Horned head. Also, head, ivy-crowned.—Rev. A he-goat.[3] Also, head of Seilenos. Seilenos, according to a legend, was made prisoner in the gardens of Midas and compelled to answer questions.[4]

---

[1] *Il.* ii. 537. [2] *Antig.* 1133. from the west.'
[3] Cf. *Dan.* viii. 5: 'An he-goat [4] Herod. viii. 138.

Magnesia. In Lydia. Dionysos, ivy-crowned, with kist and serpent.

Maroneia. Head of Dionysos, with twisted horn, ivy-crowned and with ivy-berries.—Rev. ΔΙΟΝΥΣΟΥ ΣΩΤΗΡΟΣ ΜΑΡΩΝΙΤΩΝ. Naked Dionysos, standing. Maron, priest of Apollon, who dwelt at Ismaros, near Maroneia, gave Odysseus excellent wine.[1]

Methymna. The second city of Lesbos. Head of Dionysos.

Mykonos. Head of Dionysos.—Rev. Grape-cluster.

Naxos. Head, ivy-crowned, sometimes bearded, sometimes beardless.—Rev. Kanthar, sometimes with thyrsos and ivy twined round it.

Naxos. In Sikelia. Head, ivy-crowned and bearded.—Rev. Seilenos, with kanthar and ivy.

Neapolis. In Makedonia. Head of Dionysos, a thyrsos behind it.

Parion. In Mysia. Head, ivy-crowned. Also grape-cluster.—Rev. Ear of corn.

Paros. Head, ivy-crowned.—Rev. A woman sitting on a kist, holding a thyrsos.

Peparethos. Head of Dionysos.—Rev. Kanthar. This small island off the Thessalian coast is described as abounding in grapes.[2]

Perga. Head, ivy-crowned.

Pergamos. In Mysia. Terminal Dionysos, towards which a priest leads a bull. The prophetess Phaennis alluded to Attalos I. king of Pergamos as 'the beloved son of a Zeus-nourished bull,' *i. e.*, a special votary of Dionysos Taurokeros, an epithet applied by the oracle of Apollon to the King.[3] Other coins of the place bear a bull's head, and serpent-worship also obtained there.

---

[1] Vide *sup.* IV. iii. 4.
[2] Soph. *Philok.* 540.
[3] Paus. x. 15.

Rhodos. Head of Dionysos, crowned with ivy and berries, sometimes rayed.

Sebastopolis. In Pontos. Head, ivy-crowned.—Rev. Kist of Dionysos and thyrsos.

Sidon. Head of Dionysos. On late Coins.

Sybritia. In Krete. Bearded Dionysos, half naked, sitting, with diota and thyrsos.

Tanagra. Head, ivy-crowned.—Rev. Grape-cluster.

Teos. Head, ivy-crowned and thyrsos.—Rev. Grape-cluster.

Thasos. Head of bearded Dionysos. Also ram-horned head of Dionysos, crowned with ivy and berries.

Thebai. Head of ivy-crowned and bearded Dionysos. —Rev. Boiotik buckler.

Head of ivy-crowned and bearded Dionysos.—Rev. Kanthar and thyrsos.

Coins, and more especially antonomous coins, present a singularly interesting branch of mythological and historic study. The various types, however apparently strange, were never originally chosen arbitrarily, but, like the names of places, divinities, or animals, had an appropriate history and significance. Arbitrary invention or meaningless application alike belong to a later age, which has theories to support and copies what has become famous. Thus men, ignorant who first colonized Boiotia or founded Eleusis, but possessed of a theory that every place was called after some personage, were compelled to excogitate the fabulous heroes Boiotos and Eleusis. Thus, too, any American village may *apropos* of nothing be named Babylon or Athens, according to caprice. But a real antiquity is free from such blemishes. The Sphinx of Chios or the Gryphon of Teos would be as unimportant as the animals in a child's toy ark did they not contain a meaning and a history which excite curiosity and challenge investigation. Things in themselves signify but little; the reason of their use and existence is alone of real importance. We might as well, like a weary novelist, note down and tabulate the trivialities of daily life, as crowd the brain with facts from antiquity merely regarded as dry facts. What matters it that Apollon had a bow or Athene an owl? Nothing. Who or what is Athene, what does she symbolize or signify, and why and how? This is her only important aspect, and in this respect every recorded detail of her myth, however slight, becomes replete with interest. Reason must consider nothing less than reason; its pabulum should be as god-like as itself. Thus Cause, which is invariably allied with Order, is alone worthy, Chaos alone unworthy, of consideration. Apples fall but one way (cause); did they fall any or every way (chaos) the phenomenon would have been valueless. Apparent chaos is, however, by no means always real, and to extract cause from this is the highest of achievements, the merit rising in proportion with the intricacy. To do this in the world of art is to think as men have thought; to do it in the world of nature is to think as God has thought.

Believing, then, in the truth and certainty of coin-teaching, we find on the Dionysiak Coins mentioned the following eleven symbols used in connection with the god:—The Kist or Chest of the Mysteries, Grape-cluster, Kanthar or Diota, Ivy, Thyrsos, Serpent, Panther, Horns, Rays, a Beard, and Beardlessness. It is evident from them that Dionysos is not merely a wine-god, for what has a wine-god specially to do with ivy or with a beard? It is equally evident that Dionysos is not merely a nature-god or merely a phallic god, for what have such concepts to do with rays? But as all these symbols were considered to be appropriate to the god, his real concept must have included them all. Now divide them between his true

protagonistic phases,[1] and the result is as follows:—
(1) *Theoinos*. Grape-cluster and Kanthar. (2) *Taurokeros*. Horns. (3) *Chrysopes*. Rays. (4) *Erikapeios*. Thyrsos, Panther, Ivy, Beard, Beardlessness. (5) *Zagreus*. Kist and Serpent. Of course some of these symbols harmonize also with other phases of the god besides with those under which they are here classed, but the above arrangement is sufficient for the purpose, and shows to demonstration that the god is vinal, bovine, solar, vital, and chthonian, in the proportions of $\frac{2}{11}$ths, $\frac{1}{11}$th, $\frac{1}{11}$th, $\frac{5}{11}$ths, and $\frac{2}{11}$ths. These proportions, by no means mathematically exact, are yet sufficiently accurate and fairly reflect the facts; we see at a glance that the vinal element is in a small minority, and know that the other four elements blend and change into each other harmoniously. But it may still be objected, as heretofore, that the solar, bovine, and other non-vinal phases of the god were engrafted on a simple earlier cult: an assertion incapable of proof, and to which the facts of the case as unfolded in the enquiry fully reply. Dionysos succeeded in forcing his way into the Aryan Olympos because there was room for him there; yet could he fully obtain in one only of his great aspects as the god of the life-heat and growth-power of nature. The solar seat was filled already, as was the throne of the Under-world; Apollon and Aïdes held their own against the Stranger, and the result of this is that the solar and chthonian and many other aspects of the god are crushed down and overshadowed so that, as was noticed when speaking of the early statues of Dionysos,[2] his phases and cult are frequently attributed to other divinities. Thus, for instance, localities addicted to a solar cult may naturally be connected in idea with Apollon, but the ritual which really prevailed there may have been

---

[1] Vide *inf.* IX.   [2] *Sup.* sec. ii.

frequently that of the Semitic Sun-god. Can it be supposed for an instant that the Apollon of Klaros, whose oracle declared that 'the highest of gods is Iao,' was really identical with the Apollon of Delphoi? We might as well expect to find the Delphik oracle declaring that the highest of gods was Dionysos. The matter is perfectly simple: the Sun-god of Klaros in his Pantheon corresponded with the Sun-god of Delphoi in his. No Hellene of the early ages would ever have considered that Dionysos and Apollon were identical; to him all Sun-gods were Apollon. Comparatively late philosophical enquirers considered this question of identity, but were incorrect in their attempted solution of it. Macrobius practically reasons thus: There is only one Sun; Apollon is the Sun; Liber is the Sun; therefore Apollon is Liber (Dionysos): or in numbers, there is but one Four; 2 and 2 are 4: 3 and 1 are 4: ∴ 2 and 2 are 3 and 1. But they are not; they are only equivalent to 3 and 1; so with respect to solar mythology, the Aryan Apollon is the equivalent of the Semitic Dionysos. These considerations require to be borne in mind, for it may be said: If Dionysos be a solar divinity with widely spread cult, and if coins afford most ancient and truthful representations of Religious-mythology, then we shall naturally meet with numerous numismatic examples of the solar Dionysos. But we do not meet with such; therefore, Dionysos was not solar. The answer to this is, that we should have seen numerous examples of the solar Dionysos had it not been for the brightness of the solar Apollon. However, as already noticed, we have at least one such undoubted example, and one in this case is sufficient; given a few scattered bones, and we can reconstruct the animal. Rhode the Rosy, the warm flush of the sunlight, daughter of Poseidon and Aphrodite, two Phoenician divinities, in the isle of Rhodos, to which she gave her name, bore Helios, the

Sun seven sons, who became the heads of the seven branches of the Heliadai, or Sun-children, its early or earliest inhabitants. Into this portion of the myth it is unnecessary to enter, as the connection between the island and a solar cult is the only point at present under consideration. When Rhodos was overwhelmed with a deluge, Apollon, whom we here first meet with in connection with it, raised it from the waves, and its coins show—

Head of Helios, with flowing locks, generally also with the *caput radiatum*.

Head of Dionysos, above noticed, with ivy and berries, sometimes radiate.

The infant Herakles, strangling two serpents.—Rev. A pomegranate.

Head of Helios, radiate.—Rev. Female, with stole.

Poseidon, at an altar, with trident and dolphin.

Head of Helios.—Rev. Large and small diota.

Head of Helios, with flowing locks.—Rev. Winged sphinx and the special Rhodian flower.

Now all the divinities on these coins, except Poseidon, are solar; and, moreover, are identical and without exception Semitic. The Klarian Oracle declares the identity of the 'one Helios one Dionysos,' and the coins confirm it. Helios is accompanied by the Bakchik kanthar and pomegranate,[1] and Dionysos has the *caput radiatum* of the Sun-god. The snake-entangled Herakles is not the Aryan son of Alkmene, but the Rhodian Herakles, Bouzygos or Yoke-of-oxen, in whose cult two sacred oxen were set apart, one of which was offered up with imprecations: a mode of sacrifice, as Lactantius observes, unknown to the Hellenes, but familiar to the Phoenicians and Egyptians.[2] 'Of the Hercules with whom the Greeks are familiar,' says Herodotos, 'I could hear nothing in any

---

[1] Vide *inf.* VIII. ii. *Pomegranate.* *Place,* iv. 212; Plout. *Peri Is.* lxxiii.
[2] Movers, i. 309; Bunsen, *Egypt's*

part of Egypt.'[1] Because he is a purely Aryan personage, and also has no Kamic counterpart. 'But the Egyptian Hercules is one of their ancient gods. In the wish to get the best information that I could on these matters, I made a voyage to Tyre in Phoenicia, hearing that there was a temple of Hercules at that place, very highly venerated.' The priests told him that the temple, like the city, was 2300 years old. 'In Tyre I remarked another temple where the same god was worshipped as the Thasian Hercules. So I went on to Thasos, where I found a temple of Hercules, which had been built by the Phoenicians who colonised that island when they sailed in search of Europa. Even this was five generations earlier than the time when Hercules, son of Amphitryon, was born in Greece. These researches show plainly that there is an ancient Hercules.'[2] We have already had a glimpse of the 'Tyrian Hercules' in Melikertes, this latter personage, again, being only Dionysos;[3] but in connection with the coins of Rhodos those of Thasos, where, as we have seen, his cult was established,[4] deserve attention. These latter display—

Head of bearded Dionysos, as noticed.—Rev. Herakles, clad in the lion's skin.

Head of Herakles.

Ram-horned head of Dionysos, crowned with ivy and berries.

Here, again, as at Rhodos, we have Herakles and Dionysos together, and the Hellenes have clad the Tyrian divinity in the lion's skin of the son of Alkmene. There is but one god figured on Thasian coins, Dionysos-Melikertes. Eckhel, K. O. Müller, and their followers on the question say that Dionysos is worshipped at a place

[1] Herod. ii. 43.
[2] Ibid. 44.
[3] Sup. VI. i. 2.
[4] 'Herculis cultus in haec insula vetustus fuit, nam Phoenices ei ibi statuisse templum' (Eckhel, Doct. Num. Vet. ii. 52).

because the vine flourishes there, and Eckhel explains the Dionysiak cult of Thasos on this principle, just as he says that *bos* on a coin 'laeta pascua indicat.' Unfortunately for this *simple* explanation of an obscure matter, the ox appears on the coins of places not remarkable for richness of pasturage; Dionysos is found where the vine is absent; and conversely, pastures and vine-districts exist without numismatic oxen or Dionysoi. I, of course, admit that when Dionysos is firmly established as the Wine-god, he is especially revered by vine-growers, as at Maroneia; but this circumstance, whilst illustrating his phase as Theoinos, does not interfere with his other manifestations, and but brief consideration will serve to satisfy us that his cult was introduced at Thasos not by vines, but by Phoenicians. On the Rhodian coins, as on the Thasian, there is but one god figured, Helios-Dionysos-Melikertes. The myth of Herakles strangling the snakes sent to destroy him does not belong to the earlier story of the son of Alkmene, and the snakes which encircle the Sun-god of Rhodos may be the serpents that crown Dionysos. These, according to the Natural Phenomena Theory, are 'the horrid snakes of darkness which seek to destroy their enemy,'[1] the Sun; but this explanation must be looked upon with great suspicion, for (1) the sun comes to the darkness to destroy it, not the darkness to the sun; but the snakes come to the infant Herakles: and (2) serpents, we find, are the creeping light of morning,[2] not the darkness of night. But if a serpent be a symbol of anything which creeps, darkness does not creep but falls. (I do not think the Vedic Vritra the Cloud-concealer, who is also Ahi the strangling snake who binds up the waters which the thirsty earth requires, is a *snake of darkness* principally, for the Cloud-concealer is not a snake, and the binding snake acts by day.) The coins

---

[1] *Mythol. of the Aryan Nations,* ii. 44. [2] *Ibid.* i. 410, ii. 90.

of Rhodos and Thasos thus prove on examination to belong to the Dionysiak cycle; in the former island the strong Semitic element in its mythic history prevents the intrusion of the Aryan Apollon, although it is pre-eminently a solar locality. In Thasos we find Dionysos, as in the Comedy of Aristophanes, concealed beneath the lion-skin of Herakles; but as the garment does not make the man, he is Dionysos still. But the natural question here arises, May not the coins of other localities which bear Herakles and Apollon or their attributes represent in reality the Tyrian Herakles and Helios, or in other words Dionysos-Melikertes? Far be it from me, however, to attempt to overstrain the point. I have too much respect for Apollon and his Aryan kindred to wittingly infringe upon their rightful dominions.

There is one very conspicuous coin-type, the bull, ox, or cow, which demands special notice on account of the numerous points of connection between Dionysos and this animal.[1] Of course, the type might in the abstract appear on coins for reasons unconnected with Dionysos, and each particular instance must therefore be decided on its own merits. The following is a list of some bovine coin-types:—

Akanthos. Lion tearing a bull. The solar heat drying up humidity; or, more broadly, the apparent contest in the material world between the destructive and renewing principles.[2] This is a widely spread type, a circumstance which indicates its highly symbolical nature. It appears, for instance, on ancient Phoeniko-Kilikian coins inscribed with Phoenician characters.[3] The lion is also said to be a symbol of the diurnal, the bull of the nocturnal, sun.

Akarnania. Beardless head, with bull's horns and

---

[1] Vide *inf.* VIII. ii. *Bull;* IX. iii.   [3] Vide sec. iv.; Gem, No. XX.
[2] *Inf.* VIII. ii. *Lion.*

neck.—Rev. Apollon, naked, with the cornucopiae. Akarnania is the land of Karneios, the Horned Sun,[1] but Eckhel truly observes that the 'monstrum biforme in his numis est Achelous,' the largest river in Hellas, and consequently the type of water and humidity in general.[2] And he adds, somewhat too generally, 'Fluvia taurina forma passim fueri efficti.' As to Acheloös, born of Okeanos and Tethys,[3] he fought in bovine form with Herakles for Deianira, but was conquered and had one of his horns broken off, which he recovered by giving up the horn of the Kretan goat Amaltheia, the cornucopia which was ever full. Says Deianira :—

> A river was my suitor—Acheloös.
> In triple form he sought me of my sire:
> Now would he come a bull in all his limbs;[4]
> Anon, a curling, speckled snake; anon,
> Anthropomorphic, with a bovine head.
> From his shaggy beard
> The springs of liquid fountains ever flowed.
>
> Sophokles, *Trach.* 9–14.

The myth forms an appropriate commentary on the coin of Akanthos just noticed. The Sun-god Herakles withers up the humidity of earth and takes away the horn of plenty which belongs to moisture, but the humid principle is only despoiled for a time; he can again receive from and give to the sun fresh treasures, and so the eternal apparent contest, but real harmony, ever con-

---

[1] *Sup.* sec. ii. Cf. Paus. iii. 13.

[2] Cf. Aristoph. *Lysist.* 382. Chor. of Women; 'Thy task, O Acheloös.' (*The women empty their buckets on the men's heads.*)

[3] Some said he was their eldest son, but Hesiodos very properly puts Neilos at the head of the river family (Hes. *Theog.* 340).

[4] Cf. The late imitation of Horatius, *Car.* iv. 14. 'Tauriformis Aufidus.' The sapient Scholiast in Eur *Orest.* 1372 attributes the myth to the roaring of the river waters, as a similar wise man has said that the Humber was so named from its humming sound. As to the supposed bull-roaring of Lake Onchestos, vide *Poseidon,* iv. The passage in *Il.* xxi., where the enraged river Xanthos, to whom many bulls had been offered in accordance with the principle above referred to, rushes at Achilleus, roaring like a bull, is not to the point, for a supernatural and not a natural action of the water is spoken of.

tinues. The son of Semele 'is lord of the whole humid nature,'[1] but at the same time, Sun and Bull, Herakles and Acheloös, are in truth two parts of the 'one stupendous whole,' the kosmic Dionysos.

Amphipolis. The Bull.—Rev. Head of Europe.

Also Europe carried off on the bull: over her head she holds the mystic girdle of love and darkness.[2]

Aspendos. In Pamphilia. Bull, in contorted position. 'In exactly the same attitude and gesture as when fighting with the lion.'[3]

Athenai. Theseus seizing the Minotauros, a bull-headed man, by one horn.

The same subject. Theseus forces the monster to the ground and is about to kill him with a club.[4]

Chalkedon. A Bull.—Rev. Four triangular incuses.

Chersonesos Taurika. Head of the Taurik Artemis.—Rev. Bull.

This so-called Artemis is the female 'reflection' of the Horned-god.[5]

Dyrrhachion. Cow, suckling calf.—Rev. Gardens of Alkinoös.

Euboia. Head of ox. Ox standing. 'Qui typi ad nomen insulae adludunt,' says Eckhel, apparently forgetting his theory about the pastures. Strabo tells us that there was a cave in the island called Boös Aule, or the Cow's Stall, where Io is said to have brought forth Epaphos, and that the island may have had its name of Abounding-in-oxen on that account.[6] The ancients held that it had been originally joined to Boiotia, but separated by an earthquake; the derivation of this latter name may be uncertain, but it probably signifies Ox-land. If an ox be a symbol of rich pastures, it might well be

---

[1] *Sup.* III. i. 1.
[2] Vide *inf.* X. ii.
[3] Knight, *Worship of Priapus*, 71. Vide *sup.* Akanthos.
[4] Vide *inf.* Knosos, IX. iii. *The Minotauros.*
[5] Vide *sup.* VI. i. 1.
[6] Strabo, x. 1.

applied to a region of extraordinary fertility. But, besides, the name is in exact harmony with the cult of the locality, and has reference to the wondrous ox or cow of Kadmos marked with the full moon,[1] and whose very lowing gave a name to cities.[2] This ox led Kadmos through Phokis,[3] the coins of which bear the head of an ox and also the heads of three oxen placed triangularly, and lay down on the site of Thebai; and we learn that 'the Ox is called Theba among the Syrians,'[4] a statement found elsewhere.[5] Epaphos, thus connected with Euboia, is the Hellenik idea of the Kamic Hapi, or Aigyptian Apis, and Io, herself, possibly, Aryan in origin, becomes identified with Uasi or Isis, with whom she so strikingly corresponds. In a word, the cult of the Ox-god as much or more than that of the Vine-god fills Boioto-Euboia from end to end.

Eretia. In Euboia. Ox lying down.—Rev. Two pendent grape-clusters. The type probably refers to the recumbent ox of Kadmos, and the coin presents an admirable illustration of the unity of the Ox-god and the Vine-god, the two being phases of the 'one Dionysos.'

Gela. A Sikelian colony of Rhodians and Kretans. The bearded, human-headed, demi-bull. The demi-ox also occurs on the coins of Korkyra, Syros, and Samos. —The reverse of the coin of Korkyra shows two square altars, a star between them, and on one side the field a grape-cluster, on the other a kanthar. The reverse of the Samian coin bears a lion's head. Two very curious coins, attributed to the Mardians, a Persian tribe,[6] represent a four-winged Janiform personage, one face apparently asleep and the other awake, who holds a globe, disk, or egg, which, in one instance has a bull's head in it. This figure is supported on a kneeling, human-headed demi-bull. The human head denotes man's intelligence

---

[1] Paus. ix. 12. 'It had on each side a mark like the moon' (Schol. in Aristoph. *Bat.* 1256).
[2] Paus. ix. 19.
[3] Ibid. 12.
[4] *Etymol. Magnum*, In voc. *Theba.*
[5] *Schol.* in Lykophron, 1206.
[6] Herod. i. 125.

allied with bovine force, and is frequently found, as on the coins of Neapolis, in Campania; it presents an idea essentially distinct from that of the Minotaŭrik monster. But why is the bull cut asunder, as it were? Demi-animals as coin-types are not uncommon: the demi-dog appears at Karthaia, in the isle of Keos; the demi-gryphon at Phokaia, in Ionia; the demi-stag at Ephesos; the demi-horse at Tanagra; the demi-wolf at Argos. Solar worshippers, *e.g.* the Egyptians, have ever considered the sun under a number of phases, such as the setting, rising, mid-day, diurnal, and nocturnal sun, and investigators into Hellenik symbolism have often concluded, and, I think, with great reason, that the taurik Dionysos is especially connected with the Under-world. Most of the demi-animal types appear to refer to the movements of the heavenly bodies. Take, for instance, the demi-wolf of Argos, a solar emblem;[1] on some coins the demi-wolf is represented as radiate and moving from right to left, *i.e.* from east to west, as Eliktor, the Beaming Sun. On others it is rayless and moves from left to right, that is from west to east, as the nocturnal Sun. The one wolf is divided into two, as the one sun is in thought divided into two;[2] the real unity being exactly shown in another Argeian coin, where a whole wolf stands in the centre between two dolphins, the upper dolphin moving from east to west, the lower one from west to east, and dolphins symbolize the course of sun and stars from the two sea horizons.[3] On one of the demi-bull Gelan coins, in which the bull is moving from west to east, a dolphin appears over him, apparently moving in the same direction. The demi-bull of Samos and of the Mardian coins also is moving eastward, and in the latter coins is beneath the disk-holding winged figure, and I think, therefore, that the

---

[1] Vide *sup.* VI. i. 2.
[2] And so has, or is, two eyes. 'Thy left eye is in the disk at night.
Thy right eye is in the essence' (*Inscription of Darius at El-Khargeh*).
[3] Vide VIII. ii. *Dolphin.*

course of the sun through the Under-world is implied. This is confirmed by the design on the reverse of the Korkyrean coin above mentioned; the one star, the sun, appears between the two altars sacred respectively to the Upper and Under Sun. To the former belongs the grape-cluster ripened by his beams, to the latter the kanthar or golden cup of Helios, in which he sails through the depths of the Under-world.[1] So Herakles, the Sun-god, vanquished Geryon, king of the far west, and the sacred solar oxen swam eastward into Sikelia, like the Gelan bull, and Herakles passed over after them in the cup of the sun.[2] These oxen are not the Vedic cow-clouds, but in one aspect the solar divinity himself, in another the animals sacred and offered to the Sun.[3] The curious episode of the slaughter of the sacred oxen of the Sun by the companions of Odysseus[4] presents a remarkable intertwining of Semitic and Aryan idea. The island Thrinakrie,[5] where it occurred, was always identified by the ancients with the three-cornered Sikelia or Trinakris,[6] which Horatius, in archaic affectation, calls Triquetra.[7] Helios, the lord of the oxen,[8] is just rising when Lampetie, the Dawn-gleam, *stolata* as becomes a solar priestess, hurries to him and tells him of the slaughter of his oxen, which had been done at night while Odysseus was asleep. Raising his eyes to the immortals who possess the wide heaven, Hyperion [9] the Climber exclaims:—

> O father Zeus and other blessed gods who live for aye,
> Upon Odysseus' comrades I invoke revenge to-day;
> For they have insolently slain mine oxen which were given
> To glad my heart when on my path thro' yonder starry heaven,

---

[1] *Sup.* VI. ii. 3.
[2] Paus. iii. 16. The belt of Herakles, when he came back from the West, had 'a golden goblet attached to its clasp' (Herod. iv. 10).
[3] Cf. *inf.* XI. i., the account of Melqarth and his spoil of oxen in the West.
[4] *Od.* xii.
[5] *Ibid.* xi. 107.
[6] Cf. Strabo, vi. 2.
[7] *Sat.* II. vi. 55.
[8] Cf. Apollon Nomios.
[9] *Od.* xii. 374.

And when from heaven to earth I turned, descending at the even.
Now, if they make not recompense for every single head,
I'll sink below to Hades' realm and shine amid the dead.

The idea of the resplendent subterranean sun, which is pre-eminently Kamic, seems to have been not unknown to Homeros, but it is not a feature in his Aryan Neckyomanteion. There was nothing new in the idea of the Sun sinking to the realms of Kerneter, that it did nightly; but that it should sink at morn would indeed be a prodigy. Zeus requests Helios to come on his accustomed path, and promises revenge.[1] The Sun sees all things when in the Upper-world, hears all things when in the Under-world[2] —his sight is not his hearing.

Gortyna. In Krete. Female, sitting in a leafy tree, often an eagle near her.—Rev. a Bull.

Europe[3] carried on the bull.

Female, with eagle, with spread wings.—Rev. Ox, standing.

Histiaia. In Euboia. Ox. Also demi-ox, with grape-cluster.

Ikaria. One of the Sporades, west of Samos. A woman's head.—Rev. a bull's head. The pasturage of the isle was rich,[4] and therefore it may be thought that the principle 'bos laeta pascua indicat' applies. But there was also on the island a temple of Artemis Tauropola, the Horned-goddess,[5] and the coin-type doubtless refers to her cult.

Karystos. In Euboia. Cow, suckling calf.—Rev. A Cock—'the symbol of the Sun, from proclaiming his approach in the morning.'[6]

---

[1] As to the character of the Homerik Helios, vide Gladstone, *Juv. Mundi,* 321 *et seq.*
[2] *Il.* iii. 277; *Od.* xi. 109.
[3] As to Europe, vide *inf.* X. ii.
[4] Strabo, x. 5.
[5] Ibid. xiv. 1.
[6] R. P. Knight, *Worship of Priapus,* 89.

Kleonai. The radiate androkephalic Helios.—Rev. a bull, with lowered head and lifted left foot, in the act of butting. This aspect of the bull also appears on the coins of Thourioi in Lucania. Respecting it Payne Knight remarks that the Demiurge, 'delivering the fructified seeds of things from the restraints of inert matter by his divine strength, is represented on innumerable Greek medals by the Urus, or wild Bull, in the act of butting against the Egg of Chaos, and breaking it with his horns.' He notices that the egg is not represented on the coins, but shows 'that it was no uncommon practice, in these mystic monuments, to make a part of a group represent the whole,' and alludes to examples of the egg shown by D'Hancarville, who gives[1] a specimen of the bull butting against it, while votaries beneath adore his power. The urus or *bos primigenius* existed in Germany even in the sixteenth century.[2]

Knosos. In Krete, another peculiar locality of Boukeros, the Ox-horned god. The Minotauros on one knee, holding a ball or sphere.

The *quadratum incusum* or unwrought square, within which the Labyrinth in the form of cross.

Head of Apollon.—Rev. Circular Labyrinth.

Head of Zeus.—Rev. Square Labyrinth.

The Labyrinth and Minotauros appear on coins of Augustus and Tiberius. The word Labyrinth is Egyptian.[3] The Acheloös, it will be observed, is a man-headed bull, the Minotauros a bull-headed man.[4]

Korkyra. A cow, suckling a calf. Above it the eight-rayed solar star.—Rev. The Gardens of Alkinoös.

A cow, suckling a calf.—Rev. The solar star.

The demi-ox, above noticed.[5]

---

[1] *Arts de la Grèce*, vol. iii. pl. viii.
[2] Lubbock, *Pre-historic Times*, 200.
[3] Bunsen, *Egypt's Place*, ii. 306.
[4] Vide *inf.* IX. iii. *The Minotauros.*
[5] Vide *Gela.*

Head of an ox within a crown. The crown, as noticed, was first worn by Dionysos, according to legend.

Dionysos, on a panther.—Rev. Tailed Satyr, pouring drink from one *diota* into another.

Krete. Europe on the bull. A late coin.

Magnesia. In Lydia. An Ox.

The sun radiate. Other types of the place are Artemis-Ephesia-Polymastos, the Many-breasted, the great goddess-mother of Asia Minor, who has no connection with the ever-virgin sister of Apollon; and Dionysos, with kist, serpent, and ivy-crown.

Metapontion. In southern Italia, a place of almost unknown antiquity, its earlier name being Metabon, which would seem to signify the Changing-Ox. Does this refer to the ever-varying Dionysos-Iao? A bull's head. Also three crescents with four stars. The two devices together may indicate the various aspects of day and night, considered in connection with a taurik demiurge.

Neapolis. In Campania. The human-headed bull.[1]

Olbia. Near the mouth of the Hypanis and the Taurik Chersonesos. A bull's head. The place was a seat of the Sabazios-cult.[2]

Pantikapeion. In the Taurik Chersonesos. Bull's head.

Parion. In Mysia. An Ox statant.

Head of Ox. Other types are fire burning on an altar with a kanthar below. Head of Dionysos. Grape-cluster. Female, *stolata* like the Homerik Lampetie, before an altar. The blazing altar with a kanthar forms an excellent illustration of the combined properties of heat and humidity appropriate to the demiurge.

Pergamos. Head of Ox.[3]

Perinthos. Bull, with solar disk between his horns con-

---

[1] Vide *Gela*.
[2] Vide *sup.* V. ii.
[3] Vide *sup. Pergamos.*

taining a serpent. A late coin and an Egyptian design. Although generally in Kam the solar disk is serpent-encircled, rather than serpent-containing, yet we read in the *Funereal Ritual*: 'I am the Sun. I pierce the darkness. Hidden Reptile is my name. *The soul of my body is a Uraeus.* I return to the western place.'[1] This is the Serpent of Goodness, the Agathodaimon. Among Aigyptian coins we find the crescent-marked bull, with solar disk between his horns, and a garland round his neck, standing before a conical stone, which bears a crescent and a disk.

Phaistos. In Krete. An Ox.

Herakles, with club and lion-skin, near the Hesperian dragon and tree.—Rev. an Ox passant, with feet loosely bound.

Herakles' contest with the Hydra; at his feet a crab.

Two other medals of Herakles,[2] with an Ox on the reverse.

Phokis. Head of Ox.[3]

Three bulls' heads arranged in a triangle.

Phykous. In Kyrenaia (Cyrenaica). An Ox near a palm-tree.

Polyrrhenia. In Krete. Head of an Ox.

Praisos. In Krete. Poseidon, with dolphin and trident. —Rev. Ox.

Priapos. In Mysia. Head of an Ox.

Priene. In Karia. Head of Herakles.—Rev. Bull.

Pylos. In Elis. An Ox passant; below, a dolphin. At the Messenian Pylos bulls, according to Homeros, were sacrificed to Poseidon on a very large scale.[4]

Salamis. In Kypros. Head of an Ox.—Rev. Prow of a ship.

---

[1] *Funereal Ritual,* cap. lxxxv.
[2] As to coin representations of Herakles, vide *sup.* Coins of Rhodos.
[3] Vide *Euboia.*
[4] *Od.* iii. 5.

Samos. A demi-ox.[1]
Sardis. Bull, fighting with lion.[2]
Smyrna. Gibbous bull.
Head of bull beneath crescent moon. Above two suns radiate.
Sybaris. One-horned bull, with head reverted.
Syros. A demi-ox.[3]
Tauromenion. In Sikelia. A bull, butting.[4] This place, which is comparatively modern, being founded about B.C. 358 from the neighbouring Naxos, takes its name from Mount Taurus, an eastern height of the extended chain of the Nebrodes. The Asiatic Taurus chains take their title from the Aramean *Tur*, a height, which is connected with words signifying bull and prince, and it is possible that the name of this Sikelian mountain has been copied from these, or it may simply mean Mount of the Bull; its position as first of the Nebrodes is singular.[5] Types occasionally appear on coins on account of the harmony of name or kind of pun between the type and the locality.
Thourioi. In Lucania. A bull, butting.[6]
Tyros. A bull, behind him a kind of cresset.

The Dionysiak character and connection of, at all events, the majority of these bovine coins is very fairly apparent; but with respect to the coins generally, it may be urged that even the oldest are of comparatively modern date, and that therefore types on them can make no valid pretensions to preserve the ideas and cult of a very high antiquity. If, for instance, it be conceded that Phoenicians, to whom bovine notions in religion were not unfamiliar, colonised Euboia at a remote period, it must not therefore be concluded that because in historic

---

[1] Vide *Gela.*
[2] Vide *Akanthos.*
[3] Vide *Gela.*
[4] Vide *Kleonai.*
[5] Vide *inf.* VIII. i. *Nebrodes.*
[6] Vide *Kleonai.*

times bovine types appear on Euboik coins, they necessarily indicate Phoenician influence. Certainly not; the circumstance considered alone is far from being conclusive on the matter. But in order to arrive at a just opinion, *i.e.* one which duly appreciates the preponderating probability, and gives it proper weight, the following considerations must be carefully noted: (1) The astonishing power of tradition and conservative tenacity of early times, of rural districts, and especially of the East, and of localities impregnated with her influence. (2) The general character of a great number of alleged Dionysiak coins, their connection or disconnection with Bakchik localities, and their harmony or disagreement with the leading features of the general myth. (3) The circumstance that the same or a similar type will continue for hundreds of years on the coins of a particular locality, thereby illustrating the persistence and force of the original idea: and (4) The light thrown upon Hellenik coin-types by the history and religion of other and older civilisations. These considerations make the exact date of any particular coin of not much importance; late types, *i.e.* such as appear after the conquests of Alexandros threw open the world to Hellas, are readily recognisable, and, like the disk-holding bull of Perinthos, generally stand confessed. The following additional coins present further illustrations of the Myth:—

Abdera. A gryphon sejant or couchant. The type brought from Teos.[1]

Aigai. In Aiolis. A tower-crowned, female, winged figure.

Antiochia. In Syria. A double-headed *herma*.[2] Near it the caduceus.

Apion. In Kyrenaia. A horned, beardless head. 'Ammonis cornu munitum.'

---

[1] Vide *inf. Teos.* [2] Vide *sup.* sec. ii.

Arados (Arvad). The six-rayed solar star.—Rev. a palm-tree.

Poseidon, holding a dolphin and trident.

The horned Astarte.—Rev. a Bull salient.

Helios, with radiate crown.

The tower-crowned goddess of the East.—Rev. Cornucopia. A Phoenician coin.

Askalon. Two terminal figures, with conical caps.

Helios, with radiate crown.—Rev. Prow of galley.

Tower-crowned female.—Rev. Double-prowed galley.

Assos. A gryphon rampant.[1]

Athenai. Janiform head, male and female. Attributed in local legend to Kekrops the mythic first king of Attike, who is said to have instituted marriage, and to have been half-man, half-serpent, and to whom the Dionysiak epithet of Diphues, the Two-natured, is applied.[2]

Hephaistos, with tongs.—Rev. Two torches. The Lampadephoria was a torch-race at Athenai performed in his honour at the Hephaisteia.

Automala. In Kyrenaia. Beardless ram-horned head. —Rev. Herma.

Barke. In Kyrenaia. Youthful head, with the 'cornu Ammonis.'

Head of Zeus-Ammon (Amen) within beaded circle.

Boiotia. Kanthar.—Rev. Boiotik buckler.

Chalkedon. Beardless male head.—Rev. Ivy-leaf, between four spokes of a wheel.

Wheel, with twelve spokes and a disk or globe in the centre.—Rev. Four triangular incuses.

The bull, as noticed, appears on coins of this place, and, combined with the ivy-leaf, makes certain the very interesting Dionysiak import of the four-spoked wheel or revolving seasons, and the twelve-spoked wheel or months and signs of the year, through which the sun passes and which surround the earth.

[1] Vide *Teos.* [2] Vide *inf.* VIII. i. *Diphues.*

Chalkis. There were several cities of this name, the two principal being Chalkis in Euboia and Chalkis in Syria. Eckhel gives as a coin of the former :(?) Head of Poseidon, with trident.—Rev. Double-columned temple, in which a conical stone. This is a purely Phoenician design. A coin of Chalkis in Syria bears : Bearded male head.—Rev. 'Pyramidal symbol of Astarte in a shrine.' A phallic column.[1]

Chios. Demi-lion, open-mouthed.—Rev. Winged androsphinx.

Winged androsphinx before amphora, above which a grape-cluster.—Rev. The banded *quadratum incusum*.

Sphinx and grapes in dotted circle.—Rev. Wine-jar and cornucopiae in dotted circle.

Sphinx and grapes.—Rev. Wine-jar, with solar star and crescent in the field.

Sphinx, with foot raised on prow of ship.—Rev. Two paten-bearing male figures on each side of an altar. Many similar types and combinations of sphinx, grapes, wine-jar, star, ear of corn, and prow of ship appear on other coins of the place.

When speaking of the Theban Sphinx, Mr. Cox observes, ' Neither the name nor the figures of the Hellenic sphinx have been borrowed from Egypt. The Egyptian sphinx *is never winged*, and is never represented except as prone and recumbent, or *in any form except that of a lion with a human head* and bust.'[2] So far as the name is concerned I agree with him; a sphinx in Egyptian is *akr*, *the* Sphinx Hu ; but the other statements are incorrect. Thus Sir G. Wilkinson remarks: 'The winged sphinx is rare in Egypt; but a few solitary instances occur of it on the monuments and on scarabaei ; as well as of the hawk-headed sphinx, which is winged.' Again he says: 'There were also the criosphinx, with the head of a ram ;

[1] Vide *sup.* sec. ii.   ii. 344-5.
[2] *Mythol. of the Aryan Nations,*

the hieracosphinx, with that of a hawk.'[1] 'The winged Greek sphinxes, so common on Vases, are partly Egyptian, *partly Phoenician*, in their character, the recurved tips of the wings being *evidently taken from those of Astarte.*'[2]

Ephesos. Bee.—Rev. *Quadratum incusum.* Philostratus has preserved a late fiction, perhaps his own invention, that the Muses, in the form of bees, led the Hellenik colonists to Ephesos.[3] This explanation, which explains nothing, affords a good instance of the worthlessness of arbitrary interpretations.

Bee in dotted circle.—Rev. Demi-stag couchant; behind it, palm-tree.

Bee in dotted circle.—Rev. Infant Herakles strangling serpents, as at Samos and Rhodos.

Serpent emerging from kist, the whole surrounded with ivy-wreath.

The same.—Rev. Two serpents twisted round a quiver, between their heads a bee; in the field a torch with cup and handle.

Artemis, with arrow, bow, and dog.—Rev. A cock with palm-branch, from which a crown pendent.

Draped Dionysos, in right hand kanthar, standing on kist between serpents. Temp. Antonius.

Artemis-Ephesia-Polymastos. Numerous examples. A terminal figure sometimes with the *caput radiatum*, stag and bow. Sometimes the sun and moon in the field, and at her side the horned seistron-bearing Uasi. The hands of the goddess generally supported on tridents or on many-jointed rods; she is sometimes winged.

As has been well observed, the crabs, oxen, bulls, lions, gryphons, stags, sphinxes, bees, trees, roses, and other emblems on the goddess, according to the Hellenik inscription, assist in representing 'all-varied Nature, mother

---

[1] Vide figures in Rawlinson's *Herodotus*, ii. 224-5.
[2] Rawlinson, *Herodotus*, ii. 220.
[3] *Eikones*, ii. 8.

of all things.' But each emblem has also its special meaning and appropriateness. Montfaucon gives a representation of the goddess, in which her peculiar body-covering is adorned only with bees and roses.[1] The bee-type also appears on coins of Keos[2] in connection with the cult of Aristaios,[3] a deified personage, according to one account son of Heaven and Earth, but more generally described as the son of Apollon and the Libyan nymph Kyrene, *i.e.*, Ku-Re-Ne, or Horn;[4] and the country being thus within the sway of horned divinities, the coins of Kyrenaia constantly represent the ram-horned head of Amen both bearded and beardless. Aristaios, therefore, springs from the Horned-sun, and he is further linked with Phoenician associations, as he is said to have lived at Thebai and married Autonoe, daughter of Kadmos. He taught men to keep bees, and was a fostering and beneficent protector of flocks and herds and the fruits of the earth. The bee is especially connected with the happy, peaceful earth-life. Speaking of Ephesia, Müller observes: 'Everything that is related of this deity *is singular and foreign to the Greeks.*' Doubtless,[5] 'Her constant symbol is the bee, *which is not otherwise attributed to Diana* [Artemis]. The bee appears originally to have been the symbol of nourishment; the chief priest himself was called Essen [as if akin to *hesmos*, a swarm of bees?],[6] or the King-bee.'[7] The term 'bees' was also specially applied to the priestesses of Demeter the Aryan, and Ephesia the Semitic, Earth-mother.[8] On a gem,[9] a lion appears surmounted by the eight-rayed solar star and swallowing a bee. Another gem[10] represents the same

---

[1] Montf. i. Pt. i. Pl. xcvi. fig. 1.
[2] Ibid. iii. Pt. i. pl. cxvii. fig. 3.
[3] Cf. Apollon. *Argonaut.* ii. 500; Cic. *De Divinat.* i. 57.
[4] Vide *inf.* IX. iii. *Kronos.*
[5] Vide *inf.* IX. iii. *Ephesia Polymastos.*
[6] Liddell and Scott. In voc.
[7] *Doric Race,* i. 403-4.
[8] Cf. Creuzer, *Symbolik,* iii. 354; iv. 382.
[9] Montf. ii. Pt. ii. Pl. cxlviii. fig. 5.
[10] Ibid. fig. 6.

subject,[1] but around the lion are seven stars, each surrounded with six letters. In all cases the head of the bee is in the lion's mouth; but as the Hebrew root *dbr* can be connected with words signifying 'word' and 'bee,'[2] it has been suggested that the meaning of this mystic design is to illustrate the Word of truth proceeding out of the mouth of the solar-leonine divinity. Had the bee been represented as coming out of the lion's mouth instead of going into it, there would have been more to say in favour of this view; but the ancient symbolists were very careful in matters of detail: and, as it is, the idea suggested is rather that of the burning sun, Athamas, consuming the nourishing vegetation of the earth, whose happy voice is uplifted in the ' murmuring of innumerable bees.'

Gaulos. An island near Melite. The terminal Uasar, with whip and crook; on each side a horned and disk-crowned figure with branch adoring.[3]

A bee within a laurel wreath.

A ram's head. All Phoenician coins.

Hephaistia. The chief town of Lemnos. Diademate, beardless male head.—Rev. Ram, in front torch with cup and handle.

Rev. Owl and tongs of Hephaistos.

Herakleia. In Kyrenaia. Head of Ammon.

Hierapytna. In Krete. Turreted female head. The solar star.—Rev. A palm-tree.

Histiaia. In Euboia. Female seated on prow, sometimes with the star, bird, or trident.

Ioulis. A city of Keos. Head of Zeus.—Rev. Bee.[4]

Bearded Dionysos.—Rev. Grapes.

Female head.—Rev. Grapes.

---

[1] Another representation is given in Hyde, *De Vet. Rel. Per.* 113.
[2] Cf. *Deborah.*
[3] Vide *Melite.*
[4] Vide *Ephesos.*

Issa. An island in the Adriatic, off Dalmatia. Grape-cluster.—Rev. Kanthar.

Jewish coins. Cup.—Rev. Branch.

Palm-tree.—Rev. Vine-leaf.

Sheaf of corn.—Rev. Palm-tree.

Lyre.—Rev. Grape-cluster.

Juba I., King of Numidia, ob. B.C. 46. Head of Ammon.—Rev. Elephant.

Bearded head, surrounded with dot-circle.—Rev. Grape-cluster within crown.

Juba II., King of Numidia and afterwards of Mauretania, ob. A D. 19. Bearded head.—Rev. Grape-cluster and six-rayed solar star. A frequent type.

Karthaia. A town in the isle of Keos. As the name shows, the site of a Phoenician factory.[1]

Head of Zeus.—Rev. Demi-hound radiate.

Head of Apollon.—Rev. Demi-hound radiate and bee.

Head of Apollon.—Rev. Eight-rayed star.

The hound and star represent the Dog-star so honoured and important in Phoenician and Kamic cults.

Keos. Similar types. Also grapes.

Kilikia. Lion devouring a stag.[2]

Herakles, with raised club.—Rev. Lion devouring stag.

Naked male demi-figure, with crown, and apparently a phallic emblem; below, the winged disk, as in representations of the Assyrian Assur and the Persian Ormuzd (Ahura-Mazda).

King combating monster. An Assyrian and Persian subject.—Rev. Cow, suckling calf.

Naked figure holding up a wild beast by the tail, apparently in the Bakchik phrensy.—Rev. Sheep suckling lamb.

Gryphon, devouring stag.

---

[1] Vide VI. i. 2. In voc. *Melikertes.* [2] Vide *Akanthos.*

Man riding over the waves on the fish-tailed goat.
—Rev. An owl, type of night,[1] with Uasarjan whip and crook.

A he-goat upright, with legs bent under it.

The above are Phoenician coins of the time of the Persian Empire.[2]

Korinthos. On the very numerous coins of this city are found, amongst other types and symbols:—

Thyrsos with pendent ribbons, ivy-wreath, pine-cone, pomegranate, head of gryphon, the Rhodian flower, the cock, radiate head of the Sun, the Chimaira, trident and dolphin. Also, the infant Palaimon, lying on a dolphin by a fir-tree. Two different types.

Palaimon, standing on dolphin.[3]

Korkyra. Rudder with star above.—Rev. Head of trident.

Diota.—Rev. Circular incuse.

Diota, ivy-leaf in field.—Rev. Eight-rayed star.

Prow.—Rev. Kanthar, with grapes above.

Numerous coins and variations of types.

Kossyra. A small island between Sikelia and Libye. The protagonistic type of the Phoenician coins of Kossyra is described by Gesenius as a 'Cabirus or Pataecus, *i.e.*, a deformed dwarf holding a hammer in his right hand and a serpent in his left, on his head three horns, or adorned with rays.' There are eleven types of this figure, who is generally surrounded with a dotted circle. The number of rays is either seven or eight.[4]

Kydonia. In Krete. Dog recumbent.

Star and moon. The Dog-star, Kuon-Seirios[5] or Sirius the Scorching, the Aigyptian Sothis, *i.e.*, Set (Typhon), the tutelary god of the Dog-star.[6]

---

[1] Lat. *noctua.*
[2] As to other Kilikian coins, vide *Soloi* and *Tarsos.*
[3] Vide *sup.* VI. i. 2.
[4] Vide *inf.* X. i.
[5] Ais. *Ag.* 967.
[6] Vide *Karthaia.*

Kypros. The protagonistic type of the Kypriot coins is the temple of Astarte or Aphrodite Ouranie, with the conical symbol, phallic columns, dove and crescent moon.

Lampsakos. Janiform head; under the neck a dolphin.

Bearded head of Poseidon.—Rev. Winged demi-hare.

Malaka, a Phoenician settlement in Baetica. Kabirik head, helmed and bearded, near it the fire-tongs of Hephaistos.—Rev. Bearless solar head, radiate and wreath-crowned. A Phoenician coin.

Mardoi. A four-winged Janiform personage, above noticed.[1] This Being, at once awake and asleep, is the realisation of the four-winged, four-eyed Kronos of Sanchouniathon, who saw when he slept and slept when he saw, flew when he rested and rested when he flew.[2] Symbol of the tireless energy of the Deity.

A winged, horned, and bearded goat.—Rev. The Triquetra.

A winged 'animal mihi ignotum,' said by some to be a tiger.—Rev. The Triquetra.

Two demi-bulls addorsed; above, the Triquetra.—Rev. The Triquetra.[3]

Melite (Malta). Terminal Uasar, with crook, whip, and two adorers, who are sometimes winged and triple-horned, have the legs and feet of oxen, and hold a canopy over him. Five types.[4]

Four-winged, semi-recumbent figure, with whip and crook, sometimes *mitrephoros*. Five types.[5]

Melos. Pomegranate.—Rev. Kanthar, with grapes pendent.

Pomegranate in linear circle.—Rev. Grapes in linear circle. A constant type. Melos was a Phoenician colony, and the pomegranate is sometimes called the 'malum Punicum.'[6]

---

[1] Vide *Gela.*
[2] San. i. 7.
[3] Vide *Sikelia.*
[4] Vide *Gaulos.*
[5] Vide *Mardoi.*
[6] Vide *inf.* VIII. ii. *Apples of Dionysos.*

Miletos. Head of lion with open mouth; above, a star. Lion looking back at star.—Rev. Eight-rayed star.

Mytilene. Two heads of hornless oxen, opposed. Lion's head, with open mouth and protruded tongue. Radiate solar head.

Horned head.—Rev. Bearded figure, ivy-crowned, standing on prow; in the field, grapes, with vine-branch and leaf.

Panormos. In Sikelia. Horned head, surrounded by dolphins.—Rev. Horse-head. The latter a frequent type. Also horse and palm-tree, lion and palm-tree, and palm alone. A Phoenician colony. The above are Phoenician coins.

Pantikapeion. Lion's head. Brought from its metropolis, Miletos.

Horned gryphon and demi-gryphon.[1]

Parthia. The Parthian kings, with turreted or solar-spiked crown bearing the pomegranate or globe on it.—Rev. A fire-bearing altar, generally of columnar form, with a votary on either side wearing a triple-horned or spiked cap or crown.

Persis. King combating a lion.—Rev. Galley, or battlemented city, with two lions addorsed. A Persian coin.

Ram's head.—Rev. Ram couchant within dotted circle.

Ram couchant, beneath its head a circle with cross pendent.—Rev. Dot-encircled circle with cross below, the whole within a quadratum. The two latter coins bear Persic characters.

Head of goddess called the Persic Artemis.[2]—Rev. Fire-bearing altar. The cows sacred to the goddess ranged at large, branded with a torch.

Phallic Coin types. These occasionally occur. Thus, for instance, 'it appears that the act of generation was a sort of sacrament in the island of Lesbos; for the device

---

[1] *Sup.* sec. i. Vase No. XIV.   [2] Vide Ploutarchos, *Lucullus*.

on its medals (which in the Greek Republics had always some relation to religion) is as explicit as forms can make it. The figures appear indeed to be mystic and allegorical, the male having a mixture of the goat in his beard and features, and probably represents the generative power of the universe, incorporated in universal nature. The female has all that breadth and fullness which characterise the personification of the passive power.'[1]

Phokaia. A demi-gryphon volant.

Sabrata or *Abrotnon.* A Phoenician settlement in the Regio Syrtica. Horned and fish-tailed sea-goat, dot-encircled, and with globe and cornucopia.

Sardis. Serpent emerging from kist, the whole within ivy-wreath.—Rev. Two serpents, with tails entwined around a decorated bow-case.

Sidon. Turreted female head.—Rev. Double-prowed galley. Some of the Kamic galley-types are similar.

Sikelia. One of the Sikelian emblems is the device called the Triquetra, which here takes the form of three legs issuing from a central head or circle, which in one instance is in the centre of the body of a bird. The Triquetra in the same form is also found on Etruscan coins, and the three legs appear on a coin of Aspendos, in Pamphylia, without any central circle. The Triquetra in its simpler form, *i.e.*, three crescent semi-circles emerging from a central circle, appears on a coin of Telmessos, in Lykia. These and other instances show that its signification, which is chiefly lunar, is not explained by the shape of Sikelia.[2]

Smyrna. Turreted female.—Rev. Gryphon erect, with fore-paw on wheel. The wheel is connected with time,[3] and the gryphon with the Sun.[4] A lamp, engraved

---

[1] *Worship of Priapus*, 105.
[2] Vide *Gela. Mardoi.*
[3] Vide *sup. Chalkedon.*
[4] Vide *inf. Teos.*

in Montfaucon,[1] shows the winged gryphon with one paw on the solar wheel.

Soloi. In Kilikia. Head of Pallas, with gryphon on shield.—Rev. Grape-cluster within quadratum.

Head of radiate Sun.—Rev. Pomegranate.

Syros. Radiate, bearded head.—Rev. Kanthar and goat.

Tarsos. Zeus Tarsios, enthroned.—Rev. Lion.

Herma between two animals.

Turreted female head. A constant type, as nearly all over Asia Minor the tower-bearing Great Goddess was, Demeter-like, associated with Civilisation, here expressed by the walls of the cities.

Tenedos. Two Janiform heads bearded and beardless.—Rev. Double-edged axe,[2] owl, and grapes, all in wreath.

Tenos. Youthful male head, laureate, with flowing tresses and horn round ear.—Rev. Poseidon, with dolphin and trident; in the field, the Rhodian flower.

Same type.—Rev. Grapes, in the field, trident.

Teos. Gryphon, with wings addorsed, open mouth, protruded tongue, and raised left paw; in the field, grapes and vine-branch.

Gryphon couchant.—Rev. Diota.

Gryphon passant.—Rev. Two lions in ivy-wreath.

Gryphon courant.—Rev. Triple-chord lyre, each side terminating in head of swan.

Beardless male head.—Rev. Lyre.

Teos, birthplace of the Dionysiak Anakreon, was renowned for its magnificent temple of Dionysos. 'The gryphon,' observes Col. Leake, 'was a type of the Sun or Apollo, but as Apollo [*i.e.*, the Sun-god] *was sometimes identified with Bacchus*, and in Asia Minor has generally the same feminine countenance, with long hair in ringlets,

[1] V. Pt. ii. Pl. clxii. fig. 2.   [2] Vide *sup.* sec. i. Vase No. XIII.

and distinguished only by the garland of ivy instead of bay, it is not surprising to find the gryphon on the coins of a city where Bacchus was held in the highest honour.' The above passage is very instructive, and not the less so because the learned author, whose works are models of their kind, does not sufficiently distinguish between Aryan and Semitic solar-studies. There is no original connection between Apollon and the Gryphon, nor is Apollon by any means merely the Sun; but we learn that the Gryphon is a solar type, and is found as the protagonistic type on the coins of a place specially devoted to the cult of Dionysos.[1] Apollon was not identified with Dionysos until later times, but Helios, the Sun, undoubtedly was; and the similarity of the features of Helios-Apollon and Dionysos affords an excellent illustration of the circumstance already noticed, that the overpowering influence of the Aryan Sun-god in Hellenik regions frequently threw his name over other and foreign divinities of a solar character. According to Philostratus, Apollonios of Tyana, on his return from India, 'described the gold-digging griffins; that they were *sacred to the Sun* (*his chariot is represented as drawn by them*), about the size of lions, but stronger because winged; that their wings were a reddish membrane, and hence their flight was low and spiral; and that they overpowered lions, elephants and dragons.'[2]

Thasos. Janiform head.—Rev. Two diotae.
Also bearded Herakles, wine-jar, and dolphin.
Thebai. Boiotik shield, a constant type.—Rev. Diota.
Thera. Veiled female head.
Head of bearded Herakles in lion's scalp.
Tyros. Beardless laureate head of Herakles.
Radiate head of Antiochos IV.—Rev. Galley.
Veiled and turreted female head.—Rev. Astarte on galley, holding crook and staff surmounted with cross.

[1] Vide *sup.* sec. i. Vase No. XIV. [2] Priaulx, *Apollonius of Tyana,* 52–3.

Palm-tree, with fruit.

Tree, between two rounded conical phallic pillar-stones.

Tree, with serpents round trunk, between two rounded conical stones.

Serpent twined around kosmic egg; in the field, palm-tree on the right, shell on the left.

I shall lastly notice the types of some of the Etrusco-Roman coins which are more or less illustrative of the Dionysiak Myth:—

I. Janiform head, with peaked cap.—Rev. Club, sometimes with crescent moon and several balls or globes.

II. The crescent moon pointing downwards, with a star at each of the cardinal points.—Rev. The radiate sun. Night and Day: the former the mother of the latter, as in Hesiodos, Sanchouniathon, Berosos, Moses, and other kosmogonists.

III. Grape-cluster.

IV. Cornucopia.—Rev. Fire-tongs; in the field, four globules.

V. Cornucopia and crescent moon.

VI. Club.—Rev. Diota.

VII. Cornucopia piled up with fruit and ear of wheat; in the field, grape-cluster and vine-leaf.

VIII. Conical-shaped object, possibly a spear-head.—Rev. Kanthar.

IX. Dormant animal, apparently a wolf, below crescent moon.—Rev. Trichord lyre and crescent moon.

X. Trident-head.—Rev. Bee.

XI. Thunderbolt, composed of two crescents addorsed, double-headed arrow and double zigzag lines; in the field, four globules.—Rev. Dolphin; below, four globules.

XII. Bearded Janiform head, with string of globules round the brows.—Rev. Prow of ship. A frequent type.

XIII. Globule-crowned, winged male figure in stole, with serpents twined round the arms.

XIV. Scallop-shell.—Rev. Diota.

XV. Wheel, with six divisions and globe in the centre.

XVI. Wheel, apparently representing the six-rayed solar star.—Rev. Hammer-head, with crescent in the field.

XVII. Two crescents addorsed, within each an eight-rayed star.

XVIII. The Triquetra, a ball by each foot.[1]

XIX. Lion's head, statant, with sword through the jaws.

XX. Solar wheel.[2]—Rev. Amphora.

XXI. Crescent, above eight-rayed star, below four globules.

XXII. Three crescents with globe in the centre, all within double circles, outside which, six globules.

XXIII. Shell from which dye was extracted.—Rev. Radiate globule, apparently representing the points of the compass.

XXIV. Radiate human-headed Helios.

XXV. An owl, type of Night,[3] between two globules.

XXVI. Head of Herakles, with the lion's skin as a head-covering.—Rev. Fine head of horned gryphon.[4]

XXVII. Head of bull.—Rev. Prow of ship.

XXVIII. The branch or tree stock.[5]

XXIX. Head of Herakles, with lion's skin as cap.—Rev. Horse salient; above, the eight-rayed solar star.

As we proceed in the investigation, the Myth, in itself one of almost unparalleled intricacy, becomes clearer, and from amorphousness begins to shape itself into order.

---

[1] Vide *sup. Sikelia.*
[2] Vide No. XVI.; *sup. Smyrna.*
[3] Vide *sup. Kilikia.*
[4] Vide *sup. Teos.*
[5] Vide *sup. Tyros.*

The coins, although almost infinite in variety, yet present constantly recurring types and such as illustrate the protagonistic features of this complex divinity. The reader will probably have no great difficulty in apprehending their general, and applying their special, Dionysiak significance in accordance with the previous illustrations.

An individual historian may be partial, prejudiced, ignorant, or otherwise incredible; coins, and more especially autonomous coins, present history supported by the testimony of countless witnesses, and hence their peculiar value as assistants in the investigation of the Past.

SECTION IV.

DIONYSIAK GEMS.

Dionysos, as he appears on gems, next demands attention. The specimens Nos. I.–XXXVII. are amongst those given in Mr. C. W. King's valuable work, *Antique Gems and Rings*, vol. ii. Many of these and similar subjects appear in the works of Montfaucon, Caylus, D'Hancarville, Payne, Knight, Eckhel, Worlidge, Creuzer, and others, but those here noticed are sufficient for the present purpose.

I. Dionysos, and, according to Mr. King, 'the original type of this divinity,' attired in the long saffron-coloured robe or *krokotis*, bearing a thyrsos in his right hand and the kanthar in his left, bearded and filleted. The fillet represents the solar crown or disk, and the beard the streaming rays. He moves from east to west, holding out before him his golden cup, in which he is to embark on the Western ocean; behind his back, and hanging down from the thyrsos-staff, is the robe of night which, at times appears resplendent with stars above the heads of nocturnal divinities, such as the goddess Night and Artemis-Selene, Diana-Luna.[1] His *krokotis* is the *krokopeplos* of the light-divinity, the Homerik attire of Eos-Aurora.

II. Naked, youthful Dionysos, with bunch of grapes and cup; near him a torch set in the ground referring 'to his nocturnal mysteries.' Here, as the Sun of the Under-world, he is going from west to east, holding out his cup as before.

III. Youthful Dionysos, with grape-cluster and thyrsos, gazing at the reflection of his face in the liquid in a kanthar. The pantheistic divinity 'sees himself in all he sees.'

IV. Naked, youthful Dionysos, in car drawn by two panthers.[2]

V. Drunken, hoofed and tailed Satyr, reclining on the ground grasping diota; he has the peculiar Assyrian type of beard, huge ears and brutish features, but is without horns. In the field, a large and handsome krater. 'Archaic Greek work of uncommon merit.' The treatment of the beard is remarkable, and its form closely corresponds with that ascribed to Izdubar.

VI. An obese Seilenos with four very small horns of the Assyrian type, nursing the infant Dionysos, who holds the thyrsos and grape-cluster.

VII. Beautiful, ivy-crowned head of a Bakche.

VIII. Head of excited Bakche, ivy and grape-crowned. She carries the thyrsos, the knob of which is formed of grapes.

IX. Seilenos, ivy-crowned, 'which is the sole distinction between his head and the portrait of Sokrates.'

X. Two tailed but hornless Seilenoi sacrificing a goat over a blazing altar. Holding it by the legs, they are just about to cut it in two.

---

[1] Cf. Montf. i. Pt. i. Pl. xci. fig. 1; xcii. fig. 4.; Pt. ii., Pl. ccxiv. fig. 1. [2] Vide *inf*. VIII. ii. *Panther*.

XI. Agaue in the Bakchik phrensy. Her head thrown back, hair streaming wildly, and garments fluttering in the wind.

XII. Head of Ariadne, ivy-crowned; a fawn-skin round the neck.

XIII. Faun, bearing grape-cluster and thyrsos, dancing with panther-skin on his arm. At his feet an overturned amphora.

XIV. Bakche looking into the mystic kist, out of which a serpent rises; near her a naked male figure, and behind her the *arbor vitae*.

XV. Satyr dancing for a prize against he-goat.

XVI. A winged andro-lion, 'perhaps Dionysos Leontomorphos,' with branch in right hand and large kanthar in left. 'An exquisite Greek work of the best period.'[1]

XVII. Bakchik mask, bearded and crowned with vine-leaves, and with ram's horns spreading in the Kamic fashion. 'A work,' observes Mr. King, 'superior to anything known to me in this class.'

XVIII. Boy bearing a goat to the altar of Dionysos for sacrifice.

XIX. Korinthian krater, embossed with a Bakchik procession: boy on goat led by another boy.

XX. Lion overcoming a bull. 'The *technique* of this intaglio is altogether Assyrian, and the subject justifies the conclusion that it is of Phoenician workmanship.'[2]

XXI. The Dionysiak bull, 'or rather the god himself, in the form of his own attribute.' The bull raises his right forefoot and lowers his head as if to butt; he stands upon the thyrsos, and his body is encircled with an ivy-wreath.[3]

XXII. Bull and two goats near tree. The bull lowers his head and raises his left foot; one goat standing

---

[1] Vide *Inf.* VIII. ii. *Lion.*
[2] Vide *sup.* sec. iii. *Akanthos.*
[3] Vide *sup.* sec. iii. *Kleonai*; *inf.* IX. iii. *Taurokeros.*

on its hind legs reaches upwards towards the foliage of the tree.¹

XXIII. Two gryphons devouring a stag.

XXIV. Gryphon of Apollon holding his lyre; behind, the oracular raven.²

XXV. Sphinx couchant. 'A work apparently of Asiatic Greek origin.'³

XXVI. Sphinx sedent.⁴

XXVII. Harpy between two gryphons, apparently adoring, like the Kamic ape.

XXVIII. Winged divinity between a sphinx and spotted leopard, holding a paw of each. 'Rilievo in gold, forming the face of an Etruscan ring.' The design of the wings is purely Phoenician.⁵

XXIX. The horned Zeus Ammon. 'Early Greek engraving, probably of Cyrenian workmanship.' The Roman province of Africa is also often represented as a horned female.

XXX. Conjoined heads of Dionysos and Poseidon in the Janiform type, their symbols forming a phallic talisman. A gem well illustrating their original Semitic connection.

XXXI. Double-bodied sphinx.

XXXII. Triquetric head.⁶

XXXIII. The horned and rayed Serapis.⁷

The following Gnostic gems also are connected with various ramifications of the Dionysiak Myth:—

XXXIV. The Gnostic divinity Abraxas with the head of a cock, the solar bird,⁸ the whip of Uasar in his right hand, a round shield in his left, and serpents instead of

---

¹ Cf. No. XIV.
² As to the solar gryphon, vide *sup.* sec. iii. *Teos.*
³ Vide No. XXIV.
⁴ Vide *sup.* sec. iii. *Chios.*
⁵ Vide *Ibid.*
⁶ As to the Triquetra, Vide *sup.* sec. iii. *Mardoi* and *Sikelia.*
⁷ Vide *inf.* IX. iii. *Serapis.*
⁸ 'They say that this bird is sacred to Helios, and that it announces by its crowing the rising of the sun' (Paus. v. 25). Vide *sup.* sec. iii. *Karystos.*

legs. He is placed over the car of the Sun-god, and the four horses, salient, stand two on either side; in the field are the sun and moon; below is his name ΙΑΒΑW, Sabas or Sabaoth. 'The reverse bears his name Iao-Abraxas, contained in a cartouche formed by a coiled serpent.'[1] Abraxas, or rather Abrasax, which latter is the more correct form, appears to signify in Coptic 'Holy name.'[2] A Hebrew derivation, Ab-rahak, 'fallen spirit,' has also been suggested.[3] Mr. King quotes S. Jerome in his commentary on *Amos III.* showing that Abraxas was the Sun-god, and he is at times styled the 'Eternal Sun.' In this Mansel agrees, observing 'there can be no doubt that the personified Abraxas was meant as a symbol of the Sun.'[4] Abraxas is a comparatively modern and Mithraik representation of the Iao-Uasar-Dionysos or kosmogonical Sun-god.

XXXV. The ass-headed Abraxas, with shield in right hand and dagger in the left.[5]

XXXVI. The leonto-kephalic Serpent, its head encircled with nine rays above an altar, with the inscription, 'I am Chnoubis the Eternal Sun.'[6]

XXXVII. Leonto-kephalic human figure, holding a serpent in the right hand, and a 'lustral vase' in the left, its head crowned with the solar sphere and apparently horned. 'Inscribed on the reverse with ΦPHN [*i.e.* 'Pera, le Soleil, *phra*,'[7]], Egyptian name of the sun.'

XXXVIII. Leonto-kephalic serpent Chnuphis-Abraxas, erect, with the seven-rayed nimbus.[8] Montfaucon gives nearly twenty varieties of this familiar type.

XXXIX. Radiate solar serpent, holding phallic club or

---

[1] Vide *sup.* V. ii.; *inf.* VIII. i. Sabazios.
[2] King, *The Gnostics and their Remains*, 80.
[3] S. M. Drach, *apud* W. R. Cooper, *Serpent Myths of Ancient Egypt*, 71.
[4] *Gnostic Heresies*, 153.
[5] Vide *inf.* VIII. ii. *Ass.*
[6] Vide No. XXXVIII.
[7] Chabas.
[8] Cooper, *Serpent Myths of Anct. Egypt*. Fig. 122. Vide *inf.* IX. iii. *Khnum*; VIII. ii. *Lion. Serpent.*

tree, and erect, on wheel,¹ a solar emblem.² The radiate solar serpent also appears before a blazing altar on a coin said to be Phoenician.³

XL. Leonto-kephalic serpent, erect, his head surrounded by a nimbus, from which stream seven rays.⁴

Into the abyss of Gnosticism it is unnecessary here to plunge. Its chief constituents and formative elements were:—(1) The religion of the Euphrates Valley, as reflected in the Phoiniko-Aramaic systems. (2) The Kamic system. (3) Judaism. (4) Medo-Persic ideas, tinctured also with importations from India and the far East. (5) Neo-Platonism; and (6) Christianity. A partial fusion of these heterogeneous ingredients, in unequal proportions, like parts of different animals joined together in a single form, produced a symbolic monster and a corresponding creed. The chief features to be noticed in a Dionysiak point of view are the derivative connection of the solar Abraxas with Iao-Sabazios, asinine symbolism, and the *rôle* played by the serpent and lion in reference to the sun.

XLI. Symbolic figure, consisting of horned and bearded head of the Pan type joined to a ram's head, the two being attached to the body of a cock, above whose head is a solar star.⁵ The combination represents the prolific potentiality of the world under the influence of the sun.⁶

XLII. Symbolic figure, consisting of a Seilenos-head, bald and bearded, a ram's head, and above, a horse's head and neck, the whole on a bird's legs; in the field, the

---

¹ Cooper, *Serpent Myths of Anct. Egypt*, Fig. 121. Vide *inf.* VIII. ii. *Wheel.*
² *Sup.* sec. iii. *Chalkedon.*
³ Maurice, *Indian Antiquities*, vi. 368.
⁴ Cooper, *Serpent Myths of Anct. Egypt.* Fig. 123. As to this type,
vide C. W. King, *The Gnostics and their Remains*, Pl. iii. Nos. 2, 7, Pl. v. No. 9, Pl. vii. No. 6. Vide also No. XXXVIII.
⁵ *Worship of Priapus*, Pl. iii. Fig. 1.
⁶ Cf. *inf.* VIII. ii. *Ram.*

sun and moon.[1] It is not correct to regard these designs, commonly styled Grylli or comic figures, as merely arbitrary and fantastic productions of sportive art. They are frequently deeply significant and representative. This particular gem has been explained by Böttiger as uniting the influences of all the elements for the benefit of the wearer.[2] But the only difference between it and No. XLI. is that the horse's head is here introduced instead of a cock's. The horse, in the abstract, is as much connected with the Sun-god as the cock, and is equivalent to the bird in the symbolism, in which case the two concepts embody exactly the same idea. When speaking of equine symbolism, the remarkable statue, described by Pausanias as dedicated by the inhabitants of Phigaleia in Arkadia, deserves attention. The legend, one of peculiar difficulty and intricacy, is as follows:—Near the river Ladon, in western Arkadia, was a place called Onkeion, at one time ruled over by Onkos, son of Apollon, and noted for a temple of Demeter, called Erinys the Angry, because when searching for her daughter she was pursued by Poseidon, and having changed herself into a mare he likewise changed himself into a horse and joined her amongst the horses at Onkeion. By Poseidon she became the mother of Despoina-Persephone and of the wondrous horse Areion, whose matchless swiftness saved Adrastos at the ill-omened siege of Thebai, and who was lent by Onkos to Herakles, when the latter warred against the Eleans. At Phigaleia Demeter was not described as the mother of a horse; but the tale agreed in other particulars with that told at Thelpouse, near Onkeion; and it was also said that the goddess, enraged with Poseidon and sorrowing for her daughter, clad herself in black and concealed herself in a cave, where she was

---

[1] *Antique Gems and Rings*, ii. Pl. vi. Figs. 4 and 5.   [2] *Ibid.* 72.

ultimately found by Pan, but not until the fruits of the earth were withered and the greater part of the human race had died of famine. Zeus sent the Fates to the goddess, who at length persuaded her to lay aside her anger and come forth. A cave near Phigaleia was considered the scene of the circumstance, and was therefore sacred to Demeter; and a wooden statue, the maker of which was unknown, and which had been destroyed by fire ages before the time of Pausanias, had been dedicated to her. This peculiar statue was said to be of a female figure with the head and mane of a horse; around the head were shapes of dragons and other wild beasts: a long black garment clad her to the feet, whence she was called Melainis; in one hand she held a dolphin and in the other a dove.[1] I first will give Professor Max Müller's explication of the myth. 'If the name of Erinys is sometimes applied to *Dêmêtêr*, this is because *Dêô* was Dyâvâ, and *Dêmêtêr*, Dyâvâ mâtar, the Dawn, the mother. Erinys Demeter, like Saranyû, was changed into a mare, she was followed by *Poseidon*, as a horse. *Poseidon*, if he expressed the sun rising from the sea, would approach to Varuna, who was called the father of the horse.'[2] The Vedic myth alluded to is as follows:—' Saranyû[3] had twins from Vivasvat, the sun. She placed another like her in her place, changed her form into that of a horse, and ran off. Vivasat, the sun, likewise assumed the form of a horse, followed her, and embraced her. Hence the two Asvins, or horsemen, were born.'[4] The horse, whose name is the same in many Aryan languages, is 'the runner,' the 'rapid animal.'[5] The Sun is the race-horse of the heavens,[6] and

---

[1] Paus. viii. 25, 37, 42.
[2] *Lects. on the Science of Language*, ii. 504-5.
[3] As to Saranyu, vide *sup*. VI. 3.
[4] *Lects. on the Science of Language*, ii. 528.
[5] *Ibid.* 68; Lenormant, *Les Premières Civilisations*, i. 318.
[6] Cf. *Psal*. xix. 5.

catches the Dawn, Saranyu-Erinys, and from their union spring the states of morning and evening. The parallel between parts of these two myths is most singular, and the Vedic tale might, in the absence of certain difficulties, be at once accepted as the elegant and appropriate explanation of the Hellenik. It is, however, to be observed that Professors Roth, Kuhn, and Schwartz, who are supporters of 'the meteorological theory,' which gives more prominence to clouds and tempests than to sun and dawn, discern in Saranyu 'the dark and impetuous storm-cloud,'[1] and there is, therefore, far from being a consensus of authority on her character. But to pass on; what is there of a dawn-character about the concept of Demeter? Mr. Cox apparently hesitates to follow his usual guide here, remarking 'Professor Max Müller seems to see in Demeter, not the Earth, but the Dawn-mother;' and he has laid down the judicious rule, that identification of personages is not to be made, 'unless their names, their general character, *and* their special features, carry us to this conclusion.'[2] But the general character of Demeter is undoubtedly not that of a dawn-goddess. Next as to Poseidon: '*If* he expressed the sun rising from the sea—.' Now unfortunately for this view, Poseidon, who does not appear at all in Vedic mythology, has nothing solar about him, and we, therefore, are not justified in linking him in any way with the sun. Had the personages in the Hellenik legend been Helios and Athene, for instance, anything more satisfactory than the Vedic explanation could hardly be imagined; but as it is, they are Poseidon and Demeter, and we must make the best of the facts. Creuzer deals with the tale at some length, but not happily, giving one of those explanations which leave all the chief difficulties unexplained. Waiving all dogmatism

[1] *Mythology of the Aryan Nations,* i. 423.
[2] *Ibid.* 210.

on so doubtful a matter, I will endeavour to analyze the legend, and display its underlying significance. Onkos, son of Apollon, like numberless similar mythological personages, is excogitated to furnish an explanation of the name Onkeion, and it appears that at a place called Onkeion, which in some way was especially noted for or connected with horses—(Perhaps by play of words: thus, *Hippon* is defined as 'the sexual parts of a woman or of a man; a large fish,'[1] and according to some, the word is Semitic in origin, and in accordance with the principles of occult symbolism is pictorially concealed beneath the Hellenik *hippos*, horse.)—there was an ancient temple or abode of a goddess which, as early as the time of Antimachos, B.C. 420, was connected with Demeter, for that poet writes 'There they say was the abode of Demeter Erinys.'[2] Apollodoros, too, states that Demeter, when met by Poseidon, was 'like an Erinys.'[3] Demeter, it will be observed, attempted to hide herself amongst the horses already there, and she was, at the time, wandering over the earth in search of her daughter. The original Onkeian shrine, therefore, *did not belong to Demeter*, though a temple was afterwards raised to her on the spot. Who, then, was the original goddess of Onkeion? The Phoenician Athene-Onka, I presume, whom we find located in the suburbs of Thebai.[4] Of course the name Athene is merely conferred upon the goddess, because she was supposed to correspond with the great Aryan divinity. But Onka is a horned, lunar queen of destiny and of ever-living vitality, and as the imaginary Onkos is called the son of Apollon, there was apparently a solar and lunar cult established on the spot; as elsewhere, the statues of Sun-god and Moon-goddess

---

[1] Hesych. in voc.
[2] *Thebais. Frag.* lxxxvii.
[3] Apollod. iii. 6.
[4] Vide *sup.* V. v. 3, 5; *inf.* IX. iii. *Tables of Horned Divinities of the Kamic and Phoenician Pantheons.*

stood side by side.[1] But what is the connection between Onka and the horse? Souidas tells us that Poseidon is called Hippios,[2] and observes: 'Hippeia Athena.' They say that she was the daughter of Poseidon and Polyphe, daughter of Okeanos. It is said that she was called Hippeia from having first constructed a chariot.'[3] In another work, specially devoted to the Poseidonik myth, after noticing the god's connection with the horse, I observed that his cult was introduced into Hellas from the same region as the chariot, and remarked, 'Thus the war-car, like the god Poseidon, passed over from Libye into Greece, and hence the connection of the Libyan Poseidon with the war-horse.'[4] Onka, the Phoenician goddess, comes as a stranger into Hellas, with Poseidon the Phoenician god; she not unnaturally is regarded as his daughter; but he is Hippios, Lord-of-the-horse, and similarly she becomes Hippeia. This is not the Aryan Athene who, in the great contest with Poseidon for Athenai, far from being an Hippeia, produces an olive, whilst at his command the war-horse starts up. We have seen[5] that Hellenik statuary is almost invariably anthropomorphic; and in the light of the foregoing considerations I think it nearly certain that the monstrous and very ancient statue referred to by Pausanias, and popularly connected with Demeter, was not originally that of the Aryan Earth-mother, but simply a statue of Onka-Hippeia; holding in one hand the dolphin, in allusion to the sea across which, like Palaimon, she had come,[6] and in the other a mystic bird, here called a dove.[7] Onka-Hippeia is also connected with the Phrygian Kybele, so early identified with Demeter, and who 'in Phrygia

[1] Cf. Paus. vi. 24.
[2] In voc. *Hippios*.
[3] In voc. *Hippeia Athena*.
[4] '*Poseidon*,' xxii.
[5] *Sup.* sec. ii. *Dionysiak Statuary*.
[6] Cf. *inf.* VIII. ii. *Dolphin*.
[7] Vide *sup.* sec. i. Vaso No. XXVIII.

was represented with a horse's head,[1] and here again we have a special reason for the peculiar bizarre form. In a thoughtful paper on *The Myth of Demeter and Persephone*, Mr. W. H. Pater observes, 'she is the goddess of dark caves, and is not wholly free from monstrous form.'[2] He apparently alludes to the Demeter of Phigaleia; but the examination of the myth shows that she, like other Hellenik divinities, is invariably anthropomorphic. The dark cave is in no way connected with monstrous form, being merely the hidden Under-world, into which the beautiful Persephone, who never appears as unanthropomorphic, constantly descends. Any student of the Poseidonik myth must be struck with the many contests in which the god on entering Hellenik regions is engaged with the various Aryan divinities;[3] and here we find him, in harmony with his general history, making an assault upon the Aryan Demeter. I have ventured to assert that the 'truth which underlies such legends is that, on the introduction of his foreign cultus into Hellas, it was everywhere opposed by that of rival divinities, most of whom were the already established Aryan deities of the country;' and this view has been styled 'a most ingenious piece of Euhemerism.' To me it seems very natural that disputes between opposing religionists should be poetically regarded as contests between their respective divinities.[4] Thus the campaign related on the Moabite Stone takes the form of a grand duel between Chemosh and Yahveh. Demeter repairs to the abode of Onka-Hippeia, and having thus come within the sphere of equine influence, is said to assume the form of a mare,

---

[1] Schliemann, *Troy and its Remains*, 353. Pausanias thinks that Poseidon was so very generally called Hippios from having invented the art of riding, and quotes *Il.* xxiii. 584, in illustration (Paus. vii. 21).

[2] *Fortnightly Review*, Jan. 1870, p. 72.

[3] Vide '*Poseidon*,' xxi. Territorial Contests of Poseidon.

[4] Vide *inf.* X. iv. Note on the god Zu.

DIONYSOS IN ART.

and Poseidon joins her. What is this but saying, in an occult and mystic manner, that there was a union of the rituals? Demeter is at first angry, but afterwards lays aside her anger; this expresses the feelings of her votaries; Demeter and Poseidon ultimately live peaceably together, and as she is the mother of Despoina-Kore-Persephone, so he comes to be regarded as her sire. The cult of the goddess Onka fades away in the course of time, and, as at Thebai she is swallowed up in Athene, so in Arkadia she disappears before Demeter, the tradition of the extraordinary statue, which would naturally make a deep impression on the Hellenik mind, remaining. But the goddess Hippeia reappears in Neo-Platonik mysticism as 'the universal soul,'[1] a kind of combination of Demeter-Onka, as the nurturer of Dionysos, the associate of Sabazios, the 'chthonian mother,' and dweller in the Lydian Tmolos,[2] and in Mount Ida.[3] The offspring of Poseidon Hippios and Demeter Hippeia must needs be a horse, and so we find the celebrated charger Areion, or 'More excellent,' *i.e.* than other horses. The mother of Areion varies in the legends, but all agree in making Poseidon his sire, and the myth is an old one, for it is referred to in the Homerik Poems, 'Not if he should drive behind thee godlike Areion, the swift steed of Adrastos, who had his birth from a god.'[4] Antimachos calls him Kyanochaites,[5] With-dark-blue-mane, an epithet of Poseidon, in allusion to the dark blue or kyanos-coloured sea. When Poseidon in later ages was regarded as only a sea-god, and not as a god who had come across the sea, ships are spoken of as his horses, as a camel is called the ship of the desert. 'For the poet calls ships horses, and we call Poseidon Hippios.'[6] This is illustrated by the explanation of many

[1] Proklos. In *Timaios*, Bk. ii.
[2] Cf. Eur. *Bak.* 66.
[3] *Orphik Hymn*, xlviii. 4. xlix.
[4] *Il.* xxiii. 346-7.
[5] Antim. apud Paus. viii. 25.
[6] Artemidoros. i. 58.

words in Souidas, Hesychios, and the *Etymologicum Magnum*. The dragons and other wild beasts around the head of the hippo-kephalic statue of Phigaleia remind us of the animals which surround the statue of Ephesia Polymastos. Onka is a lunar goddess, like Hekate the Far-shooter, who 'assumes three heads or faces, which denote the monthly phases of the moon—the horse, with its streaming mane pointing, to the moon at its full, and the snake and the dog representing its waxing and waning.'[1] There is nothing originally unanthropomorphic about Hekate. The statues of Hekate Triformis are merely three females *addorsed*, if I may so express it, a fashion first introduced by Alkamenes, the pupil of Pheidias.[2] An ancient statue of the goddess at Aigina, where she was especially revered, was purely anthropomorphic. I merely quote this passage to show the parallel between the lunar divinities in their both being connected with the horse. For it is not at all apparent how the full moon resembles a streaming mane, which might rather be regarded as comet-like, nor how waxing and waning are symbolized by snake and dog. But to pursue this obscure subject further would take us beyond the limits of the Dionysiak Myth.

XLIII. Tree, in vineyard, with four *oscilla*[3] hanging from it.[4]

XLIV. Tree, with three *oscilla* hanging from it; in the field Iao.[5] A remarkable illustration of the unity of Dionysos, the only divinity connected with the *oscillum*, and the solar Iao.[6]

XLV. Various Gnostic specimens of the time-serpent, tail in mouth.[7]

---

[1] *Mythol. of the Aryan Nations*, ii. 142.
[2] Paus. ii. 30.
[3] Vide *sup.* VI. i. 1.
[4] Smith, *Smaller Dictionary of Antiquities*, 278.
[5] Montfaucon, ii. Pt. ii. Pl. clx. Fig. 3.
[6] *Sup.* II. iii. 3.
[7] Montfaucon, ii. Pt. ii. Pl. clxiv. Inf. VIII. ii. Serpent, No. III.

XLVI. Tauro-kephalic personage, standing between two inscribed columns, apparently holding the lotus in one hand, and the *ankh* or *crux ansata* in the other.[1]

XLVII. The sport of the *askoliasmos*.[2]—Three filleted Satyrs, with short tails, but otherwise anthropomorphic, are leaping and endeavouring to stand on the full wine-skin.

The other Dionysiak gems referred to require no further special notice; the incidents they pourtray will be found to harmonize with the vase-scenes and coin-emblems relating to the Myth. Some gems give scenes which represent the reproductive power in nature under phallic types, but contribute no new general idea.

In the subsequent portion of this work, I shall continue the Hellenik analysis of Dionysos; and, that completed, shall next attempt to trace his concept back to its historical starting-point. Lastly, as the enquiry vastly widens, I shall consider the basis-ideas of the archaic Religious-mythology of Western Asia, in connection with some prominent theories and opinions which exercise many thoughtful minds in the present age. The investigation of the Dionysiak Myth is not merely the history of a second-class divinity of a single remarkable nation; in its true extent, it embraces almost the entire cycle of early religious belief.

---

[1] Montfaucon, i. Pt. ii. Pl. cxlviij. Fig. 1. Vide *inf.* IX. iii.

[2] Smith, *Smaller Dict. of Antiquities*, 44; *sup.* VI. i. 1.

END OF THE FIRST VOLUME.